Elegant Glassware of the Depression Era

of the

IDENTIFICATION
AND
VALUE GUIDE

ELEVENTH
EDITION

Gene & Cathy Florence

Cambridge
Fostoria
Heisey
&
others

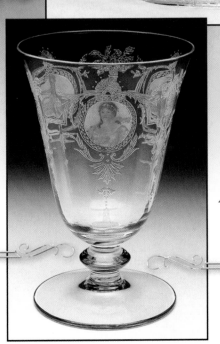

COLLECTOR BOOKS
A Division of Schroeder Publishing Co., Inc.

On the front cover: Candlewick urn candleholder, #400/129; Cleo gravy boat with liner, #1091; Cambridge Rose Point three-footed candy with cover, ebony, gold-encrusted, 7".

On the back cover: Fostoria Versailles 2375½ oval centerpiece, blue, 13", with #2371 flower holder and #2375½ candlesticks, 2½" high.

Cover design by Beth Summers
Book design by Terri Hunter

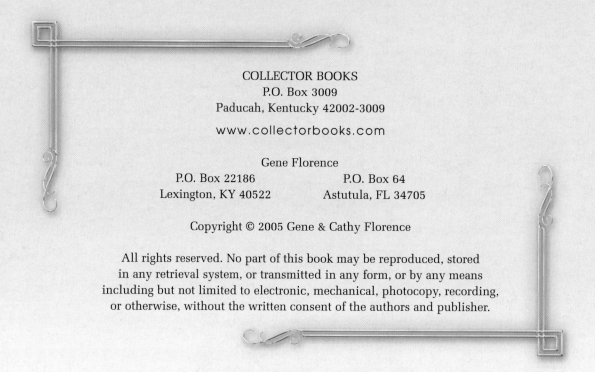

COLLECTOR BOOKS
P.O. Box 3009
Paducah, Kentucky 42002-3009

www.collectorbooks.com

Gene Florence

P.O. Box 22186   P.O. Box 64
Lexington, KY 40522   Astutula, FL 34705

The current values in this book should be used only as a guide. They are not intended to set prices, which vary from one section of the country to another. Auction prices as well as dealer prices vary greatly and are affected by condition as well as demand. Neither the authors nor the publisher assumes responsibility for any losses that might be incurred as a result of consulting this guide.

Searching For A Publisher?

We are always looking for people knowledgeable within their fields. If you feel that there is a real need for a book on your collectible subject and have a large comprehensive collection, contact Collector Books.

Gene M. Florence, Jr., a native Kentuckian, graduated from the University of Kentucky in 1967. He held a double major in mathematics and English that he immediately put to use in industry and subsequently, in teaching junior and senior high school.

A collector since childhood, Mr. Florence progressed from baseball cards, comic books, coins, and bottles to glassware. His buying and selling glassware "hobby" began to override his nine-year teaching career. In the summer of 1972, he wrote a book on Depression glassware that was well received by collectors in the field, persuading him to leave teaching in 1976 and pursue the antique glass business full time. This allowed time to travel to glass shows throughout the country, where he assiduously studied the prices of glass being sold... and of that remaining unsold.

Cathy Gaines Florence, also a native Kentuckian, graduated with honors and a coveted voice award from high school, attended Georgetown College where she obtained a French major and an English minor, then married her middle-school sweetheart Gene Florence.

She taught four years at the middle school level, then worked part-time while raising two boys. It was then that she typed her husband's first manuscript, written in "chicken scratch." The first three or four letters of each word would be legible and then it was up to her to guess what the last was. To their astonishment, the book sold well and a new career was born for her husband and their lives took different turns from the teaching careers they'd planned.

In the mid-80s she authored a book on collecting quilts, harking back to skills taught her by her grandmothers; and she has since co-authored books on glass with husband Gene.

Books written by the Florences include the following titles: *The Collector's Encyclopedia of Depression Glass, Stemware Identification, The Collector's Encyclopedia of Akro Agate, Pocket Guide to Depression Glass & More, Kitchen Glassware of the Depression Years, Collectible Glassware from the 40s, 50s, and 60s, Glass Candlesticks of the Depression Era, Anchor Hocking's Fire-King & More,* three volumes of *Florences' Glassware Pattern Identification Guide, Florence's Big Book of Salt and Pepper Shakers, Standard Baseball Card Price Guide,* six editions of *Very Rare Glassware of the Depression Years,* and *Treasures of Very Rare Depression Glass.* Gene has also written six volumes of *The Collector's Encyclopedia of Occupied Japan* and a book on Degenhart glassware for that museum. Mr. and Mrs. Florence's most recent books are *Florences' Glass Kitchen Shakers, 1930 – 1950s,* and *The Hazel-Atlas Glass Identification and Value Guide.*

PRICING

All prices quoted are retail for mint condition glassware. This book is intended only as a guide to prices. There continue to be regional price disparities that cannot be adequately dealt with herein.

You may expect dealers to pay approximately 30 to 60 percent less than the prices listed. My personal knowledge of prices comes from buying and selling glass for 36 years and from traveling to and selling at shows in various parts of the United States. Strangely, I am working even harder at markets and shows, today, to remain current with the ever-fluctuating prices. You can find me on the Internet at www.gene florence.com. I readily admit that I solicit price information from persons known to be authorities in certain wares in order to provide you with the latest, most accurate pricing information. However, final pricing judgments are always mine!

MEASUREMENTS AND TERMS

All measurements and terminology in this book are from factory catalogs and advertisements or actual measurements from the piece. It has been my experience that actual measurements vary slightly from those listed in most factory catalogs; so, do not get unduly concerned over slight variations. For example, Fostoria always seems to have measured plates to the nearest inch, but I have found that most Fostoria plates are never exact inches in measurement.

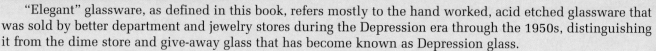

"Elegant" glassware, as defined in this book, refers mostly to the hand worked, acid etched glassware that was sold by better department and jewelry stores during the Depression era through the 1950s, distinguishing it from the dime store and give-away glass that has become known as Depression glass.

The rise in collecting Elegant glassware has been extraordinary the past few years. Many dealers who would dare not stock that crystal glass a few years ago are buying as much or more Elegant than basic Depression glass today. Glass shows used to display 15% to 20% Elegant glass; now, there is more than 50% at most shows. Many collectors who have completed sets of Depression glassware have now switched to acquiring sets of Elegant.

Ten photography sessions for this book were spread over a two-year period with one session lasting almost two weeks. I hope you enjoy this book, and will feel my 34 years of working to furnish you the best books possible on glassware were well spent.

ACKNOWLEDGMENTS

There are generous people behind the scenes in the production of this book. Some lent glass, some, their time; others lent their talents and expertise. These people somehow have continued to be friends and contributors even after exhausting hours of packing, unpacking, arranging, sorting, and repacking glass. Some traveled hundreds of miles to bring their valuable glass to share with you. Others spent hours discussing and listing their prices, often late at night after long show hours. Some never made it to the studio, but sent lists of additional pieces from their personal collections that we had not yet documented. Without these fabulous people, this book would not be the caliber their contributions made it. These extraordinary people include John and Evelyn Knowles, Dan and Geri Tucker, Charles and Maxine Larson, Rosemary Trietsch, Carrie Domitz, Bud and Kathy Stultz, Ray Sibley, Jr., Frank Fenton, and numerous unnamed readers from throughout the U.S. and Canada who shared pictures and tidbits of information about their collections and findings. Richard Walker and Charles R. Lynch, with help arranging by Jane White and Zibby Walker, did most of the photography for this book. Richard and Zibby travel from New York each fall to "enjoy" long studio hours, ending after dark. Thanks, also, to Terri Hunter of Collector Books for transcribing all my Microsoft words into Quark and my scribbled prices into existence.

A special note of gratitude is due Dick and Pat Spencer, not only for lending their glass, but also for gathering up and transporting other collectors' patterns to the photography sessions. They provided their knowledge of pricing, plus numbering and labeling pictured pieces of Heisey and Duncan patterns in this book. This was in addition to their own book on glass animals they were trying to get finished. We hope you will benefit from those long, tedious days of numbering and labeling pieces herein. Requests have been received to do this; so, we tried to fulfill that.

Two surgeries in the last six months have really slowed me down writing. Anesthesia created a bit of havoc with my memory at first, and my body healed at its own speed — not my more impatient one. Thus, Cathy, who has always worked long hours as editor, sounding board, and proofreader, has worked even harder filling in the gaps for these last three manuscripts due at the publishers by April. This didn't exactly help her stress level. Yet, somehow, we made it through. If I even knew the names of all the people who prayed for us both, I couldn't thank them enough. Thanks to you readers whose generous response to my books have made this career possible. Too, many pieces have been added to lists over the years simply via your efforts, and collectors as a whole have benefited. If you have sent a postcard with prices or shared your particular bit of knowledge, give yourself a well-deserved pat on the back.

HOW TO USE THE PHOTO LEGENDS

To make this book easier to use and to provide more information, you will find photo legends with each pattern. Each piece is now identified either through the use of photo legends or through the use of numbers on shelf shots and individual shots. Each piece is numbered in the photo legends with corresponding numbers alongside the listings. Now you can tell exactly which piece is in the photo, and then refer to the listing to find size, color, price, and other information.

	Candlestick, 3⅛", #7951 Stafford	100.00
	Pitcher, 48 oz. 8"	195.00
5	Plate, 7½", #1511	12.50
	Stem, ¾ oz. cordial, #7565 Astrid	55.00
3	Stem, 3 oz., 5" cocktail, Monroe cut stem	45.00

1	Stem, 3½ oz. cocktail, #7669 Grandure	20.00
2	Stem, 5½ oz. saucer champagne, #7565 Astrid	20.00
	Stem, 6 oz., champagne	20.00
	Stem, 8½ oz., #7565 Astrid	30.00
4	Stem, 9 oz., 7", water	32.50

CONTENTS

CONTENTS BY COMPANY

Color: crystal

Achilles and Adonis are two Cambridge engraved patterns that seem to be the most sought. Achilles has a "shield" type design with a floral cut at its top. Think of "hill" within the name Achilles and the point of the shield as a "hill." That may help you distinguish between Achilles and Adonis.

The vase pictured on the right stands 18" high. My publisher saw it while we were photographing and wanted to buy it. He thought it gorgeous — and it is!

Achilles is a beautiful cutting, and it is a shame that not more of it was made. Cambridge cut patterns were expensive and more admirers were into Rose Point because that was the pattern so heavily marketed.

Item	Price		Item	Price
Bonbon, 7½", 2-hdld., ftd. bowl, 3900/130	50.00		Plate, 13½", 2-hdld. cake, #3900/35	85.00
Bowl, 12", 4-toed, flared, #3900/62	75.00		Plate, 14", rolled edge, #3900/166	75.00
Candlestick, double, #399/72	65.00	5	Saucer, demi, #3400/69	20.00
Candy box & cover, #3900/165	135.00		Stem, 1 oz., cordial, #3121	75.00
Celery & relish, 8", 3-pt, #3900/125	65.00		Stem, 3½ oz., wine, #3121	65.00
Celery & relish, 12", 3-pt, #3900/126	75.00		Stem, 3 oz., cocktail, #3121	35.00
Celery & relish, 12", 5-pt, #3900/120	85.00		Stem, 4½ oz., claret, #3121	65.00
1 Cigarette holder, oval, #1066	85.00		Stem, 4½ oz., oyster cocktail, #3121	25.00
Cocktail icer w/liner, #968	85.00		Stem, 5 oz., café parfait, #3121	65.00
Comport, 5⅜", blown, #3121	75.00		Stem, 6 oz., high sherbet, #3121	17.00
Comport, 5½", #3900/136	65.00		Stem, 6 oz., low sherbet, #3121	27.00
Creamer, #3900/41	25.00		Stem, 10 oz., water goblet, #3121	55.00
5 Cup, demi, #3400/69	65.00		Sugar, #3900/41	25.00
Mayonnaise, 2 part, #3900/11	35.00		Tumbler, 5 oz., ftd. juice, #3121	35.00
Mayonnaise liner, #3900/11	15.00		Tumbler, 10 oz., ftd. water, #3121	40.00
3 Mayonnaise, #3900/129	35.00		Tumbler, 12 oz., ftd. tea, #3121	45.00
Mayonnaise liner, #3900/129	15.00		Vase, 11", ftd., #278	225.00
4 Pitcher, 80 oz., ball jug, #3400/38	250.00		Vase, 11", floral, ftd., #278	225.00
Plate, 8", 2-hdld. ftd. bonbon, #3900/111	50.00	6	Vase, 18", floor vase, #1336	1,100.00
2 Plate, 8½", luncheon, #3900/22	16.00			

Color: crystal

Adonis is beautiful Cambridge pattern, and it is easier to find than Achilles. It has an oval in the design with a flower within the oval. You may note that most tumblers and stems in Adonis are on the #3500 line. The covered urn and ice bucket are my favorite pieces! Gracious collectors loaned these for photography.

You will rarely find one of the cut patterns a piece at a time. Usually, they will be found in sets or a partial set. Adonis and Achilles are superb, so do not shy from them should you see some for sale.

19	Bonbon, 7½", 2-hdld., ftd. bowl, 3900/130	45.00
18	Bowl, 9" ram's head, #3500/25	395.00
14	Bowl, 12", 4-toed, #3400/4	95.00
	Bowl, 12", 4-toed, flared, #3900/62	95.00
13	Candlestick, #627	35.00
	Candlestick, double, #399/72	65.00
12	Candlestick, double, ram's head, #657	95.00
	Candy box & cover, #3900/165	135.00
	Celery & relish, 8", 3-pt, #3900/125	65.00
	Celery & relish, 12", 3-pt, #3900/126	75.00
	Celery & relish, 12", 5-pt, #3900/120	85.00
	Cocktail icer w/liner, #968	85.00
	Comport, 5⅜", blown, #3500	75.00
	Comport, 5½", #3900/136	65.00
17	Comport, 8", 2-hdld., #3500	125.00
	Creamer, #3900/41	25.00
15	Cup, demi, #3400	70.00
9	Decanter, 28 oz., #1321	295.00
11	Ice pail, #1402/52	135.00
	Mayonnaise, 2 pt., #3900/11	35.00
	Mayonnaise liner, #3900/11	15.00
	Mayonnaise, #3900/129	35.00
	Mayonnaise liner, #3900/129	15.00
20	Plate, 6", bread, #3500	12.00
	Plate, 8", 2-hdld. ftd. bonbon, #3900/111	50.00
21	Plate, 8½", luncheon, #3500	16.00
10	Plate, 13", ftd., #3500/110	75.00
	Plate, 13½", 2-hdld. cake, #3900/35	85.00
	Plate, 14", rolled edge, #3900/166	75.00
23	Relish, 2-hdld., 2-pt.	85.00
15	Saucer, demi, #3400	15.00
22	Shaker, pr.	85.00
6	Stem, 1 oz., cordial, #3500	75.00
	Stem, 2 oz., sherry, #7966	65.00
4	Stem, 2½ oz., wine, #3500	65.00
5	Stem, 3 oz., cocktail, #3500	35.00
	Stem, 4½ oz., claret, #3500	65.00
	Stem, 4½ oz., oyster cocktail, #3500	25.00
	Stem, 5 oz., café parfait, #3500	65.00
7	Stem, 7 oz., high sherbet, #3500	17.00
8	Stem, 7 oz., low sherbet, #3500	27.00
1	Stem, 10 oz., water goblet, #3500	55.00
	Sugar, #3900/41	25.00
	Tumbler, 5 oz., ftd. juice, #3500	35.00
2	Tumbler, 10 oz., ftd. water, #3500	40.00
3	Tumbler, 13 oz., ftd. tea, #3500	45.00
16	Urn, 10" w/cover, #3500/41	395.00
	Vase, 10", ftd., bud, #274	85.00
	Vase, 11", ftd., #278	225.00
	Vase, 20", ftd.	1,295.00

ADONIS

Color: crystal

Alexis is an older Fostoria pattern that was concluding its production period about the time that the majority of patterns in this book were getting started. Alexis is a simple pattern with a classic style that has always sold well for us at shows across the country. Surprisingly, it is not yet a pricey pattern to collect. As with any other pattern, there are hard to find items that will be costly. These include pitchers, water bottles, and syrups or cruets. Many pressed wares are gathering momentum in the collectibles market especially now that it's nearly a century old. Further, it's a long-lived pattern of a major company that is no longer in business. Alexis is a link from the pattern glass era to that of Depression glass.

Besides glass shows, antique malls, and antique shows, you will find a few pieces of Alexis showing up on Internet auctions.

1	Bowl, 4½", high foot	15.00
9	Bowl, 4½", nappy	12.50
	Bowl, 5", nappy	15.00
	Bowl, 7", nappy	20.00
	Bowl, 8", nappy	22.50
10	Bowl, 8", nappy, shallow	22.50
	Bowl, 9", nappy	25.00
	Bowl, crushed ice	25.00
	Bowl, finger (flat edge)	15.00
	Butter dish w/cover	75.00
	Catsup bottle	65.00
	Celery, tall	32.50
	Comport, 4½" high	22.50
4	Cream, short, hotel	25.00
	Cream. tall	22.50
11	Cup, hdld. custard	10.00
	Decanter w/stopper	110.00
	Horseradish jar w/spoon	60.00
	Molasses can ewer, drip cut	65.00
	Mustard w/slotted cover	35.00
	Nut bowl	15.00
	Oil, 2 oz.	30.00
	Oil, 4 oz.	35.00
7	Oil, 6 oz.	40.00
	Oil, 9 oz.	50.00
	Pitcher, 16 oz.	45.00
	Pitcher, 32 oz.	75.00
	Pitcher, 64 oz., ice	85.00
	Pitcher, 64 oz., tall	100.00
	Plate, crushed ice liner	10.00
	Salt shaker, pr. (2 styles)	35.00
8	Salt, individual, flat	22.50

	Salt, individual, ftd.	15.00
	Salt, table, flat	15.00
2	Spooner	30.00
	Stem, claret, 5 oz.	15.00
	Stem, cocktail, 3 oz.	12.50
	Stem, cordial, 1 oz.	15.00
	Stem, crème de menthe, 2½ oz.	15.00
	Stem, egg cup	12.50
5	Stem, ice cream, high foot	15.00
	Stem, pousse café, ¾ oz.	16.00
	Stem, sherbet, high	15.00
	Stem, sherbet, low	12.50
	Stem, water, 10 oz.	15.00
6	Stem, wine, 2½ oz.	15.00
	Stem, wine, 3 oz.	15.00
	Sugar shaker	65.00
	Sugar, hdld., hotel	25.00
	Sugar, no handles w/lid	40.00
	Toothpick	30.00
	Tray, celery	25.00
	Tray, olive	20.00
	Tray, pickle	22.50
	Tumbler, ice tea	17.50
	Tumbler, ice tea, ftd., 10 oz.	20.00
	Tumbler, water	15.00
	Tumbler, water, ftd., 8½ oz.	20.00
	Tumbler, whiskey	15.00
	Tumbler, wine	15.00
	Vase, 7", sweet pea, ftd.	50.00
3	Vase, 9", ftd.	65.00
	Vase, Nasturium (sic)	37.50
	Water bottle	85.00

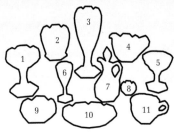

Colors: crystal; some amber, blue, green, yellow, pink tinting to purple in late 1920s; white, red in 1980s; and being newly made in crystal for Lancaster Colony

American was Fostoria's most recognizable pattern, having been made from 1915 until Fostoria's closing in 1986. After that, American continued to be made under the backing of the new owner, Lancaster Colony. Many items (particularly red colored) were subcontracted to Viking Glass Company (later Dalzell-Viking) and sold labeled Fostoria American by Lancaster Colony. Don't be bamboozled by the recently designed Whitehall pattern that was created by Indiana Glass Company and is similar to American. Whitehall's quality is inferior to that of American and shapes and sizes are dissimilar as well. Still, neophytes often confuse the two patterns.

American, though respected by collectors, is beginning to be slighted by some dealers because it is, presently, a slow seller due to its significant availability. Rarely found items sell well if priced within reason, but many of the expensively priced items are also faltering due, in part, to the economy. In addition, the continuing manufacture of commonly found pieces by Lancaster Colony keeps adding to the abundant supply. A wealth of Whitehall is found in colors of pink, avocado green, and several shades of blue. The glassware section of your local discount store is a good place to scrutinize colors and items recently made. Various specialty catalogs suggest this new colored glassware to be Depression glass in an effort to enhance its value. Whitehall's pink colored ware is frequently confused with Jeannette's Depression era Cube pattern judging by the numerous letters and e-mails I receive. There are no footed pitchers or tumblers in Jeannette's Cube. *Current American or look-alike American pieces are not marked in any way.* American pieces that have been produced in recent years are indicated with an asterisk (*) in the price listing below.

Many auction advertisements publicize Fostoria is being sold when they actually mean American pieces. These were the "good" dishes used by Mom or Grandma. When Fostoria was no longer available in the department or jewelry stores then the secondary market (glass shows, flea markets, local antique or thrift shops) became the focal point to replace absent wares. The Internet has added to the adventure of finding American, but the risk there is that many sellers are inexperienced or unscrupulous regarding glass condition (or identification). Try to buy only from those who guarantee their merchandise. I have been told often that the shysters will not accept returns.

Today, an abundant supply of American pattern keeps most of the prices within the range of the average collector. Harder to find pieces are almost out of the realm of the general collector. Notice there are obvious price adjustments for American items being found in England. The Internet has European antique dealers watchful of our glass collecting inclinations. Those once hard-to-find English Fostoria American pieces are easier to find here, since so many have been imported! Reissued cookie jars continue to create a problem. A *majority* of the newer issues have wavy lines in the pattern itself and crooked knobs on the top. Old cookie jars do not. (A telling point that works about 80% of the time is to try to turn the lid around while it rests inside the cookie jar. The new lids seem to hang up and stop somewhere along the inside making the whole cookie jar turn. The old jars will allow you to turn the lid completely around without catching on the sides.)

If you enjoy the beauty the American pattern exudes, then definitely go for it. Collecting what you like has always been a major factor; and little pleasures in life should be pandered to when possible!

	*Crystal			*Crystal
Appetizer, tray, 10½", w/6 inserts	300.00		Bottle, cologne, w/stopper, 6 oz., 5¾"	72.50
Appetizer, insert, 3¼"	32.50	26	Bottle, cologne, w/stopper, 7¼", 8 oz.	80.00
Ashtray, 2⅞", sq.	7.50		Bottle, cordial, w/stopper, 7¼", 9 oz.	90.00
Ashtray, 3⅞", oval	9.00		Bottle, water, 44 oz., 9¼"	625.00
Ashtray, 5", sq.	45.00		Bowl, banana split, 9" x 3½"	595.00
Ashtray, 5½", oval	20.00		Bowl, finger, 4½" diam., smooth edge	40.00
Basket, w/reed handle, 7" x 9"	95.00		Bowl, 3½", rose	20.00
Basket, 10", new in 1988	40.00		Bowl, 3¾", almond, oval	18.00
Bell	495.00		Bowl, 4¼", jelly, 4¼" h.	15.00
Bottle, bitters, w/tube, 5¾", 4½ oz.	72.50		*Bowl, 4½", 1 hdld.	10.00
Bottle, condiment/ketchup w/stopper	145.00	18	Bowl, 4½", 1 hdld., sq.	11.00

*See note in second paragraph above.

11

	*Crystal
Bowl, 4½", jelly, w/cover, 6¾" h.	30.00
*Bowl, 4½", nappy	13.00
Bowl, 4½", oval	15.00
Bowl, 4¾", fruit, flared	15.00
Bowl, 5", cream soup, 2 hdld.	45.00
Bowl, 5", 1 hdld., tri-corner	12.00
*Bowl, 5", nappy	10.00
Bowl, 5", nappy, w/cover	30.00
Bowl, 5", rose	30.00

	*Crystal
Bowl, 5½", lemon, w/cover	55.00
Bowl, 5½", preserve, 2 hdld., w/cover	100.00
Bowl, 6", bonbon, 3 ftd.	15.00
*Bowl, 6", nappy	15.00
Bowl, 6", olive, oblong	12.00
Bowl, 6½", wedding, w/cover, sq., ped. ft., 8" h.	110.00
Bowl, 6½", wedding, sq., ped. ft., 5¼" h.	75.00
Bowl, 7", bonbon, 3 ftd.	13.00

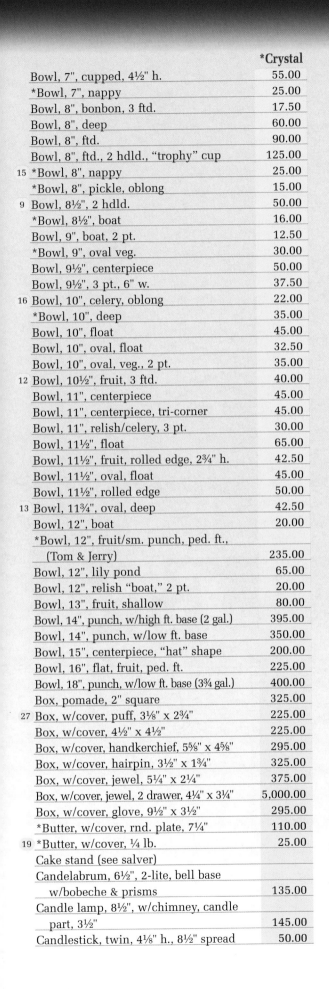

		*Crystal
	Bowl, 7", cupped, 4½" h.	55.00
	*Bowl, 7", nappy	25.00
	Bowl, 8", bonbon, 3 ftd.	17.50
	Bowl, 8", deep	60.00
	Bowl, 8", ftd.	90.00
	Bowl, 8", ftd., 2 hdld., "trophy" cup	125.00
15	*Bowl, 8", nappy	25.00
	*Bowl, 8", pickle, oblong	15.00
9	Bowl, 8½", 2 hdld.	50.00
	*Bowl, 8½", boat	16.00
	Bowl, 9", boat, 2 pt.	12.50
	*Bowl, 9", oval veg.	30.00
	Bowl, 9½", centerpiece	50.00
	Bowl, 9½", 3 pt., 6" w.	37.50
16	Bowl, 10", celery, oblong	22.00
	*Bowl, 10", deep	35.00
	Bowl, 10", float	45.00
	Bowl, 10", oval, float	32.50
	Bowl, 10", oval, veg., 2 pt.	35.00
12	Bowl, 10½", fruit, 3 ftd.	40.00
	Bowl, 11", centerpiece	45.00
	Bowl, 11", centerpiece, tri-corner	45.00
	Bowl, 11", relish/celery, 3 pt.	30.00
	Bowl, 11½", float	65.00
	Bowl, 11½", fruit, rolled edge, 2¾" h.	42.50
	Bowl, 11½", oval, float	45.00
	Bowl, 11½", rolled edge	50.00
13	Bowl, 11¾", oval, deep	42.50
	Bowl, 12", boat	20.00
	*Bowl, 12", fruit/sm. punch, ped. ft., (Tom & Jerry)	235.00
	Bowl, 12", lily pond	65.00
	Bowl, 12", relish "boat," 2 pt.	20.00
	Bowl, 13", fruit, shallow	80.00
	Bowl, 14", punch, w/high ft. base (2 gal.)	395.00
	Bowl, 14", punch, w/low ft. base	350.00
	Bowl, 15", centerpiece, "hat" shape	200.00
	Bowl, 16", flat, fruit, ped. ft.	225.00
	Bowl, 18", punch, w/low ft. base (3¾ gal.)	400.00
	Box, pomade, 2" square	325.00
27	Box, w/cover, puff, 3⅛" x 2¾"	225.00
	Box, w/cover, 4½" x 4½"	225.00
	Box, w/cover, handkerchief, 5⅝" x 4⅝"	295.00
	Box, w/cover, hairpin, 3½" x 1¾"	325.00
	Box, w/cover, jewel, 5¼" x 2¼"	375.00
	Box, w/cover, jewel, 2 drawer, 4¼" x 3¼"	5,000.00
	Box, w/cover, glove, 9½" x 3½"	295.00
	*Butter, w/cover, rnd. plate, 7¼"	110.00
19	*Butter, w/cover, ¼ lb.	25.00
	Cake stand (see salver)	
	Candelabrum, 6½", 2-lite, bell base w/bobeche & prisms	135.00
	Candle lamp, 8½", w/chimney, candle part, 3½"	145.00
	Candlestick, twin, 4⅛" h., 8½" spread	50.00

		*Crystal
	Candlestick, 2", chamber with fingerhold	45.00
	**Candlestick, 3", rnd. ft.	15.00
	Candlestick, 4⅜", 2-lite, rnd. ft.	40.00
	Candlestick, 6", octagon ft.	25.00
2	Candlestick, 6½", 2-lite, bell base	120.00
	Candlestick, 6¼", round ft.	195.00
	*Candlestick, 7", sq. column	115.00
	Candlestick, 7¼", "Eiffel" tower	150.00
	Candy box, w/cover, 3 pt., triangular	90.00
	Candy, w/cover, ped. ft.	37.50
	Cheese (5¾" compote) & cracker (11½" plate)	65.00
	Cigarette box, w/cover, 4¾"	40.00
	Coaster, 3¾"	9.00
	Comport, 4½", jelly	15.00
	*Comport, 5", jelly, flared	15.00
	*Comport, 6¾", jelly, w/cover	35.00
	Comport, 8½", 4" high	45.00
	Comport, 9½", 5¼" high	85.00
	Comport, w/cover, 5"	25.00
	**Cookie jar, w/cover, 8⅞" h.	295.00
	Creamer, tea, 3 oz., 2⅜" (#2056½)	9.00
	Creamer, individual, 4¾ oz.	9.00
	Creamer, 9½ oz.	12.50
	Crushed fruit, w/cover & spoon, 10"	2,500.00
	Cup, flat	7.50
21	Cup, ftd., 7 oz.	8.00
	Cup, punch, flared rim	11.00
	Cup, punch, straight edge	10.00
28	Decanter, w/stopper, 24 oz., 9¼" h.	85.00
	Dresser set: powder boxes w/covers & tray	475.00
1	Flower pot, w/perforated cover, 9½" diam., 5½" h.	1,995.00
5	Goblet, #2056, 2½ oz., wine, hex ft., 4⅜" h.	12.00
	Goblet, #2056, 4½ oz., oyster cocktail, 3½" h.	17.50
	Goblet, #2056, 4½ oz., sherbet, flared, 4⅜" h.	8.00
	Goblet, #2056, 4½ oz., fruit, hex ft., 4¾" h.	8.00
	Goblet, #2056, 5 oz., low ft., sherbet, flared, 3¼" h.	8.00
	Goblet, #2056, 6 oz., low ft., sundae, 3⅛" h.	8.00
	Goblet, #2056, 7 oz., claret, 4⅞" h.	55.00
	*Goblet, #2056, 9 oz., low ft., 4⅜" h.	10.00
	Goblet, #2056, 10 oz., hex ft., water, 6⅞" h.	12.00
	Goblet, #2056, 12 oz., low ft., tea, 5¾" h.	15.00
	Goblet, #2056½, 4½ oz., sherbet, 4½" h.	9.00
	Goblet, #2056½, 5 oz., low sherbet, 3½" h.	9.00

13

**Amber, May 2000

26   27   26   22

24   25   28

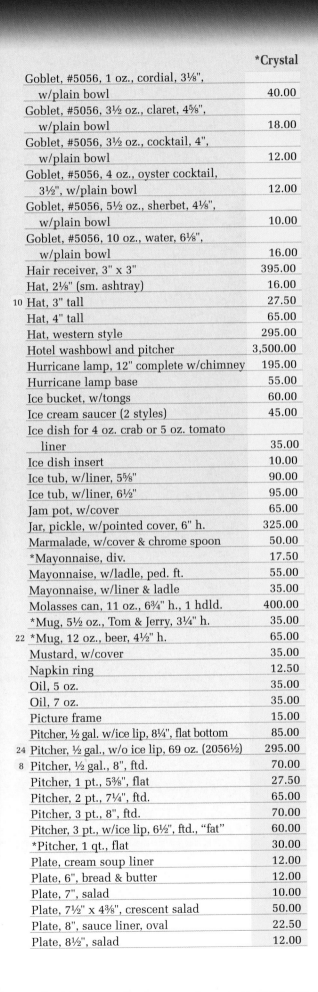

	*Crystal
Goblet, #5056, 1 oz., cordial, 3⅛",	
w/plain bowl	40.00
Goblet, #5056, 3½ oz., claret, 4⅝",	
w/plain bowl	18.00
Goblet, #5056, 3½ oz., cocktail, 4",	
w/plain bowl	12.00
Goblet, #5056, 4 oz., oyster cocktail,	
3½", w/plain bowl	12.00
Goblet, #5056, 5½ oz., sherbet, 4⅛",	
w/plain bowl	10.00
Goblet, #5056, 10 oz., water, 6⅛",	
w/plain bowl	16.00
Hair receiver, 3" x 3"	395.00
Hat, 2⅛" (sm. ashtray)	16.00
10 Hat, 3" tall	27.50
Hat, 4" tall	65.00
Hat, western style	295.00
Hotel washbowl and pitcher	3,500.00
Hurricane lamp, 12" complete w/chimney	195.00
Hurricane lamp base	55.00
Ice bucket, w/tongs	60.00
Ice cream saucer (2 styles)	45.00
Ice dish for 4 oz. crab or 5 oz. tomato	
liner	35.00
Ice dish insert	10.00
Ice tub, w/liner, 5⅝"	90.00
Ice tub, w/liner, 6½"	95.00
Jam pot, w/cover	65.00
Jar, pickle, w/pointed cover, 6" h.	325.00
Marmalade, w/cover & chrome spoon	50.00
*Mayonnaise, div.	17.50
Mayonnaise, w/ladle, ped. ft.	55.00
Mayonnaise, w/liner & ladle	35.00
Molasses can, 11 oz., 6¾" h., 1 hdld.	400.00
*Mug, 5½ oz., Tom & Jerry, 3¼" h.	35.00
22 *Mug, 12 oz., beer, 4½" h.	65.00
Mustard, w/cover	35.00
Napkin ring	12.50
Oil, 5 oz.	35.00
Oil, 7 oz.	35.00
Picture frame	15.00
Pitcher, ½ gal. w/ice lip, 8¼", flat bottom	85.00
24 Pitcher, ½ gal., w/o ice lip, 69 oz. (2056½)	295.00
8 Pitcher, ½ gal., 8", ftd.	70.00
Pitcher, 1 pt., 5⅜", flat	27.50
Pitcher, 2 pt., 7¼", ftd.	65.00
Pitcher, 3 pt., 8", ftd.	70.00
Pitcher, 3 pt., w/ice lip, 6½", ftd., "fat"	60.00
*Pitcher, 1 qt., flat	30.00
Plate, cream soup liner	12.00
Plate, 6", bread & butter	12.00
Plate, 7", salad	10.00
Plate, 7½" x 4⅜", crescent salad	50.00
Plate, 8", sauce liner, oval	22.50
Plate, 8½", salad	12.00

	*Crystal
Plate, 9", sandwich (sm. center)	14.00
Plate, 9½", dinner	22.00
Plate, 10", cake, 2 hdld.	27.50
Plate, 10½", sandwich (sm. center)	20.00
Plate, 11½", sandwich (sm. center)	20.00
Plate, 12", cake, 3 ftd.	25.00
Plate, 13½", oval torte	50.00
Plate, 14", torte	80.00
Plate, 18", torte	145.00
Plate, 20", torte	225.00
Plate 24", torte	250.00
*Platter, 10½", oval	40.00
14 Platter, 12", oval	55.00
Ring holder	200.00
Salad set: 10" bowl, 14" torte, wood	
fork & spoon	135.00
Salt, individual	9.00
23 Salver, 10", sq., ped. ft. (cake stand)	175.00
17 Salver, 10", rnd., ped. ft. (cake stand)	110.00
*Salver, 11", rnd., ped. ft. (cake stand)	35.00
Sauce boat & liner	55.00
21 Saucer	3.00
Set: 2 jam pots w/tray	150.00
Set: decanter, 6 – 2 oz. whiskeys on	
10½" tray	245.00
Set: toddler, w/baby tumbler & bowl	110.00
Set: youth, w/bowl, hdld. mug, 6" plate	110.00
Set: condiment, 2 oils, 2 shakers,	
mustard w/cover & spoon w/tray	350.00
Shaker, 3", ea.	10.00
*Shaker, 3½", ea.	7.00
Shaker, 3¼", ea.	10.00
Shakers w/tray, individual, 2"	22.00
Sherbet, handled, 3½" high, 4½ oz.	120.00
Shrimp bowl, 12¼"	325.00
29 Soap dish	975.00
Spooner, 3¾"	35.00
**Strawholder, 10", w/cover	295.00
Sugar, tea, 2¼" (#2056½)	13.00
Sugar, hdld., 3¼" h.	12.00
Sugar shaker	65.00
Sugar, w/o cover	10.00
Sugar, w/cover, no hdl., 6¼" (cover	
fits strawholder)	65.00
Sugar, w/cover, 2 hdld.	20.00
Syrup, 6½ oz., #2056½, Sani-cut server	80.00
Syrup, 6 oz., non pour screw top, 5¼" h.	225.00
11 Syrup, 10 oz., w/glass cover &	
6" liner plate	235.00
Syrup, w/drip proof top	35.00
Toothpick	25.00
Tray, cloverleaf for condiment set	155.00
Tray, tid bit, w/question mark metal	
handle	40.00
Tray, 5" x 2½", rect.	80.00

AMERICAN

	*Crystal
Tray, 6" oval, hdld.	35.00
Tray, pin, oval, 5½" x 4½"	210.00
Tray, 6½" x 9" relish, 4 part	45.00
Tray, 9½", service, 2 hdld.	35.00
Tray, 10", muffin (2 upturned sides)	32.50
Tray, 10", square, 4 part	75.00
Tray, 10", square	175.00
Tray, 10½", cake, w/question mark metal hdl.	32.00
Tray, 10½" x 7½", rect.	70.00
Tray, 10½" x 5", oval hdld.	45.00
Tray, 10¾", square, 4 part	155.00
Tray, 12", sand. w/ctr. handle	37.50
Tray, 12", round	175.00
Tray, 13½", oval, ice cream	185.00
Tray for sugar & creamer, tab. hdld., 6¾"	12.00
Tumbler, hdld. iced tea	395.00
Tumbler, #2056, 2 oz., whiskey, 2½" h.	11.00
Tumbler, #2056, 3 oz., ftd. cone, cocktail, 2⅞" h.	12.50
Tumbler, #2056, 5 oz., ftd., juice, 4¾"	12.00
6 Tumbler, #2056, 6 oz., flat, old-fashion, 3⅜" h.	15.00
Tumbler, #2056, 8 oz. flat, water, flared, 4⅛" h.	14.00
7 *Tumbler, #2056, 9 oz. ftd., water, 4⅞" h.	12.50
Tumbler, #2056, 12 oz., flat, tea, flared, 5¼" h.	15.00
Tumbler, #2056½, 5 oz., straight side, juice	13.00

	*Crystal
25 Tumbler, #2056½, 8 oz., straight side, water, 3⅞" h.	13.00
Tumbler, #2056½, 12 oz., straight side, tea, 5" h.	18.00
Tumbler, #5056, 5 oz., ftd., juice, 4⅛" w/plain bowl	10.00
Tumbler, #5056, 12 oz., ftd., tea, 5½" w/plain bowl	10.00
Urn, 6", sq., ped. ft	30.00
20 Urn, 7½", sq. ped. ft.	37.50
Vase, 4½", sweet pea	80.00
4 Vase, 6", bud, ftd., cupped	18.00
*Vase, 6", bud, flared	18.00
Vase, 6", straight side	35.00
Vase, 6½", flared rim	15.00
Vase, 7", flared	80.00
*Vase, 8", straight side	40.00
*Vase, 8", flared	80.00
Vase, 8", porch, 5" diam.	450.00
Vase, 8½", bud, flared	25.00
Vase, 8½", bud, cupped	25.00
3 Vase, 9", w/sq. ped. ft.	45.00
Vase, 9½", flared	150.00
Vase, 10", cupped in top	295.00
Vase, 10", porch, 8" diam.	750.00
*Vase, 10", straight side	90.00
Vase, 10", swung	225.00
Vase, 10", flared	90.00
Vase, 12", straight side	250.00
Vase, 12", swung	250.00
Vase, 14", swung	250.00
Vase, 20", swung	395.00

29

Colors: amber, blue, crystal, green, and pink

American Beauty is one of those patterns that is often brought into shows for me to identify. So, it is apparent, it was widely distributed on a multitude of stems! My favorite stem #7575 has the rose vine climbing along the stem. It is represented by a cordial here.

		*Crystal
	Candlestick, 3⅛", #7951 Stafford	100.00
	Compote, 5" w/8" diameter	37.50
	Compote, 6½" high, w/cover, #7941 Helena	175.00
	Custard liner, 5⅛"	15.00
	Custard, hdld. #8851	75.00
	Finger bowl liner	10.00
	Finger bowl, 4⅜", #2927	45.00
	Nappy, 6" diameter, w/cover, #7557 Savoy	155.00
	Nut, 4½" master w/cover, #7556	165.00
	Pitcher, 48 oz. 8"	195.00
	Pitcher, 54 oz. w/lid, #2 Arcadia	295.00
	Plate, 7¼"	12.50
5	Plate, 7½", #1511	12.50
	Stem, ¾ oz. cordial, #7565 Astrid	55.00
6	Stem, ¾ oz., 4⅜" cordial, #7575	85.00
	Stem, 1½ oz. port, #7565 Astrid	30.00
	Stem, 1oz. pousse cafe, #7565 Astrid	50.00
	Stem, 2½ oz. sherry, #7565 Astrid	25.00
	Stem, 3 oz., 6" sherry, #7695 trumpet	50.00
3	Stem, 3 oz., 5" cocktail, Monroe cut stem	45.00
	Stem, 3 oz. wine, #7565 Astrid	25.00
	Stem, 3½ oz. cocktail, #7565 Astrid	15.00

		*Crystal
1	Stem, 3½ oz. cocktail, #7669 Grandure	20.00
	Stem, 4½ oz. parfait, #7565 Astrid	20.00
	Stem, 4½ oz., 5⅝", tall champagne, #7565 Astrid	20.00
	Stem, 4¼ oz. claret, #7565 Astrid	25.00
	Stem, 5 oz. deep champagne, #7565 Astrid	20.00
	Stem, 5 oz. hot whiskey, #7565 Astrid	15.00
	Stem, 5 oz. sherbet, #7565 Astrid	15.00
2	Stem, 5½ oz. saucer champagne, #7565 Astrid	20.00
	Stem, 6 oz., champagne	20.00
	Stem, 6½ oz., 4⅝", bowl champagne, #7565 Astrid	20.00
	Stem, 8½ oz., #7565 Astrid	30.00
4	Stem, 9 oz., 7", water	32.50
	Stem, 10 oz. water, #7565 Astrid	40.00
	Stem, 11 oz., 7½" water, #7695 trumpet	45.00
	Tumbler, 2¾ oz., 2¼" bar, #8107 Sherman	35.00
	Tumbler, 8 oz., 4⅛" water, #9001 Billings	30.00
	Tumbler, 9 oz, ftd. w/handle, #9069 Hopper	50.00
	Tumbler, 9 oz., 4⅝" water, #8701 Garrett	30.00
	Tumbler, 12 oz. 4⅞", #9715 Calhoun	30.00
	Tumbler, 12 oz, ftd. w/handle, #9069 Hopper	60.00
	Vase, 10", #25 Olympic	165.00
	Vase, 12" #25 Olympic	200.00

* Add 40% for colors

Colors: amber, amethyst, crystal, crystal w/ebony stem, light and dark Emerald, Gold Krystol, Heatherbloom, Peach Blo, Royal blue, Willow blue

Cambridge's Apple Blossom attracts new collectors predominantly in Cambridge's yellow, known as Gold Krystol. It is the copiously found color of Apple Blossom and the most reasonably priced except for crystal. You can acquire a small set; however difficult to find items and serving pieces are now expensive. Beverage items can still be attained in most colors. Latch onto any serving pieces or dinner plates whenever you have the opportunity.

Colors other than yellow and crystal can be found with patience (and capital); however, availability of pink, green, blue, and Heatherbloom is quite inadequate in contrast to yellow or crystal. Very little dark Emerald green, amethyst, or amber is found. Settings of blue when exhibited at a show, produce a lot of "ooh and ahs," but typically, the price makes viewers waver at buying.

Note the Royal blue, gold encrusted pitcher used as a pattern shot. This was found in Florida. When trimmed in this fashion, it's known as Decoration #970. Apple Blossom is found on several Cambridge stemware lines, but the #3130 line is normally found and collected. Some collectors blend stem lines, but the bowl shapes differ and others will not combine them. I once asked a collector why she was mixing several stem lines simultaneously and was informed that she liked the pattern and bought anything she could find. I think that collecting mode may become more and more customary in the future, particularly in Elegant patterns like this.

14

	Crystal	Yellow Amber	Pink *Green
13 Ashtray, 6", heavy	50.00	125.00	150.00
Bowl, #3025, ftd., finger, w/plate	45.00	65.00	75.00
Bowl, #3130, finger, w/plate	40.00	60.00	70.00
Bowl, 3", indiv. nut, 4 ftd.	55.00	75.00	80.00
Bowl, 5¼", 2 hdld., bonbon	25.00	40.00	45.00
9 Bowl, 5½", 2 hdld., bonbon	25.00	40.00	40.00
Bowl, 5½", fruit "saucer"	20.00	28.00	30.00
Bowl, 6", 2 hdld., "basket" (sides up)	30.00	48.00	50.00
Bowl, 6", cereal	35.00	50.00	55.00
Bowl, 9", pickle	30.00	55.00	60.00
Bowl, 10", 2 hdld.	55.00	95.00	110.00
Bowl, 10", baker	60.00	100.00	110.00
Bowl, 11", fruit, tab hdld.	65.00	110.00	125.00
Bowl, 11", low ftd.	60.00	100.00	120.00
3 Bowl, 12", relish, 5 pt.	45.00	70.00	75.00
Bowl, 12", 4 ftd.	60.00	100.00	125.00
Bowl, 12", flat	55.00	90.00	95.00
Bowl, 12", oval, 4 ftd.	65.00	95.00	125.00
Bowl, 12½", console	55.00	75.00	80.00
Bowl, 13"	55.00	90.00	100.00
Bowl, cream soup, w/liner plate	35.00	55.00	60.00
Butter w/cover, 5½"	195.00	395.00	495.00
Candelabrum, 3-lite, keyhole	35.00	50.00	75.00
7 Candlestick, 1-lite, keyhole	24.00	35.00	40.00
Candlestick, 2-lite, keyhole	30.00	45.00	50.00
Candy box w/cover, 4 ftd. "bowl"	85.00	145.00	195.00
Cheese (compote) & cracker (11½" plate)	45.00	85.00	110.00
Comport, 4", fruit cocktail	20.00	28.00	30.00
Comport, 7", tall	45.00	70.00	95.00
17 Creamer, ftd., 3400/68	20.00	26.00	30.00

* Blue prices 25% to 30% more.

	Crystal	Yellow Amber	Pink *Green
Creamer, tall, ftd.	22.00	30.00	35.00
15 Cup, 3400/75	16.00	28.00	35.00
16 Cup, A.D., 3400/83	50.00	75.00	110.00
Ice bucket	95.00	150.00	235.00
Fruit/oyster cocktail, #3025, 4½ oz.	20.00	25.00	30.00
Mayonnaise, w/liner & ladle (4 ftd. bowl)	45.00	65.00	80.00
Pitcher, 50 oz., ftd., flattened sides	195.00	295.00	395.00
Pitcher, 64 oz., #3130	215.00	325.00	400.00
Pitcher, 64 oz., #3025	215.00	325.00	400.00
Pitcher, 67 oz., squeezed middle, loop hdld.	225.00	375.00	425.00
Pitcher, 76 oz.	125.00	350.00	425.00
14 Pitcher, 80 oz., ball	225.00	395.00	550.00
Pitcher w/cover, 76 oz., ftd., #3135	250.00	395.00	595.00
Plate, 6", bread/butter	8.00	10.00	12.00
Plate, 6", sq., 2 hdld.	10.00	20.00	22.00
Plate, 7½", tea	12.00	22.00	25.00
Plate, 8½"	20.00	25.00	30.00
Plate, 9½", dinner	55.00	90.00	115.00
4 Plate, 10", grill, 3400/66, club luncheon	35.00	55.00	75.00

* Blue prices 25% to 30% more.

APPLE BLOSSOM

	Crystal	Yellow Amber	Pink *Green
Plate, sandwich, 11½", tab hdld.	30.00	45.00	50.00
Plate, sandwich, 12½", 2 hdld.	32.00	50.00	60.00
Plate, sq., bread/butter	8.00	10.00	12.00
Plate, sq., dinner	55.00	90.00	115.00
Plate, sq., salad	12.00	22.00	25.00
Plate, sq., servce	30.00	45.00	50.00
Platter, 11½	55.00	95.00	120.00
Platter, 13½" rect., w/tab handle	65.00	125.00	195.00
6 Salt & pepper, pr., 3400/77	50.00	95.00	125.00
Saucer, 3400/540 rnd.	5.00	7.00	8.00
16 Saucer, A.D., squared, 3400/83	20.00	30.00	35.00
Stem, #1066, parfait	45.00	110.00	150.00
Stem, #3025, 7 oz., low fancy ft., sherbet	17.00	25.00	28.00
Stem, #3025, 7 oz., high sherbet	18.00	30.00	33.00
Stem, #3025, 10 oz.	24.00	35.00	45.00
Stem, #3130, 1 oz., cordial	65.00	110.00	175.00
8 Stem, #3130, 3 oz., cocktail	18.00	32.00	35.00
Stem, #3130, 6 oz., low sherbet	16.00	24.00	28.00
2 Stem, #3130, 6 oz., tall sherbet	18.00	30.00	33.00
1 Stem, #3130, 8 oz., water	22.00	30.00	45.00
Stem, #3135, 3 oz., cocktail	18.00	32.00	35.00
Stem, #3135, 6 oz., low sherbet	16.00	24.00	28.00
Stem, #3135, 6 oz., tall sherbet	18.00	30.00	33.00
Stem, #3135, 8 oz., water	22.00	30.00	33.00
Stem, #3400, 6 oz., ftd., sherbet	15.00	22.00	26.00
Stem, #3400, 9 oz., water	22.00	35.00	50.00
10 Sugar, ftd., 3400/68	20.00	26.00	30.00
Sugar, tall ftd.	20.00	30.00	35.00
Tray, 7", hdld. relish	25.00	40.00	45.00
5 Tray, 11", ctr. hdld. sand., 3400/10	35.00	50.00	60.00
Tumbler, #3025, 4 oz.	16.00	24.00	28.00
Tumbler, #3025, 10 oz.	20.00	30.00	35.00
Tumbler, #3025, 12 oz.	25.00	40.00	45.00
11 Tumbler, #3130, 5 oz., ftd.	16.00	28.00	33.00
Tumbler, #3130, 8 oz., ftd.	22.00	30.00	35.00
Tumbler, #3130, 10 oz., ftd.	25.00	35.00	40.00
Tumbler, #3130, 12 oz., ftd.	30.00	40.00	50.00
Tumbler, #3135, 5 oz., ftd.	16.00	30.00	35.00
Tumbler, #3135, 8 oz., ftd.	22.00	35.00	40.00
Tumbler, #3135, 10 oz., ftd.	25.00	35.00	45.00
Tumbler, #3135, 12 oz., ftd.	30.00	40.00	50.00
12 Tumbler, #3400, 2½ oz., flat	35.00	75.00	85.00
Tumbler, #3400, 12 oz., flat	22.00	30.00	35.00
Tumbler, #3400, 14 oz., flat	30.00	40.00	50.00
Tumbler, 12 oz., flat (2 styles) – 1 mid indent to match 67 oz. pitcher	25.00	50.00	60.00
Tumbler, 6"	25.00	45.00	50.00
18 Vase, 5"	65.00	110.00	145.00
Vase, 6", rippled sides	95.00	145.00	195.00
Vase, 8", 2 styles	100.00	175.00	225.00
Vase, 12", keyhole base w/neck indent	125.00	195.00	265.00

* Blue prices 25% to 30% more.

Note: See pages 252 – 253 for stem identification.

Colors: Amber, Amethyst, blue, crystal, green, pink

We understand "Balda" to be a Central Glass Works pattern that was designed by Joseph Balda who was widely acclaimed for his Heisey designs. Up until now, no one has uncovered a bona fide name from Central except Etch #410; hence its designer's appellation thus far. Stems are the most found items, the usual circumstance with most Elegant patterns. Amethyst (lilac) is the often found color and consequently the most collected.

I have added only four pieces to the listings since last book. Fellow dealers and collectors have supplied the information presented. There are likely additional pieces and/or colors to those currently listed. You are unlikely to discover large batches of "Balda," except for stemware, but it does happen periodically.

Another Central Glass pattern, Morgan is also found on the same #1428 stem and tumbler line shown here in Amethyst. The Morgan pattern is etched on at least two additional stem lines (page 149), but may be found etched on several other Central lines. Let us know what you find.

	Blue Amethyst	Pink Green Amber			Blue Amethyst	Pink Green Amber
7 Bowl, 7" soup	65.00	45.00		Saucer	6.00	4.00
Candy and lid, cone shaped, 7⅝" tall	250.00	195.00		Shaker, pr		150.00
Candlestick	65.00	45.00	9 Stem, champagne/sherbet	25.00	20.00
Cup	25.00	20.00		Stem, claret	75.00	40.00
1 Decanter and stopper	495.00	395.00	6 Stem, cordial	95.00	65.00
Ice bucket	295.00	195.00		Stem, water	45.00	30.00
Pitcher	995.00	795.00	5 Stem, wine	45.00	30.00
3 Plate, 6"	12.50	10.00		Tumbler, ftd. juice	25.00	20.00
8 Plate, lunch	20.00	14.00		Tumbler, ftd. tea	35.00	30.00
4 Plate, dinner	65.00	45.00	2 Tumbler, ftd. water	30.00	25.00
Platter	95.00	65.00		Tumbler, ftd. whiskey	50.00	35.00
				Vase, 9"	195.00	150.00

Colors: crystal, Azure blue, Topaz yellow, amber, green, pink, red, cobalt blue, black amethyst

Baroque has seven different candlesticks and that is one item that new collectors seek regardless of the pattern. There are many books out addressing this candlestick-collecting phenomenon, one of which is mine. It is called *Glass Candlesticks of the Depression Era* and the second volume is in the works. It had been almost 20 years since a candlestick book had been available and now there have been at least seven I know of since my first one appeared.

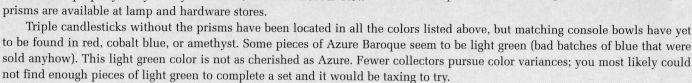

You will find both 4" and 5½" single light candles and a 4½" double candle. The 6" three-light (triple) candlesticks are called candelabra with prisms attached. Many collectors desire these elusive candelabra with older prism wires attached. Some collectors are substituting modern wires for the old, rusty ones. Once prisms are secured properly, they rarely come off, even if moved. New prisms are available at lamp and hardware stores.

Triple candlesticks without the prisms have been located in all the colors listed above, but matching console bowls have yet to be found in red, cobalt blue, or amethyst. Some pieces of Azure Baroque seem to be light green (bad batches of blue that were sold anyhow). This light green color is not as cherished as Azure. Fewer collectors pursue color variances; you most likely could not find enough pieces of light green to complete a set and it would be taxing to try.

Baroque cream soups and individual shakers are elusive in colors, and to some extent, crystal. They have always been expensive. Speaking of shakers, the regular size came with both metal and glass tops. Today, most collectors fancy glass lids. Glass lids were easily broken by over tightening them. Fostoria changed to metal lids before Baroque production was halted. Replacement lids were always metal. Metal tops are normally found on the later crystal patterns of Navarre, Chintz, Lido, and Meadow Rose that were etched onto Baroque blanks. Pitchers and punch bowls are not abundant; but blue ones are virtually impossible to find. Straight tumblers are more onerous to find than footed ones, but are preferred over cone-shaped, footed pieces even though they are more expensive. The photo above illustrates the larger sweetmeats as compared to the smaller covered jelly.

I have received numerous letters and e-mails about Wisteria Baroque vases, bowls, and candlesticks being discovered. Lancaster Colony produced a few pieces of Baroque in a color similar to Wisteria for Tiara. I have seen the bowl and vase, but not the candle. My old Tiara catalog does not show the candle. These items have a purple/pink tint; do not pay an "antique" price for Baroque pieces in this color. Baroque was never originally made in this color, which, by the way, does not change tints in natural or artificial light, as does the original Fostoria Wisteria.

			Crystal	Blue	Yellow
		Ashtray	10.00	22.00	15.00
	5	Bowl, cream soup	35.00	95.00	77.50
		Bowl, ftd., punch, 1½ gal., 8¼" x 13¼"	400.00	1,300.00	
	10	Bowl, 3¾", rose	32.00	110.00	70.00
22 23	26	Bowl, 4", hdld. (4 styles: sq., rnd., tab hdld. mint, 4⅝" tricorn)	12.50	30.00	25.00
		Bowl, 5", fruit	15.00	38.00	30.00
		Bowl, 6", cereal	22.00	60.00	42.00
		Bowl, 6", sq., sweetmeat	12.00	30.00	25.00
	34	Bowl, 6", 3-toe nut	12.00	33.00	20.00
	20	Bowl, 6", 2-part relish, sq.	14.00	30.00	22.00
		Bowl, 6½", oblong sauce	14.00	30.00	20.00
		Bowl, 6½", 2 pt. mayonnaise, oval tab hdl.	15.00	35.00	23.00
		Bowl, 7", 3 ftd.	12.50	25.00	25.00
	2	Bowl, 7½", jelly, w/cover	45.00	165.00	100.00
		Bowl, 8", pickle	15.00	32.50	25.00
		Bowl, 8½", hdld.	30.00	75.00	50.00
	31	Bowl, 9½", veg., oval	40.00	95.00	65.00
		Bowl, 10", hdld.	35.00	110.00	75.00

		Crystal	Blue	Yellow
	Bowl, 10" x 7½", hdld.	30.00		
13	Bowl, 10", relish, 3 pt.	22.00	45.00	30.00
32	Bowl, 10½", hdld., 4 ftd.	35.00	85.00	65.00
19	Bowl, 11", celery	28.00	45.00	35.00
29	Bowl, 10½", salad	35.00	75.00	65.00
	Bowl, 11", rolled edge	30.00	80.00	60.00
	*Bowl, 12", flared	30.00	45.00	35.00

*Pink just discovered.

		Crystal	Blue	Yellow
	Candelabrum, 8¼", 2-lite, 16 lustre	115.00	200.00	145.00
14	Candelabrum, 9½", 3-lite, 24 lustre	165.00	250.00	185.00
	Candle, 7¾", 8 lustre	50.00	90.00	80.00
41	Candlestick, 4"	15.00	52.50	35.00
	Candlestick, 4½", 2-lite	20.00	60.00	50.00
38	Candlestick, 5½"	30.00	65.00	45.00
	*Candlestick, 6", 3-lite	32.50	100.00	75.00
25	Candy, 3 part w/cover	55.00	140.00	95.00
	Comport, 4¾"	20.00	50.00	33.00
	Comport, 6½"	22.00	55.00	40.00
7	Creamer, 3¼", indiv.	10.00	30.00	25.00
33	Creamer, 3¾", ftd.	12.00	30.00	20.00
3	Cup	10.00	33.00	24.00
	Cup, 6 oz., punch	15.00	30.00	
28	Ice bucket	60.00	135.00	85.00
9	Mayonnaise, 5½", w/liner	30.00	95.00	70.00
16	Mustard, w/cover	50.00	110.00	85.00
21	Oil, w/stopper, 5½"	85.00	400.00	225.00
	Pitcher, 6½"	100.00	800.00	450.00
	Pitcher, 7", ice lip	100.00	750.00	550.00
	Plate, 6"	5.00	12.00	10.00
	Plate, 7½"	8.00	17.00	11.00
	Plate, 8½"	9.00	22.50	18.00
	Plate, 9½"	20.00	67.50	47.50
40	Plate, 10", cake, hdld.	30.00	45.00	35.00
	Plate, 11", ctr. hdld., sandwich	30.00		
30	Plate, 14", torte	28.00	65.00	40.00
	Platter, 12", oval	40.00	85.00	52.50
4	Salt & pepper, 2¾", pr.	60.00	165.00	120.00
	Salt & pepper, indiv., 2", pr.	60.00	250.00	200.00
39	Sauce dish	30.00	85.00	70.00
36	Sauce dish, divided	25.00	75.00	65.00
	Saucer	2.00	7.00	6.00
11	Sherbet, 3¾", 5 oz.	12.00	27.50	20.00
15	Stem, 6¾", 9 oz., water	18.00	40.00	28.00
6	Sugar, 3", indiv.	10.00	30.00	25.00
	Sugar, 3½", ftd.	12.00	30.00	20.00
1	Sweetmeat, covered, 9"	100.00	225.00	175.00
24	Tidbit, 3-toe flat	20.00	35.00	30.00
	Tray, 8" oblong, 7" w, tab hdl.	25.00	45.00	35.00
	Tray, 12½", oval	40.00	85.00	52.50
8	Tray, 6¼" for indiv. cream/sugar	15.00	25.00	20.00
35	Tumbler, 3½", 6½ oz., old-fashion	22.50	95.00	60.00
17	Tumbler, 3", 3½ oz., ftd., cocktail	12.00	30.00	22.00
12	Tumbler, 6", 12 oz., ftd., tea	20.00	40.00	30.00
18	Tumbler, 3¾", 5 oz., juice	15.00	50.00	33.00
	Tumbler, 5½", 9 oz., ftd., water	12.00	30.00	25.00
	Tumbler, 4¼", 9 oz., water	25.00	55.00	37.50
	Tumbler, 5¾", 14 oz., tea	35.00	95.00	62.00
37	Vase, 6½"	50.00	145.00	110.00
27	Vase, 7"	60.00	175.00	135.00

* Red $150.00; Green $120.00; Black Amethyst $140.00; Cobalt Blue $140.00; Amber $75.00

BLACK FOREST, possibly Paden City for Van Deman & Son, late 1920s – early 1930s

Colors: amber, black, ice blue, crystal, green, pink, red, cobalt

Internet auctions have blown the former standard prices of Black Forest out of the water. Prices for many pieces have jumped to previously unknown realms. Internet activity has also stimulated sales in Deerwood, a pattern often advertised wrongly as Black Forest. Black Forest portrays moose and trees, while deer and trees are on Deerwood.

I am frequently asked about the etched, heavy goblets pictured here, that were made in the 1970s in amber, amberina, dark green, blue, crystal, and ruby by L. G. Wright. These are retailing in the $18.00 to $30.00 range with red and blue on the upper side of that price. These newer goblets have a heavy, prevalent "Daisy and Button" cubed stem and are not accepted as Black Forest by most long-time collectors. However, newer collectors have no such qualms and buy because "They're neat!" as one enthusiast put it.

		Amber	*Black	Crystal	Green	Pink	Red
	Batter jug			250.00			
	Bowl, 4½", finger				40.00		
	Bowl, 9¼", center hdld.				125.00	125.00	
	Bowl, 11", console	95.00	150.00	65.00	125.00	125.00	
	Bowl, 11", fruit		150.00		125.00	125.00	
	Bowl, 13", console		195.00				
	Bowl, 3 ftd.			100.00			
	Cake plate, 2" pedestal	95.00	150.00		125.00	125.00	
9	Candlestick, mushroom style, Line 210, 2⅜"		50.00	95.00	50.00	85.00	85.00
	Candlestick double			100.00			
8 11	Candy dish, w/cover, several styles	155.00	250.00		225.00	225.00	
14	Creamer, 2 styles, Line 210 shown	50.00	75.00	35.00	65.00	65.00	
6	Comport, 4", low ftd.				75.00	75.00	
	Comport, 5½", high ftd.		125.00		100.00	100.00	
10	Cup and saucer, 3 styles		150.00		125.00	125.00	175.00
	Decanter, w/stopper, 8½", 28 oz., bulbous				395.00	395.00	395.00
	Decanter w/stopper, 8¾", 24 oz., straight				295.00	395.00	395.00
3	Egg cup, Line 210				195.00		
	Ice bucket		225.00		125.00	125.00	
	Ice pail, 6", 3" high	150.00					
2	Ice tub, 2 styles (ice blue $1,000.00), Line 210	160.00	250.00		195.00	195.00	
	Mayonnaise, with liner		175.00		125.00	125.00	
	Night set: pitcher, 6½", 42 oz. & tumbler				695.00	695.00	
	Pitcher, 8", 40 oz. (cobalt $1,500.00)						
1	Pitcher, 8", 62 oz., night set			265.00			
5	Pitcher, 9", 80 oz.					500.00	
	Pitcher, 10½", 72 oz., T-neck, bulbous bottom				625.00	625.00	
	Plate, 6½", bread/butter		35.00		30.00	30.00	
	Plate, 8", luncheon		50.00		40.00	40.00	
	Plate, 10", dinner		225.00				
	Plate, 11", 2 hdld.		125.00		65.00	65.00	
18	Plate, 13¾", 2 hdld., Line 210				100.00	100.00	
	Relish, 10½", 5 pt. covered				595.00	595.00	
	Salt and pepper, pr.			125.00		175.00	
4	Server, center hdld.	50.00	40.00	35.00	50.00	35.00	
	Shot glass, 2 oz., 2½"	40.00					
	Stem, 2 oz., wine, 4¼"			17.50	50.00		
	Stem, 6 oz., champagne, 4¾"			17.50		30.00	
	Stem, 9 oz., water, 6"			22.50			
15	Sugar, 2 styles, Line 210 shown	50.00	75.00	35.00	65.00	65.00	
12 13	Tumbler, 3 oz., juice, flat or footed, 3½"			50.00	95.00	95.00	
7	Tumbler, 8 oz., old fashion, 3⅞"				95.00	95.00	
	Tumbler, 9 oz., ftd., 5½"	50.00					
	Tumbler, 12 oz., tea, 5½"				125.00	125.00	
16	Vase, 6½" (cobalt $300.00)		195.00	100.00	175.00	175.00	
19	Vase, 8½", Line 210						
17	Vase, 10", 2 styles in black, Line 210		250.00		195.00	195.00	
	Whipped cream pail	95.00					

*Add 20% for gold decorated.

26

BO PEEP, Design #854, Monongah, late 1920s

Colors: pink, amber, pink and green with crystal, green, all with Optic

Monongah was squeezed out of business in the economic decline of the late 20s by the larger, more mechanized glass firms who were able to "hang on" after the Depression. It was taken over by Hocking Glass Company. Bo Peep was made by Monongah, although the shapes are very analogous to those we identify as Tiffin. Perhaps these moulds were sold to Tiffin in an effort to stay afloat or maybe Hocking sold them after the takeover, as they did not then make glass of this quality. Cathy found the green-footed juice tumbler pictured about 25 years ago and asked me to gather other pieces in the pattern. Bo Peep is not bountiful and I have spent those years accumulating what you see here.

I have seen one large set of Bo Peep for sale in an antique mall. Prices were more than I was willing to pay for stems then. Even today, I would have trouble selling them had I purchased them. I did buy the vase and pitcher depicted here. The pitcher lid is undecorated, as are Tiffin pitchers. Another collector was pleased I turned down the set; he ultimately bought it. One of the toughest lessons as a dealer is a desire to buy pieces you like. You have a tendency to pay too much and not be able to profit. Frankly, over the years I have probably made more money from buying things I do not like because I am never tempted to buy them for more than I can sell profitably.

	Pink Green			Pink Green
Finger bowl, ftd., #6102	95.00	9	Stem, low sherbet, #6102	70.00
7 Jug w/cover, #20	995.00		Stem, parfait, #6102	110.00
Jug w/o cover, #20	895.00	1	Stem, water, #6102	135.00
3 Plate, 7½", salad	40.00		Stem, wine, #6102	135.00
Stem, cocktail, #6102	75.00	8	Tumbler, 5 oz., ftd., juice/seltzer, #6102	95.00
4 Stem, high sherbet, #6102	75.00	5	Tumbler, 9 oz., ftd., water/table, #6102	75.00
		6	Tumbler, 12 oz., ftd., iced tea, #6102	95.00
		2	Vase, 9", ruffled edge, #0713	495.00

Colors: Azure blue, crystal, Ebony, green, Orchid, Rose

Pictured are several Fostoria Brocades, illustrating that you can simply blend the different designs rather than buy only one. Designs are shown separately here and on pages 30 – 31. With any luck, the labeled small group shots will make identification easier. You should know that Oak Leaf pattern with iridescence is correctly referred to as Oak Wood, and Paradise with iridescence is called Victoria, Decoration #71.

Grape

Grape

	#290 Oakleaf			#72 Oakwood	#289 Paradise	#73 Palm Leaf		#287 Grape	
	Crystal	Green/Rose	Ebony	Orchid/Azure	Green/Orchid	Rose/Green	Blue	Green	Orchid
Bonbon, #2375	30.00	45.00		50.00		50.00		40.00	
Bowl, finger, #869	60.00	70.00		75.00					
Bowl, 4½", mint, #2394	30.00	40.00							
Bowl, 7½", "D," cupped rose, #2339							85.00	60.00	110.00
Bowl, 10", scroll hdld, #2395	90.00	155.00	145.00			200.00			
12 Bowl, 10", 2 hdld, #2375	80.00	125.00		175.00		165.00			
Bowl, 10½", "A," 3 ftd., #2297					95.00		95.00	70.00	120.00
Bowl, 10½", "C," sm roll rim, deep, #2297							95.00	70.00	120.00
Bowl, 10½", "C," pedestal ftd., #2315					95.00				
Bowl, 11", roll edge ctrpiece, #2329					100.00		155.00	135.00	175.00
Bowl, 11", ctrpiece, #2375				195.00		155.00			
Bowl, 11", cornucopia hdld, #2398	100.00	135.00							
8 Bowl, 12", 3 toe, flair rim, #2394	100.00	125.00		195.00		150.00			
Bowl, 12", console, #2375	85.00	115.00							
2 Bowl, 12" low, "saturn rings," #2362					85.00		115.00	90.00	135.00
Bowl, 12", hexagonal, 3 tab toe, #2342	110.00	135.00		210.00	100.00				
4 Bowl, 12", "A," 3 tab toe, #2297					115.00		125.00	110.00	135.00
Bowl, 12½", "E," flat, shallow, #2297							125.00	100.00	135.00
Bowl, 13", ctrpiece rnd., #2329					140.00		225.00	195.00	235.00
Bowl, ctrpiece oval, #2375½		135.00		175.00		295.00			
Bowl, 13", oval, roll edge w/grid frog, #2371					175.00		225.00	185.00	250.00
Bowl, #2415 comb, candle hdld.	120.00	175.00	185.00	295.00		250.00			
Candlestick, 2", mushroom, #2372					25.00		35.00	30.00	35.00
Candlestick, 2", 3 toe, #2394	40.00	55.00				70.00			
Candlestick, 3", scroll, #2395	50.00	65.00	75.00						
Candlestick, 3", #2375	45.00	60.00		65.00		75.00			
Candlestick, 3", stack disc, #2362					40.00		35.00	30.00	35.00
1 Candlestick, 4", #2324					35.00		35.00	30.00	35.00
13 Candlestick, 5", 2395½						95.00			
Candlestick, hex mushroom, #2375½	45.00	55.00		75.00					
Candlestick, trindle, #2383 ea.						145.00			
9 Candy box, cov., 3 pt, #2331	100.00	150.00	200.00	250.00			185.00	145.00	200.00
11 Candy, box, cone lid, #2380	100.00	145.00			115.00				

BROCADE

Oakwood

Oak Leaf

	#290 Oakleaf			#72 Oakwood	#289 Paradise	#73 Palm Leaf	#287 Grape		
	Crystal	Green/Rose	Ebony	Orchid/Azure	Green/Orchid	Rose/Green	Blue	Green	Orchid
Candy, cov,, oval, #2395		135.00		200.00					
Cheese & cracker, #2368	65.00	75.00							
Cigarette & cov. (small), #2391	65.00	135.00	120.00	175.00					
Cigarette & cov. (large), #2391	85.00	135.00	125.00	185.00					
Comport, 6", #2400						125.00			
Comport, 7" tall, twist stem, #2327					75.00		75.00	55.00	75.00
Comport, 8", short, ftd, #2350					65.00				
Comport, 8", pulled stem, #2400				115.00					
Comport, 11", stack disc stem, ftd., #2362					100.00		125.00	100.00	120.00
10 Ice bucket, #2378	100.00	145.00		225.00		155.00	100.00	90.00	95.00
Ice bucket, w/drainer, handle & tongs, #2378				150.00		140.00	125.00	130.00	
Jug, #5000	395.00	595.00		995.00	695.00				
6 Lemon, "bow" or open hdld, #2375	30.00	45.00		65.00	60.00	40.00		40.00	
Mayonnaise, #2315	55.00	70.00		225.00					
Plate, mayonnaise, #2332	20.00	30.00		35.00					
Plate, 6", #2283	15.00	20.00							
Plate, 7", #2283	20.00	25.00		35.00					
Plate, 8", sq., #2419						35.00			
Plate, 8", #2283	22.00	30.00		45.00					
Plate, 10", cake, #2375	65.00	90.00		125.00		155.00			
Plate, 12", salver, #2315	100.00	125.00		160.00					
Plate, 13", lettuce, #2315	60.00	90.00		145.00					
Stem, ¾ oz., cordial, #877	65.00			165.00					
Stem, 2¾ oz., wine, #877	35.00			95.00					
Stem, 3½ oz., cocktail, #877	25.00			65.00					
Stem, 4 oz., claret, #877	35.00			95.00					
Stem, 6 oz., hi sherbet, #877	32.50			65.00					
5 Stem, 6 oz., low sherbet, #877	22.50			55.00					
Stem, 10 oz., water, #877	45.00			100.00					
Sugar pail, #2378	105.00	150.00		225.00		250.00			
7 Sweetmeat, hex 2 hdld bowl, #2375	35.00	45.00		60.00		60.00		40.00	
Tray, rnd, fleur de lis hdld., #2387							95.00	90.00	95.00
3 Tray, ctr, hdld., #2342, octagonal	65.00	95.00		160.00	75.00	140.00	95.00	90.00	95.00
Tumbler, 2½ oz., ftd. whiskey, #877	30.00	75.00							
Tumbler, 4½ oz., ftd. oyster cocktail	22.50								
Tumbler, 5 oz., ftd. juice, #877	30.00								
Tumbler, 5½ oz., parfait, #877	40.00	65.00							
Tumbler, 9 oz., ftd., #877				85.00	60.00				
Tumbler, 12 oz., ftd. tea, #877				110.00	65.00				
Urn & cover, #2413		200.00		410.00		495.00			
Vase, 3", 4", #4103, bulbous	50.00	60.00	75.00		70.00		85.00	70.00	80.00
Vase, 5", 6", #4103, optic					75.00		105.00	90.00	100.00
Vase, 6", #4100, flat straight side optic					85.00		105.00	90.00	100.00

Palm Leaf

Paradise

	#290 Oakleaf			#72 Oakwood	#289 Paradise	#73 Palm Leaf	#287 Grape		
	Crystal	Green/Rose	Ebony	Orchid/Azure	Green/Orchid	Rose/Green	Blue	Green	Orchid
Vase, 6", #4105, scallop rim	65.00	85.00		140.00	85.00				
Vase, 7", 9", ftd. urn, #2369	85.00	100.00		140.00	120.00	150.00			
Vase, 8", cupped melon, #2408						255.00			
Vase, 8", #2292, ftd. flair flat, straight side	85.00	100.00	125.00						
Vase, 8", #4100					95.00		125.00	115.00	135.00
Vase, 8", #4105	70.00	95.00		265.00		250.00			
Vase, 8", melon, #2387	90.00	115.00		210.00					
Vase, 8½" fan, #2385	150.00	200.00		450.00		285.00			
Vase, 10½" ftd., #2421						295.00			
Vase, sm. or lg. window & cov., #2373	150.00	200.00	350.00	365.00		350.00			
Whip cream, scallop 2 hdld bowl, #2375	35.00	50.00		55.00		40.00			
Whip cream pail, #2378	90.00	135.00		195.00				40.00	

Colors: pink and green

McKee's Brocade only came in the one pattern unlike Fostoria's many. I have heard it referred to many times by collectors as "Poinsettia" and even "Palm Tree" though I have no official reference for either name. I did find a few more pieces to show. Usually sellers of this pattern do not know what it is but price it rather exorbitantly.

		Pink/Green
	Bowl, 12", flared edge	55.00
	Bowl, center, hdld. nut	45.00
2	Bowl, 12", console, rolled edge	55.00
5	Candlestick, roll edge, octagonal	20.00
1	Candlestick, octagonal ft.	25.00
	Candy box/cover	75.00
	Candy jar, ftd., w/cover	65.00
	Cheese and cracker	55.00
	Compote, 10", flared edge	65.00
	Compote, cone shape, octagonal	65.00
3 4	Mayonnaise, 3 pc., w/liner & spoon	50.00
	Salver, ftd. (cake stand)	45.00
	Server, center hdld.	40.00
	Vase, 11", bulbous	165.00

Colors: pink, crystal

"Bubble Girl" has been a mystery for glass dealers and collectors for over 25 years. In the early 80s, several dealers discussed this pattern over dinner in Cambridge, Ohio. Plates were showing up marked Cambridge, but the stems all looked like Fry blanks which confused us terribly then. "Bubble Girl" was the name proposed as the reclining woman looks to be blowing bubbles. I remember jokes about Lawrence Welk and several other references to bubbles and champagne, but "Bubble Girl" seemed to stick from that time.

I bought several stems hoping to research it in the future, but they were boxed up and forgotten. A few years ago, I found a Heisey candle and a friend found a Heisey Octagon bowl for me. It took some doing to uncover the stems, and meantime we found some footed water and tea tumblers to match. In any case, the listing is what we have been able to find and can only surmise that this is a Lotus (or another company's) etching on molds of at least three glassmakers.

Most plates are unmarked, but others have Cambridge's triangle in a "C." Stems and tumblers are Fry with bowls and candles being Heisey. The five-part relish was an unknown entity so that would make a possible fourth maker. This pattern needs your input; so if you see additional items, let me know.

		Pink, Crystal			Pink, Crystal
1	Bowl, 5⅜", 2-hdld., Heisey, Octagon, 1229 Jelly	55.00		Stem, 3 oz., 4¾", wine	37.50
3	Bowl, 11½", Octagon, 1229 Floral	65.00	5	Stem, 3½ oz., 4⅜", cocktail	30.00
4	Candlestick, 3½", Heisey, Pluto #114	37.50	6	Stem, 7 oz., 5⅛", Fry stem, high sherbet	22.50
	Plate, 6¼", sherbet	12.50	7	Stem, 9 oz., 7", Fry stem, water	35.00
	Plate, 6⅝", Octagon, 2-hdld.	45.00	8	Tumbler, 10 oz., 5⅛", Fry blank, ftd. water	25.00
2	Plate, 8½" luncheon	18.00	9	Tumbler 15 oz., 6¼", Fry blank, ftd. ice tea	35.00
	Relish, 5-part	75.00			

Colors: crystal, yellow; some pink

Cadena stemware is a collector's dream, but finding serving pieces is a nightmare. Even if you are willing to pay the price for them, they will only appear infrequently. I have never been able to buy a bowl of any size in 25 years of looking. Oh, I have seen some, but they have been more highly prized by their owners even with a thumb-sized piece missing in one case. Never leave a piece you discover at a reasonable price. Someone wants it, even if you are not interested.

A few pieces of pink have been surfacing, but not enough yet to make a set — even a small one. Tiffin pitchers were sold either with or without a lid. The top edge of pitchers without lids were often curved in or "cupped" so much that a lid will not fit inside the lip. Thus, buying a lid separately may be a bit premature unless you have the pitcher available to see if it fits. Remember that the pitcher cover does not have an etching, even though the Cadena pitcher itself will.

		Crystal	Pink Yellow
	Bowl, cream soup, #5831	25.00	45.00
	Bowl, finger, ftd., #041	25.00	45.00
	Bowl, grapefruit, ftd., #251	50.00	110.00
	Bowl, 6", hdld., #5831	20.00	30.00
	Bowl, 10", pickle, #5831	30.00	45.00
	Bowl, 12", console, ftd., #5831	35.00	65.00
	Candlestick, #5831	30.00	55.00
1	Creamer, #5831	20.00	30.00
	Cup, #5831	45.00	100.00
	Decanter w/stopper	150.00	300.00
	Mayonnaise, ftd., w/liner, #5831	50.00	85.00
	Oyster cocktail, #065	20.00	32.00
3	Pitcher, ftd., #194	225.00	325.00
	Pitcher, ftd., w/cover, #194	295.00	425.00
	Plate, 6", #8814	8.00	12.00
	Plate, 7¾", #5831	10.00	20.00
	Plate, 9¼"	45.00	75.00

		Crystal	Pink Yellow
	Saucer, #5831	15.00	25.00
9	Stem, 4¾", sherbet/sundae	18.00	25.00
6	Stem, 5¼", cocktail	22.00	30.00
	Stem, 5¼", ¾ oz., cordial	75.00	150.00
	Stem, 6", wine	30.00	60.00
	Stem, 6⁵⁄₁₆", 8 oz., parfait	35.00	70.00
5	Stem, 6½", champagne	25.00	32.00
4	Stem, 7½", water, #065	35.00	40.00
2	Sugar, #5831	20.00	30.00
	Tumbler, 3¼", ftd., bar, #065	20.00	30.00
8	Tumbler, 4¼", ftd., juice, #065	22.00	30.00
7	Tumbler, 5¼", ftd., water, #065	25.00	33.00
	Vase, 9"	115.00	165.00

Colors: crystal, crystal and Crown Tuscan with gold decoration

Between pamphlet pages and the identifying each item in the photograph, we hope we have solved recognition questions asked over the years. Pictured is a 1951 Candlelight brochure of the type usually given to people who were registering a pattern for bridal gifts. We have opened it to show you the #3776 stems usually found in Candlelight.

The photo below shows mostly #3114 stemware. Candlelight is not as abundant as other Cambridge patterns. Candlelight was made in two ways. The pattern was *cut* into some pieces, but was acid *etched* on others. The cut items are scarce, but there are fewer collectors for cut pieces. To illustrate the difference, there are two icers and liners in the photograph below: one etched, the other cut. The pattern is harder to see on the cut one at the right. There is cutting on the foot, but the etched has no design on the foot. Etching was accomplished by covering the glass except where the design was desired and then dipping the glass into acid.

With many collectors searching for this pattern, there is a scarcity of shakers (both footed and flat), butter dishes, basic serving pieces, candlesticks, and even cups and saucers. Do not pass any of those items if you have a chance to buy them. Again, even if you don't want them, someone does.

Dealers remember that, today, when people ask for wine goblets, you need to find out if they want water goblets. Originally, wine goblets held 2½ to 4 ounces; but now, many people think of wine goblets as holding 8 or 9 ounces. Thus, what they want for serving wine is a water goblet.

	Crystal		Crystal
Bonbon, 7", ftd., 2 hdld., #3900/130	40.00	Bowl, 11½", ftd., 2 hdld., #3900/28	85.00
Bowl, 10", 4 toed, flared, #3900/54	85.00	Bowl, 12", 4 ftd., flared, #3400/4	85.00
Bowl, 11", 2 hdld., #3900/34	95.00	Bowl, 12", 4 ftd., oblong, #3400/160	90.00
Bowl, 11", 4 ftd., fancy edge, #3400/48	100.00	Bowl, 12", 4 toed, flared, #3900/62	90.00

	Crystal
Bowl, 12", 4 toed, oval, hdld., #3900/65	110.00
Butter dish, 5", #3400/52	325.00
Candle, 5", #3900/67	60.00
Candle, 6", 2-lite, #3900/72	75.00
Candle, 6", 3-lite, #3900/74	95.00
Candlestick, 5", #646	65.00
Candlestick, 6", 2-lite, #647	75.00
Candlestick, 6", 3-lite, #1338	95.00
Candy box and cover, 3-part, #3500/57	165.00
Candy w/lid*, rnd., div., #3900/165	60.00
Cocktail shaker, 36 oz., #P101	245.00
Comport, 5", cheese, #3900/135	45.00
Comport, 5⅜", blown, #3121	80.00
Comport, 5½", #3900/136	70.00
Creamer, #3900/41	25.00
Creamer, indiv., #3900/40	25.00
Cruet, 6 oz., w/stopper, #3900/100	175.00
Cup, #3900/17	33.00
Decanter, 28 oz., ftd., #1321	265.00
6 Ice bucket, #3900/671	175.00
5 Icer, 2 pc., cocktail, #968	120.00
Lamp, hurricane, #1617	225.00
Lamp, hurricane, keyhole, w/bobeche, #1603	275.00
Lamp, hurricane, w/bobeche, #1613	325.00
Mayonnaise, 3 pc., #3900/129	75.00
Mayonnaise, div., 4 pc., #3900/111	85.00
Mayonnaise, ftd., 2 pc., #3900/19	75.00
Nut cup, 3", 4 ftd., #3400/71	70.00
Oil, 6 oz., #3900/100	125.00
11 Pitcher, Doulton, #3400/141	435.00
Plate, 6½", #3900/20	14.00
Plate, 8", 2 hdld., #3900/131	30.00
Plate, 8", salad, #3900/22	22.00
Plate, 10½", dinner, #3900/24	95.00
Plate, 12", 4 toed, #3900/26	75.00
Plate, 13", torte, 4 toed, #3900/33	85.00
Plate, 13½", cake, 2 hdld., #3900/35	85.00
Plate, 13½", cracker, #3900/135	75.00
Plate, 14", rolled edge, #3900/166	85.00
Relish, 7", 2 hdld., #3900/123	45.00
Relish, 7", div., 2 hdld., #3900/124	50.00
8 Relish, 8", 3 part, #3400/91	65.00
Relish, 9", 3 pt., #3900/125	65.00
Relish, 12", 3 pt., #3900/126	75.00
Relish, 12", 5 pt., #3900/120	85.00
1 Salt & pepper, pr., #3900/1177	150.00
13 Salt & pepper, ftd., #3400/77	140.00
Saucer, #3900/17	7.00
Stem, 1 oz., cordial, #3776	95.00
Stem, 2 oz., sherry, trumpet, #7966	90.00
15 Stem, 2½ oz., wine, #3111, w/ball, 3114, w/rings	80.00
Stem, 3 oz., cocktail, #3114	40.00
Stem, 3 oz., cocktail, #3776	40.00
2 Stem, 3½ oz., wine, #3776	65.00

	Crystal
Stem, 4 oz., cocktail, #7801	35.00
Stem, 4½ oz., claret, #3776	90.00
Stem, 4½ oz., oyster cocktail, #3114	40.00
Stem, 4½ oz., oyster cocktail, #3776	40.00
Stem, 7 oz., low sherbet, #3114	23.00
Stem, 7 oz., low sherbet, #3776	24.00
Stem, 7 oz., tall sherbet, #3114	30.00
Stem, 7 oz., tall sherbet, #3776	28.00
Stem, 9 oz., water, #3776	50.00
10 Stem, 10 oz., water, #3114	50.00
7 Sugar, #3900/41	25.00
Sugar, indiv., #3900/40	35.00
4 Tumbler, 5 oz., ftd., juice, #3114	30.00
Tumbler, 5 oz., juice, #3776	30.00
3 Tumbler, 10 oz., ftd., #3114	37.50
14 Tumbler, 12 oz., ftd., iced tea, #3114	45.00
Tumbler, 12 oz., iced tea, #3776	45.00
Tumbler, 13 oz., #3900/115	50.00
Vase, 5", ftd., bud, #6004	95.00
12 Vase, 5", globe, #1309	85.00
Vase, 6", ftd., #6004	100.00
Vase, 8", ftd., #6004	120.00
Vase, 9", ftd., keyhole, #1237	125.00
Vase, 10", bud, #274	95.00
Vase, 11", ftd., pedestal, #1299	185.00
9 Vase, 11", ftd., #278	135.00
Vase, 12", ftd., keyhole, #1238	175.00
Vase, 13", ftd, #279	195.00

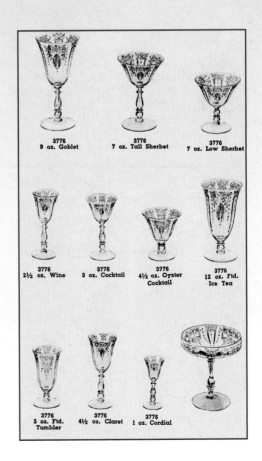

Colors: crystal, blue, pink, yellow, black, red, cobalt blue, green, caramel slag

New collectors should know that not all Candlewick has a ball in its stem. Note the Ritz blue oyster cocktail shown on page 39. After explaining the story of finding these at an antique show where no one recognized them, I have had other dealers tell me that they had found these priced inexpensively since seeing them pictured in my book.

Tumbler and stemware identification is a primary concern of new collectors of Candlewick. Stemware line 400/190 comes with a hollow stem. These are not pictured this time, but should be self-explanatory. The tumblers designated 400/19 have flat bases with knobs around that base as opposed to 400/18 that has a domed foot. The 400/... was Imperial's factory listing for each piece. If you can find a copy of my first *Elegant Glassware of the Depression Era* book, there is a 15-page reprint of Imperial's Catalog B showing Candlewick listings as distributed by the factory.

Viennese (light blue) Candlewick is selling well if priced appropriately, but higher priced red and black items have presently leveled off. One of the problems has been the many reproductions of Candlewick coming into the market. *Candlewick was never made by Imperial in Jadite.* Dalzell Viking made red and cobalt blue pieces before they went bankrupt and many people rushed to their outlet store to buy these pieces including punch sets.

For now, prices have slowed down due to the many colored reproductions. Ruby and black fancy bowls sell in the ballpark of $225.00 – 250.00 with the Viennese blue pieces bringing 50 to 60 percent of that. Ruby stems continue to be found in the 3400 and 3800 lines with most of these selling in the $85.00 – 120.00 range. However, cordials are selling in Ruby and Ritz blue (cobalt) from $125.00 to $175.00. Other Ritz blue stems are fetching $125.00 – 175.00. All of these original colored pieces of Candlewick, except black, were made before 1940.

Collectors and non-collectors alike admire the 72-hole birthday cake plate. One woman told me she was looking for a second one as she ran out of holes for candles since she was turning 73 years young.

Be sure to notice the hanging lamp on page 37. It was fascinating watching the photographers figure how to support it for a photo, although fascinating is not one of the adjectives I heard used while trying to hang it. It was heftier than it looked.

	Crystal
Ashtray, eagle, 6½", 1776/1	55.00
Ashtray, heart, 4½", 400/172	10.00
Ashtray, heart, 5½", 400/173	12.00
Ashtray, heart, 6½", 400/174	15.00
Ashtray, indiv., 400/64.	8.00
Ashtray, oblong, 4½", 400/134/1	6.00
Ashtray, round, 2¾", 400/19	9.00
Ashtray, round, 4", 400/33	12.00
Ashtray, round, 5", 400/133	10.00
Ashtray, square, 3¼", 400/651	35.00
Ashtray, square, 4½", 400/652	35.00
Ashtray, square, 5¾", 400/653	45.00
Ashtray, 6", matchbook holder center, 400/60	165.00
Ashtray set, 3 pc. rnd. nesting (crys. or colors), 400/550	35.00
Ashtray set, 3 pc. sq. nesting, 400/650	115.00
Ashtray set, 4 pc. bridge (cigarette holder at side), 400/118	50.00
Basket, 5", beaded hdld., 400/273	265.00
Basket, 6½", hdld., 400/40/0	37.50
Basket, 11", hdld., 400/73/0	285.00
Bell, 4", 400/179	85.00
Bell, 5", 400/108	95.00
Bottle, bitters, w/tube, 4 oz., 400/117	75.00
Bowl, bouillon, 2 hdld., 400/126	50.00
Bowl, #3400, finger, ftd.	35.00
Bowl, #3800, finger	35.00
Bowl, 4½", nappy, 3 ftd., 400/206	80.00
Bowl, 4¾", round, 2 hdld., 400/42B	12.50
Bowl, 5", cream soup, 400/50	45.00
Bowl, 5", fruit, 400/1F	12.00
Bowl, 5", heart w/hand., 400/49H	22.00
Bowl, 5", square, 400/231	95.00
51 Bowl, 5½", heart, 400/53H	22.00
Bowl, 5½", jelly, w/cover, 400/59	75.00

	Crystal
Bowl, 5½", sauce, deep, 400/243	40.00
Bowl, 6", baked apple, rolled edge, 400/53X	35.00
Bowl, 6", cottage cheese, 400/85	25.00
Bowl, 6", fruit, 400/3F	12.00
Bowl, 6", heart w/hand., 400/51H	30.00
Bowl, 6", mint w/hand., 400/51F	23.00
20 Bowl, 6", round, div., 2 hdld., 400/52	25.00
Bowl, 6", 2 hdld., 400/52B	15.00
Bowl, 6", 3 ftd., 400/183	60.00
Bowl, 6", sq., 400/232	125.00
Bowl, 6½", relish, 2 pt., 400/84	25.00
Bowl, 6½", 2 hdld., 400/181	30.00
Bowl, 7", round, 400/5F	25.00
Bowl, 7", round, 2 hdld., 400/62B	17.50
Bowl, 7", relish, sq., div., 400/234	165.00
Bowl, 7", ivy, high, bead ft., 400/188	235.00
Bowl, 7", lily, 4 ft., 400/74J	75.00
Bowl, 7", relish, 400/60	25.00
Bowl, 7", sq., 400/233	155.00
Bowl, 7¼", rose, ftd. w/crimp edge, 400/132C	550.00
Bowl, 7½", pickle/celery, 400/57	27.50
Bowl, 7½", lily, bead rim, ftd., 400/75N	325.00
Bowl, 7½", belled (console base), 400/127B	85.00
Bowl, 8", round, 400/7F	37.50
Bowl, 8", relish, 2 pt., 400/268	20.00
Bowl, 8", cov. veg., 400/65/1	395.00
Bowl, 8½", rnd., 400/69B	35.00
Bowl, 8½", nappy, 4 ftd., 400/74B	75.00
Bowl, 8½", 3 ftd., 400/182	135.00
Bowl, 8½", 2 hdld., 400/72B	22.00
Bowl, 8½", pickle/celery, 400/58	20.00
Bowl, 8½", relish, 4 pt., 400/55	22.00
Bowl, 9", round, 400/10F	50.00
Bowl, 9", crimp, ftd., 400/67C	175.00
Bowl, 9", sq., fancy crimp edge, 4 ft., 400/74SC	85.00
Bowl, 9", heart, 400/49H	125.00
Bowl, 9", heart w/hand., 400/73H	160.00
Bowl, 10", 400/13F	45.00
Bowl, 10", banana, 400/103E	1,995.00
Bowl, 10", 3 toed, 400/205	175.00
Bowl, 10", belled (punch base), 400/128B	95.00
Bowl, 10", cupped edge, 400/75F	45.00
Bowl, 10", deep, 2 hdld., 400/113A	165.00
Bowl, 10", divided, deep, 2 hdld., 400/114A	185.00
Bowl, 10", fruit, bead stem (like compote), 400/103F	235.00
Bowl, 10", relish, oval, 2 hdld., 400/217	40.00
Bowl, 10", relish, 3 pt., 3 ft., 400/208	115.00
Bowl, 10", 3 pt., w/cover, 400/216	695.00
Bowl, 10½", belled, 400/63B	60.00
Bowl, 10½", butter/jam, 3 pt., 400/262	235.00
50 Bowl, 10½", salad, 400/75B	40.00
21 Bowl, 10½", relish, 3 section, 400/256	30.00
Bowl, 11", celery boat, oval, 400/46	65.00
Bowl, 11", centerpiece, flared, 400/13B	55.00
Bowl, 11", float, inward rim, ftd., 400/75F	40.00
Bowl, 11", oval, 400/124A	295.00
Bowl, 11", oval w/partition, 400/125A	350.00
Bowl, 12", round, 400/92B	45.00
Bowl, 12", belled, 400/106B	100.00

11

30

		Crystal
55	Bowl, 12", cupped, float, console, rnd., 400/92F	40.00
	Bowl, 12", hdld., 400/113B	165.00
	Bowl, 12", shallow, 400/17F	47.50
	Bowl, 12", relish, oblong, 4 sect., 400/215	125.00
	Bowl, 13", centerpiece, mushroom, 400/92L	60.00
	Bowl, 13", float, 1½" deep, 400/101	65.00
	Bowl, 13½", relish, 5 pt., 400/209	82.50
	Bowl, 14", belled, 400/104B	110.00
	Bowl, 14", oval, flared, 400/131B	295.00
	Butter and jam set, 5 piece, 400/204	495.00
	Butter, w/ cover, rnd., 5½", 400/144	35.00
	Butter, w/ cover, no beads, California, 400/276	150.00
	Butter, w/ bead top, ¼ lb., 400/161	30.00
53	Cake stand, 10", low foot, 400/67D	60.00
1	Cake stand, 11", high foot, 400/103D	75.00
	Calendar, 1947, desk	250.00
	Candleholder, 3 way, beaded base, 400/115	135.00
	Candleholder, 2-lite, 400/100	24.00
	Candleholder, flat, 3½", 400/280	40.00
	Candleholder, 3½", rolled edge, 400/79R	17.50
	Candleholder, 3½", w/fingerhold, 400/81	60.00
	Candleholder, flower, 4", 2 bead stem, 400/66F	65.00
	Candleholder, flower, 4½", 2 bead stem, 400/66C	65.00
	Candleholder, 4½", 3 toed, 400/207	110.00
	Candleholder, 3-lite on cir. bead. ctr., 400/147	45.00
	Candleholder, 5", hdld./bowled up base, 400/90	65.00
	Candleholder, 5", heart shape, 400/40HC	110.00
	Candleholder, 5½", 3 bead stems, 400/224	165.00
	Candleholder, flower, 5" (epergne inset), 400/40CV	195.00
	Candleholder, 5", flower, 400/40C	35.00
	Candleholder, 6½", tall, 3 bead stems, 400/175	185.00
	Candleholder, flower, 6", round, 400/40F	40.00
	Candleholder, urn, 6", holders on cir. ctr. bead, 400/129R	185.00
	Candleholder, flower, 6½", square, 400/40S	85.00
	Candleholder, mushroom, 400/86	40.00
	Candleholder, flower, 9", centerpiece, 400/196FC	245.00
	Candy box, round, 5½", 400/59	50.00
	Candy box, sq., 6½", rnd. lid, 400/245	350.00
	Candy box, w/ cover, 7", 400/259	165.00
54	Candy box, w/ cover, 7" partitioned, 400/110	125.00
	Candy box, w/ cover, round, 7", 3 sect., 400/158	250.00
	Candy box, w/ cover, beaded, ft., 400/140	495.00
	Cigarette box w/cover, 400/134	35.00
44	Cigarette holder, 3", bead ft., 400/44	40.00
	Cigarette set: 6 pc. (cigarette box & 4 rect. ashtrays), 400/134/6	67.50
	Clock, 4", round	295.00
	Coaster, 4", 400/78	10.00
	Coaster, w/spoon rest, 400/226	18.00
	Cocktail, seafood w/bead ft., 400/190	90.00
	Cocktail set: 2 pc., plate w/indent; cocktail, 400/97	40.00
	Compote, 4½", 400/63B	40.00
	Compote, 5", 3 bead stems, 400/220	90.00

		Crystal
	Compote, 5½", 4 bead stem, 400/45	30.00
56	Compote, 5½, low, plain stem, 400/66B	22.00
	Compote, 5½", 2 bead stem, 400/66B	22.00
	Compote, 8", bead stem, 400/48F	110.00
	Compote, 10", ftd. fruit, crimped, 40/103C	225.00
	Compote, ft. oval, 400/137	1,750.00
31	Condiment set, 4 pc., 400/1769	80.00
	Creamer, domed foot, 400/18	135.00
	Creamer, 6 oz., bead handle, 400/30	8.00
60	Creamer, indiv. bridge, 400/122	9.00
49	Creamer, plain ft., 400/31	9.00
33	Creamer, flat, bead handle, 400/126	35.00
29	Cruet set, 3 pc., 400/2911	95.00
39	Cruet w/stopper, 4 oz., 400/70	55.00
	Cup, after dinner, 400/77	20.00
10	Cup, coffee, 400/37	7.50
4	Cup, punch, 400/211	8.00
	Cup, tea, 400/35	8.00
	Decanter, w/stopper, 15 oz. cordial, 400/82/2	495.00
	Decanter, w/stopper, 18 oz., 400/18	365.00
	Decanter, w/stopper, 26 oz., 400/163	425.00
28	Deviled egg server, 12", ctr. hdld., 400/154	130.00
	Egg cup, bead. ft., 400/19	60.00
	Fork & spoon, set, 400/75	35.00
	Hurricane lamp, 2 pc. candle base, 400/79	135.00
	Hurricane lamp, 2 pc., hdld. candle base, 400/76	210.00
	Hurricane lamp, 3 pc. flared & crimped edge globe, 400/152	225.00
	Ice tub, 5½" deep, 8" diam., 400/63	135.00
	Ice tub, 7", 2 hdld., 400/168	265.00
	Icer, 2 pc., seafood/fruit cocktail, 400/53/3	100.00
	Icer, 2 pc., seafood/fruit cocktail, #3800 line, one bead stem	75.00
	Jam set, 5 pc., oval tray w/2 marmalade jars w/ladles, 400/1589	120.00
	Jar tower, 3 sect., 400/655	495.00
	Knife, butter, 4000	500.00

	Crystal
Ladle, marmalade, 3 bead stem, 400/130	12.00
58 Ladle, mayonnaise, 3 knob, 400/165	12.00
Ladle, mayonnaise, 6¼", 400/135	12.00
11 Lamp shade	85.00
Marmalade set, 3 pc., beaded ft. w/cover & spoon, 400/1989	45.00
Marmalade set, 3 pc. tall jar, domed bead ft., lid, spoon, 400/8918	100.00
43 Marmalade set, 4 pc., liner saucer, jar, lid, spoon, 400/89	55.00
Mayonnaise set, 2 pc. scoop side bowl, spoon, 400/23	40.00
Mayonnaise set, 3 pc. hdld. tray/hdld. bowl/ladle, 400/52/3	55.00
Mayonnaise set, 3 pc. plate, heart bowl, spoon, 400/49	40.00
Mayonnaise set, 3 pc. scoop side bowl, spoon, tray, 400/496	135.00
58 Mayonnaise, 4 pc., plate, divided bowl, 2 ladles, rnd., 400/84	45.00
Mirror, 4½", rnd., standing	150.00
Mustard jar, w/spoon, 400/156	40.00
Oil, 4 oz., bead base, 400/164	55.00
Oil, 6 oz., bead base, 400/166	75.00
26 Oil, 4 oz., bulbous bottom, 400/274	55.00
Oil, 4 oz., hdld., bulbous bottom, 400/278	75.00

	Crystal
Oil, 6 oz., hdld., bulbous bottom, 400/279	90.00
Oil, 6 oz., bulbous bottom, 400/275	65.00
Oil, w/stopper, etched "Oil," 400/121	75.00
Oil, w/stopper, etched "Vinegar," 400/121	75.00
Party set, 2 pc., oval plate w/indent for cup, 400/98	27.50
Pitcher, 14 oz., short rnd., 400/330	210.00
37 Pitcher, 16 oz., low ft., Liliputian, 400/19	265.00
Pitcher, 16 oz., no ft., 400/16	200.00
Pitcher, 20 oz., plain, 400/416	40.00
Pitcher, 40 oz., juice/cocktail, 400/19	215.00
38 Pitcher, 40 oz., manhattan, 400/18	250.00
Pitcher, 40 oz., plain, 400/419	50.00
Pitcher, 64 oz., plain, 400/424	60.00
Pitcher, 80 oz., plain, 400/424	70.00
Pitcher, 80 oz., 400/24	165.00
Pitcher, 80 oz., beaded ft., 400/18	265.00
Plate, 4½", 400/34	8.00
Plate, 5½", 2 hdld., 400/42D	12.00
Plate, 6", bread/butter, 400/1D	8.00
5 Plate, 6", canape w/off ctr. indent, 400/36	18.00
Plate, 6¾", 2 hdld. crimped, 400/52C	30.00
47 Plate, 7", salad, 400/3D	9.00
Plate, 7½", 2 hdld., 400/52D	15.00
Plate, 7½", triangular, 400/266	100.00

		Crystal
	Plate, 8", oval, 400/169	25.00
	Plate, 8", salad, 400/5D	10.00
	Plate, 8", w/indent, 400/50	12.00
6	Plate, 8¼", crescent salad, 400/120	67.50
	Plate, 8½", 2 hdld., crimped, 400/62C	30.00
	Plate, 8½", 2 hdld., 400/62D	13.00
	Plate, 8½", salad, 400/5D	12.00
	Plate, 8½", 2 hdld. (sides upturned), 400/62E	30.00
	Plate, 9", luncheon, 400/7D	15.00
	Plate, 9", oval, salad, 400/38	45.00
3	Plate, 9", w/indent, oval, 400/98	24.00
	Plate, 10", 2 hdld., sides upturned, 400/72E	40.00
	Plate, 10", 2 hdld. crimped, 400/72C	42.00
	Plate, 10", 2 hdld., 400/72D	35.00
	Plate, 10½", dinner, 400/10D	45.00
	Plate, 12", 2 hdld., 400/145D	45.00
	Plate, 12", 2 hdld. crimp., 400/145C	55.00
	Plate, 12", service, 400/13D	35.00
	Plate, 12½", cupped edge, torte, 400/75V	35.00
	Plate, 12½", oval, 400/124	90.00
	Plate, 13½", cracker, 400/145	40.00
	Plate, 13½", cupped edge, serving, 400/92V	47.00
7	Plate, 14" birthday cake (holes for 72 candles), 400/160	550.00
	Plate, 14", 2 hdld., sides upturned, 400/113E	50.00
	Plate, 14", 2 hdld., torte, 400/113D	50.00
	Plate, 14", service, 400/92D	50.00
	Plate, 14", torte, 400/17D	50.00
	Plate, 17", cupped edge, 400/20V	95.00

		Crystal
	Plate, 17", torte, 400/20D	95.00
	Platter, 13", 400/124D	110.00
	Platter, 16", 400/131D	245.00
	Punch ladle, small 2 lip, 400/259	30.00
8	Punch set, family, 8 demi cups, ladle, lid, 400/139/77	750.00
2	Punch set, 15 pc. bowl on 18" plate, 12 cups, ladle, 400/20	300.00
	Relish & dressing set, 4 pc. (10½" 4 pt. relish w/marmalade), 400/1112	115.00
16	Relish, 10½", 5 pt., 5 hndl., 400/56	75.00
15	Relish, 10½", 6 pt., 5 hndl., 400/112	50.00
18	Relish, 13", 5 pt., 400/102	75.00
22	Relish, 6½", 2 pt., 400/54	20.00
23	Relish, 7" sq., div., 2 pt., 400/234	125.00
19	Relish, 10½", oval, 400/256	30.00
	Salad set, 4 pc. (buffet; lg. rnd. tray, div. bowl, 2 spoons), 400/17	135.00
	Salad set, 4 pc. (rnd. plate, flared bowl, fork, spoon), 400/75B	110.00
35	Salt & pepper pr., bead ft., straight side, chrome top, 400/247	20.00
	Salt & pepper pr., bead ft., bulbous, chrome top, 400/96	18.00
42	Salt & pepper, 400/167	16.00
	Salt & pepper pr., bulbous w/bead stem, plastic top, 400/116	100.00
45	Salt & pepper, pr., indiv., 400/109	15.00

CANDLEWICK

		Crystal
	Salt & pepper, pr., ftd. bead base, 400/190	65.00
41	Salt dip, 2", 400/61	11.00
	Salt dip, 2¼", 400/19	10.00
40	Salt "type" dip, 2¾", nut or sugar, 400/64	12.00
	Salt spoon, 3, 400/616	11.00
	Salt spoon, w/ribbed bowl, 4000	11.00
	Sauce boat, 400/169	115.00
	Sauce boat liner, 400/169	40.00
	Saucer, after dinner, 400/77AD	5.00
10	Saucer, tea or coffee, 400/35 or 400/37	3.00
	Set: 2 pc. hdld. cracker w/cheese compote, 400/88	65.00
	Set: 2 pc. rnd. cracker plate w/indent; cheese compote, 400/145	65.00
36	Snack jar w/cover, bead ft., 400/139/1	795.00
	Stem, 1 oz., cordial, 400/190	90.00
	Stem, 4 oz., cocktail, 400/190	20.00
	Stem, 5 oz., tall sherbet, 400/190	15.00
	Stem, 5 oz., wine, 400/190	22.00
	Stem, 6 oz., sherbet, 400/190	15.00
	Stem, 10 oz., water 400/190	22.00
27	Stem, #3400, 1 oz., cordial	40.00
13	Stem, #3400, 4 oz., cocktail	18.00
30	Stem, #3400, 4 oz., oyster cocktail	16.00
14	Stem, #3400, 4 oz., wine	24.00
24	Stem, #3400, 5 oz., claret	55.00
	Stem, #3400, 5 oz., low sherbet	10.00
	Stem, #3400, 6 oz., parfait	60.00
	Stem, #3400, 6 oz., sherbet/saucer champagne	16.00
25	Stem, #3400, 9 oz., goblet, water	20.00
	Stem, #3800, low sherbet	28.00
	Stem, #3800, brandy	60.00
	Stem, #3800, 1 oz., cordial	48.00
	Stem, #3800, 4 oz., cocktail	24.00
	Stem, #3800, 4 oz., wine	30.00
	Stem, #3800, 6 oz., champagne/sherbet	28.00
	Stem, #3800, 5 oz. claret	75.00
	Stem, #3800, 9 oz., water goblet	38.00
	Stem, #4000, 1¼ oz., cordial	40.00
	Stem, #4000, 4 oz., cocktail	22.00
	Stem, #4000, 5 oz., wine	32.00
	Stem, #4000, 6 oz., tall sherbet	22.00
	Stem, #4000, 11 oz., goblet	35.00
	Stem, #4000, 12 oz., tea	35.00
	Strawberry set, 2 pc. (7" plate/sugar dip bowl), 400/83	50.00
	Sugar, domed foot, 400/18	135.00
	Sugar, 6 oz., bead hdld., 400/30	8.00
	Sugar, flat, bead handle, 400/126	35.00
32	Sugar, indiv. bridge, 400/122	9.00
52	Sugar, plain ft., 400/31	7.00
	Tete-a-tete 3 pc. brandy, a.d. cup, 6½" oval tray, 400/111	125.00
9	Tidbit server, 2 tier, cupped, 400/2701	60.00
	Tidbit set, 3 pc., 400/18TB	225.00
	Toast, w/cover, set, 7¾", 400/123	365.00
	Tray, 5½", hdld., upturned handles, 400/42E	25.00
	Tray, 5½", lemon, ctr. hdld., 400/221	35.00
	Tray, 5¼" x 9¼", condiment, 400/148	48.00

		Crystal
	Tray, 6½", 400/29	18.00
	Tray, 6", wafer, handle bent to ctr. of dish, 400/51T	25.00
34	Tray, 9", oval, 400/159	40.00
	Tray, 10½", ctr. hdld. fruit, 400/68F	135.00
	Tray, 11½", ctr. hdld. party, 400/68D	65.00
48	Tray, 11½", 2 hdld., 400/145E	50.00
	Tray, 13½", 2 hdld., celery, oval, 400/105	35.00
	Tray, 13", relish, 5 sections, 400/102	65.00
	Tray, 14", hdld., 400/113E	95.00
	Tumbler, 3½ oz., cocktail, 400/18	55.00
57	Tumbler, 3½ oz., juice, 400/112	12.00
	Tumbler, 5 oz., juice, 400/18	60.00
	Tumbler, 6 oz., sherbet, 400/18	60.00
	Tumbler, 7 oz., old-fashion, 400/18	70.00
	Tumbler, 7 oz., parfait, 400/18	85.00
	Tumbler, 9 oz., water, 400/18	75.00
	Tumbler, 12 oz., tea, 400/18	80.00
	Tumbler, 3 oz., ftd., cocktail, 400/19	16.00
	Tumbler, 3 oz., ftd., wine, 400/19	22.00
	Tumbler, 5 oz., low sherbet, 400/19	14.00
	Tumbler, 5 oz., juice, 400/19	10.00
	Tumbler, 7 oz., old-fashion, 400/19	38.00
	Tumbler, 10 oz., 400/19	12.00
	Tumbler, 12 oz., 400/19	22.00
	Tumbler, 14 oz., 400/19, tea	22.00
17	Tumbler, #3400, 5 oz., ft., juice	18.00
	Tumbler, #3400, 6 oz., parfait	70.00
	Tumbler, #3400, 9 oz., ftd.	20.00
	Tumbler, #3400, 10 oz., ftd.	20.00
12	Tumbler, #3400, 12 oz., ftd.	20.00
	Tumbler, #3800, 5 oz., juice	30.00
	Tumbler, #3800, 9 oz.	28.00
	Tumbler, #3800, 12 oz.	35.00
	Vase, 4", bead ft., sm. neck, ball, 400/25	65.00
	Vase, 5¾", bead ft., bud, 400/107	65.00
	Vase, 5¾", bead ft., mini bud, 400/107	65.00
	Vase, 6", flat, crimped edge, 400/287C	50.00
	Vase, 6", ftd., flared rim, 400/138B	195.00
	Vase, 6" diam., 400/198	350.00
	Vase, 6", fan, 400/287 F	40.00
	Vase, 7", ftd., bud, 400/186	310.00
	Vase, 7", ftd., bud, 400/187	325.00
	Vase, 7", ivy bowl, 400/74J	165.00
	Vase, 7", rolled rim w/bead hdld., 400/87 R	45.00
	Vase, 7", rose bowl, 400/142 K	300.00
	Vase, 7¼", ftd., rose bowl, crimped top, 400/132C	525.00
	Vase, 7½", ftd., rose bowl, 400/132	495.00
	Vase, 8", fan, w/bead hdld., 400/87F	35.00
	Vase, 8", flat, crimped edge, 400/143C	95.00
46	Vase, 8", fluted rim w/bead hdlds., 400/87C	40.00
	Vase, 8½", bead ft., bud, 400/28C	110.00
	Vase, 8½", bead ft., flared rim, 400/21	325.00
	Vase, 8½", bead ft., inward rim, 400/27	325.00
	Vase, 8½", hdld. (pitcher shape), 400/227	595.00
	Vase, 10", bead ft., straight side, 400/22	295.00
	Vase, 10", ftd., 400/193	295.00

Colors: crystal, Sapphire blue, Cape Cod blue, Chartreuse, Ruby, Cranberry pink, Jasmine yellow

First introduced in 1937, Canterbury had its principal production output through the 1940s and early 1950s. Canterbury exudes that 50s love of fluid shapes. Later, molds were relocated to Tiffin where most of the colored Canterbury was made. I see the yellow-green colored Canterbury (called Chartreuse) more than any other color in my travels. Many of the items being found in this color are Tiffin pieces manufactured from Duncan's moulds sometime after 1955.

Canterbury, or Line No. 115, was the mold blank Duncan incorporated for several of their etched patterns; First Love is the most known. You can find First Love listed in my *Collectible Glassware of the 40s, 50s, and 60s* book. In order to have space for the new patterns in this book I've removed all of the copies of original catalog pages of Canterbury that were included in previous editions. If you are a new collector and wish to see Canterbury listings by Duncan, you will have to track down one of those earlier editions. You should know that older editions have become collectible themselves and sell at a premium price.

Duncan's light blue was called Sapphire and the opalescent blue was christened Cape Cod blue. The red was Ruby. You may find opalescent pieces of Canterbury in pink, called Cranberry, or yellow, called Jasmine. In Florida, Canterbury pieces are often found cloudy or stained, which almost certainly indicates the hard water from wells here leaves residue that will not remove easily. Be aware of this problem especially when buying in the early morning dew by flashlight. Water hides the cloudiness until it dries out later and you see your serious error. If you know of additional pieces not listed or wish to relate prices on colored wares, just drop me a postcard. The 64-ounce water pitcher and candlesticks seem to be the quick sell items for me.

I have only shown Canterbury crystal except for the ice buckets pictured on page 45. Note the silver decorated one. I have not seen enough Canterbury in other colors to get a feel for those prices although 15 – 20% more than crystal seems to be normal. I see Ruby pieces that are priced either very high or rather low. There does not seem to be any consensus. Time will determine whether this color is rare. Opalescent items seem to be priced three to four times those for crystal, but I have not met many customers for those either.

Moderately priced when compared to patterns made by Cambridge, Heisey, or Fostoria, Canterbury is beginning to inch up in price with new collectors on the lookout for it. Pieces are heavier than most patterns, which bothers some, but which has also meant greater survival over the years. A major concern is scratches from heavy use.

	Crystal		Crystal
6 Ashtray, 3"	6.00	Bowl, 8" x 2½", flared	17.50
Ashtray, 3", club	8.00	Bowl, 8½" x 4"	22.00
Ashtray, 4½", club	10.00	Bowl, 9" x 2", gardenia	27.50
Ashtray, 5"	12.00	Bowl, 9" x 4¼", crimped	27.50
Ashtray, 5½", club	15.00	Bowl, 9" x 6" x 3", oval	30.00
Basket, 3" x 3" x 3¼", oval, hdld.	22.00	12 Bowl, 10" x 5", salad	30.00
Basket, 3" x 4", crimped, hdld.	30.00	Bowl, 10" x 8½" x 5", oval	27.50
Basket, 3½", crimped, hdld.	35.00	Bowl, 10¾" x 4¾"	27.50
Basket, 3½", oval, hdld.	26.00	Bowl, 10½" x 5", crimped	32.50
Basket, 4½" x 4¾" x 4¾", oval, hdld.	42.00	Bowl, 11½" x 8¼", oval	32.50
Basket, 4½" x 5" x 5", crimped, hdld.	48.00	Bowl, 12" x 2¾", gardenia	30.00
Basket, 9¼" x 10" x 7¼"	58.00	Bowl, 12" x 3½", flared	30.00
Basket, 10" x 4¼" x 7", oval, hdld.	75.00	Bowl, 12" x 3¾", crimped	32.50
Basket, 10" x 4½" x 8", oval, hdld.	78.00	Bowl, 13" x 8½" x 3¼", oval, flared	35.00
Basket, 11½", oval, hdld.	78.00	Bowl, 13" x 10" x 5", crimped, oval	40.00
Bowl, 4¼" x 2", finger	12.00	Bowl, 15" x 2¾", shallow salad	42.00
Bowl, 5" x 3¼", 2 part, salad dressing	12.50	Candle, 3", low	12.50
Bowl, 5" x 3¼", salad dressing	12.50	Candle, 3½"	15.00
Bowl, 5½" x 1¾", one hdld., heart	9.00	Candlestick, 6", 3-lite	39.00
Bowl, 5½" x 1¾", one hdld., square	9.00	Candlestick, 6"	25.00
Bowl, 5½" x 1¾", one hdld., star	10.00	Candlestick, 7", w/U prisms	75.00
Bowl, 5½" x 1¾", one hdld., fruit	7.00	Candy and cover, 8" x 3½", 3 hdld., 3 part	35.00
Bowl, 5½" x 1¾", one hdld., round	7.00	Candy, 6½", w/5" lid	32.50
5 Bowl, 5", fruit nappy	8.00	Celery and relish, 10½" x 6¾" x 1¼", 2 hdld., 2 part	32.50
Bowl, 6" x 2", 2 hdld., round	10.00	
Bowl, 6" x 2", 2 hdld., sweetmeat, star	15.00	Celery and relish, 10½" x 6¾" x 1¼", 2 hdld., 3 part	32.50
Bowl, 6" x 3¼", 2 part, salad dressing	14.00	
Bowl, 6" x 3¼", salad dressing	14.00	Celery, 9" x 4" x 1¼", 2 hdld.	22.50
Bowl, 6" x 5¼" x 2¼", oval olive	10.00	Cheese stand, 5½" x 3½" high	15.00
22 Bowl, 7½" x 2¼", crimped	15.00	Cigarette box w/cover, 3½" x 4½"	22.50
Bowl, 7½" x 2¼", gardenia	17.50	Cigarette jar w/cover, 4"	30.00
Bowl, 8" x 2¾", crimped	22.50	Comport, high, 6" x 5½" high	20.00

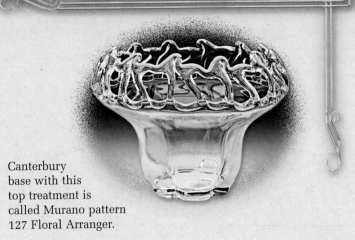

		Crystal
3	Comport, low, 6" x 4½" high	18.00
18	Creamer, 2¾", 3 oz., individual	9.00
9	Creamer, 3¾", 7 oz.	9.00
10	Cup	8.00
	Decanter w/stopper, 12", 32 oz.	80.00
11	Ice bucket or vase, 6"	35.00
	Ice bucket or vase, 7"	38.00
	Lamp, hurricane, w/prisms, 15"	125.00
	Marmalade, 4½" x 2¾", crimped	20.00
	Mayonnaise, 5" x 3¼"	20.00
	Mayonnaise, 5½" x 3¼", crimped	22.00
	Mayonnaise, 6" x 3¼"	24.00
21	Pitcher, 16 oz., pint	55.00
20	Pitcher, 9¼", 32 oz., hdld., martini	90.00
	Pitcher, 9¼", 32 oz., martini	80.00
1	Pitcher, 64 oz.	265.00
	Plate, 6½", one hdld., fruit	6.00
	Plate, 6", finger bowl liner	6.00
	Plate, 7½"	9.00
	Plate, 7½", 2 hdld., mayonnaise	12.00
	Plate, 8½"	12.00
	Plate, 11¼", dinner	27.50
	Plate, 11", 2 hdld. w/ring, cracker	20.00
	Plate, 11", 2 hdld., sandwich	22.00
	Plate, 13½", cake, hdld.	40.00
16	Plate, 14", cake	25.00
	Relish, 6" x 2", 2 hdld., 2 part, round	14.00
	Relish, 6" x 2", 2 hdld., 2 part, star	14.00
	Relish, 7" x 5¼" x 2¼", 2 hdld., 2 part, oval	16.00
23	Relish, 8" x 1¾", 3 hdld., 3 part	17.50
	Relish, 9" x 1½", 3 hdld., 3 part	22.00
2	Relish, 11" x 2", 5 part	33.00
	Rose bowl, 5"	20.00
	Rose bowl, 6"	25.00
	Salt and pepper	22.50
	Sandwich tray, 12" x 5¼", center handle	50.00
10	Saucer	3.00
	Sherbet, crimped, 4½", 2¾" high	10.00
	Sherbet, crimped, 5½", 2¾" high	11.00
	Stem, 3¾", 6 oz., ice cream	6.00
	Stem, 4", 4½ oz., oyster cocktail	12.50
	Stem, 4¼", 1 oz., cordial, #5115	30.00
	Stem, 4¼", 3½ oz., cocktail	12.00
	Stem, 4½", 6 oz., saucer champagne	12.00
	Stem, 5", 4 oz., claret or wine	20.00
	Stem, 5¼", 3 oz., cocktail, #5115	14.00

Canterbury
base with this
top treatment is
called Murano pattern
127 Floral Arranger.

		Crystal
	Stem, 5½", 5 oz., saucer champagne, #5115	12.00
	Stem, 6", 3½ oz., wine, #5115	27.50
	Stem, 6", 9 oz., water	15.00
	Stem, 6¾", 5 oz., claret, #5115	27.00
	Stem, 7¼", 10 oz., water, #5115	20.00
17	Sugar, 2½", 3 oz., individual	9.00
7	Sugar, 3", 7 oz.	9.00
	Top hat, 3"	20.00
19	Tray, 9", individual cr/sug	10.00
	Tray, 9" x 4" x 1¼", 2 part, pickle and olive	17.50
8	Tumbler, 2½", 1½ oz., whiskey	12.50
	Tumbler, 2½", 5 oz., ftd., ice cream, #5115	10.00
	Tumbler, 3¼", 4 oz., ftd., oyster cocktail, #5115	12.50
14	Tumbler, 3¾", 5 oz., flat, juice	8.00
	Tumbler, 4¼", 5 oz., ftd., juice	10.00
	Tumbler, 4¼", 5 oz., ftd., juice, #5115	12.00
4	Tumbler, 4½", 9 oz., flat, table, straight	14.00
	Tumbler, 4½", 10 oz., ftd., water, #5115	14.00
15	Tumbler, 5½", 9 oz., ftd., luncheon goblet	14.00
	Tumbler, 5¾", 12 oz., ftd., ice tea, #5115	17.50
	Tumbler, 6¼", 13 oz., flat, ice tea	18.00
	Tumbler, 6¼", 13 oz., ftd., ice tea	20.00
	Urn, 4½" x 4½"	15.00
	Vase, 3", crimped violet	15.00
	Vase, 3½", clover leaf	15.00
	Vase, 3½", crimped	15.00
	Vase, 3½", crimped violet	15.00
	Vase, 3½", oval	15.00
	Vase, 4", clover leaf	17.50
	Vase, 4", crimped	17.50
	Vase, 4", flared rim	17.50
	Vase, 4", oval	17.50
	Vase, 4½" x 4¾"	15.00
	Vase, 4½", clover leaf	20.00
13	Vase, 4½", crimped violet	17.50
	Vase, 4½", oval	17.50
	Vase, 5" x 5", crimped	17.50
	Vase, 5", clover leaf	25.00
	Vase, 5", crimped	17.50
	Vase, 5½", crimped	20.00
	Vase, 5½", flower arranger	27.50
	Vase, 6½", clover leaf	38.00
	Vase, 7", crimped	35.00
	Vase, 7", flower arranger	45.00
	Vase, 8½" x 6"	55.00
	Vase, 12", flared	80.00

11

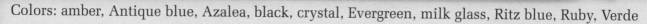

Colors: amber, Antique blue, Azalea, black, crystal, Evergreen, milk glass, Ritz blue, Ruby, Verde

Crystal Cape Cod is most pursued, since it can still be found whereas colored wares are difficult to accumulate. There are several hundred different pieces in crystal giving collectors a wide range of choices. Colored items were mostly made in the late 1960s and 1970s although Ruby and Ritz Blue first appeared in the 1930s. You can see examples of most Cape Cod colors pictured here. Below is Verde (green) and the dark green goblet is Emerald. The pitcher and tumbler on the end of the top row were made for Tiara and are not considered true Imperial Cape Cod by well-informed collectors. Rounding out the second row are pieces in milk glass, ebony, and crystal trimmed in red. The latter items were made in the early 1940s and trimmed pieces are difficult to find with that red flashing undamaged. The top row on page 47 is all Azalea with Ruby, amber and Antique blue filling in the bottom row. As can be seen by those photos, stems and tumblers are what turn up regularly in color as well as crystal. This is causing them to sell for lower prices than a few years ago. For those who have difficulty discerning stem types, I have included some new catalog pages. Rarely found items continue to soar in price, but commonly found items have weakened of late.

Perhaps, the color in which you could put a small set together would be Ruby. Most of the Ritz Blue has disappeared into collections. It won't come cheaply, but there was enough made to find it. I mentioned last book that Ruby old fashions had been selling for $75.00 and suddenly they started raining from everywhere. Now, half of that is hard to get since everyone who wanted them are saturated with them. You can buy most of the fundamental pieces of Cape Cod inexpensively. How long that will hold true is a question. If you like it, buy it now.

Item	Crystal
Ashtray, 4", 160/134/1	14.00
Ashtray, 5½", 160/150	17.50
Basket, 9", handled, crimped, 160/221/0	235.00
Basket, 11" tall, handled, 160/40	165.00
Bottle, bitters, 4 oz., 160/235	60.00
Bottle, cologne, w/stopper, 1601	60.00
Bottle, condiment, 6 oz., 160/224	65.00
Bottle, cordial, 18 oz., 160/256	125.00
Bottle, decanter, 26 oz., 160/244	155.00
Bottle, ketchup, 14 oz., 160/237	245.00
Bowl, 3", handled mint, 160/183	20.00
Bowl, 3", jelly, 160/33	12.00

Item	Crystal
Bowl, 4", finger, 1602	12.00
Bowl, 4½", finger, 1604½A	12.00
Bowl, 4½", handled spider, 160/180	22.50
Bowl, 4½", dessert, tab handled, 160/197	24.00
Bowl, 5", dessert, heart shape, 160/49H	22.00
Bowl, 5", flower, 1605N	25.00
Bowl, 5½", fruit, 160/23B	10.00
Bowl, 5½", handled spider, 160/181	25.00
Bowl, 5½", tab handled, soup, 160/198	22.50
Bowl, 6", fruit, 160/3F	10.00
Bowl, 6", baked apple, 160/53X	11.00
Bowl, 6", handled, round mint, 160/51F	22.00

	Crystal
Bowl, 6", handled heart, 160/40H	22.00
Bowl, 6", handled mint, 160/51H	22.00
Bowl, 6", handled tray, 160/51T	30.00
Bowl, 6½", handled portioned spider, 160/187	27.50
Bowl, 6½", handled spider, 160/182	32.50
Bowl, 6½", tab handled, 160/199	30.00
Bowl, 7", nappy, 160/5F	22.00
Bowl, 7½", 160/7F	22.00
Bowl, 7½", 2-handled, 160/62B	27.50
Bowl, 8¾", 160/10F	33.00
Bowl, 9", footed fruit, 160/67F	65.00
Bowl, 9½", 2 handled, 160/145B	40.00
Bowl, 9½", crimped, 160/221C	100.00
Bowl, 9½", float, 160/221F	65.00
Bowl, 10", footed, 160/137B	75.00
Bowl, 10", oval, 160/221	80.00
Bowl, 11", flanged edge, 1608X	165.00
Bowl, 11", oval, 160/124	80.00
Bowl, 11", oval divided, 160/125	90.00
Bowl, 11", round, 1608A	95.00
Bowl, 11", salad, 1608D	60.00
Bowl, 11¼", oval, 1602	80.00
Bowl, 12", 160/75B	40.00
Bowl, 12", oval, 160/131B	95.00
Bowl, 12", oval crimped, 160/131C	165.00
Bowl, 12", punch, 160/20B	65.00
Bowl, 13", console, 160/75L	42.50
Bowl, 15", console, 1601/0L	75.00
Butter, 5", w/cover, handled, 160/144	30.00
Butter, w/cover, ¼ lb., 160/161	45.00
Cake plate, 10", 4 toed, 160/220	90.00
Cake stand, 10½", footed, 160/67D	50.00
Cake stand, 11", 160/103D	85.00
Candleholder, twin, 160/100	95.00
7 Candleholder, 3", single, 160/170	17.50
Candleholder, 4", 160/81	27.50
Candleholder, 4", Aladdin style, 160/90	165.00

	Crystal
Candleholder, 4½", saucer, 160/175	30.00
Candleholder, 5", 160/80	20.00
Candleholder, 5", flower, 160/45B	60.00
Candleholder, 5½", flower, 160/45N	120.00
Candleholder, 6", centerpiece, 160/48BC	110.00
Candy, w/cover, 160/110	85.00
Carafe, wine, 26 oz., 160/185	225.00
Celery, 8", 160/105	30.00
Celery, 10½", 160/189	55.00
Cigarette box, 4½", 160/134	45.00
Cigarette holder, ftd., 1602	12.50
Cigarette holder, Tom & Jerry mug, 160/200	32.50
9 Cigarette lighter, 1602	30.00
Coaster, w/spoon rest, 160/76	12.00
Coaster, 3", square, 160/85	20.00
Coaster, 4", round, 160/78	15.00
Coaster, 4½", flat, 160/1R	10.00
Comport, 5¼", 160F	27.50
Comport, 5¾", 160X	30.00
Comport, 6", 160/45	25.00
Comport, 6", w/cover, ftd., 160/140	85.00
Comport, 7", 160/48B	37.50
Comport, 11¼", oval, 1602, 6½" tall	210.00
Creamer, 160/190	30.00
Creamer, 160/30	8.00
Creamer, ftd., 160/31	15.00
15 Cruet, w/stopper, 4 oz., 160/119	25.00
Cruet, w/stopper, 5 oz., 160/70	30.00
Cruet, w/stopper, 6 oz., 160/241	40.00
Cup, tea, 160/35	6.00
Cup, coffee, 160/37	6.00
Cup, bouillon, 160/250	30.00
Decanter, bourbon, 160/260	100.00
Decanter, rye, 160/260	100.00
Decanter w/stopper, 30 oz., 160/163	65.00
Decanter w/stopper, 24 oz., 160/212	70.00
Egg cup, 160/225	30.00

CAPE COD

	Crystal
Epergne, 2 pc., plain center, 160/196	265.00
Fork, 160/701	12.00
Gravy bowl, 18 oz., 160/202	85.00
Horseradish, 5 oz. jar, 160/226	95.00
Ice bucket, 6½", 160/63	195.00
Icer, 3 pc., bowl, 2 inserts, 160/53/3	60.00
Jar, 12 oz., hdld. peanut w/lid, 160/210	75.00
Jar, 10", "Pokal," 160/133	85.00
Jar, 11", "Pokal," 160/128	90.00
Jar, 15", "Pokal," 160/132	150.00
Jar, candy w/lid, wicker hand., 5" h., 160/194	125.00
Jar, cookie, w/lid, wicker hand., 6½" h., 160/195	150.00
Jar, peanut butter w/lid, wicker hand., 4" h., 160/193	110.00
Ladle, marmalade, 160/130	10.00
Ladle, mayonnaise, 160/165	10.00
Ladle, punch	25.00
Lamp, hurricane, 2 pc., 5" base, 160/79	100.00
Lamp, hurricane, 2 pc., bowl-like base, 1604	145.00
Marmalade, 3 pc. set, 160/89/3	32.50
Marmalade, 4 pc. set, 160/89	40.00
Mayonnaise, 3 pc. set, 160/52H	37.50
Mayonnaise, 3 pc., 160/23	27.50
Mayonnaise, 12 oz., hdld., spouted, 160/205	55.00
Mug, 12 oz., handled, 160/188	65.00
Mustard, w/cover & spoon, 160/156	35.00
Nut dish, 3", hdld., 160/183	35.00
Nut dish, 4", hdld., 160/184	35.00
Pepper mill, 160/236	30.00
Pitcher, milk, 1 pt., 160/240	55.00
5 Pitcher, 36 oz., refrig. jug open lip, Tiars pro.	60.00
Pitcher, ice lipped, 40 oz., 160/19	85.00
Pitcher, martini, blown, 40 oz., 160/178	210.00
Pitcher, ice lipped, 2 qt., 160/239	100.00
Pitcher, 2 qt., 160/24	100.00
Pitcher, blown, 5 pt., 160/176	210.00
Plate, 4½" butter, 160/34	8.00
Plate, 6", cupped (liner for 160/208 salad dressing), 160/209	30.00
Plate, 6½", bread & butter, 160/1D	7.00
Plate, 7", 160/3D	8.00
Plate, 7", cupped (liner for 160/205 Mayo), 160/206	40.00
Plate, 8", center handled tray, 160/149D	40.00
Plate, 8", crescent salad, 160/12	80.00
Plate, 8" cupped (liner for gravy), 160/203	35.00
Plate, 8", salad, 160/5D	9.00
Plate, 8½", 2 handled, 160/62D	30.00
Plate, 9", 160/7D	20.00
Plate, 9½", 2 hdld., 160/62D	40.00
Plate, 10", dinner, 160/10D	37.50
Plate, 11½", 2 handled, 160/145D	40.00
Plate, 12½" bread, 160/222	70.00
Plate, 13", birthday, 72 candle holes, 160/72	410.00
Plate, 13", cupped torte, 1608V	35.00
Plate, 13", torte, 1608F	40.00
Plate, 14", cupped, 160/75V	50.00
Plate, 14", flat, 160/75D	50.00
Plate, 16", cupped, 160/20V	80.00
Plate, 17", 2 styles, 160/10D or 20D	95.00
Platter, 13½", oval, 160/124D	80.00
18 Puff Box, w/cover, 1601	60.00
Relish, 8", hdld., 2 part, 160/223	37.50

	Crystal
Relish, 9½", 4 pt., 160/56	35.00
Relish, 9½", oval, 3 part, 160/55	25.00
Relish, 11", 5 part, 160/102	55.00
Relish, 11¼", 3 part, oval, 1602	75.00
Salad dressing, 6 oz., hdld., spouted, 160/208	65.00
Salad set, 14" plate, 12" bowl, fork & spoon, 160/75	110.00
Salt & pepper, individual, 160/251	20.00
8 Salt & pepper, pr., ftd., 160/117	20.00
Salt & pepper, pr., ftd., stemmed, 160/243	40.00
Salt & pepper, pr., 160/96	18.00
Salt & pepper, pr. square, 160/109	27.50
Salt dip, 160/61	20.00
Salt spoon, 1600	8.00
Saucer, tea, 160/35	2.00
Saucer, coffee, 160/37	2.00
Server, 12", ftd. or turned over, 160/93	85.00
Spoon, 160/701	12.00
10 Stem, 1½ oz., cordial, 1602	6.00
17 Stem, 3 oz., wine, 1602	5.00
Stem, 3½ oz., cocktail, 1602	5.00
11 Stem, 3½ oz., cocktail, 1600	5.00
13 Stem, 5 oz., claret, 1602	7.00
16 Stem, 6 oz., low sundae, 1602	3.00
14 Stem, 6 oz., ftd., juice, 1602	6.00
Stem, 6 oz., sherbet, 1600	14.00
1 Stem, 6 oz., tall sherbet, 1602	6.00
19 Stem, 8 oz., goblet, 160	8.00
Stem, 9 oz., water, 1602	6.00
Stem, 10 oz., water, 1600	18.00
3 Stem, 11 oz., dinner goblet, 1602	7.00
4 Stem, 14 oz., goblet, magnum, 160	38.00
Stem, oyster cocktail, 1602	8.00
Sugar, 160/190	30.00
Sugar, 160/30	7.00
Sugar, ftd., 160/31	15.00
Toast, w/cover, 160/123	235.00
Tom & Jerry footed punch bowl, 160/200	375.00
Tray, sq. cov. sugar & creamer, 160/25/26	160.00
Tray, 7", for creamer/sugar, 160/29	15.00
Tray, 11", pastry, center hdld., 160/68D	70.00
Tumbler, 2½ oz., whiskey, 160	10.00
Tumbler, 6 oz., ftd., juice, 1602	5.00
6 Tumbler, 6 oz., juice, Tiara productions, 1600	5.00
Tumbler, 7 oz., old-fashion, 160	8.00
2 Tumbler, 10 oz., ftd., water, 1602	6.00
Tumbler, 10 oz., water, 160	6.00
Tumbler, 12 oz., ftd., ice tea, 1602	8.00
Tumbler, 12 oz., ftd., tea, 160	12.00
12 Tumbler, 12 oz., ice tea, 160	12.00
Tumbler, 14 oz., double old-fashion, 160	32.00
Tumbler, 16 oz., 160	35.00
Vase, 6¼", ftd., 160/22	35.00
Vase, 6½", ftd., 160/110B	70.00
Vase, 7½", ftd., 160/22	40.00
Vase, 8", fan, 160/87F	235.00
Vase, 8½", flip, 160/143	60.00
Vase, 8½", ftd., 160/28	45.00
Vase, 10", cylinder, 160/192	75.00
Vase, 10½", hdld., urn, 160/186	200.00
Vase, 11", flip, 1603	185.00
Vase, 11½", ftd., 160/21	75.00

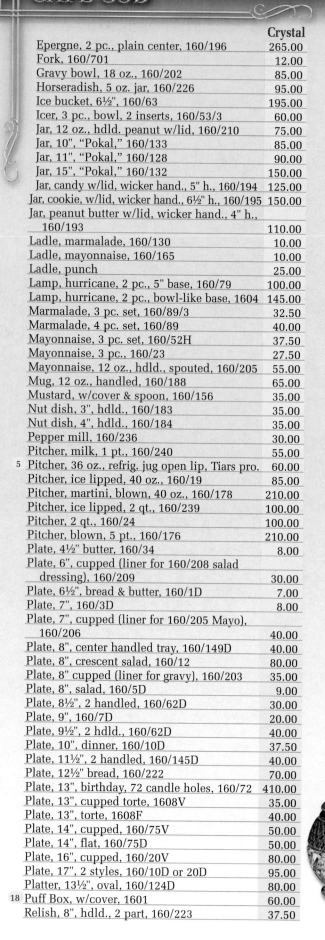

18

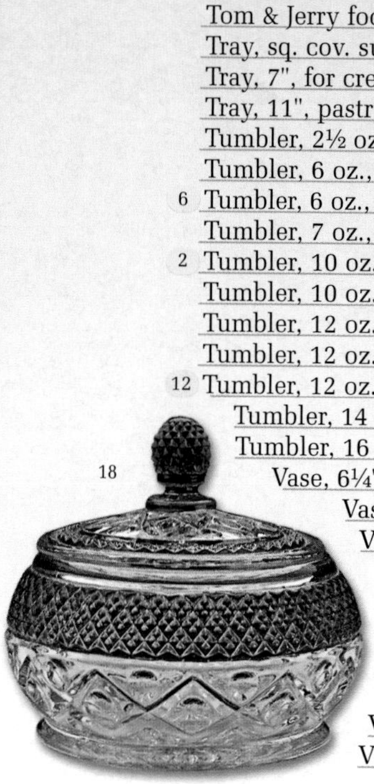

IMPERIAL GLASS CORPORATION, BELLAIRE, OHIO

IMPERIAL CAPE COD

160 12 oz.
Iced Tea Tumbler
or Highball

160 10 oz.
Water Tumbler

160 6 oz.
Juice Tumbler

160 7 oz.
O/F Cocktail

160 2½ oz.
Whiskey

1602 11 oz.
Goblet

1602 9 oz.
Luncheon Goblet

1602 6 oz.
Tall Sherbert or
Saucer Champagne

1602 6 oz.
Sundae

1602 5 oz.
Claret

1602 3½ oz.
Cocktail

1602 3 oz.
Wine

1602 1½ oz.
Cordial

1602
12 oz. Ftd. Ice tea
10 oz. Ftd. Tumbler

1602 6 oz.
Ftd. Juice Tumbler

1602
Oyster or Fruit Cocktail

1602 Finger Bowl

IMPERIAL GLASS CORPORATION, BELLAIRE, OHIO

IMPERIAL CAPE COD

160/87F 8"
Fan Vase

160/110B 6½"
Ftd. Vase

160/143 8½"
Flip Vase

160/27 7"
Bud Vase

160/110
One pound Candy Jar and Cover

160/22 7½"
Ftd. Flip Vase

160/132 15"
Covered Pokal

160/133 10"
Covered Pokal

160/21 11½"
Ftd. Flip Vase

Page 9

IMPERIAL GLASS CORPORATION, BELLAIRE, OHIO

IMPERIAL
CAPE COD

160/73/0
11" Basket

160/186   10½"
2 Handled Urn Vase

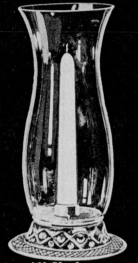

160/79   2 pc.
Hurrican Lamp 9 inches Overall

160/24   60 oz.
Ice Lipped Pitcher

160/19   40 oz.
Ice Lipped Pitcher

160/196   2 pc. Epergne
Height-12·inches Overall

160/40   11"
Basket

160/63   6½"
Ice Bucket with Handle & Ice Tongs

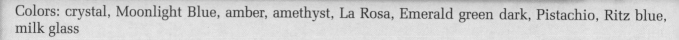

Colors: crystal, Moonlight Blue, amber, amethyst, La Rosa, Emerald green dark, Pistachio, Ritz blue, milk glass

Moonlight Blue and crystal Caprice are the colors usually collected. Numerous pieces made in crystal and blue were never made in (La Rosa) pink, which limits people's options of collecting that color. Caprice can be found in a variety of colors; only luncheon sets, a few stems, vases, bowls, and candles can be amassed in any color besides crystal, Moonlight Blue, and pink.

Pink is the color many new collectors first select, but most have given up the task of putting a set together. Pink is not as expensive as buying blue, but you will only locate a piece or two infrequently.

Prices for seldom seen colors of Caprice are similar to those of blue. Collectors searching for amber or amethyst, should know those particular colors are priced closer to their crystal counterparts.

Some blue Caprice items have become hard to sell at the level of prices that they were once bringing. Some items turned out to be more common than previously thought and the Internet auctions pointed this out vividly. Rare pieces were bought by the four or five serious collectors willing to pay whatever price was being asked. When those collectors filled their needs, others scorned those asking prices. Today, clarets, moulded, straight side, nine and twelve-ounce tumblers, footed whiskeys, and finger bowls are sitting in dealers' inventories instead of being purchased for collections. Things will most likely change, but right now, I'm finding more collectors are willing to settle on not owning every piece in a pattern than in the past.

Blue bitters bottles and covered cracker jars have appeared and most major collections now have a Doulton pitcher. The dearth of those has become apparent and their price shocks all!

Once shunned Alpine Caprice items are being collected by beginners. Alpine pieces have satinized panels or bases that are found in both crystal and blue items. You should be aware that collecting tastes change as more people come into our collecting society. It is now possible to attain this finish with equipment from a craft shop. The satinized decoration on newly embellished pieces is rough and not as smooth a finish as it was originally — but the point is that it can be done.

Crystal Caprice candle reflectors and punch bowls are seldom found; but there is serious money waiting for those that do find them. Should you desire, you could put a large set of crystal together for a reasonable figure when compared to other patterns of this quality — if you avoid buying those rarely found items.

Be aware that the non-designed centers on all flat pieces had a tendency to scratch with use. Do not pay mint condition prices for items that are not mint.

Item	Crystal	Blue Pink
Ashtray, 2¾", 3 ftd., shell, #213	7.00	12.50
*Ashtray, 3", #214	6.00	11.00
*Ashtray, 4", #215	8.00	15.00
*Ashtray, 5", #216	10.00	22.00
Bonbon, 6", oval, ftd., #155	22.00	50.00
Bonbon, 6", sq., 2 hdld., #154	18.00	40.00
Bonbon, 6", sq., ftd., #133	20.00	45.00
Bottle, 7 oz., bitters, #186	235.00	695.00
Bowl, 2", 4 ftd., almond, #95	25.00	55.00
*Bowl, 5", 2 hdld., jelly, #151	15.00	35.00
14 Bowl, 5", mayonnaise, #127	25.00	50.00
Bowl, 5", fruit, #18	30.00	75.00
27 Bowl, 5", fruit, crimped, #19	30.00	95.00
20 Bowl, 6", low ftd., compote, #130	22.00	55.00
24 Bowl, 6", 2 hndl. bonbon	22.00	55.00
Bowl, 8", 4 ftd., #49	45.00	120.00
Bowl, 8", sq., 4 ftd., #50	55.00	130.00
*Bowl, 8", 3 pt., relish, #124	20.00	45.00
Bowl, 9½", crimped, 4 ftd., #52	45.00	110.00
Bowl, 9", pickle, #102	25.00	60.00
Bowl, 10", salad, 4 ftd., #57	45.00	125.00
Bowl, 10", sq., 4 ftd., #58	50.00	125.00
Bowl, 10½", belled, 4 ftd., #54	40.00	85.00
Bowl, 10½", crimped, 4 ftd., #53	40.00	110.00
Bowl, 11", crimped, 4 ftd., #60	45.00	110.00
*Bowl, 11", 2 hdld., oval, 4 ftd., #65	45.00	110.00
Bowl, 11½", shallow, 4 ftd., #81	40.00	110.00
*Bowl, 12", 4 pt. relish, oval, #126	90.00	225.00
*Bowl, 12", relish, 3 pt., rect., #125	50.00	160.00
Bowl, 12½", belled, 4 ftd., #62	40.00	100.00

Item	Crystal	Blue Pink
1 Bowl, 12½", crimped, 4 ftd., #61	40.00	100.00
Bowl, 13", cupped, salad, #80	75.00	175.00
Bowl, 13", crimped, 4 ftd., #66	45.00	120.00
Bowl, 13½", 4 ftd., shallow cupped, #82	50.00	125.00
Bowl, 15", salad, shallow, #84	60.00	175.00
Bridge set:		
*Cloverleaf, 6½", #173	32.00	110.00
*Club, 6½", #170	32.00	110.00
Diamond, 6½", #171	32.00	110.00
*Heart, 6½", #169	38.00	120.00
*Spade, 6½", #172	32.00	110.00
*Butterdish, ¼ lb., #52	235.00	
Cake plate, 13", ftd., #36	150.00	350.00
Candle reflector, #73	350.00	
Candlestick, 2½", ea., #67	15.00	30.00
Candlestick, 2-lite, keyhole, 5", #647	20.00	60.00
Candlestick, 3-lite, #74	50.00	110.00
Candlestick, 3-lite, keyhole, #638	25.00	70.00
Candlestick, 3-lite, #1338	45.00	90.00
Candlestick, 5-lite, #1577	150.00	
Candlestick, 5", ea., keyhole, #646	20.00	35.00
6 Candlestick, 6", 2-lite, ea., arch, #72	40.00	95.00
Candlestick, 7", ea., w/prism, #70	25.00	75.00
Candlestick, 7½", dbl., ea., #69	195.00	575.00
Candy, 6", 3 ftd., w/cover, #165	42.50	120.00
Candy, 6", w/cover (divided), #168	90.00	175.00
Celery & relish, 8½", 3 pt., #124	20.00	45.00
2 Cheese stand comport, Alpine		250.00
Cigarette box, w/cover, 3½" x 2¼", #207	20.00	45.00

*Moulds owned by Summit Art Glass; many pieces have been remade. 52

	Crystal	Blue Pink
Cigarette box, w/cover, 4½" x 3½", #208	25.00	65.00
Cigarette holder, 2" x 2¼", triangular, #205	20.00	65.00
Cigarette holder, 3" x 3", triangular, #204	22.00	50.00
16 Coaster, 3½", #13	15.00	35.00
Comport, 6", low ftd., #130	22.00	50.00
Comport, 7", low ftd., #130	35.00	75.00
Comport, 7", tall, #136	40.00	100.00
Cracker jar & cover, #202	495.00	1,995.00
*Creamer, large, #41	13.00	25.00
*Creamer, medium, #38	11.00	20.00
30 *Creamer, ind., #40	12.00	22.00
15 Cup, #17	14.00	35.00
9 Decanter, w/stopper, 35 oz., #187	195.00	595.00
Finger bowl & liner, #16	45.00	85.00
Finger bowl and liner, blown, #300	50.00	85.00
Ice bucket, #201	75.00	175.00
Marmalade, w/cover, 6 oz., #89	75.00	200.00
*Mayonnaise, 6½", 3 pc. set, #129	42.00	110.00
*Mayonnaise, 8", 3 pc. set, #106	55.00	125.00
26 Mustard, w/cover, 2 oz., #87	60.00	160.00
Nut Dish, 2½", #93	22.00	45.00
Nut Dish, 2½", divided, #94	25.00	50.00
25 *Oil, 3 oz., w/stopper, #101	35.00	80.00
28 *Oil, 3 oz., w/stopper, belled skirt, #117	35.00	80.00
4 *Oil, 3 oz., w/stopper, #98	35.00	80.00
19 *Oil, 5 oz., w/stopper, #100	70.00	235.00
Pitcher, 32 oz., ball shape, #179	135.00	335.00
Pitcher, 80 oz., ball shape, #183	125.00	350.00
Pitcher, 90 oz., tall Doulton style, #178	750.00	3,995.00
Plate, 5½", bread & butter, #20	12.00	20.00
Plate, 6½", bread & butter, #21	11.00	20.00
Plate, 6½", hdld., lemon, #152	15.00	26.00
11 Plate, 7½", salad, #23	15.00	25.00
12 Plate, 8½", luncheon, #22	15.00	30.00
*Plate, 9½", dinner, #24	50.00	175.00
Plate, 11", cabaret, 4 ftd., #32	30.00	65.00
Plate, 11½", cabaret, #26	30.00	65.00
Plate, 14", cabaret, 4 ftd., #33	40.00	80.00
Plate, 14", 4 ftd., #28	35.00	75.00
Plate, 16", #30	45.00	135.00
Punch bowl, ftd., #498	2,750.00	
*Salad dressing, 3 pc., ftd. & hdld., 2 spoons, #112	195.00	465.00
31 Salt & pepper, pr., ball, #91	45.00	125.00
*Salt & pepper, pr., flat, #96	35.00	80.00
Salt & pepper, indiv., ball, pr., #90	50.00	140.00
Salt & pepper, indiv., flat, pr., #92	40.00	125.00
Salver, 13", 2 pc. (cake atop pedestal), #31	165.00	600.00
15 Saucer, #17	2.50	5.50
17 Stem, #300, blown, 1 oz., cordial	52.50	135.00
Stem, #300, blown, 2½ oz., wine	25.00	65.00
10 Stem, #300, blown, 3 oz., cocktail	25.00	45.00
Stem, #300, blown, 4½ oz., claret	80.00	150.00
7 Stem, #300, blown, 4½ oz., low oyster cocktail	20.00	40.00
Stem, #300, blown, 5 oz., parfait	95.00	175.00
5 Stem, #300, blown, 6 oz., low sherbet	14.00	20.00
8 Stem, #300, blown, 6 oz., tall sherbet	14.00	28.00
Stem, #300, blown, 9 oz., water	20.00	45.00
Stem, #301, blown, 1 oz., cordial	40.00	
Stem, #301, blown, 2½ oz., wine	20.00	

	Crystal	Blue Pink
Stem, #301, blown, 3 oz., cocktail	22.00	
Stem, #301, blown, 4½ oz., claret	40.00	
Stem, #301, blown, 6 oz., sherbet	15.00	
Stem, #301, blown, 9 oz., water	20.00	
*Stem, 3 oz., wine, #6	40.00	100.00
*Stem, 3½ oz., cocktail, #3	25.00	55.00
*Stem, 4½ oz., claret, #5	80.00	200.00
Stem, 4½ oz., fruit cocktail, #7	30.00	75.00
Stem, 5 oz., low sherbet, #4	25.00	40.00
*Stem, 7 oz., tall sherbet, #2	17.50	30.00
Stem, 10 oz., water, #1	27.50	45.00
*Sugar, large, #41	12.50	22.00
*Sugar, medium, #38	10.00	20.00
29 *Sugar, indiv., #40	12.00	22.00
*Tray, for sugar & creamer, #37	17.50	35.00
Tray, 9" oval, #42	22.00	50.00
*Tumbler, 2 oz., flat, #188	25.00	70.00
Tumbler, 3 oz., ftd., #12	27.50	75.00
Tumbler, 5 oz., ftd., #11	22.00	55.00
23 Tumbler, 5 oz., flat, #180	22.00	55.00
Tumbler, #300, 2½ oz., whiskey	55.00	175.00
3 Tumbler, #300, 5 oz., ftd., juice	20.00	40.00
Tumbler, #300, 10 oz., ftd. water	20.00	42.00
Tumbler, #300, 12 oz., ftd. tea	20.00	44.00
Tumbler, #301, blown, 4½ oz., low oyster cocktail	17.50	
Tumbler, #301, blown, 5 oz., juice	15.00	
Tumbler, #301, blown, 12 oz., tea	20.00	
*Tumbler, 9 oz., straight side, #14	40.00	110.00
*Tumbler, 10 oz., ftd., #10	20.00	40.00
18 Tumbler, 12 oz., flat., #184	53.00	53.00
Tumbler, 12 oz., ftd., #9	22.50	45.00
*Tumbler, 12 oz., straight side, #15	37.50	95.00
Tumbler, #310, 5 oz., flat, juice	25.00	75.00
21 Tumbler, #310, 7 oz., flat, old-fashion	45.00	135.00
Tumbler, #310, 10 oz., flat, table	25.00	65.00
Tumbler, #310, 11 oz., flat, tall, 4¹³⁄₁₆"	25.00	80.00
Tumbler, #310, 12 oz., flat, tea	30.00	120.00
Vase, 3½", #249	70.00	175.00
Vase, 4", blown, #251, blown	70.00	175.00
Vase, 4¼", #241, ball	60.00	105.00
Vase, 4½", #237, ball	75.00	195.00
Vase, 4½", #252, blown	55.00	160.00
Vase, 4½", #337, crimped top	55.00	130.00
Vase, 4½", #344, crimped top	85.00	175.00
Vase, 4½", #244	60.00	150.00
Vase, 5", ivy bowl, #232	90.00	210.00
22 Vase, 5½", #245	65.00	165.00
Vase, 5½", #345, crimped top	90.00	210.00
Vase, 6", #242, ftd.	80.00	195.00
Vase, 6", blown, #254	185.00	425.00
Vase, 6", #342, crimped top	95.00	200.00
Vase, 6", #235, ftd., rose bowl	75.00	150.00
13 Vase, 6½", #238, ball	65.00	165.00
Vase, 6½", #338, crimped top	100.00	250.00
Vase, 7½", #246	65.00	195.00
Vase, 7½", #346, crimped top	115.00	325.00
Vase, 8", #236, ftd., rose bowl	100.00	250.00
Vase, 8½", #243	110.00	225.00
Vase, 8½", #239, ball	125.00	325.00
Vase, 8½", #339, crimped top	125.00	300.00
Vase, 8½", #343, crimped top	150.00	300.00
Vase, 9¼" #240, ball	140.00	310.00
Vase, 9½" #340, crimped top	175.00	450.00

Colors: Amber, blue, cobalt blue, crystal, red

A combination of blue and crystal Caribbean makes a pleasing arrangement. Collectors started combining colors due to a decorating scheme featured in women's magazines. Currently, mixing glass colors has come about from necessity (due to lack of finding just one color) as much as anything. However, it's generating some delightfully creative collections. I've seen pictures of imaginative table arrangements using this wonderful older glassware.

Blue Caribbean dinner plates are challenging to find, but even more exasperating is finding them worn and scratched with mint condition prices on them. Collectors shopping for fundamental Caribbean dinnerware items (dinner plates, cups, and saucers) are not finding many. When basic items are not found in any quantity, new collectors tend to avoid the pattern. Prices for blue have remained rather stable as so little is available for sale. Neither do I see the crystal on the market that I once did. Of course, dealers have a propensity to avoid buying patterns that few collectors seek, creating a second difficulty for collecting crystal Caribbean. The blue punch bowl, pitchers, and some of the stemware, particularly cordials, will all cost you big time — if you can find them.

Amber Caribbean is rarely seen except for the cigarette jar and ashtrays. Other pieces are unusual; keep that in mind.

Crystal punch sets can be found with all crystal cups or with crystal cups with colored handles of red, cobalt blue, or amber. With the colored handled punch cup and ladle, these sets sell for about $75.00 more than the plain crystal set priced below. Red and cobalt blue handled pieces appear to be more desirable than amber. Many collectors mix the colored punch cups so that they have four of each colored handle with their set. In fact, I have seen so many with four of each cup that I'm speculating that was the way they were promoted in some areas.

		Crystal	Blue
	Ashtray, 6", 4 indent	15.00	30.00
	Bowl, 3¾" x 5", folded side, hdld.	16.00	35.00
17	Bowl, 4½", finger	16.00	30.00
	Bowl, 5", fruit nappy (takes liner), hdld.	12.50	25.00
	Bowl, 5" x 7", folded side, hdld.	20.00	40.00
18	Bowl, 6½", soup (takes liner)	16.00	40.00
	Bowl, 7", hdld.	25.00	50.00
	Bowl, 7¼", ftd., hdld., grapefruit	20.00	50.00
19	Bowl, 8½"	30.00	75.00
	Bowl, 9", salad	30.00	75.00
	Bowl, 9¼", veg., flared edge	32.50	75.00
	Bowl, 9¼", veg., hdld.	40.00	85.00
	Bowl, 9½", epergne, flared edge	37.50	95.00
	Bowl, 10", 6¼ qt., punch	90.00	475.00
6	Bowl, 10", 6¼ qt., punch, flared top (catalog lists as salad)	90.00	425.00
	Bowl, 10¾", oval, flower, hdld.	40.00	95.00
	Bowl, 12", console, flared edge	50.00	125.00
	Candelabrum, 4¾", 2-lite	40.00	90.00
	Candlestick, 7¼", 1-lite, w/blue prisms	65.00	195.00
	Candy dish w/cover, 4" x 7"	50.00	115.00
	Cheese/cracker crumbs, 3½" h., plate 11", hdld.	50.00	100.00
	Cigarette holder (stack ashtray top)	35.00	80.00
	Cocktail shaker, 9", 33 oz.	100.00	275.00
	Creamer	14.00	25.00
	Cruet	45.00	95.00
5	Cup, tea	15.00	65.00
	Cup, punch	10.00	22.50
	Epergne, 4 pt., flower (12" bowl, 9½" bowl, 7¾" vase, 14" plate)	225.00	450.00
	Ice bucket, 6½", hdld.	75.00	225.00

		Crystal	Blue
	Ladle, punch	35.00	100.00
	Mayonnaise, w/liner, 5¾", 2 pt., 2 spoons, hdld.	42.50	100.00
	Mayonnaise, w/liner, 5¾", hdld., 1 spoon	35.00	80.00
	Mustard, 4", w/slotted cover	35.00	65.00
	Pitcher, 4¾" 16 oz., milk	95.00	250.00
	Pitcher, w/ice lip, 9", 72 oz., water	225.00	595.00
	Plate, 6", hdld., fruit nappy liner	4.00	12.00
13	Plate 6¼", bread/butter	5.00	12.00
	Plate, 7¼", rolled edge, soup liner	5.00	12.50
	Plate, 7½", salad	10.00	20.00
	Plate, 8", hdld., mayonnaise liner	6.00	14.00
15	Plate, 8½", luncheon	15.00	35.00
4	Plate, 10½", dinner	65.00	150.00
	Plate, 11", hdld., cheese/cracker liner	20.00	42.50
14	Plate, 12", salad liner, rolled edge	22.00	55.00
	Plate, 14"	25.00	75.00
	Plate, 16", torte	35.00	110.00
	Plate, 18", punch underliner	40.00	110.00
	Relish, 6", round, 2 pt.	12.00	25.00
	Relish, 9½", 4 pt., oblong	30.00	65.00
	Relish, 9½", oblong	27.50	60.00
	Relish, 12¾", 5 pt., rnd.	40.00	95.00
	Relish, 12¾", 7 pt., rnd.	40.00	95.00
	Salt dip, 2½"	11.00	25.00
	Salt & pepper, 3", metal tops	32.00	95.00
16	Salt & pepper, 5", metal tops	37.50	125.00
5	Saucer	4.00	8.00
	Server, 5¾", ctr. hdld.	13.00	45.00
	Server, 6½", ctr. hdld.	22.00	50.00
	Stem, 3", 1 oz., cordial	60.00	240.00
3	Stem, 3½", 3½ oz., ftd., ball stem, wine/coctail	20.00	65.00
1	Stem, 3⅝", 2½ oz., wine (egg cup shape)	22.50	40.00
	Stem, 4", 6 oz., ftd., ball stem, champagne	14.00	27.50
8	Stem, 4¼", ftd., sherbet	10.00	26.00
7	Stem, 4¾", 3 oz., ftd., ball stem, wine	22.00	65.00
2	Stem, 5¾", 8 oz., ftd., ball stem	20.00	50.00
9	Sugar	11.00	25.00
	Syrup, metal cutoff top	125.00	275.00
	Tray, 6¼", hand., mint, div.	14.00	30.00
	Tray, 12¾", rnd.	25.00	50.00
12	Tumbler, 2¼", 2 oz., shot glass	25.00	65.00
10	Tumbler, 3½", 5 oz., flat	20.00	55.00
11	Tumbler, 5¼", 11½ oz., flat	20.00	55.00
	Tumbler, 5½", 8½ oz., ftd.	22.00	55.00
	Tumbler, 6½", 11 oz., ftd., ice tea	27.50	65.00
	Vase, 5¾", ftd., ruffled edge	22.00	55.00
	Vase, 7¼", ftd., flared edge, ball	27.50	75.00
	Vase, 7½", ftd., flared edge, bulbous	32.50	85.00
	Vase, 7¾", flared edge, epergne	40.00	125.00
	Vase, 8", ftd., straight side	40.00	85.00
21	Vase, 9", ftd., ruffled top	50.00	225.00
	Vase, 10", ftd.	55.00	195.00

Brilliant Colors: Emerald Green, Spanish Rose, and Crystal (color of the glass itself)
Soft Colors: Honey, Amethyst, and Jade (ceramic wash over crystal)
Rare Colors: Ruby Stained (on crystal), Red (Ruby glass), Blue (ceramic wash), and Rainbow (multiple color washed on crystal)

Catalonian was handmade glass introduced in January 1927 and advertised as "a replica of seventeenth-century glass." Original labels read "Catalonian, A Reproduction of Old Spanish Glass."

Catalonian is characterized by bubbled and spiral ridges on the outer surface of the piece. The gather of glass was sprinkled with raw "batch" and then dipped back into the molten glass. This caused the granules to bubble. As the glassmaker worked the glass, the bubbles would stretch and become larger.

Blown items always have a rough pontil mark on the base. The edges of Catalonian were generally not polished or beveled. The only exception to this is Ruby glass items, which commanded higher prices at the time of production and thus demanded extra attention. If you find a piece of Catalonian other than Ruby with a ground edge, someone tried to repair a chip.

The Spanish Knobs line was based on the Catalonian shapes and same glass formula. In addition to the bubbles, Spanish Knobs pieces have raised knobs molded into the glass. This line was sold along with Catalonian and original company ads combine the two in table settings. It's considered part of the Catalonian line, not a separate pattern.

In general, vases, candlesticks, and 8" plates are common. Other tableware is harder to find, and cup and saucer sets, decanters, toilet bowls, covered cigarette boxes and the whiskey set trays are very hard to find.

8

Rainbow color was done in the early 1940s. Crystal pieces are highlighted with one or more colors. These colors were applied in bands, so that crystal became one of the colors in the "rainbow." On rare items, you find only three colors: blue, green, and red with no crystal band.

Pricing at present is the same for all the brilliant and soft colors (with crystal about 50% less than the others). Spanish Rose is the hardest of the regular production colors to find. Ruby Stained items are about 50% higher. Blue ceramic, Rainbow colors, and Ruby glass are at least 100% more. Rare colors are primarily found on vases and occasional pieces such as console sets and pitchers.

Milk glass vases in Catalonian shapes were made in the 1950s, but are not collected as Catalonian. Catalonian has been known to sell in art glass markets for more than in Depression glass ones.

13

	Item	Price		Item	Price
	Ashtray, #1125	45.00		Creamer or mayonnaise boat, #1106	40.00
	Basket (made from fingerbowl), #1114	125.00		Creamer, 7 oz., triangular, #1103P	45.00
	Bottle, toilet water w/lid, #1175	135.00		Creamer, footed, SK, #1147	65.00
	Bowl, bulb, #1178	75.00		Cup, #1179	75.00
10	Bowl, 4½" finger or mayo, #1114	48.00		Goblet, parfait, low ftd., SK, #1141	75.00
11	Bowl, 9", straight-sided salad, #1115	135.00	1	Goblet, 10 oz., low ftd., #1120	40.00
	Bowl, 9½", flared salad, #1115B	125.00		Goblet, 10 oz., low ftd., SK, #1142	65.00
	Bowl, 12", Lily, cupped, #1108	350.00	2	Goblet, 12 oz., low ftd. iced tea, #1121	45.00
	Bowl, 12¾", flared, #1185	200.00		Jug, 20 oz., 6", triangular, #1102P	150.00
	Bowl, flower or low centerpiece, SK, #1130	375.00		Jug, 72 oz., cylindrical, #1100P	250.00
	Candlestick, mushroom, SK, #1131, pr.	150.00		Jug, 72 oz., 10", triangular, #1101P	250.00
7	Candlestick, ftd., #1124, pr.	120.00		Jug, 72 oz., squat triangular, #1109	250.00
	Cigarette box and cover, #1107	165.00		Jug, whiskey decanter & stopper, #1127	300.00
	Comport, 6½", SK, #1145	85.00		Plate, 6", bread & butter, #1181	22.00

	Plate, 7", bread & butter, #1113	26.00
3	Plate, 8", salad, #1112	30.00
	Plate, 10", service, #1177	75.00
	Plate, 13", charger, #1111	125.00
	Plate, 16", #1194	175.00
	Relish tray, 3 part, #1191	350.00
	Relish tray, 6 part, #1192	450.00
	Saucer, #1180	50.00
	Sugar, no handles, #1105B	35.00
	Sugar, two handles, #1105	45.00
	Sugar, footed SK, #1146	65.00
12	Sundae (sherbet), 7 oz., ftd., #1123	48.00
	Sundae (sherbet), ftd. SK, #1140	65.00
	Tray, round whiskey set, #1128	300.00
9	Tumbler, 2 oz., whiskey, flat, #1119	45.00
	Tumbler, 2½ oz., whiskey, ftd., #1122	55.00
	Tumbler, 7 oz., flat, #1118	35.00
	Tumbler, 8 oz., flat, SK, #1138	75.00
6	Tumbler, 9 oz., flat, #1110	35.00
13	Tumbler, 12. oz., tea, flat, #1117	45.00
5	Tumbler, 12. oz., hdld. tea, flat, #1117B	65.00

	Vase, 3 bulge rolled edge, #1182	300.00
	Vase, 3 bulge cupped edge, #1183	300.00
	Vase, 3 bulge flared edge, #1184	300.00
8	Vase, Nasturtium, 4 openings, bulbous, #1170	300.00
	Vase, 3¾", Violet, SK, #1171	110.00
	Vase, 4", fan, SK, #1174	110.00
	Vase, 4", flared (hat) SK, #1153	110.00
	Vase, 4", Sweet Pea SK, #1154	110.00
	Vase, 4", triangular, #1103	65.00
	Vase, 6", flared (hat shape), #1116C	100.00
	Vase, 6", ftd., flared, SK, #1148	125.00
	Vase, 6", pillow (oblong), #1104	100.00
	Vase, 6", pinch bottle, triangular, SK, #1167	175.00
	Vase, 6", pinch bottle, 4-sided, SK, #1166	175.00
	Vase, 6", pinch bottle, 4 openings, SK, #1169	225.00
4	Vase, 6", triangular, #1102	100.00
	Vase, 6½", ftd. fan, #1172	100.00
	Vase, 7", fan, #1168	100.00
	Vase, 7", tumbler, #1116	100.00
	Vase, 8", fan, #1100B	125.00
	Vase, 8", flared (hat shape), #1100C	125.00
	Vase, 8", rose jar, #1109B	175.00
	Vase, 8", rose jar, SK, #1173	225.00
	Vase, 8", tumbler, #1100	125.00
	Vase, 10", triangular, #1101	175.00

Colors: crystal, Ebony (gold encrusted)

There is a more complete inventory for Cambridge pieces under Rose Point later in this book (pgs. 190 – 195). Many Chantilly pieces are not listed here, as my main interest is to familiarize you with the pattern itself. When pricing missing Chantilly items using the Rose Point list, you must remember that Rose Point items are currently a minimum of 30% to 50% higher due to collector demand.

Although Chantilly was made and sold along with the popular Rose Point, it never attracted the quantity of customers then or today as did Rose Point. I have included a couple of fold out pages from a pamphlet showing the readily available #3625 Chantilly stems and an array of vases at the top of page 61. Maybe this will help those having trouble distinguishing stems or line numbers. There are two pages to help identify Cambridge stemware lines in the back of this book (pgs. 252 – 253).

Item	Crystal
Bowl, 7", bonbon, 2 hdld., ftd.	25.00
Bowl, 7", relish/pickle, 2 pt.	30.00
Bowl, 7", relish/pickle	32.00
Bowl, 9", celery/relish, 3 pt.	38.00
Bowl, 10", 4 ftd., flared	50.00
Bowl, 11", tab hdld.	50.00
Bowl, 11½", tab hdld. ftd.	55.00
Bowl, 12", celery/relish, 3 pt.	50.00
Bowl, 12", 4 ftd., flared	55.00
Bowl, 12", 4 ftd., oval	60.00
Bowl, 12", celery/relish, 5 pt.	55.00
Butter, w/cover, round	210.00
Butter, ¼ lb.	325.00
Candlestick, 5"	28.00
Candlestick, 6", 2-lite, "keyhole"	40.00
Candlestick, 6", 3-lite	50.00
Candy box, w/cover, ftd.	175.00
Candy box, w/cover, rnd.	95.00
Cocktail icer, 2 pc.	65.00
Comport, 5½"	35.00
Comport, 5⅜", blown	40.00
Creamer	18.00
Creamer, indiv., #3900, scalloped edge	15.00
20 Cup, #3900/17	17.50
Decanter, ftd.	210.00
Decanter, ball	250.00
Hat, small	225.00
Hat, large	325.00
Hurricane lamp, candlestick base	160.00
Hurricane lamp, keyhole base w/prisms	295.00
3 Ice bucket, w/chrome handle	125.00
Marmalade & cover	60.00
Mayonnaise (sherbet type bowl w/ladle)	40.00
Mayonnaise, div. w/liner & 2 ladles	65.00
Mayonnaise, w/liner & ladle	50.00
Mustard & cover	95.00
Oil, 6 oz., hdld., w/stopper	135.00
Pitcher, ball	225.00
Pitcher, Doulton	395.00
Pitcher, upright	250.00
8 Pitcher, 32 oz., martini jug, #3900/114	195.00
Plate, crescent, salad	135.00
Plate, 6½", bread/butter	8.00
7 Plate, 8", salad	12.50
Plate, 8", tab hdld., ftd., bonbon	20.00
Plate, 10½", dinner	75.00
Plate, 12", 4 ftd., service	50.00
Plate, 13", 4 ftd.	60.00
Plate, 13½", tab hdld., cake	65.00
Plate, 14", torte	45.00
Salad dressing bottle	175.00
Salt & pepper, pr., flat	35.00
Salt & pepper, footed	40.00
Salt & pepper, handled	40.00
20 Saucer, #3900/17	4.00
9 Stem, #3080, 9 oz., water	45.00
12 Stem, #3138, 6 oz., tall sherbet	18.00
Stem, #3600, 1 oz., cordial	50.00

Item	Crystal
Stem, #3600, 2½ oz., cocktail	22.00
Stem, #3600, 2½ oz., wine	32.00
Stem, #3600, 4½ oz., claret	40.00
Stem, #3600, 4½ oz., low oyster cocktail	16.00
Stem, #3600, 7 oz., tall sherbet	18.00
Stem, #3600, 7 oz., low sherbet	16.00
Stem, #3600, 10 oz., water	32.00
Stem, #3625, 1 oz., cordial	50.00
Stem, #3625, 3 oz., cocktail	26.00
Stem, #3625, 4½ oz., claret	40.00
Stem, #3625, 4½ oz., low oyster cocktail	16.00
Stem, #3625, 7 oz., low sherbet	16.00
Stem, #3625, 7 oz., tall sherbet	18.00
Stem, #3625, 10 oz., water	32.00
Stem, #3775, 1 oz., cordial	50.00
19 Stem, #3775, 2½ oz., wine	32.00
16 Stem, #3775, 3 oz., cocktail	24.00
Stem, #3775, 4½ oz., claret	40.00
Stem, #3775, 4½ oz., oyster cocktail	16.00
17 Stem, #3775, 6 oz., low sherbet	16.00
18 Stem, #3775, 6 oz., tall sherbet	18.00
6 Stem, #3779, 1 oz., cordial	65.00
4 Stem, #3779, 2½ oz., wine	32.00
5 Stem, #3779, 3 oz., cocktail	24.00
Stem, #3779, 4½ oz., claret	40.00
Stem, #3779, 4½ oz., low oyster cocktail	16.00
1 Stem, #3779, 6 oz., tall sherbet	18.00
Stem, #3779, 6 oz., low sherbet	16.00
2 Stem, #3779, 9 oz., water	32.00
Stem, #7801, 10 oz., goblet	28.00
Sugar	18.00
Sugar, indiv., #3900, scalloped edge	15.00
14 Syrup, 1670, drip cut top	250.00
Tumbler, #3600, 5 oz., ftd., juice	18.00
Tumbler, #3600, 12 oz., ftd., tea	25.00
11 Tumbler, #3625, 5 oz., ftd., juice	18.00
10 Tumbler, #3625, 10 oz., ftd., water	20.00
Tumbler, #3625, 12 oz., ftd., tea	26.00
Tumbler, #3775, 5 oz., ftd., juice	18.00
Tumbler, #3775, 10 oz., ftd., water	20.00
Tumbler, #3775, 12 oz., ftd., tea	24.00
Tumbler, #3779, 5 oz., ftd., juice	20.00
Tumbler, #3779, 12 oz., ftd., tea	25.00
Tumbler, 13 oz.	26.00
Vase, 5", globe	65.00
Vase, 6", high ftd., flower	50.00
Vase, 8", high ftd., flower	55.00
Vase, 9", keyhole base	60.00
Vase, 10", bud	95.00
Vase, 11", ftd., flower	95.00
Vase, 11", ped. ftd., flower	115.00
Vase, 12", keyhole base	110.00
Vase, 13", ftd., flower	165.00
21 Cordial, Sterling base	75.00
15 Wine, Farberware Trims	25.00
22 Sugar, Farberware Trims	25.00
13 Creamer, Farberware Trims	30.00

1237

6004-8

6004-6

274

3625
10 oz. Goblet

3625
12 oz. Ftd. Ice Tea

1617

1603

1238

3625
10 oz. Ftd. Tumbler

3625
4½ oz. Claret

3625
3 oz. Cocktail

3625
5 oz. Ftd. Tumbler

278

279

1299

3625
2½ oz. Wine

3625
7 oz. Tall Sherbet

3625
1 oz. Cordial

3625
7 oz. Low Sherbet

3625
4½ oz. Oyster Cocktail

Colors: Crystal, Flamingo, Moongleam, Hawthorne, Marigold

Flamingo (pink) Charter Oak pieces are offered sporadically, but I rarely see other colors. Stemware, however, seems to materialize in small batches rather than a piece or two. Prices have remained stable over the last few years, which normally means there has been sufficient supply for collector demand. Price increases frequently signal not enough being found to supply all who want it. Many pieces of Charter Oak are unmarked, however, and bargains can still be discovered with a canny eye. Acorns are the hallmark of the pattern. Plantation with its pineapple and Charter Oak with its acorn stems are hard to miss.

You can see that clever "Acorn" #130, one lite candleholder in the *Pattern Identification II* book. The base is an oak leaf with stem curled up and an acorn for the candle cup. Actually, this is not Charter Oak pattern, but a number of Charter Oak collectors try to acquire these to go with their sets. Heisey designed a number of candles to "blend" (their words) with numerous patterns. This candle was made during the same time as Charter Oak and mostly in the same colors. Yeoman cups and saucers are often used with this set since there were no cups and saucers made. A Yeoman cup and saucer set is pictured here, but not priced in the Charter Oak listing. I mention that since several readers have wanted to know why I did not price the cup and saucer in my listings. These are priced under Yeoman.

I have pictured Flamingo over the years because that is what I have been able to borrow, but notice that Charter Oak came in several other colors.

		Crystal	Flamingo	Moongleam	Hawthorne	Marigold
	Bowl, 11", floral, #116 (oak leaf)	50.00	50.00	70.00	85.00	
7	Bowl, finger, #3362	10.00	17.50	20.00		
	Candleholder, 1-lite, #130, "Acorn"	150.00	300.00	450.00		
	Candlestick, 3", #116 (oak leaf)	25.00	35.00	45.00	90.00	
2	Candlestick, 5", 3-lite, #129, "Tricorn"	100.00	110.00	140.00	160.00	200.00+
6	Coaster, #10 (Oak Leaf)	10.00	20.00	25.00	35.00	

		Crystal	Flamingo	Moongleam	Hawthorne	Marigold
	Comport, 6", low ft., #3362	45.00	55.00	60.00	80.00	100.00
13	Comport, 7", ftd., #3362	50.00	65.00	70.00	160.00	175.00
4	Cup and Saucer (#1231 Yeoman)	15.00	25.00	25.00	35.00	
	Lamp, #4262 (blown comport/water filled to magnify design & stabilize lamp)	1,000.00	1,500.00	1,500.00		
16	Pitcher, flat, #3362		160.00	180.00		
1	Plate, 6", salad, #1246 (Acorn & Leaves)	5.00	10.00	12.50	20.00	
	Plate, 7", luncheon/salad, #1246 (Acorn & Leaves)	8.00	12.00	17.50	22.50	
	Plate, 8", luncheon, #1246 (Acorn & Leaves)	10.00	15.00	20.00	25.00	
17	Plate, 10½", dinner, #1246 (Acorn & Leaves)	30.00	45.00	55.00	70.00	
11	Stem, 3 oz., cocktail, #3362	10.00	25.00	25.00	45.00	40.00
9	Stem, 3½ oz., low ft., oyster cocktail, #3362	8.00	20.00	20.00	40.00	35.00
14	Stem, 4½ oz., parfait, #3362	15.00	25.00	35.00	60.00	50.00
10	Stem, 6 oz., saucer champagne, #3362	10.00	15.00	20.00	50.00	40.00
5	Stem, 6 oz., sherbet, low ft., #3362	10.00	15.00	22.00	50.00	40.00
15	Stem, 8 oz., goblet, high ft., #3362	20.00	35.00	35.00	95.00	60.00
3	Stem, 8 oz., luncheon goblet, low ft., #3362	20.00	40.00	40.00	95.00	60.00
8	Tumbler, 10 oz., flat, #3362	10.00	20.00	25.00	35.00	30.00
12	Tumbler, 12 oz., flat, #3362	12.50	20.00	25.00	40.00	35.00

Colors: crystal

Cherokee Rose stemware line #17399 is the teardrop style in the photo, while the #17403 stem is represented by the footed juice in the center. Should you find a Cherokee Rose cup or saucer, please let me know. The 5902 line had scalloped and beaded edges on serving pieces. A few are found with gold trim.

13

	Item	Price
	Bowl, 5", finger	30.00
	Bowl, 6", fruit or nut, #5902	30.00
	Bowl, 7", nappy, #5902	45.00
	Bowl, 10", deep salad, cupped, #5902	75.00
	Bowl, 10½", celery, rectangular, #5902	50.00
	Bowl, 12", crimped, #5902	65.00
	Bowl, 12½", centerpiece, flared, #5902	65.00
	Bowl, 13", centerpiece, cone shape, #5902	75.00
	Cake plate, 12½", center hdld., #5902	55.00
5	Candlesticks, pr., double branch, 7¼"	100.00
	Comport, 6", #15082	52.50
6	Creamer, also bead hndl., #5902	22.00
	Icer w/liner	125.00
	Mayonnaise, liner and ladle, #5902	65.00
	Pitcher, sleek top dips to hndl., #5859	650.00
	Pitcher, 2 qt., straight top, ftd., #14194	500.00+
	Plate, 6", sherbet	8.00
4	Plate, 8", luncheon, plain or beaded rim, #5902	15.00
	Plate, 13½", turned-up edge, lily, #5902	50.00
	Plate, 14", sandwich, #5902	55.00
13	Relish, 6½", 3 pt., #5902	38.00
	Relish, 12½", 3 pt., #5902	60.00
	Shaker, pr.	150.00+
	Stem, 1 oz., cordial, #17399	45.00
	Stem, 2 oz., sherry, #17399	33.00

	Item	Price
10	Stem, 3½ oz., cocktail, #17399	18.00
7	Stem, 3½ oz., wine, #17399	33.00
9	Stem, 4 oz., claret, #17399	45.00
	Stem, 4½ oz., parfait	48.00
12	Stem, 5½ oz., sherbet/champagne, #17399	18.00
1	Stem, 9 oz., water, #17399	28.00
	Sugar, also w/beaded hndl., #5902	22.00
	Table bell, #9742 – lg.; #9743 – sm.	75.00
11	Tumbler, 4½ oz., oyster cocktail, #14198	24.00
8	Tumbler, 5 oz., ftd., juice, #17399	24.00
	Tumbler, 8 oz., ftd., water, #17399	25.00
	Tumbler, 10½ oz., ftd., ice tea, #17399	40.00
	Vase, 6", bud, #14185	25.00
3	Vase, 8", bud, #14185	35.00
	Vase, 8½", tear drop	85.00
	Vase, 9¼", tub, #17350, (1) ball stem, ftd.	95.00
2	Vase, 10", bud, #14185	45.00
	Vase, 11", bud, 6 beaded stem, flare rim	50.00
	Vase, 11", urn, #5943, (1) ball stem, ftd.	110.00
	Vase, 12", flared, #5855	135.00

Colors: crystal, Sahara yellow (Chintz only), Moongleam green, Flamingo pink, and Alexandrite orchid (all colors made in Formal Chintz)

Heisey's Chintz pattern is found as two distinct motifs on assorted Heisey blanks. Pieces pictured below are known as Chintz. Pieces with encompassing circles are pictured at the bottom of page 66 and are designated Formal Chintz. These patterns are similarly priced. I have never been fortunate enough to find any tumblers or stemware in Formal Chintz though they were made on the #3390 Carcassone stem line.

Collectors have reported Chintz shakers in #1401 Empress line. Items do sneak by my listings until someone writes to correct omissions. (If you have pieces that are not in any pattern's listing, please let me know.) Sahara is the color most desired, but a few collectors search for crystal. Alexandrite Formal Chintz is quite uncommon. It is very striking when displayed in quantity. There is so little of Alexandrite color that putting a set together would be a tremendously expensive challenge. However, a lucky someone did run into a large set a few years ago.

Do not confuse this pattern with the Fostoria or Tiffin Chintz; and realize that you must also specify the company name when you ask for any pattern named Chintz. It was a fashionable designation used by many glass and pottery companies for their wares.

		Crystal	Sahara
8	Bowl, cream soup	18.00	35.00
14	Bowl, finger, #4107	10.00	20.00
	Bowl, 5½", ftd., preserve, hdld.	15.00	30.00
	Bowl, 6", ftd., mint	20.00	32.00
	Bowl, 6", ftd., 2 hdld., jelly	17.00	35.00
	Bowl, 7", triplex relish	20.00	40.00
	Bowl, 7½", Nasturtium	20.00	40.00
	Bowl, 8½", ftd., 2 hdld., floral	35.00	70.00
15	Bowl, 10", oval, vegetable	20.00	35.00
	Bowl, 11", dolphin ft., floral	45.00	110.00
	Bowl, 13", 2 pt., pickle & olive	15.00	35.00
	Comport, 7", oval	45.00	85.00
7	Creamer, 3 dolphin ft.	20.00	50.00
	Creamer, individual	12.00	30.00
9	Cup	15.00	25.00
	Grapefruit, ftd., #3389, Duquesne	30.00	60.00
	Ice bucket, ftd.	85.00	155.00
	Mayonnaise, 5½", dolphin ft.	35.00	65.00

	Crystal	Sahara
Oil, 4 oz.	60.00	135.00
Pitcher, 3 pint, dolphin ft.	200.00	300.00
Plate, 6", sq. or rnd., bread	6.00	15.00
Plate, 7", sq. or rnd., salad	8.00	18.00
16 Plate, 8", sq. or rnd., luncheon	10.00	22.00
Plate, 10½", sq. or rnd., dinner	40.00	85.00
Plate, 12", two hdld.	25.00	47.50
11 Plate, 13", hors d' oeuvre, two hdld.	30.00	65.00
12 Platter, 14", oval	35.00	90.00
Salt and pepper, pr.	40.00	95.00
9 Saucer	3.00	5.00
Stem, #3389, Duquesne, 1 oz., cordial	100.00	200.00
6 Stem, #3389, 2½ oz., wine	25.00	50.00
Stem, #3389, 3 oz., cocktail	17.50	35.00
Stem, #3389, 4 oz., claret	25.00	50.00
Stem, #3389, 4 oz., oyster cocktail	12.50	25.00
5 Stem, #3389, 5 oz., parfait	17.50	35.00
1 Stem, #3389, 5 oz., saucer champagne	12.50	22.00
3 Stem, #3389, 5 oz., sherbet	10.00	15.00
2 Stem, #3389, 9 oz., water	17.50	35.00
Sugar, 3 dolphin ft.	20.00	50.00
13 Sugar, individual	12.00	30.00
Tray, 10", celery	15.00	30.00
Tray, 12", sq., ctr. hdld., sandwich	35.00	65.00
Tray, 13", celery	18.00	45.00
Tumbler, #3389, 5 oz., ftd., juice	12.00	22.00
Tumbler, #3389, 8 oz., soda	13.00	24.00
10 Tumbler, #3389, 10 oz., ftd., water	14.00	25.00
4 Tumbler, #3389, 12 oz., iced tea	16.00	30.00
Vase, 9", dolphin ft.	95.00	185.00

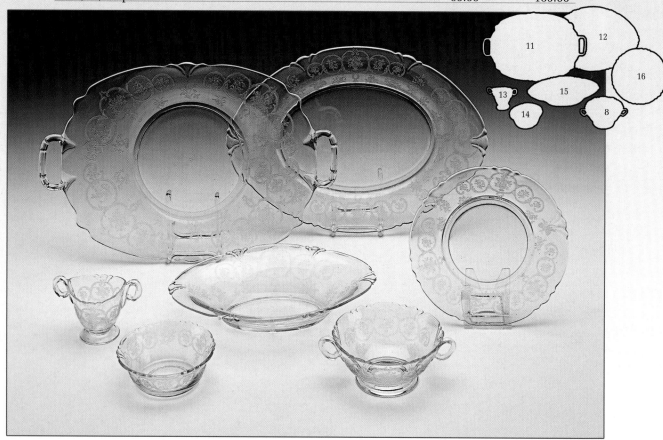

Colors: crystal, pink; crystal with Nile green trim

Classic is an older pattern that I have had fun finding over the years. When you start with few listings, you can discover an assortment of surprises in your travels. Dinner plates shocked me several years ago, as did a pink cup. Alas, I have never found a saucer to go with it, but I'm confident it will turn up. Note the decorated vase that was found right at this book's deadline.

I prefer the pink Classic, but only stemmed beverage items are surfacing in that color. Tiffin pitchers (one pictured in pink) came with and without a lid. The one here has the top curved in so it will not take a lid. Remember that Tiffin pitcher lids have no pattern etched on them.

Note the crystal pitcher at the bottom of page 68, which is a different style, but holds approximately 60 ounces. I have priced both pitchers in the same listing. As with all glass dinner plates with no pattern in the center, you need to check for blemishes and scratches from use. Of course, finding any mint condition dinner plate 70 or 80 years after its manufacture is nearly impossible. I, personally, have found few serving pieces save for a two-handled bowl and a cheese and cracker.

Pink Classic stems are found on the #17024 line that is also found with Tiffin's Flanders pattern. Crystal stemmed items seem to surface on the #14185 line. There are some size discrepancies within these two stemware lines. We have measured both colors and noted them in the listings.

Nile green trim is found on the #15011 stem line which has a wafer beneath the flared rim bowl. On 15016, the bowl is cupped at the rim.

12

		Crystal	Pink
13	Bowl, 9½" Nouvelle, #15361	110.00	
	Bowl, 2 hdld., 8" x 9¼"	140.00	
	Bowl, 11" centerpiece, #14185	120.00	
	Bowl, 13" centerpiece, rolled edge	135.00	
	Candy jar w/cover, ½ lb., ftd	150.00	
	Candle, 5", #9758	50.00	
	Cheese & cracker set	110.00	
	Comport, 6" wide, 3¼" tall	75.00	
	Creamer, flat, #6	45.00	95.00
23	Creamer, ftd., #5931	35.00	
	Creamer, ftd., cone, #14185	35.00	
	Cup, #8869	75.00	
	Finger bowl, ftd., #14185	25.00	50.00
	Mayonnaise, or whipped cream w/ladle, ftd.		75.00
	Pitcher, ftd., hld, #194 (bulbous)	250.00	
17	Pitcher, 61 oz., (2 qt.) #114	295.00	595.00
6	Pitcher, 61 oz., w/cover, #145 (subtract $50 w/out cover)	395.00	695.00
27	Plate, 6⅜", champagne liner, #23	10.00	

			Crystal	Pink
		Plate, 7½", #8814	12.50	
		Plate, 8", #8833	12.50	25.00
18		Plate, 10", dinner, #8818	125.00	
		Saucer, #8869	15.00	
11		Sherbet, 3⅛", 6½ oz., short	17.50	*38.00
5		Stem, 3⅞", 1 oz., cordial	65.00	
3		Stem, 4¹⁵⁄₁₆", 3 oz., wine	32.50	*65.00
9		Stem, 4⅞", 3¾ oz., cocktail	40.00	
		Stem, 4⅞", 4 oz., cocktail	25.00	
21	2	Stem, 6½", 5 oz., parfait	40.00	*75.00
7		Stem, 6", 7½ oz., saucer champagne	22.50	*50.00
20	8	Stem, 7¼", 9 oz., water	35.00	*70.00
		Stem, 22 oz., grapefruit w/liner	75.00	
		Sugar, flat, #6	35.00	95.00
		Sugar, ftd.	35.00	
		Sugar, ftd., covered, #14185	22.50	
16		Tumbler, 3½", 5 oz., ftd., juice	22.00	
4		Tumbler, 4½", 8½ oz., ftd., water	25.00	60.00
15		Tumbler, 4⅛", 10½ oz., flat, water	28.00	
		Tumbler, 5⁹⁄₁₆", 14 oz., ftd., tea	35.00	
22		Tumbler, 6", 13 oz., ftd., iced tea		75.00
1		Tumbler, 6¹⁄₁₆", 14 oz., ftd., iced tea	35.00	
		Tumbler, 6¼", 6½ oz., ftd., Pilsner	40.00	
14		Tumbler, 10 oz., flat, table	30.00	
10		Tumbler, 12 oz., flat, tea	35.00	
		Tumbler, tea, hndl, #14185	30.00	
24		Vase, bud, 6½", #14185	35.00	
12		Vase, 8", wide optic	175.00	
	19	Vase, bud, 10½", #14185	42.50	

Colors: amber, Willow blue, crystal, Ebony, Emerald green light, Gold Krystol, Peach Blo

Cleo Peach Blo (pink) and Emerald prices have remained steady and supplies of those colors continue to be found. Emerald Cleo has seen little action of late and is remaining in dealer supplies. Cleo can be collected in large sets of pink or green, but not all pieces were made in the other colors. The blue, a predecessor of Moonlight blue, was named Willow by Cambridge and is shown below. Some huge collections of Willow have materialized in the market the last few years, and most have quickly been absorbed into new collections. Original owners made a tidy profit at today's prices from their long years of patient collecting. Hopefully, you will run into a large set for a reasonable price; but those chances are not as frequent as in the past.

There are more collectors looking for blue than supplies turning up. Thus, prices for Willow Cleo continue upward, albeit at a slower pace than in the past. Most blue is found on Cambridge's Decagon blank. Rarely seen Cleo items fetch some serious prices. There is always a market for rare and unusual glassware.

I have found rare pieces of Cleo in the past but they were usually amber rather than colors that charm collectors. This pattern will continue to attract new collectors as long as the supply lasts. You might consider mixing colors or even collecting one particular item such as the ice buckets and pails like those pictured on page 71. Not often will you have the opportunity to see that many at one time.

	Blue	Pink Green Yellow Amber
Almond, 2½", individual	110.00	75.00
Basket, 7", 2 hdld. (upturned sides), Decagon	60.00	30.00
Basket, 11", 2 hdld. (upturned sides), Decagon	95.00	50.00
Bouillon cup, w/saucer, 2 hdld., Decagon	95.00	55.00
Bowl, 2 pt., relish	40.00	22.00
Bowl, 3½", cranberry	70.00	50.00
Bowl, 5½", fruit	40.00	25.00

	Blue	Pink Green Yellow Amber
Bowl, 5½" 2 hdld., bonbon, Decagon	60.00	22.00
Bowl, 6", 4 ft., comport	60.00	35.00
Bowl, 6", cereal, Decagon	60.00	40.00
Bowl, 6½", 2 hdld., bonbon, Decagon	40.00	22.00
Bowl, 7½", tab hdld., soup	75.00	35.00
Bowl, 8", miniature console		195.00
Bowl, 8½"	90.00	40.00
Bowl, 8½" 2 hdld., Decagon	100.00	40.00
Bowl, 9", covered vegetable		295.00
Bowl, 9½", oval veg., Decagon	145.00	75.00
8 Bowl, 9", pickle, Decagon, #1082	75.00	45.00

CLEO

13

	Blue	Pink Green Yellow Amber
Bowl, 10", 2 hdld., Decagon	125.00	75.00
3 Bowl, 11", oval, celery, #1083	125.00	75.00
Bowl, 11½", oval	125.00	75.00
Bowl, 12", console	140.00	75.00
7 Bowl, 12", #842	125.00	65.00
22 Bowl, 15½", oval, Decagon		225.00
Bowl, cream soup w/saucer, 2 hdld., Decagon	85.00	55.00
Bowl, finger w/liner, #3077	75.00	50.00
Bowl, finger w/liner, #3115	75.00	50.00
5 Candlestick, 1-lite, 2 styles, 4", #627	40.00	30.00
Candlestick, 2-lite	110.00	65.00
Candlestick, 3-lite	150.00	85.00
Candy box w/lid	295.00	195.00
Candy & cover, tall	325.00	225.00
Comport, 7", tall, #3115	110.00	75.00
1 Comport, 12", #877	145.00	95.00
11 Creamer, Decagon/"Lightning"	35.00	25.00
Creamer, ewer style, 6"	195.00	125.00
9 Creamer, ftd., #867	40.00	22.00
14 Cup, Decagon, #865	30.00	15.00
Decanter, w/stopper		325.00
13 Gravy boat, w/liner plate, Decagon, #1091	550.00	325.00
20 Gravy boat, 2 spout, #917	185.00	
21 Gravy boat liner, #167	75.00	
16 Ice bowl, #844		
17 Ice pail, #851	250.00	125.00
15 Ice tub, #394	225.00	125.00
19 Mayonnaise, w/liner and ladle, Decagon, #983	145.00	90.00
Mayonnaise, ftd.	75.00	45.00
Oil, 6 oz., w/stopper, Decagon	750.00	185.00
Pitcher, 3½ pt., #38		235.00
Pitcher, w/cover, 22 oz.		275.00
Pitcher, w/cover, 60 oz., #804		495.00
Pitcher, w/cover, 62 oz., #955	550.00	395.00
Pitcher, w/cover, 63 oz., #3077	895.00	425.00
Pitcher, w/cover, 68 oz., #937		395.00
2 Plate, 6½", bread & butter, #809	15.00	10.00
Plate, 7"	28.00	18.00
Plate, 7", 2 hdld., Decagon	30.00	20.00

	Blue	Pink Green Yellow Amber
24 Plate, 8½", luncheon, Decagon	40.00	20.00
Plate, 9½", dinner, Decagon	175.00	65.00
Plate, 9½", grill		100.00
Plate, 11", 2 hdld., Decagon	120.00	50.00
Platter, 12"	195.00	125.00
23 Platter, 15", #1079	325.00	225.00
Platter, w/cover, oval (toast)		425.00
Platter, asparagus, indented, w/sauce & spoon		395.00
Salt dip, 1½"	145.00	95.00
14 Saucer, Decagon, #865	8.00	5.00
Server, 12", ctr. hand.	65.00	45.00
Stem, #3077, 1 oz., cordial	225.00	195.00
Stem, #3077, 2½ oz., cocktail		35.00
Stem, #3077, 3½ oz., wine	95.00	70.00
Stem, #3077, 6 oz., low sherbet	35.00	20.00
Stem, #3077, 6 oz., tall sherbet	45.00	25.00
Stem, #3115, 9 oz.		30.00
Stem, #3115, 3½ oz., cocktail		25.00
Stem, #3115, 6 oz., fruit		16.00
Stem, #3115, 6 oz., low sherbet		16.00
Stem, #3115, 6 oz., tall sherbet		18.00
Stem, #3115, 9 oz., water		27.50
Sugar cube tray		185.00
4 Sugar, Decagon/"Lightning"	35.00	25.00
10 Sugar, ftd., #867	40.00	22.00
Sugar sifter, ftd., 6¾"	850.00	325.00
Syrup pitcher, drip cut		195.00
Syrup pitcher, glass lid		250.00
Toast & cover, round		500.00
Tobacco humidor		500.00
Tray, 12", handled serving		155.00
Tray, 12", oval service, Decagon	225.00	145.00
Tray, creamer & sugar, oval		50.00
12 Tray, hdld. for creamer/sugar	35.00	20.00
Tumbler, #3077, 2½ oz., ftd.	125.00	65.00
6 Tumbler, #3077, 5 oz., ftd.	60.00	25.00
Tumbler, #3077, 8 oz., ftd.	60.00	28.00
Tumbler, #3077, 10 oz., ftd.	65.00	30.00
Tumbler, #3022, 12 oz., ftd.	95.00	40.00
Tumbler, #3115, 2½ oz., ftd.		55.00
Tumbler, #3115, 5 oz., ftd.		25.00
Tumbler, #3115, 8 oz., ftd.		25.00
Tumbler, #3115, 10 oz., ftd.		37.50
Tumbler, #3115, 12 oz., ftd.		35.00
Tumbler, 12 oz., flat		65.00
Vase, 5½"		95.00
18 Vase, 9", ftd., #3450, Nautilis		225.00
Vase, 9½"		155.00
Vase, 11"		195.00

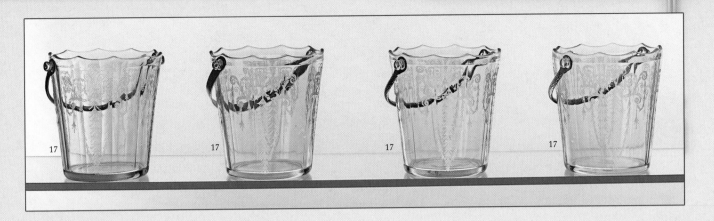

17   17   17   17

15   16   17

18   24
19   22   7
20
21   23   14

Colors: crystal; some yellow, opaque blue, green, white, amber, red in 1980s as Maypole

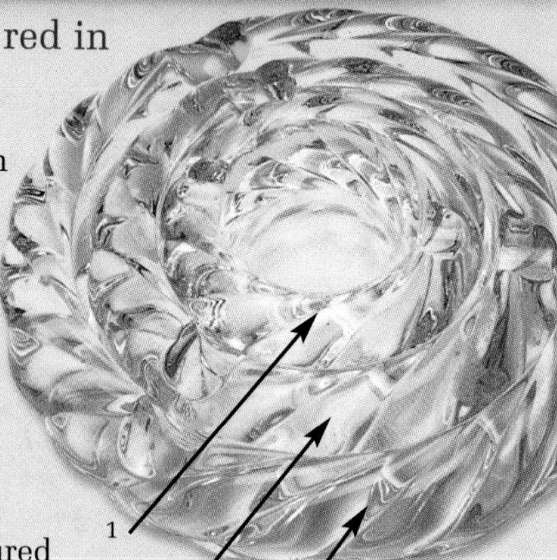

Fostoria's stately Colony was developed from a previous Fostoria pattern named Queen Ann. A few Colony pieces were made as late as 1983. Fostoria listed colored pieces of Colony Maypole in the 1980s catalogs. Red vases, candlesticks, and bowls being noticed were fashioned by Viking for Fostoria in the early 1980s. Note the red bud vase pictured. Dalzell Viking later made red for Lancaster Colony who now owns these Fostoria moulds.

Stems and tumblers with a thin, plain bowl and a Colony patterned foot (sold to go with this pattern) were called Colonial Dame. You might even find these stems with colored bowls in dark emerald green or amethyst.

Note the round stacking set of three ashtrays containing a 3", 4½", and 6", pictured here. These were the first round ones I had seen outside of catalogs, though the square ones appear commonly.

Experimental pieces such as the blue goblets (pictured on pg. 74) turn up sporadically, but you could never accumulate many pieces in that color. Colony prices have been holding their own, indicating there are new collectors searching for it. As with other Elegant patterns, stemware abounds. Some pieces you may have trouble locating include finger bowls, cream soups, punch bowl, ice tub with flat rim, flat tumblers, and cigarette boxes. The supply of pitchers is adequate for now. All the flat pieces with plain centers need to be checked closely for abrasions, but that is true for any pattern. When stacking these today, place a paper plate between each one to protect them for future generations.

		Crystal
14	Ashtray, 2⅞", sq.	12.00
1	Ashtray, 3", round, #2412½	15.00
13	Ashtray, 3½", sq.	16.00
2	Ashtray, 4½", round, #2412½	20.00
3	Ashtray, 6", round, #2412½	25.00
	Bowl, 2¾" ftd., almond	20.00
	Bowl, 4½", rnd.	12.00
	Bowl, 4¾", finger	50.00
12	Bowl, 4¾", hdld., whip cream	12.00
28	Bowl, 5", bonbon, rolled edge	12.00
	Bowl, 5", cream soup	60.00
10	Bowl, 5", hdld., sweet meat	15.00
	Bowl, 5½", sq.	22.00
21	Bowl, 5⅝", 3 toe nut	20.00
	Bowl, 5¾", high ft.	16.00
	Bowl, 5", rnd.	15.00
	Bowl, 6", rose	25.00
24	Bowl, 7", 2 pt., relish, 2 hndl.	14.00
	Bowl, 7", bonbon, 3 ftd.	14.00
	Bowl, 7", olive, oblong	14.00
	Bowl, 7¾", salad	25.00
	Bowl, 8", cupped	47.50
17	Bowl, 8½", hdld.	40.00
	Bowl, 9", rolled console	40.00
	Bowl, 9½", pickle	22.00
	Bowl, 9¾", salad	50.00
18	Bowl, 8¾" x 9¾", w/rolled edge, muffin tray	32.00
	Bowl, 10", fruit	40.00
	Bowl, 10½", low ft.	85.00
16	Bowl, 10½", high ft., #2412½, 6½T	125.00

		Crystal
	Bowl, 10½", oval	60.00
	Bowl, 10½", oval, 2 part	55.00
	Bowl, 11", oval, ftd.	75.00
19	Bowl, 11", flared	40.00
	Bowl, 11½", celery	32.00
	Bowl, 13", console	40.00
	Bowl, 13¼", punch, ftd.	425.00
	Bowl, 14", fruit	60.00
	Butter dish, ¼ lb.	45.00
	Candlestick, 3½"	17.50
	Candlestick, 6½", double	45.00
	Candlestick, 7"	37.50
	Candlestick, 7½", w/8 prisms	95.00
	Candlestick, 9"	40.00
	Candlestick, 9¾", w/prisms	125.00
	Candlestick, 14½", w/10 prisms	195.00
	Candy, w/cover, 6½"	45.00
	Candy, w/cover, ftd., ½ lb.	75.00
	Cheese & cracker	55.00
	Cigarette box	58.00
4	Comport, 4", low foot	17.50
23	Comport, cover, 6½"	45.00
15	Comport, 7"	65.00
25	Comport, 7", w/plain top	75.00
5	Creamer, 3¼", indiv.	12.50
	Creamer, 3¾"	9.00
	Cup, 6 oz., ftd.	6.50
	Cup, punch	15.00
	Ice bucket	95.00
	Ice bucket, plain edge	225.00

1
2
3

		Crystal
	Lamp, electric	195.00
	Mayonnaise, 3 pc.	35.00
	Oil w/stopper, 4½ oz.	45.00
	Pitcher, 16 oz., milk	65.00
	Pitcher, 48 oz., ice lip	195.00
	Pitcher, 2 qt., ice lip	115.00
	Plate, ctr. hdld., sandwich	32.00
	Plate, 6", bread & butter	6.00
29	Plate, 6½", lemon, hdld.	12.00
	Plate, 7", salad	9.00
	Plate, 8", luncheon	12.00
	Plate, 9", dinner	25.00
	Plate, 10", hdld., cake	27.50
	Plate, 12", ftd., salver	85.00
	Plate, 13", torte	30.00
	Plate, 15", torte	60.00
	Plate, 18", torte	95.00
	Platter, 12"	52.50
11	Relish, 10", 3 part	27.50
	Salt, 2½" indiv., pr.	20.00

		Crystal
	Salt & pepper, pr., 3⅝"	28.00
	Saucer	2.00
20	Stem, 3½ oz., cocktail	10.00
30	Stem, 3⅜", 4 oz., oyster cocktail	10.00
	Stem, 3⅝", 5 oz., sherbet	8.00
	Stem, 4", 3½ oz., cocktail	11.00
	Stem, 4¼", 3¼ oz., wine	20.00
22	Stem, 5¼", 9 oz., goblet	15.00
6	Sugar, 2¾", indiv.	12.50
	Sugar, 3½"	9.00
7	Tray for indiv. sugar/cream, 6¾"	15.00
26	Tumbler, 3⅝", 5 oz., juice	25.00
27	Tumbler, 3⅞", 9 oz., water	22.00
	Tumbler, 4⅞", 12 oz., tea	40.00
	Tumbler, 4½", 5 oz., ftd.	18.00
	Tumbler, 5¾", 12 oz., ftd.	22.00
9	Vase, 6", bud, flared	15.00
8	Vase, 7", cupped	45.00
	Vase, 7½", flared	60.00
	Vase, 9", cornucopia	80.00
	Vase, 12", straight	195.00

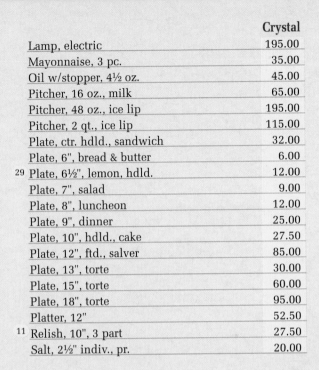

73

COLONY PATTERN
No. 2412 LINE

2412—Sweetmeat
Diameter 5 in.
Height 1½ in.

2412—Bon Bon
Length 5 in.
Width 6 in.

2412 Whip Cream
Diameter 4¾ in.
Height 1¾ in.

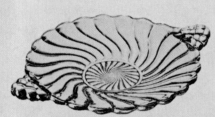

2412—Lemon
Diameter 6½ in.

2412—3 Piece Ash Tray Set
Consisting of:
1/12 Doz. 2412—3 in. Ind. Ash Tray
1/12 Doz. 2412—3½ in. Small Ash Tray
1/12 Doz. 2412—4½ in. Large Ash Tray

2412—Oblong Cigarette Box and Cover
Length 6 in.   Width 4¾ in.
Height 1⅜ in.   Holds 38 Cigarettes

2412—3 in. Individual Ash Tray

2412—3½ in. Small Ash Tray

2412—4½ in. Large Ash Tray

Fostoria Glass Company, Moundsville, West Virginia, January 1, 1941

Colors: blue, crystal with blue

"Columbine Variant" is a name we first used for this cutting, which was very close to Tiffin's Columbine and Double Columbine patterns. However, in researching, Cathy found the pattern called Bluebell in a 1928 Butler Brothers merchandising catalog.

In any case, this cutting was apparently placed on both Fostoria and Tiffin blanks suggesting a separate decorating firm rather than either of these companies per se. The early color blue of Fostoria and the blue of Tiffin are almost identical, so this would have made for a diversity of pieces, which could be used for the pattern. The name obviously came from the bluebell-like cutting as well as the color. Frankly, there does not seem to be much of this about in the marketplace today, which lends credence to its not being a major company's production.

The candlestick and comport are Fostoria mold blanks, but all the other pieces we have found have been on Tiffin blanks. Additional pieces could be found, but our listing only includes those we could document at the present.

Let me know what other items you find.

		Blue
5	Candlestick, 4", #2324, Fostoria	25.00
4	Comport, 6¼" h x 7¼" w, #2327, Fostoria	67.50
	Creamer	37.50
2	Pitcher w/cover, 2 qt., #14194	250.00
3	Plate, 7⅛", #2350, Fostoria	12.50
	Stem, 3 oz. wine #50001	45.00
	Stem, 6 oz, low sherbet #50001	20.00
	Stem, 6 oz. high sherbet #50001	25.00
1	Stem, 9 oz., 7¼" water #50001	35.00
	Sugar	37.50

Colors: crystal, Zircon/Limelight, Sahara, and rare in amber

Striking Crystolite is one of the most acknowledged Heisey patterns since nearly all pieces are marked with the well-known H inside a diamond. That easily distinguished mark means you will seldom find a deal on a piece of Crystolite in today's market. Many pieces of Heisey are not marked. They had paper labels that were detached with use.

One question with an answer that seems obvious is "What constitutes the swan handled Heisey pitcher?" It is found only in crystal and pictured below, right. If you spot colored pitchers, they are reproductions by Imperial from Heisey's moulds bought when Heisey closed its plant in 1957.

You can note the harder to find items by their higher prices. Non-scratched dinner plates, 5" comport, 6" basket, rye bottle, cocktail shaker, and pressed tumblers have always been difficult to locate.

		Crystal
	Ashtray, 3½", sq.	6.00
	Ashtray, 4½", sq.	6.00
9	Ashtray, 4" x 6", oblong	85.00
12	Ashtray, 5", w/book match holder	45.00
	Ashtray (coaster), 4", rnd.	8.00
15	Basket, 6", hdld.	550.00
	Bonbon, 7", shell	22.00
	Bonbon, 7½", 2 hdld.	15.00
2	Bottle, 1 qt., rye, #107 stopper	300.00
	Bottle, 4 oz., bitters, w/short tube	175.00
	Bottle, 4 oz., cologne, w/#108 stopper	75.00
	w/drip stop	150.00
	Bottle, syrup, w/drip & cut top	135.00
	Bowl, 7½ quart, punch	120.00
	Bowl, 2", indiv. swan nut (or ashtray)	20.00
	Bowl, 3", indiv. nut, hdld.	20.00
	Bowl, 4½", dessert (or nappy)	20.00
	Bowl, 5", preserve	20.00
	Bowl, 5", 1000 island dressing, ruffled top	30.00
	Bowl, 5½", dessert	14.00
	Bowl, 6", oval jelly, 4 ft.	60.00
	Bowl, 6", preserve, 2 hdld.	20.00
19	Bowl, 7", shell praline	35.00
	Bowl, 8", dessert (sauce)	30.00
	Bowl, 8", 2 pt. conserve, hdld.	55.00
	Bowl, 9", leaf pickle	30.00

		Crystal
	Bowl, 10", salad, rnd.	50.00
17	Bowl, 11", w/attached mayonnaise (chip 'n dip)	200.00
	Bowl, 12", gardenia, shallow	65.00
	Bowl, 13", oval floral, deep	60.00
	Candle block, 1-lite, sq.	25.00
	Candle block, 1-lite, swirl	25.00
	Candlestick, 1-lite, ftd.	25.00
	Candlestick, 1-lite, w/#4233, 5", vase	35.00
	Candlestick, 2-lite	35.00
	Candlestick, 2-lite, bobeche & 10 "D" prisms	65.00
	Candlestick and vase, 3-lite	45.00
	Candlestick, w/#4233, 5", vase, 3-lite	55.00
	Candy, 5½", shell and cover	55.00
	Candy box, w/cover, 7", 3 part	70.00
	Candy box, w/cover, 7"	60.00
	Cheese, 5½", ftd.	27.00
	Cigarette box, w/cover, 4"	35.00
	Cigarette box, w/cover, 4½"	40.00
11	Cigarette holder, ftd.	35.00
	Cigarette holder, oval	25.00
	Cigarette holder, rnd.	25.00
	Cigarette lighter	30.00
	Coaster, 4"	12.00
3	Cocktail shaker, 1 qt. w/#1 strainer; #86 stopper	325.00
	Comport, 5", ftd., deep, #5003, blown rare	300.00

CRYSTOLITE

	Crystal
Creamer, indiv.	20.00
Creamer, reg.	30.00
Creamer, round	40.00
Cup	22.00
Cup, punch or custard	9.00
Hurricane block, 1-lite, sq.	40.00
Hurricane block, w/#4061, 10" plain globe, 1-lite, sq.	120.00
Ice tub, w/silver plate handle	100.00
Jar, covered cherry	110.00
Jam jar, w/cover	70.00
Ladle, glass, punch	35.00
Ladle, plastic	10.00
Mayonnaise, 5½", shell, 3 ft.	35.00
Mayonnaise, 6", oval, hdld.	40.00
Mayonnaise ladle	12.00
Mustard & cover	55.00
20 Nut, oval, footed	55.00
Oil bottle, 3 oz.	45.00
Oil bottle, w/stopper, 2 oz.	35.00
Oval creamer, sugar, w/tray, set	70.00
1 Pitcher, ½ gallon, ice, blown	140.00
4 Pitcher, 2 quart swan, ice lip	700.00
Plate, 7", salad	15.00
Plate, 7", shell	32.00
Plate, 7", underliner for 1000 island dressing bowl	20.00
Plate, 7½", coupe	40.00
Plate, 8", oval, mayonnaise liner	20.00
Plate, 8½", salad	20.00
Plate, 10½", dinner	100.00
Plate, 11", ftd., cake salver	350.00
Plate, 11", torte	40.00
Plate, 12", sandwich	45.00
Plate, 13", shell torte	100.00
Plate, 14", sandwich	55.00

	Crystal
Plate, 14", torte	50.00
Plate, 20", buffet or punch liner	125.00
Puff box, w/cover, 4¾"	75.00
Salad dressing set, 3 pc.	38.00
Salt & pepper, pr.	45.00
Saucer	6.00
Stem, 1 oz., cordial, wide optic, blown, #5003	130.00
Stem, 3½ oz., cocktail, w.o., blown, #5003	25.00
Stem, 3½ oz., claret, w.o., blown, #5003	38.00
Stem, 3½ oz., oyster cocktail, w.o. blown, #5003	25.00
Stem, 6 oz., sherbet/saucer champagne, #5003	18.00
7 Stem, 10 oz., water, #1503, pressed	500.00
Stem, 10 oz., w.o., blown, #5003	35.00
Sugar, indiv.	20.00
Sugar, reg.	30.00
Sugar, round	40.00
Syrup pitcher, drip cut	135.00
Tray, 5½", oval, liner indiv. creamer/sugar set	40.00
Tray, 9", 4 pt., leaf relish	40.00
Tray, 10", 5 pt., rnd. relish	45.00
Tray, 12", 3 pt., relish, oval	35.00
Tray, 12", rect., celery	38.00
Tray, 12", rect., celery/olive	35.00
5 Tumbler, 5 oz., juice, blown	30.00
Tumbler, 5 oz., ftd., juice, w.o., blown, #5003	38.00
6 Tumbler, 8 oz., blown	35.00
10 Tumbler, 8 oz., pressed, #5003	60.00
Tumbler, 10 oz., pressed	70.00
8 Tumbler, 10 oz., iced tea, w.o., blown, #5003	40.00
Tumbler, 12 oz., ftd., iced tea, w.o., blown, #5003	38.00
13 Urn, 7", flower	75.00
18 Vase, 3", short stem	45.00
21 Vase, 6", ftd.	40.00
14 Vase, 12"	225.00
16 Vase, spittoon (whimsey)	400.00

Colors: crystal, crystal w/gold encrusting

Daffodil is a later Cambridge pattern that is beginning to attract new collectors. I will be relocating it to my *Collectible Glassware from the 40s, 50s, and 60s* book with the next edition; so this will be the last time you will find it in this book. I am adjusting patterns to fit the time frames set in our books.

		Crystal
	Basket, 6", 2 hdld., low ft., #55	40.00
	Bonbon, #1181	30.00
1	Bonbon, 5¼", 2 hdld., #3400/1180	40.00
2	Bowl, 11" oval, tuck hdld., #384	80.00
	Bowl, 12", belled, #430	85.00
	Candle, 2 lite, arch, #3900/72	65.00
	Candlestick, 3½", #628	50.00
	Candy box & cover, cut hexagon knob, #306	150.00
11	Celery, 11", #248	65.00
	Comport, 5½", ftd., #533	45.00
	Comport, 6½", 2 hdld., low ftd., #54	55.00
3	Comport, 6" tall, pulled stem, #532	65.00
	Creamer, #254	25.00
9	Creamer, indiv., #253	30.00
	Cup, #11770	25.00
	Jug, #3400/140	295.00
	Jug, 76 oz., #3400/141	325.00
	Mayonnaise, 3 pc., ftd., w/ladle & liner plate, #533	95.00
7	Mayonnaise, ftd., w/ladle and plate	95.00
	Oil, 6 oz., #293	145.00
	Plate, #1174	30.00
	Plate, 6", 2 hdld., bonbon, #3400/1181	22.50
	Plate, 8½", salad	18.00
4	Plate, 8", sq., #1176	20.00
	Plate, 8", 2 hdld., low ft., #56	30.00
	Plate, 11½" cake, #1495	80.00
	Plate, 13½", cabaret, #166	100.00
12	Relish, 10", 3 pt., #214	65.00
6	Salad dressing set, twin, 4 pc. w/ladles & liner, #1491	115.00

		Crystal
	Salt & pepper, squat, pr., #360	65.00
	Saucer, #1170	5.00
	Stem, brandy, ¾ oz., #1937	80.00
	Stem, claret, 4½ oz., #3779	60.00
	Stem, claret, 4½ oz., #1937	60.00
	Stem, cocktail, 3½ oz., #1937	32.00
	Stem, cocktail, 3 oz., #3779	32.00
13	Stem, cordial, 1 oz., #3779	100.00
	Stem, cordial, 1 oz., #1937	100.00
	Stem, oyster cocktail, 5 oz., #1937	20.00
	Stem, oyster cocktail, 4½ oz., #3779	20.00
	Stem, sherbet, 6 oz., low, #1937	18.00
	Stem, sherbet, 6 oz., low, #3779	18.00
	Stem, sherbet, 6 oz., tall, #1937	22.00
	Stem, sherbet, 6 oz., tall, #3779	22.00
	Stem, sherry, 2 oz., #1937	70.00
	Stem, water, 9 oz., low, #3779	32.00
	Stem, water, 9 oz., tall, #3779	38.00
	Stem, water, 11 oz., #1937	50.00
	Stem, wine, 2½ oz., #3779	60.00
	Stem, wine, 3 oz., #1937	55.00
	Sugar, #254	25.00
8	Sugar, indiv., #253	30.00
	Tumbler, ftd., 5 oz., #1937	24.00
10	Tumbler, ftd., 5 oz., #3779	24.00
	Tumbler, ftd., 10 oz., #1937	28.00
5	Tumbler, ftd., 12 oz., iced tea, #3779	40.00
	Tumbler, ftd., 12 oz., #1937	40.00
	Vase, 8", ftd., #6004	125.00
	Vase, 11", ftd., #278	150.00

Colors: crystal, French crystal, frosted crystal, green and frosted green, pink and frosted pink, Ruby flashed, white, and assorted ceramic colors

Dancing Nymph is the Consolidated name for this pattern that has been referred to as "Dance of the Nudes" for as long as I have been researching glassware. Traditional names are nearly impossible to toss aside in the collecting world, once they have been established, even after the precise name has become known. When Consolidated's Deco-looking Ruba Rombic was first listed in this book twelve years ago, bargains in that pattern soon became infrequent. Dancing Nymph price hikes have not been quite so breathtaking, since glassware illustrating nude women has always been popular. People may not have known its proper name, but it captured their attention and few priced it cheaply. Dancing Nymph prices are actually reasonable when weighed against other Consolidated patterns. This pattern is one of a few three-dimensional patterns that exist in this collecting field and was influenced by the graceful curves of the Art Nouveau movement — particularly Lalique wares, popular at that time.

We searched for this pattern for years trying to find enough to picture. I have been unable to find one new piece not pictured in the last two years.

Dancing Nymph was introduced in 1926 and made until Consolidated closed in 1932. In 1936, the plant was reopened and a cupped saucer and sherbet plates were added to this production. You can see the cupped saucer in row 2 and the cupped sherbet plates in several colors. These sherbet plates are like a shallow bowl and were often referred to as ice cream plates in other patterns of the time. The flatter version is shown in row 1 as sherbet liners. Salad plates usually came with basic sets, but sherbet plates were special order items, which makes them harder to find now. Dancing Nymph candlesticks are rare. Notice the two different styles pictured. I have been counseled the crystal items were never sold by the factory, but were designed to be frosted. I have seen enough crystal to wonder about that. However, one story was that the crystal was carried out of the factory when it closed for good in the 1940s. It was scheduled to be frosted, but had not received the treatment when the plant closed.

Green color has an aqua cast to it as shown in the photograph. French Crystal is clear nudes with satin background like the plate in the bottom row, really illustrating the Lalique influence. Other colors are self-explanatory except for the unusual ceramic colors. Ceramic colors were obtained by covering the bottom of a crystal piece with color, wiping the nude designs clear, and firing the piece. The Honey (yellow) plate in row 3 is an example. (Older glassware often involved several hand processes that would be prohibitive to perform today due to labor costs.) Ceramic colors are highly desirable and costly. Other colors with this process are Sepia (brown), white, dark blue, light blue, pinkish lavender, and light green.

		Crystal	Frosted Crystal French Crystal	*Frosted Pink or Green	Ceramic Colors
5	Bowl, 4½", #3098	35.00	65.00	85.00	110.00
1	Bowl, 8", #3098½	75.00	125.00	200.00	275.00
	Bowl, 16", palace, #2795B	600.00	1,250.00		1,600.00
9	Candle, pr., #2840	395.00	600.00		750.00
6	Cup, #3099	35.00	55.00	85.00	110.00
10	Plate, 6", cupped, #3099½	15.00	25.00	35.00	45.00
4	Plate, 6", sherbet, flat, #3099½	25.00	45.00	75.00	100.00
11	Plate, 8", salad, #3096	35.00	65.00		125.00
8	Plate, 10", #3097	65.00	95.00	150.00	195.00
7	Platter, 18", palace	600.00	1,000.00		1,250.00
6	Saucer, coupe	15.00		35.00	
3	Sherbet, #3094	35.00	65.00	85.00	
12	Tumbler, 3½", cocktail, #3094½	45.00	65.00		
2	Tumbler, 5½", goblet, #3080	55.00	75.00	125.00	175.00
	Vase, 5½", crimped, #3080C	75.00	135.00		165.00
	Vase, 5½", fan, #3080F	75.00	135.00		165.00

*Subtract 10% to 15% for unfrosted.

Colors: Amber, amethyst, crystal Emerald green, Peach-Blo, Carmen, Royal blue, Willow blue, Ebony

Decagon is Cambridge's name for the ten-sided mold blank on which many of its etchings were added. The blank makes little difference when etchings like Cleo, Rosalie, and Imperial Hunt Scene are added to it. Collectors definitely see the pattern decoration rather than the Decagon blank. Yet, there are some enthusiastic admirers of this plain, geometric Decagon "pattern." Amber Decagon has devotees too, but not as many as for the Willow (blue) color. Some Cleo collectors pursue Decagon to enrich their etched collections. Why spend $500.00 for a blue gravy and liner when you can buy an undecorated Decagon one for 25% of that?

You will discover that Peach-Blo (pink), Emerald (green), and amber are more abundant, but Willow (blue) is the preferred color, and therefore is more expensive to obtain. Pattern availability is only one important issue in collecting. Color also plays an extremely important part, and blue colors win collector interest more frequently.

Flat soups, cordials, and pitchers are not easily attained. Many collectors are searching for serving pieces for both Decagon and their etched wares. This makes finding what you need doubly demanding.

	Item	Pastel Colors	Blue
	Basket, 7", 2 hdld. (upturned sides), #760	15.00	30.00
	Bowl, bouillon, w/liner, #866	15.00	35.00
	Bowl, cream soup, w/liner, #1075	22.00	35.00
	Bowl, 2½", indiv., almond, #611	30.00	50.00
	Bowl, 3¾", flat rim, cranberry	20.00	35.00
	Bowl, 3½" belled, cranberry, #1102	20.00	35.00
	Bowl, 5½", 2 hdld., bonbon, #758	12.00	22.00
	Bowl, 5½", belled, fruit, #1098	10.00	20.00
	Bowl, 5¾", flat rim, fruit, #1099	10.00	20.00
	Bowl, 6", belled, cereal, #1011	20.00	30.00
	Bowl, 6", flat rim, cereal, #807	22.00	40.00
	Bowl, 6", ftd., almond, #612	30.00	45.00
	Bowl, 6¼", 2 hdld., bonbon	12.00	22.00
20	Bowl, 8½", flat rim, soup, #808	25.00	45.00
	Bowl, 9", rnd., veg., #1085	30.00	55.00
	Bowl, 9", 2 pt., relish, #1067	30.00	40.00
	Bowl, 9½", oval, veg., #1087	35.00	50.00
	Bowl, 10", berry, #1087	35.00	50.00
	Bowl, 10½", oval, veg., #1088	35.00	50.00
	Bowl, 11", rnd. veg., #1086	40.00	48.00
	Bowl, 11", 2 pt., relish, #1068	38.00	40.00
	Comport, 5¾", #869	20.00	35.00
	Comport, 6½", low ft., #608	20.00	32.00
	Comport, 7", tall, #1090	25.00	45.00
	Comport, 9½", #877	35.00	60.00
15	Comport, 11½", #877	50.00	75.00
5	Creamer, ftd., #979	10.00	20.00
	Creamer, bulbous, ftd., #867	9.00	18.00
	Creamer, lightning bolt handles, #1096	10.00	15.00
	Creamer, tall, lg. ft., #814	10.00	22.00
11	Cup, #865	6.00	11.00
14	Finger bowl	20.00	25.00
	Gravy boat, w/2 hdld. liner (like spouted cream soup), #917/1167	100.00	125.00
	French dressing bottle, "Oil/Vinegar," #1263, ftd., #1261	90.00	150.00
10	Ice pail, #851	45.00	75.00
	Ice tub	45.00	65.00
	Mayonnaise, 2 hdld., w/2 hdld. liner and ladle, #873	27.00	45.00

	Item	Pastel Colors	Blue
	Mayonnaise, w/liner & ladle, #983	25.00	65.00
	Oil, 6 oz., tall, w/hdld. & stopper, #197	70.00	175.00
	Plate, 6¼", bread/butter	5.00	10.00
	Plate, 7", 2 hdld.	9.00	15.00
	Plate, 7½"	8.00	12.00
8	Plate, 8½", salad, #597	14.00	22.00
12	Plate, 8½", snack w/ring		35.00
	Plate, 9½", dinner	40.00	60.00
	Plate, 10", grill, #1200	35.00	50.00
4	Plate, 10", service, #812	35.00	50.00
2	Plate, 12½", service, #598	30.00	60.00
16	Relish, 6 inserts	90.00	110.00
	Salt dip, 1½", ftd., #613	25.00	40.00
7	Salt & pepper, #396	50.00	85.00
	Sauce boat & plate, #1091	90.00	110.00
11	Saucer, #866	3.00	4.00
	Stem, 1 oz., cordial, #3077	40.00	60.00
	Stem, 3½ oz., cocktail, #3077	14.00	22.00
	Stem, 6 oz., low sherbet, #3077	10.00	16.00
18	Stem, 6 oz., high sherbet, #3077	15.00	22.00
1	Stem, 9 oz., water, #3077	20.00	35.00
17	Sugar, lightning bolt handles, #1096	10.00	15.00
6	Sugar, ftd., #979	9.00	20.00
	Sugar, bulbous, ftd., #867	9.00	20.00
	Sugar, tall, sifter, #813	20.00	35.00
	Tray, 8", 2 hdld., flat pickle, #1167	25.00	40.00
	Tray, 9", pickle, #1082	25.00	40.00
	Tray, 11", oval, service	30.00	50.00
	Tray, 11", celery, #1083	30.00	50.00
19	Tray, 12", center handled, #870	30.00	45.00
3	Tray, 12", oval, service, #1078	25.00	45.00
	Tray, 13", 2 hdld., service, #1084	35.00	50.00
9	Tray, 15", oval, service, #1079	45.00	75.00
	Tumbler, 2½ oz., ftd., #3077	20.00	25.00
	Tumbler, 5 oz., ftd., #3077	15.00	20.00
	Tumbler, 8 oz., ftd., #3077	16.00	22.00
	Tumbler, 10 oz., ftd., #3077	18.00	25.00
13	Tumbler, 12 oz., ftd., #3077	20.00	30.00

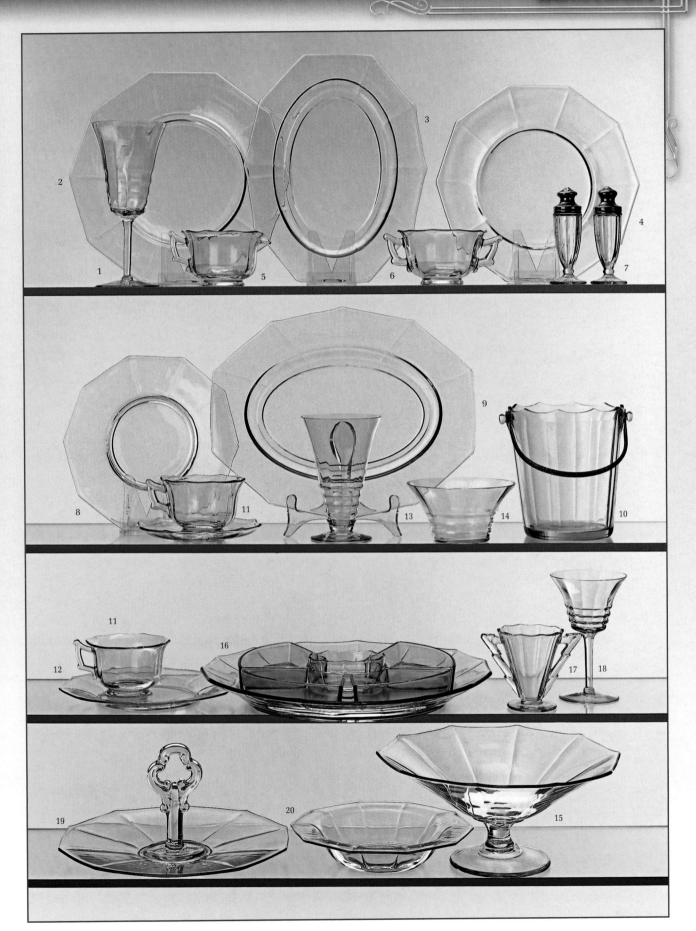

Colors: light amber, green, pink, black, crystal

Look on page 27 for the Black Forest pattern photo if you tend to confuse these two patterns. Deer and trees are illustrated on "Deerwood"; moose and trees are illustrated on Black Forest.

Know that some pieces similar to Deerwood (made at the Tiffin plant of U.S. Glass) have turned up on Paden City blanks. I was told by a Paden City scholar that they are "Deerwood-like" and not precisely the same. However, I do not have pieces of each to compare at this time.

Gold decorated, black "Deerwood" is being bought by connoisseurs of "that look" who are not necessarily glass collectors per se, but who just admire it. Those searching Internet auctions have also noticed "Deerwood." These occurrences have caused some price modifications. "Deerwood" itself is not commonly found, but gold decoration on black really makes the pattern stand out, and pieces of this are particularly hard to acquire. Remember that if gold is missing in the design, you will have to be cautious of the price you pay. Large sets can only be assembled in green and pink with patience (and money). You will have to settle for an infrequent piece or two in other colors.

There is some catalog documentation for "Deerwood," but not nearly enough. That is why unfamiliar pieces keep turning up after 30 years of serious collecting.

The familiar mayonnaise was listed by Tiffin as a whipped cream rather than a mayonnaise. Terminology within the old glass companies often differed from their competitors. Perhaps Tiffin thought whipped cream dishes would sell more readily than mayonnaise ones in the timing of the market.

	*Black	Amber	Green	Pink
Bowl, breakfast/cereal w/attched liner, #8133			60.00	60.00
Bowl, 10", ftd.	185.00			
Bowl, 10", straight edge, flat rim, salad, #8105			75.00	75.00
Bowl, 12", centerpiece, flat rim ftd.	65.00			
9 Bowl, 12", centerpiece, #8177, cupped	125.00		85.00	80.00
Cake plate, low pede., 10", #330, #8177			75.00	75.00
Candlestick, 2½"	75.00		40.00	
6 Candlestick, 5"				60.00
1 Candy dish, w/cover, 3 part, flat, #329, 6"	170.00			150.00
Candy jar, w/cover, ftd. cone, #330			165.00	165.00
Celery, 12", #151			75.00	
Cheese and cracker, #330			125.00	125.00
3 Comport, 7", #8177	110.00			75.00
5 Comport, 9", low, ftd.	150.00			
Comport, 10", low, ftd., flared, #330	150.00			75.00
10 Creamer, 2 styles, #179	70.00		45.00	45.00
Cup, #9395				95.00
Plate, 5½", #8836			15.00	15.00
Plate, 7½", salad, #8836				25.00
Plate, 9½", dinner, #8859				110.00
Plate, 10¼", 2 hdld., cake, #336	155.00			
Saucer, #9395				20.00
Server, center hdld., 10", #330			75.00	75.00
Stem, 2 oz., cocktail, 4½", #2809				60.00
Stem, 3 oz., wine, 4¾", #2809			30.00	
Stem, 6 oz., saucer champagne, 5", #2809			40.00	
Stem, 9 oz., water, 7", #2809			65.00	65.00
8 Sugar, 2 styles, #179	70.00		45.00	45.00
Tumbler, 9 oz., ftd., table, #2808			37.50	37.50
2 Tumbler, 12 oz., ftd., tea, 5½", #2808			55.00	
4 Tumbler, 12 oz., flat, tea		55.00	65.00	
Vase, 7", sweet pea, rolled edge, #151			195.00	195.00
Vase, 10", ruffled top, #6471			195.00	195.00
7 Vase, 10", 2 handles, #15319	225.00			
Whipped cream pail, w/ladle			75.00	75.00

*Add 20% for gold decorated.

Colors: crystal; some pink, yellow, blue, Heatherbloom, Emerald green, amber, Crown Tuscan w/gold

Cambridge's Diane pattern can be found in all the colors listed; but only crystal can be collected in a large set. You may be able to obtain a small luncheon set in color, but after that only an occasional bowl, candlestick, or tumbler will be seen. Seemingly, the price of making this colored, handmade glass contributed to its scarcity. In any case, colored Diane is in very short supply today.

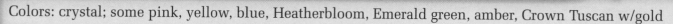

Crystal is currently pictured; you will have to search earlier books for Diane in color. As with other Cambridge patterns in this book, you will have to look at Rose Point listings for pricing any unlisted Diane items you come across. Notice the pamphlet reproduced here to help you identify Cambridge factory designations. Diane will run 30% to 40% less than similar items listed in Rose Point. Remember that Rose Point is currently the highest priced Cambridge pattern and other patterns sell for less. Demand for Rose Point pushes prices to new levels; other patterns increase in price gradually.

The bitters bottle, cabinet flask, and pitchers are in demand. You have several choices for stemware collecting in Diane; pick whichever you like. Each line enhances the set. In my travels, I see more #3122 stems than other stem lines; they might be the easiest to find. Items 5, 6, and 7 below are the more unusual #3575 Regency (or Stradavari) stem line.

	Crystal
Basket, 6", 2 hdld., ftd.	35.00
Bottle, bitters	195.00
Bowl, #3106, finger, w/liner	47.50
Bowl, #3122	25.00
Bowl, #3400, cream soup, w/liner	55.00
Bowl, 3", indiv. nut, 4 ftd.	60.00
Bowl, 5", berry	32.00
Bowl, 5¼", 2 hdld., bonbon	25.00
Bowl, 6", 2 hdld., ftd., bonbon	25.00
Bowl, 6", 2 pt., relish	25.00
Bowl, 6", cereal	40.00
Bowl, 6½", 3 pt., relish	35.00
Bowl, 7", 2 hdld., ftd., bonbon	38.00
Bowl, 7", 2 pt., relish	35.00
Bowl, 7", relish or pickle	35.00
Bowl, 9", 3 pt., celery or relish	40.00
Bowl, 9½", pickle (like corn)	40.00
Bowl, 10", 4 ft., flared	65.00
Bowl, 10", baker	60.00
10 Bowl, 11", 2 hdld., 2 pt. relish, #3400/89	65.00
4 Bowl, 11", 4 ftd., fancy top, #3400/45	65.00
Bowl, 11½", tab hdld., ftd.	62.00
Bowl, 12", 3 pt., celery & relish	55.00
Bowl, 12", 4 ft.	70.00
Bowl, 12", 4 ft., flared	80.00
Bowl, 12", 4 ft., oval	80.00
Bowl, 12", 4 ft., oval, w/"ears," hdld.	85.00
Bowl, 12", 5 pt., celery & relish	65.00
11 Bowl, 15", 3 pt. relish, #3500/112	75.00
Butter, rnd.	165.00
Cabinet flask	295.00
Candelabrum, 6", 2-lite, keyhole	40.00
Candelabrum, 6", 3-lite, keyhole	50.00
Candlestick, 1-lite, keyhole	30.00
Candlestick, 5"	30.00
2 Candy, 5½", blown, #3121/3	135.00
Candy box, w/cover, rnd.	125.00
Cigarette urn	75.00
Cocktail shaker, glass top	250.00
Cocktail shaker, metal top	150.00
Cocktail icer, 2 pc.	85.00

	Crystal
Comport, 5½"	40.00
Comport, 5⅜", blown	60.00
Creamer	20.00
Creamer, indiv., #3500 (pie crust edge)	22.00
Creamer, indiv., #3900, scalloped edge	22.00
Creamer, scroll handle, #3400	22.00
Cup	20.00
9 Decanter, ball, 16 oz., cordial, #3400/92	250.00
Decanter, lg. ftd.	225.00
Decanter, short ft., cordial	265.00
Hurricane lamp, candlestick base	195.00
Hurricane lamp, keyhole base w/prisms	250.00
Ice bucket, w/chrome hand	120.00
Mayonnaise, div., w/liner & ladles	65.00
Mayonnaise (sherbet type w/ladle)	55.00
Mayonnaise, w/liner, ladle	50.00
Oil, 6 oz., w/stopper	135.00
Pitcher, ball	225.00
Pitcher, Doulton	395.00
Pitcher, martini	795.00
Pitcher, upright	235.00
Plate, 6", 2 hdld., plate.	15.00
Plate, 6", sq., bread/butter	10.00
Plate, 6½", bread/butter	8.00
Plate, 8", 2 hdld., ftd., bonbon	18.00
Plate, 8", salad	14.00
Plate, 8½"	20.00
8 Plate, 10½", dinner, #3400/1177, sq.	95.00
Plate, 12", 4 ft., service	55.00
Plate, 13", 4 ft., torte	60.00
Plate, 13½", 2 hdld.	60.00
Plate, 14", torte	75.00
Platter, 13½"	110.00
Salt & pepper, ftd., w/glass tops, pr.	50.00
Salt & pepper, pr., flat	50.00
Saucer	6.00
Stem, #1066, 1 oz., cordial	60.00
Stem, #1066, 3 oz., cocktail	25.00
Stem, #1066, 3 oz., wine	35.00
Stem, #1066, 3½ oz., tall cocktail	28.00
Stem, #1066, 4½ oz., claret	50.00

	Crystal
Stem, #1066, 5 oz., oyster/cocktail	25.00
Stem, #1066, 7 oz., low sherbet	20.00
Stem, #1066, 7 oz., tall sherbet	22.00
Stem, #1066, 11 oz., water	35.00
Stem, #3122, 1 oz., cordial	60.00
Stem, #3122, 2½ oz., wine	35.00
Stem, #3122, 3 oz., cocktail	22.00
Stem, #3122, 4½ oz., claret	50.00
Stem, #3122, 4½ oz., oyster/cocktail	20.00
Stem, #3122, 7 oz., low sherbet	20.00
Stem, #3122, 7 oz., tall sherbet	22.00
1 Stem, #3122, 9 oz., water goblet	35.00
7 Stem, #3575, tall sherbert/champagne	22.00
Sugar, indiv., #3500 (pie crust edge)	22.00
Sugar, indiv., #3900, scalloped edge	22.00
Sugar, scroll handle, #3400	22.00
Tumbler, 2½ oz., sham bottom	60.00
Tumbler, 5 oz., ft., juice	40.00
Tumbler, 5 oz., sham bottom	45.00
Tumbler, 7 oz., old-fashion, w/sham bottom	55.00
Tumbler, 8 oz., ft.	30.00
Tumbler, 10 oz., sham bottom	35.00
Tumbler, 12 oz., sham bottom	40.00
Tumbler, 13 oz.	35.00
Tumbler, 14 oz., sham bottom	45.00

	Crystal
Tumbler, #1066, 3 oz.	30.00
Tumbler, #1066, 5 oz., juice	25.00
Tumbler, #1066, 9 oz., water	22.00
Tumbler, #1066, 12 oz., tea	28.00
Tumbler, #3106, 3 oz., ftd.	26.00
Tumbler, #3106, 5 oz., ftd., juice	22.00
Tumbler, #3106, 9 oz., ftd., water	20.00
Tumbler, #3106, 12 oz., ftd., tea	26.00
Tumbler, #3122, 2½ oz.	40.00
Tumbler, #3122, 5 oz., juice	20.00
Tumbler, #3122, 9 oz., water	25.00
Tumbler, #3122, 12 oz., tea	30.00
Tumbler, #3135, 2½ oz., ftd., bar	45.00
Tumbler, #3135, 10 oz., ftd., tumbler	22.00
Tumbler, #3135, 12 oz., ftd., tea	33.00
6 Tumbler, #3575, 5 oz., ftd., juice	22.00
5 Tumbler, #3575, 12 oz., ftd., tea	28.00
Vase, 5", globe	65.00
Vase, 6", high ft., flower	55.00
Vase, 8", high ft., flower	70.00
Vase, 9", keyhole base	95.00
3 Vase, 10", ftd., #1301	75.00
Vase, 10", bud	65.00
Vase, 11", flower	115.00
Vase, 11", ped. ft., flower	110.00
Vase, 12", keyhole base	125.00
Vase, 13", flower	165.00

Note: See pages 252 – 253 for stem identification.

GENUINE HAND MADE
Cambridge
MADE IN U.S.A.

LIST OF DIANE ITEMS

3122	9 oz. Goblet
3122	7 oz. Tall Sherbet
3123	7 oz. Low Sherbet
3122	3 oz. Cocktail
3122	2½ oz. Wine
3122	4½ oz. Claret
3122	4½ oz. Oyster Cockta
3122	1 oz. Cordial
3122	12 oz. Ftd. Ice Tea
3122	9 oz. Ftd. Tumbler
3122	5 oz. Ftd. Tumbler
477	9½ in. Pickle
3400/1180	5¼ in. 2 Hdl. Bonbon
3400/1181	6 in. 2 Hdl. Plate
3400/90	6 in. 2 part Relish
3500/15	Ind. Sugar & Cream
3500/54	6 in. 2 Hdl. Ftd. Bonbon
3500/55	6 in. 2 Hdl. Ftd. Basket
3500/69	6½ in. 3 part Relish
3500/161	8 in. 2 Hdl. Ftd. Plate
3500/57	8 in. 3 part Candy Box & Cover (not illus.)
3900/17	Cup & Saucer
3900/19	2 pc. Mayonnaise Set
3900/20	6½ in. Bread & Butter Plate
3900/22	8 in. Salad Plate
3900/24	10½ in. Dinner Plate
3900/26	12 in. 4 Ftd. Plate
3900/28	11½ in. Ftd. Bowl
3900/33	13 in. 4 Ftd. Torte Plate, R. E.
3900/34	11 in. 2 Handled Bowl
3900/35	13½ in. 2 Handled Cake Plate
3900/40	Ind. Sugar & Cream
3900/41	Sugar & Cream
3900/54	10 in. 4 Ftd. Bowl, flared
3900/62	12 in. 4 Ftd. Bowl, flared
3900/65	12 in. 4 Ftd. Oval Bowl
3900/67	5 in. Candlestick
3900/72	6 in. 2 lite Candlestick
3900/74	6 in. 3 lite Candlestick
3900/100	6 oz. Oil, g.s.
3900/111	4 pc. Mayonnaise Set
3900/115	13 oz. Tumbler
3900/120	12 in. 5 part Celery & Relish
3900/123	7 in. Relish or Pickle
3900/124	7 in. 2 part Relish
3900/125	9 in. 3 part Celery & Relish
3900/126	12 in. 3 part Celery & Relish
3900/129	3 pc. Mayonnaise Set
3900/130	7 in. 2 handled Ftd. Bonbon
3900/131	8 in. 2 handled Ftd. Bonbon Plate
3900/136	5½ in. Comport
3900/165	Candy Box & Cover
3900/166	14 in. Plate, r.e.
3900/671	Ice Bucket
3900/671	Ice Bucket with chrome handle Chrome Ice Tongs (long)
3900/1177	Salt & Pepper Shaker (doz. pr.)
274	10 in. Bud Flower Holder
278	11 in. Ftd. Flower Holder
279	13 in. Ftd. Flower Holder
968	2 pc. Cocktail Icer
1237	9 in. Ftd. Flower Holder
1238	12 in. Ftd. Flower Holder
1299	11 in. Ftd. Flower Holder
1309	5 in. Glode Flower Holder
1603	Hurricane Lamp (Etch. Chimney only)
1617	Hurricane Lamp (Etch. Chimney only)
3121	5-⅜ in. Blown Comport
6004	6 in. Ftd. Flower Holder
6004	8 in. Ftd Flower Holder

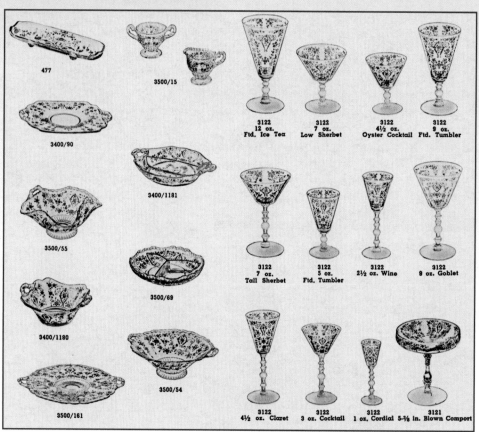

477

3500/15

3400/90

3400/1181

3500/55

3500/69

3500/54

3400/1180

3500/161

3122
12 oz.
Ftd. Ice Tea

3122
7 oz.
Low Sherbet

3122
4½ oz.
Oyster Cocktail

3122
9 oz.
Ftd. Tumbler

3122
7 oz.
Tall Sherbet

3122
5 oz.
Ftd. Tumbler

3122
2½ oz. Wine

3122
9 oz. Goblet

3122
4½ oz. Claret

3122
3 oz. Cocktail

3122
1 oz. Cordial

3121
5-⅜ in. Blown Comport

GENUINE
HAND MADE
Cambridge
MADE IN U.S.A.

3900/17

3900/19

3900/115

968

3900/1177

3900/20

3900/22

3900/67

3900/124

3900/65

3900/28

3900/24

3900/123

3900/120

3900/34

3900/26

3900/111

3900/100

3900/40

3900/40

3900/35

3900/54

3900/126

3900/131

3900/165

3900/130

3900/74

3900/166

1603

3900/62

3900/136

3900/125

3900/33

3900/72

3900/671

274

1299

3900/129

1617

1237

6004-6

6004-8

1238

278

279

Color: crystal

Elaine is repeatedly confused with Chantilly. The Elaine design has a thin and angled scroll like the top of the capital script letter "E." Compare the design here with the one on page 60.

Elaine is most often found on Cambridge's #3500 Gadroon line that has the ornate "pie crust" edge. You will find accessory pieces not listed here. Many pieces listed under Rose Point etch exist in Elaine. However, bear in mind that prices for Elaine will be 30% to 40% lower than those shown for Rose Point, which is more in demand in the market.

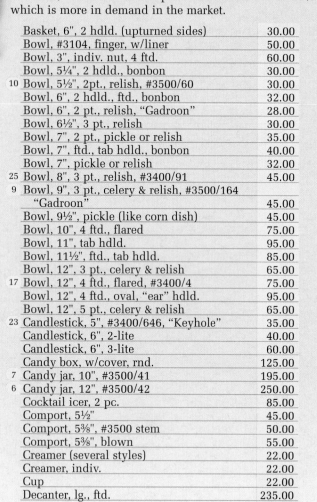

1

	Item	Price
	Basket, 6", 2 hdld. (upturned sides)	30.00
	Bowl, #3104, finger, w/liner	50.00
	Bowl, 3", indiv. nut, 4 ftd.	60.00
	Bowl, 5¼", 2 hdld., bonbon	30.00
10	Bowl, 5½", 2pt., relish, #3500/60	30.00
	Bowl, 6", 2 hdld., ftd., bonbon	32.00
	Bowl, 6", 2 pt., relish, "Gadroon"	28.00
	Bowl, 6½", 3 pt., relish	30.00
	Bowl, 7", 2 pt., pickle or relish	35.00
	Bowl, 7", ftd., tab hdld., bonbon	40.00
	Bowl, 7", pickle or relish	32.00
25	Bowl, 8", 3 pt., relish, #3400/91	45.00
9	Bowl, 9", 3 pt., celery & relish, #3500/164 "Gadroon"	45.00
	Bowl, 9½", pickle (like corn dish)	45.00
	Bowl, 10", 4 ftd., flared	75.00
	Bowl, 11", tab hdld.	95.00
	Bowl, 11½", ftd., tab hdld.	85.00
	Bowl, 12", 3 pt., celery & relish	65.00
17	Bowl, 12", 4 ftd., flared, #3400/4	75.00
	Bowl, 12", 4 ftd., oval, "ear" hdld.	95.00
	Bowl, 12", 5 pt., celery & relish	65.00
23	Candlestick, 5", #3400/646, "Keyhole"	35.00
	Candlestick, 6", 2-lite	40.00
	Candlestick, 6", 3-lite	60.00
	Candy box, w/cover, rnd.	125.00
7	Candy jar, 10", #3500/41	195.00
6	Candy jar, 12", #3500/42	250.00
	Cocktail icer, 2 pc.	85.00
	Comport, 5½"	45.00
	Comport, 5⅜", #3500 stem	50.00
	Comport, 5⅜", blown	55.00
	Creamer (several styles)	22.00
	Creamer, indiv.	22.00
	Cup	22.00
	Decanter, lg., ftd.	235.00
	Hat, 9"	395.00
	Hurricane lamp, candlestick base	190.00
	Hurricane lamp, keyhole ft., w/prisms	250.00
	Ice bucket, w/chrome handle	125.00
20	Mayonnaise (cupped sherbet w/ladle)	50.00
24	Mayonnaise (div. bowl, liner, 2 ladles), #3900/111	60.00
22	Mayonnaise, w/liner & ladle, #1532, "Pristine"	55.00
	Oil, 6 oz., hdld., w/stopper	125.00
	Pitcher, ball, 80 oz.	295.00
	Pitcher, Doulton	395.00
18	Pitcher, 78 oz., #3900/115	250.00
	Plate, 6", 2 hdld.	15.00
	Plate, 6½", bread/butter	12.00
5	Plate, 7½", dessert, #3500/4, "Gadroon"	14.00
21	Plate, 8", 2 hdld., ftd., bonbon, #3500/131	22.00
	Plate, 8", salad	22.00
	Plate, 8", tab hdld., bonbon	25.00
4	Plate, 8½", salad, #3500, "Gadroon"	20.00
	Plate, 10½", dinner	85.00
	Plate, 11½" 2 hdld., ringed "Tally Ho" sandwich	65.00
	Plate, 12", 4 ftd., service	60.00
	Plate, 13", 4 ftd., torte	55.00
	Plate, 13½", tab hdld., cake	75.00

	Item	Price
16	Plate, 14", service, #3900/166, rolled edge	70.00
	Salt & pepper, flat, pr.	50.00
	Salt & pepper, ftd., pr	45.00
	Salt & pepper, hdld., pr	50.00
	Saucer	5.00
	Stem, #1402, 1 oz., cordial	125.00
	Stem, #1402, 3 oz., wine	45.00
	Stem, #1402, 3½ oz., cocktail	35.00
	Stem, #1402, 5 oz., claret	45.00
	Stem, #1402, low sherbet	20.00
	Stem, #1402, tall sherbet	22.00
	Stem, #1402, goblet	40.00
19	Stem, #3035, cordial	60.00
	Stem, #3104 (very tall stems), ¾ oz., brandy	225.00
	Stem, #3104, 1 oz., cordial	225.00
	Stem, #3104, 1 oz., pousse-cafe	225.00
	Stem, #3104, 2 oz., sherry	225.00
	Stem, #3104, 2½ oz., creme de menthe	175.00
	Stem, #3104, 3 oz., wine	175.00
	Stem, #3104, 3½ oz., cocktail	110.00
	Stem, #3104, 4½ oz., claret	175.00
	Stem, #3104, 5 oz., roemer	175.00
	Stem, #3104, 5 oz., tall hock	175.00
	Stem, #3104, 7 oz., tall sherbet	135.00
	Stem, #3104, 9 oz., goblet	175.00
	Stem, #3121, 1 oz., cordial	60.00
	Stem, #3121, 3 oz., cocktail	30.00
	Stem, #3121, 3½ oz., wine	40.00
	Stem, #3121, 4½ oz., claret	45.00
	Stem, #3121, 4½ oz., oyster cocktail	28.00
	Stem, #3121, 5 oz., parfait, low stem	40.00
	Stem, #3121, 6 oz., low sherbet	20.00
	Stem, #3121, 6 oz., tall sherbet	22.00
1	Stem, #3121, 10 oz., water	35.00
12	Stem, #3500, 1 oz., cordial	60.00
2	Stem, #3500, 2½ oz., wine	40.00
	Stem, #3500, 3 oz., cocktail	30.00
	Stem, #3500, 4½ oz., claret	45.00
	Stem, #3500, 4½ oz., oyster cocktail	28.00
	Stem, #3500, 5 oz., parfait, low stem	40.00
	Stem, #3500, 7 oz., low sherbet	20.00
	Stem, #3500, 7 oz., tall sherbet	22.00
3	Stem, #3500, 10 oz., water	38.00
11	Sugar (several styles), #3500/14 (shown)	22.00
	Sugar, indiv.	22.00
	Tumbler, #1402, 9 oz., ftd., water	25.00
	Tumbler, #1402, 12 oz., tea	40.00
	Tumbler, #1402, 12 oz., tall ftd., tea	40.00
	Tumbler, #3121, 5 oz., ftd., juice	30.00
	Tumbler, #3121, 10 oz., ftd., water	40.00
	Tumbler, #3121, 12 oz., ftd., tea	40.00
	Tumbler, #3500, 5 oz., ftd., juice	30.00
13	Tumbler, #3500, 10 oz., ftd., water	35.00
8	Tumbler, #3500, 12 oz., ftd., tea	40.00
	Vase, 6", ftd.	75.00
	Vase, 8", ftd.	100.00
	Vase, 9", keyhole, ftd.	165.00
15	Vase, 10", cornucopia, #3900/575	195.00
14	Vase, 12", #3400	175.00

LIST OF ELAINE ITEMS

3121	10 oz. Goblet
3121	6 oz. Tall Sherbet
3121	6 oz. Low Sherbet
3121	3 oz. Cocktail
3121	3½ oz. Wine
3121	4½ oz. Claret
3121	4½ oz. Oyster Cocktail
3121	1 oz. Cordial
3121	5 oz. Cafe Parfait
3121	12 oz. Ftd. Ice Tea
3121	10 oz. Ftd. Tumbler
3121	5 oz. Ftd. Tumbler
477	9½ in. Pickle
3400/1180	5¼ in. 2 Hdl. Bonbon
3400/1181	6 in. 2 Hdl. Plate
3400/90	6 in. 2 part Relish
3500/15	Ind. Sugar & Cream
3500/54	6 in. 2 Hdl. Ftd. Bonbon
3500/55	6 in. 2 Hdl. Ftd. Basket
3500/69	6½ in. 2 part Relish
3500/161	8 in. 2 Hdl. Plate
3500/57	8 in. 3 part Candy Box & Cover (not illus.)
3900/17	Cup & Saucer
3900/19	2 pc. Mayonnaise Set
3900/20	6½ in. Bread & Butter Plate
3900/22	8 in. Salad Plate
3900/24	10½ in. Dinner Plate
3900/26	12 in. 4 Ftd. Plate
3900/28	11½ in. Ftd. Bowl
3900/33	13 in. 4 Ftd. Torte Plate, R.E.
3900/34	11 in. 2 Handled Bowl
3900/35	13½ in. 2 Handled Cake Plate
3900/40	Ind. Sugar & Cream
3900/41	Sugar & Cream
3900/54	10 in. 4 Ftd. Bowl, flared
3900/62	12 in. 4 Ftd. Bowl, flared
3900/65	12 in. 4 Ftd. Oval Bowl
3900/67	5 in. Candlestick
3900/72	6 in. 2 lite Candlestick
3900/74	6 in. 3 lite Candlestick
3900/100	6 oz. Oil, g.s.
3900/111	4 pc. Mayonnaise Set
3900/115	13 oz. Tumbler
3900/120	12 in. 5 part Celery & Relish
3900/123	7 in. Relish or Pickle
3900/124	7 in. 2 part Relish
3900/125	9 in. 3 part Celery & Relish
3900/126	12 in. 3 part Celery & Relish
3900/129	3 pc. Mayonnaise Set
3900/130	7 in. 2 handled Ftd. Bonbon
3900/131	8 in. 2 handled Ftd. Bonbon Plate
3900/136	5½ in. Comport
3900/165	Candy Box & Cover
3900/166	14 in. Plate, r.e.
3900/671	Ice Bucket
3900/671	Ice Bucket with chrome Handle
	Chrome Ice Tongs (long)
3900/1177	Salt & Pepper Shaker (doz. pr.)
274	10 in. Bud Flower Holder
278	11 in. Ftd. Flower Holder
279	13 in. Ftd. Flower Holder
968	2 pc. Cocktail Icer
1237	9 in. Ftd. Flower Holder
1238	12 in. Ftd. Flower Holder
1299	11 in. Ftd. Flower Holder
1309	5 in. Glode Flower Holder
1603	Hurricane Lamp (Etch., Chimney only)
1617	Hurricane Lamp (Etch., Chimney only)
3121	5-⅜ in. Blown Comport
6004	6 in. Ftd. Flower Holder
6004	8 in. Ftd. Flower Holder

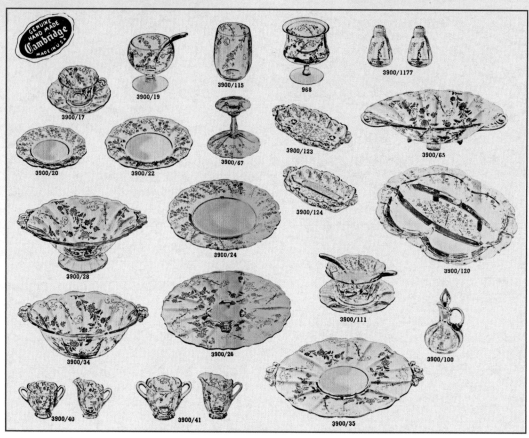

3900/54

3900/126

3900/131

3900/165

3900/130

3900/72

3900/166

1603

3900/62

3900/74

3900/125

3900/33

3900/136

3900/671

274

1299

1309

3900/129

1617

1237

6004-6

6004-9

1238

278

279

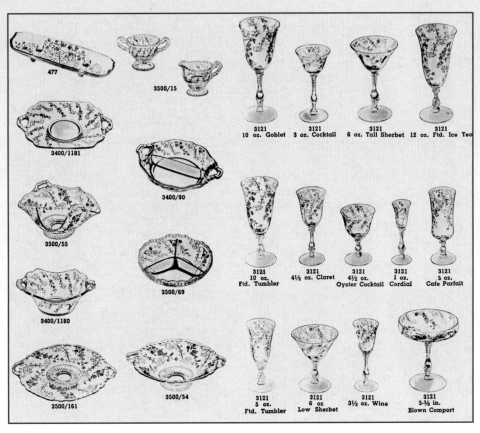

477

3500/15

3121
10 oz. Goblet

3121
3 oz. Cocktail

3121
6 oz. Tall Sherbet

3121
12 oz. Ftd. Ice Tea

3400/1181

3400/90

3500/55

3121
10 oz.
Ftd. Tumbler

3121
4½ oz. Claret

3121
4½ oz.
Oyster Cocktail

3121
1 oz.
Cordial

3121
5 oz.
Cafe Parfait

3500/69

3400/1180

3500/161

3500/54

3121
5 oz.
Ftd. Tumbler

3121
6 oz
Low Sherbet

3121
3½ oz. Wine

3121
5-3½ in.
Blown Comport

Colors: Flamingo pink, Sahara yellow, Moongleam green, cobalt, and Alexandrite; some Tangerine

Crystal listings of Empress are now located under the pattern Queen Ann on page 182. When the colors were made, this pattern was called Empress; but later on, when crystal was produced, the pattern's name was changed to Queen Ann. Observe that Empress can be found on both round and square mold blanks. I have always favored square plates because they seem more unusual as well as hold more food.

Empress is shown in Sahara on page 94 and Alexandrite on page 95. Alexandrite is Heisey's purple/pink color that changes colors depending upon the lighting source. Under natural light, it appears pink; under florescent light, it appears blue. My photographers and printers have always done a remarkable job in showing it just right. That is not easily accomplished.

	Flamingo	Sahara	Moongleam	Cobalt	Alexandrite
Ashtray	175.00	185.00	250.00	300.00	225.00
Bonbon, 6"	20.00	25.00	30.00		
Bowl, cream soup	30.00	30.00	50.00		110.00
Bowl, cream soup, w/sq. liner	40.00	40.00	55.00		175.00
Bowl, frappe, w/center	45.00	60.00	75.00		
17 Bowl, nut, dolphin ftd., indiv.	30.00	32.00	45.00		170.00
Bowl, 4½", nappy	40.00	40.00	60.00		
Bowl, 5", preserve, 2 hdld.	20.00	25.00	30.00		
16 Bowl, 6", ftd., jelly, 2 hdld.	20.00	25.00	30.00		
Bowl, 6", dolphin ftd., mint	35.00	40.00	45.00		325.00
Bowl, 6", grapefruit, sq. top, grnd. bottom	12.50	20.00	25.00		
Bowl, 6½", oval, lemon, w/cover	65.00	80.00	150.00		
15 Bowl, 7", 3 pt., relish, triplex	40.00	45.00	50.00		300.00
Bowl, 7", 3 pt., relish, ctr. hand.	45.00	50.00	75.00		
Bowl, 7½", dolphin ftd., nappy	65.00	65.00	80.00	300.00	350.00
2 Bowl, 7½", dolphin ftd., nasturtium	130.00	130.00	150.00	350.00	425.00
Bowl, 8", nappy	35.00	37.00	45.00		

	Flamingo	Sahara	Moongleam	Cobalt	Alexandrite
Bowl, 8½", ftd., floral, 2 hdld	45.00	50.00	70.00		
Bowl, 9", floral, rolled edge	40.00	42.00	50.00		
Bowl, 9", floral, flared	70.00	75.00	90.00		
Bowl, 10", 2 hdld., oval dessert	50.00	60.00	70.00		
Bowl, 10", lion head, floral	550.00	550.00	700.00		
Bowl, 10", oval, veg.	50.00	55.00	75.00		
Bowl, 10", square, salad, 2 hdld.	55.00	60.00	80.00		
Bowl, 10", triplex, relish	50.00	55.00	65.00		
13 Bowl, 11", dolphin ftd., floral	65.00	75.00	100.00	400.00	500.00
Bowl, 13", pickle/olive, 2 pt.	35.00	45.00	50.00		
Bowl, 15", dolphin ftd., punch	900.00	900.00	1,250.00		
Candlestick, low, 4 ftd., w/2 hdld.	100.00	100.00	170.00		
20 Candlestick, 6", #135		50.00	190.00		275.00
Candlestick, 6", dolphin ftd.	170.00	125.00	155.00	260.00	350.00
Candy, w/cover, 6", dolphin ftd.	150.00	150.00	200.00	450.00	
Comport, 6", ftd.	110.00	70.00	100.00		
Comport, 6", square	70.00	75.00	85.00		
5 Comport, 7", oval	85.00	80.00	90.00		
Compotier, 6", dolphin ftd.	260.00	225.00	275.00		
Creamer, dolphin ftd.	50.00	45.00	45.00		250.00
9 Creamer, indiv.	45.00	45.00	50.00		210.00
12 Cup	30.00	30.00	35.00		115.00
14 Cup, after dinner	60.00	60.00	70.00		
Cup, bouillon, 2 hdld.	35.00	35.00	45.00		
Cup, 4 oz., custard or punch	30.00	35.00	45.00		
Cup, #1401½, has rim as demi-cup		28.00	32.00	40.00	
Grapefruit, w/square liner		30.00	30.00	35.00	

EMPRESS

	Flamingo	Sahara	Moongleam	Cobalt	Alexandrite
Ice tub, w/metal handles, dolphin ftd.	100.00	150.00	350.00		300.00
8 Hors d'oeuvre, 10", 7 compartments		75.00			
Jug, 3 pint, ftd.	200.00	210.00	250.00		
Jug, flat			175.00		
Marmalade, w/cover, dolphin ftd.	200.00	200.00	225.00		
1 Mayonnaise, 5½", ftd. with ladle	85.00	90.00	110.00		400.00
Mustard, w/cover	85.00	80.00	95.00		
7 Oil bottle, 4 oz.	125.00	125.00	135.00		
Plate, bouillon liner	12.00	15.00	17.50		25.00
Plate, 4½"	10.00	15.00	20.00		
Plate, 6"	11.00	14.00	16.00		40.00
Plate, 6", sq.	10.00	13.00	15.00		40.00
Plate, 7"	12.00	15.00	17.00		50.00
4 Plate, 7", sq.	12.00	15.00	17.00	60.00	65.00
3 Plate, 8", sq.	18.00	22.00	35.00	80.00	75.00
19 Plate, 8"	16.00	20.00	24.00	70.00	75.00
Plate, 9"	25.00	35.00	40.00		
Plate, 10½"	100.00	100.00	140.00		335.00
18 Plate, 10½", sq.	100.00	100.00	140.00		335.00
Plate, 12"	45.00	55.00	65.00		
Plate, 12", muffin, sides upturned	55.00	80.00	90.00		
Plate, 12", sandwich, 2 hdld.	35.00	45.00	60.00		180.00
Plate, 13", hors d'oeuvre, 2 hdld.	50.00	60.00	70.00		
Plate, 13", sq., 2 hdld.	40.00	45.00	55.00		
Platter, 14"	40.00	45.00	80.00		
22 Salt & pepper, pr.	100.00	110.00	135.00		450.00
12 Saucer, sq.	10.00	10.00	15.00		25.00
14 Saucer, after dinner	10.00	10.00	15.00		
12 Saucer, rnd.	10.00	10.00	15.00		25.00
Stem, 2½ oz., oyster cocktail	20.00	25.00	30.00		
Stem, 4 oz., saucer champagne	35.00	40.00	60.00		
Stem, 4 oz., sherbet	22.00	28.00	35.00		
Stem, 9 oz., Empress stemware, unusual	55.00	65.00	75.00		
10 Sugar, indiv.	45.00	45.00	50.00		210.00
Sugar, dolphin ftd., 3 hdld.	50.00	45.00	45.00		250.00
11 Tray, condiment & liner for indiv. sugar/creamer	75.00	75.00	85.00		
Tray, 10", 3 pt., relish	50.00	55.00	65.00		
Tray, 10", 7 pt., hors d'oeuvre	160.00	150.00	200.00		
Tray, 10", celery	25.00	35.00	40.00		150.00
Tray, 12", ctr. hdld., sandwich	48.00	57.00	65.00		
Tray, 12", sq. ctr. hdld., sandwich	52.00	60.00	67.50		
Tray, 13", celery	30.00	40.00	45.00		
Tray, 16", 4 pt., buffet relish	75.00	75.00	86.00		160.00
Tumbler, 8 oz., dolphin ftd., unusual	150.00	170.00	160.00		
6 Tumbler, 8 oz., grnd. bottom	60.00	50.00	70.00		
Tumbler, 12 oz., tea, grnd. bottom	70.00	65.00	75.00		
Vase, 8", flared	140.00	150.00	190.00		
21 Vase, 9", dolphin ftd.	200.00	200.00	220.00		850.00

Colors: Blue, crystal, Azure blue, Orchid, amber, Rose, green, Topaz; some Ruby, Ebony, and Wisteria

Fairfax (the name of this #2375 mould blank) was the mold shape used by Fostoria for many of their most popular etchings, including June, Versailles, and Trojan. Illustrated below is Rose (pink) and on page 98 amber and Topaz are shown. Orchid and Azure blue are the colors most collected in Fairfax. Amber and yellow are readily available, but typically have had fewer collectors seeking them. Some collectors of blue or pink June and Versailles are buying Fairfax to fill holes in their sets. Many Fairfax fill-in pieces can be bought for 25% – 40% of the cost of an etched piece. Some collectors would rather have a non-etched piece than none at all.

Happily, Fairfax collectors have a choice of two stemware lines, which does not happen in some etched patterns. The Fostoria stems and shapes shown on page 99 are the #5298 stem and tumbler line (even though the pieces shown are etched June and Versailles). More collectors adopt this line especially in pink and blue. The other stem line, #5299, is commonly found in yellow with Trojan etch. Collectors call this stem "waterfall." All Wisteria stems are found on the #5299 line. Some collectors mix stems, but tumblers are more difficult to mix because they have noticeably different shapes. The #5299 tumblers (oyster cocktail on page 99) are more flared at the top than the #5298 (all other tumblers on page 99).

I have shown an array of Fostoria's stemware on page 99 so that all shapes can be seen. The claret and high sherbets are major concerns. Each is 6" high. The claret is shaped like the wine. I recently had to show that difference to someone who told me he had some blue June clarets, which turned out to be crystal high sherbets. The parfait is also taller than the juice, although shaped similarly.

		Rose, Blue, Orchid	Amber	Green, Topaz
	Ashtray, 2½"	14.00	6.00	10.00
	Ashtray, 4"	16.00	8.00	11.00
	Ashtray, 5½"	18.00	11.00	12.00
	Baker, 9", oval	45.00	16.00	30.00
	Baker, 10½", oval	50.00	20.00	30.00
	Bonbon	12.50	9.00	10.00
23	Bottle, salad dressing	210.00	75.00	110.00
12	Bouillon, ftd.	15.00	8.00	10.00
	Bowl, 9", lemon, 2 hdld.	20.00	10.00	13.00
	Bowl, sweetmeat	22.00	12.00	16.00
	Bowl, 5", fruit	20.00	8.00	10.00
15	Bowl, 6", cereal	30.00	10.00	15.00
16	Bowl, 6⅞", 3 ftd.	25.00	15.00	20.00
	Bowl, 7", soup	50.00	24.00	33.00
	Bowl, 8", rnd., nappy	45.00	20.00	30.00
18	Bowl, 8½", 2 pt., relish	45.00	20.00	30.00
	Bowl, lg., hdld., dessert	45.00	20.00	30.00
	Bowl, 12"	50.00	25.00	35.00

		Rose, Blue, Orchid	Amber	Green, Topaz
10	Bowl, 12", centerpiece, #2394	50.00	25.00	35.00
	Bowl, 13", oval, centerpiece	50.00	25.00	35.00
	Bowl, 15", centerpiece	55.00	30.00	40.00
14	Butter dish, w/cover	150.00	70.00	100.00
	Candlestick, flattened top	25.00	12.00	15.00
	Candlestick, 3"	22.00	12.00	16.00
	Candy w/cover, flat, 3 pt.	85.00	45.00	55.00
	Candy w/cover, ftd.	95.00	50.00	65.00
	Celery, 11½"	30.00	15.00	18.00
6	Cheese comport (2 styles), #2368	25.00	10.00	12.50
	Cheese & cracker set (2 styles)	45.00	20.00	25.00
	Cigarette box	32.00	20.00	25.00
	Comport, 5"	35.00	15.00	25.00
11	Comport, 7"	40.00	15.00	25.00
	Cream soup, ftd.	23.00	10.00	15.00
20	Creamer, flat		10.00	14.00
13	Creamer, ftd.	15.00	7.00	10.00
31	Creamer, tea	25.00	8.00	12.00

	Rose, Blue, Orchid	Amber	Green, Topaz
32 Cup, after dinner	30.00	12.00	18.00
Cup, flat		3.00	5.00
19 Cup, ftd.	12.00	4.00	6.00
Flower holder, oval, window box w/frog	135.00	85.00	95.00
Grapefruit	35.00	18.00	25.00
Grapefruit liner	30.00	12.00	20.00
Ice bucket	95.00	50.00	65.00
1 Ice bowl, #2451	25.00	15.00	20.00
Ice bowl liner	20.00	12.00	* 15.00
2 Lemon dish, 6¾", 2 hndl.	25.00	15.00	20.00
Mayonnaise	25.00	12.00	15.00
Mayonnaise ladle	30.00	15.00	20.00
Mayonnaise liner, 7"	10.00	5.00	6.00
28 Nut cup, blown	25.00	15.00	18.00
25 Oil, ftd.	175.00	85.00	110.00
Pickle, 8½"	25.00	8.00	12.00
21 Pitcher, #5000	250.00	110.00	160.00
Plate, canape	20.00	10.00	10.00
Plate, whipped cream	11.00	8.00	9.00
Plate, 6", bread/butter	8.00	3.00	4.00
Plate, 7½", salad	10.00	4.00	5.00
Plate, 7½", cream soup or mayonnaise liner	10.00	5.00	6.00
Plate, 8¾", salad	14.00	7.00	8.00
24 Plate, Mah Jongg (w/sherbet), #2321	250.00	110.00	160.00
Plate, 9½", luncheon	17.00	7.00	10.00
22 Plate, 10¼", dinner	45.00	18.00	28.00
3 Plate, 10¼", grill	40.00	15.00	24.00
Plate, 10", cake	22.00	13.00	15.00
Plate, 12", bread, oval	45.00	25.00	27.50
Plate, 13", chop	30.00	15.00	20.00
Platter, 10½", oval	38.00	20.00	30.00
Platter, 12", oval	65.00	30.00	45.00
Platter, 15", oval	110.00	35.00	60.00
Relish, 3 part, 8½"	30.00	10.00	15.00
Relish, 11½"	22.00	11.00	13.00
8 Sauce boat	50.00	20.00	30.00
9 Sauce boat liner	20.00	10.00	15.00
32 Saucer, after dinner	8.00	4.00	5.00
19 Saucer	4.00	2.50	3.00
29 Shaker, ftd., pr	70.00	30.00	45.00
Shaker, indiv., ftd., pr.		20.00	25.00
33 Stem, 4", ¾ oz., cordial, #5098	65.00	25.00	45.00
7 Stem, 5½ oz., oyster cocktail	16.00	9.00	11.00
Stem, 4¼", 6 oz., low sherbet	16.00	9.00	11.00
5 Stem, 5¼", 3 oz., cocktail	22.00	12.00	18.00
27 Stem, 5½", 3 oz., wine, #5098	30.00	16.00	20.00
Stem, 6", 4 oz., claret	40.00	22.00	33.00
4 Stem, 6", 6 oz., high sherbet, #5098	20.00	10.00	15.00
Stem, 8¼", 10 oz., water	35.00	16.00	20.00
Sugar, flat		10.00	12.00
17 Sugar, ftd.	15.00	6.00	8.00
17 Sugar cover	35.00	20.00	25.00
Sugar pail	80.00	35.00	55.00
30 Sugar, tea	25.00	8.00	12.00
Tray, 11", ctr. hdld.	40.00	20.00	30.00
Tumbler, 2½ oz., ftd.	32.00	12.00	18.00
34 Tumbler, 4½", 5½ oz., ftd., oyster cocktail, #5099	18.00	10.00	11.00
Tumbler, 5¼", 9 oz., ftd.	22.00	12.00	13.00
26 Tumbler, 6", 12 oz., ftd., #5098	28.00	13.50	18.00
Vase, 8" (2 styles)	95.00	40.00	60.00
Whipped cream pail	75.00	35.00	50.00

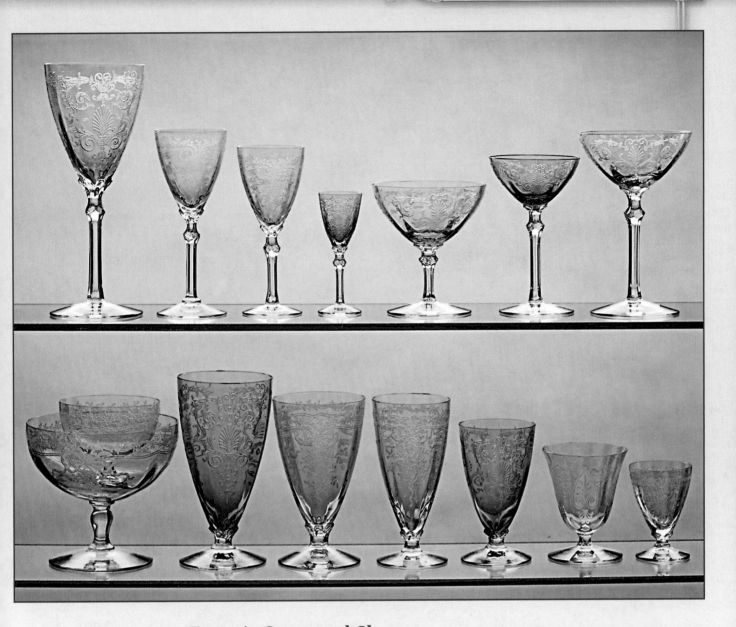

Fostoria Stems and Shapes

All are on #5098 "Petal" stems unless otherwise indicated.

Top Row: Left to Right
1. Water, 10 oz., 8¼", #5098
2. Claret, 4 oz., 6", #5098
3. Wine, 3 oz., 5½", #5098
4. Cordial, ¾ oz., 4", #5098
5. Sherbet, low, 6 oz., 4¼", #5098
6. Cocktail, 3 oz., 5¼", #5098
7. Sherbet, high, 6 oz., 6", #5098

Bottom Row: Left to Right
1. Grapefruit and liner, #877
2. Ice tea tumbler, 12 oz., 6", #5098
3. Water tumbler, 9 oz., 5¼", #5098
4. Parfait, 6 oz., 5¼", #5098
5. Juice tumbler, 5 oz., 4½", #5098
6. Oyster cocktail, 5½ oz., #5099 "Waterfall" stemline
7. Bar tumbler, 2½ oz., #5098

Cordial, 3⅞",
#5099 "Waterfall" stemline

Color: crystal

First Love is likely the most recognized Duncan & Miller etching. Various mold lines were incorporated into this large pattern. Among those are #30 (Pall Mall), #111 (Terrace), #115 (Canterbury), #117 (Three Feathers), #126 (Venetian), and #5111½ (Terrace blown stemware). Canterbury can be found on pages 43 to 45 and Terrace can be seen on pages 221 to 223. You will have to explore earlier editions of this book for catalog pages showing details of those other lines. Most pieces of First Love will be found on lines #111 or #115.

This etching was made to go with Roger Bros. First Love silverplate.

1

Ashtray, 3½", sq., #111	17.50	
Ashtray, 3½" x 2½", #30	16.50	
Ashtray, 5" x 3", #12, club	37.50	
Ashtray, 5" x 3¼", #30	24.00	
Ashtray, 6½" x 4¼", #30	35.00	
Basket, 9¼" x 10" x 7¼", #115	185.00	
2 Basket, 10" x 4¼" x 7", oval hdld., #115	200.00	
Bottle, oil w/stopper, 8", #5200	60.00	
Bowl, 3" x 5", rose, #115	40.00	
Bowl, 4" x 1½", finger, #30	32.00	
Bowl, 4¼", finger, #5111½	35.00	
Bowl, 6" x 2½", oval, olive, #115	25.00	
Bowl, 6¾" x 4¼", ftd., flared rim, #111	30.00	
Bowl, 7½" x 3", 3 pt., ftd., #117	35.00	
Bowl, 8" sq. x 2½", hdld., #111	60.00	
Bowl, 8½" x 4", #115	37.50	
Bowl, 9" x 4½", ftd., #111	42.00	
Bowl, 9½" x 2½", hdld., #111	45.00	
Bowl, 10" x 3¾", ftd., flared rim, #111	55.00	
Bowl, 10" x 4½", #115	45.00	
Bowl, 10½" x 5", crimped, #115	44.00	
Bowl, 10½" x 7" x 7", #126	62.00	
Bowl, 10¾" x 4¾", #115	42.50	
Bowl, 11" x 1¾", #30	55.00	
Bowl, 11" x 3¼", flared rim, #111	62.50	
Bowl, 11" x 5¼", flared rim, #6	70.00	
Bowl, 11½" x 8¼", oval, #115	45.00	
Bowl, 12" x 3½", #6	70.00	
Bowl, 12" x 3¼", flared, #115	60.00	
Bowl, 12" x 4" x 7½", oval, #117	65.00	
Bowl, 12½", flat, ftd., #126	75.00	
Bowl, 13" x 3¼" x 8¾", oval, flared, #115	55.00	
Bowl, 13" x 7" x 9¼", #126	67.50	
Bowl, 13" x 7", #117	62.50	
Bowl, 14" x 7½" x 6", oval, #126	65.00	
Box, candy w/lid, 4¾" x 6¼"	60.00	
Butter or cheese, 7" sq. x 1¼", #111	130.00	
Candelabra, 2-lite, #41	35.00	
Candelabrum, 6", 2-lite w/prisms, #30	60.00	
8 Candle, 3", 1-lite, #111	25.00	
Candle, 3", low, #115	25.00	
Candle, 3½", #115	25.00	
Candle, 4", cornucopia, #117	25.00	
Candle, 4", low, #111	25.00	
Candle, 5¼", 2-lite, globe, #30	35.00	
Candle, 6", 2-lite, #30	35.00	
Candy box, 6" x 3½", 3 hdld., 3 pt., w/lid, #115	85.00	
Candy box, 6" x 3½", 3 pt., w/lid, crown finial, #106	90.00	
Candy jar, 5" x 7¼", w/lid, ftd., #25	85.00	
Candy, 6½", w/5" lid, #115	75.00	
Carafe, w/stopper, water, #5200	195.00	
Cheese stand, 3" x 5¼", #111	25.00	
5 Cheese stand, 5¾" x 3½", #115	25.00	
Cigarette box w/lid, 4" x 4¼"	32.00	
Cigarette box w/lid, 4½" x 3½", #30	35.00	
Cigarette box w/lid, 4¾" x 3¾"	35.00	
Cocktail shaker, 14 oz., #5200	135.00	
Cocktail shaker, 16 oz., #5200	135.00	
Cocktail shaker, 32 oz., #5200	175.00	
Comport w/lid, 8¾" x 5½", #111	135.00	
Comport, 3½" x 4¾"w, #111	30.00	
Comport, 5" x 5½", flared rim, #115	32.00	
Comport, 5¼" x 6¾", flat top, #115	32.00	
Comport, 6" x 4¾", low #115	37.50	
Creamer, 2½", individual, #115	18.00	
Creamer, 3", 10 oz., #111	18.00	
11 Creamer, 3¾", 7 oz., #115	15.00	
Creamer, sugar w/butter pat lid, breakfast set, #28	75.00	
Cruet, #25	90.00	
Cruet, #30	90.00	
Cup, #115	15.00	
Decanter w/stopper, 16 oz., #5200	150.00	
4 Decanter w/stopper, 32 oz., #30	175.00	
Decanter w/stopper, 32 oz., #5200	175.00	
Hat, 4½", #30	395.00	
Hat, 5½" x 8½" x 6¼", #30	350.00	
Honey dish, 5" x 3", #91	30.00	
13 Ice bucket, 6", #30	110.00	
Lamp, hurricane, w/prisms, 15", #115	165.00	
Lamp shade only, #115	110.00	
Lid for candy urn, #111	35.00	
Mayonnaise, 4¾" x 4½", div. w/7½" underplate	35.00	
Mayonnaise, 5¼" x 3", div. w/6½" plate, #115	35.00	
Mayonnaise, 5½" x 2½", ftd., hdld., #111	35.00	
12 Mayonnaise, 5½" x 2¾", #115	35.00	
Mayonnaise, 5½" x 3½", crimped, #111	32.00	
Mayonnaise, 5¾" x 3", w/dish hdld. tray, #111	35.00	
Mayonnaise, w/7" tray hdld., #111	35.00	
Mustard w/lid & underplate	57.50	
Nappy, 5" x 1", w/bottom star, #25	20.00	
Nappy, 5" x 1¾", one hdld., #115	18.00	
Nappy, 5½" x 2", div., hdld., #111	18.00	
Nappy, 5½" x 2", one hdld., heart, #115	28.00	
Nappy, 6" x 1¾", hdld., #111	22.00	

FIRST LOVE

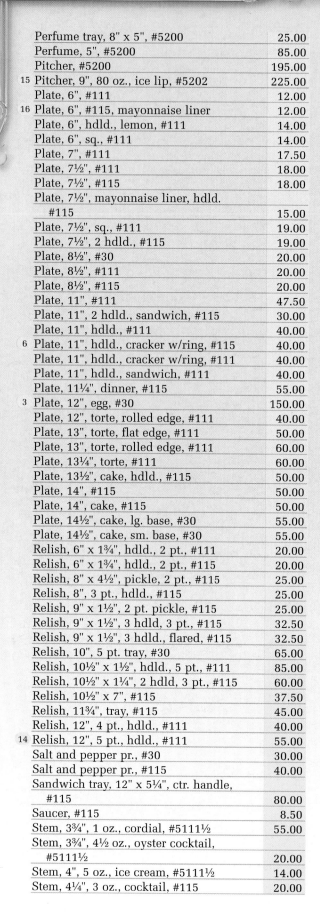

	Perfume tray, 8" x 5", #5200	25.00
	Perfume, 5", #5200	85.00
	Pitcher, #5200	195.00
15	Pitcher, 9", 80 oz., ice lip, #5202	225.00
	Plate, 6", #111	12.00
16	Plate, 6", #115, mayonnaise liner	12.00
	Plate, 6", hdld., lemon, #111	14.00
	Plate, 6", sq., #111	14.00
	Plate, 7", #111	17.50
	Plate, 7½", #111	18.00
	Plate, 7½", #115	18.00
	Plate, 7½", mayonnaise liner, hdld. #115	15.00
	Plate, 7½", sq., #111	19.00
	Plate, 7½", 2 hdld., #115	19.00
	Plate, 8½", #30	20.00
	Plate, 8½", #111	20.00
	Plate, 8½", #115	20.00
	Plate, 11", #111	47.50
	Plate, 11", 2 hdld., sandwich, #115	30.00
	Plate, 11", hdld., #111	40.00
6	Plate, 11", hdld., cracker w/ring, #115	40.00
	Plate, 11", hdld., cracker w/ring, #111	40.00
	Plate, 11", hdld., sandwich, #111	40.00
	Plate, 11¼", dinner, #115	55.00
3	Plate, 12", egg, #30	150.00
	Plate, 12", torte, rolled edge, #111	40.00
	Plate, 13", torte, flat edge, #111	50.00
	Plate, 13", torte, rolled edge, #111	60.00
	Plate, 13¼", torte, #111	60.00
	Plate, 13½", cake, hdld., #115	50.00
	Plate, 14", #115	50.00
	Plate, 14", cake, #115	50.00
	Plate, 14½", cake, lg. base, #30	55.00
	Plate, 14½", cake, sm. base, #30	55.00
	Relish, 6" x 1¾", hdld., 2 pt., #111	20.00
	Relish, 6" x 1¾", hdld., 2 pt., #115	20.00
	Relish, 8" x 4½", pickle, 2 pt., #115	25.00
	Relish, 8", 3 pt., hdld., #115	25.00
	Relish, 9" x 1½", 2 pt. pickle, #115	25.00
	Relish, 9" x 1½", 3 hdld., 3 pt., #115	32.50
	Relish, 9" x 1½", 3 hdld., flared, #115	32.50
	Relish, 10", 5 pt. tray, #30	65.00
	Relish, 10½" x 1½", hdld., 5 pt., #111	85.00
	Relish, 10½" x 1¼", 2 hdld, 3 pt., #115	60.00
	Relish, 10½" x 7", #115	37.50
	Relish, 11¾", tray, #115	45.00
	Relish, 12", 4 pt., hdld., #111	40.00
14	Relish, 12", 5 pt., hdld., #111	55.00
	Salt and pepper pr., #30	30.00
	Salt and pepper pr., #115	40.00
	Sandwich tray, 12" x 5¼", ctr. handle, #115	80.00
	Saucer, #115	8.50
	Stem, 3¾", 1 oz., cordial, #5111½	55.00
	Stem, 3¾", 4½ oz., oyster cocktail, #5111½	20.00
	Stem, 4", 5 oz., ice cream, #5111½	14.00
	Stem, 4¼", 3 oz., cocktail, #115	20.00
	Stem, 4½", 3½ oz., cocktail, #5111½	20.00
	Stem, 5", 5 oz., saucer champagne, #5111½	18.00
7	Stem, 5¼", 3 oz., wine, #5111½	30.00
	Stem, 5¼", 5 oz., ftd. juice, #5111½	22.00
	Stem, 5¾", 10 oz., low luncheon goblet, #5111½	17.50
	Stem, 6", 4½ oz., claret, #5111½	45.00
	Stem, 6½", 12 oz., ftd. ice tea, #5111½	30.00
	Stem, 6¾", 14 oz., ftd. ice tea, #5111½	30.00
	Stem, cordial, #111	18.00
	Sugar, 2½", individual, #115	15.00
10	Sugar, 3", 7 oz., #115	14.00
1	Sugar, 3", 10 oz., #111	15.00
	Tray, 8" x 2", hdld. celery, #111	17.50
	Tray, 8" x 4¾", individual sug/cr., #115	17.50
	Tray, 8¾", celery, #91	30.00
	Tray, 11", celery, #91	40.00
	Tumbler, 2", 1½ oz., whiskey, #5200	55.00
	Tumbler, 2½" x 3⅜", sham, Teardrop, ftd.	50.00
	Tumbler, 3", sham, #5200	30.00
	Tumbler, 4¾", 10 oz., sham, #5200	33.00
	Tumbler, 5½", 12 oz., sham, #5200	33.00
	Tumbler, 6", 14 oz., sham, #5200	33.00
	Tumbler, 8 oz., flat, #115	28.00
	Urn, 4½" x 4½", #111	27.50
	Urn, 4½" x 4½", #115	27.50
	Urn, 4¾", rnd ft.	27.50
	Urn, 5", #525	37.50
	Urn, 5½", ring hdld, sq. ft.	65.00
	Urn, 5½", sq. ft.	37.50
9	Urn, 7", sq. hdld., #545	70.00
	Urn, 7", #529	37.50
	Vase, 4", flared rim, #115	25.00
	Vase, 4½" x 4¾", #115	30.00
	Vase, 5" x 5", crimped, #115	35.00
	Vase, 6", #507	55.00
	Vase, 8" x 4¾", cornucopia, #117	65.00
	Vase, 8", ftd., #506	90.00
	Vase, 8", ftd., #507	90.00
	Vase, 8½" x 2¾", #505	110.00
	Vase, 8½" x 6", #115	90.00
	Vase, 9" x 4½", #505	95.00
	Vase, 9", #509	90.00
	Vase, 9", bud, #506	80.00
	Vase, 9½" x 3½", #506	125.00
	Vase, 10" x 4¾", #5200	90.00
	Vase, 10", #507	95.00
	Vase, 10", ftd., #111	115.00
	Vase, 10", ftd., #505	115.00
	Vase, 10", ftd., #506	115.00
	Vase, 10½" x 12 x 9½", #126	155.00
	Vase, 10½", #126	175.00
	Vase, 11" x 5¼", #505	145.00
	Vase, 11½ x 4½", #506	140.00
	Vase, 12", flared #115	145.00
	Vase, 12", ftd., #506	145.00
	Vase, 12", ftd., #507	155.00

Colors: crystal, pink, yellow, and rare in green

I find that Tiffin's Flanders is often incorrectly identified as Cambridge's Gloria. Look at Gloria on pages 111 – 112 to see that curved stem floral design. My mom once called me all excited to tell me she had just bought a pink Gloria pitcher! That "Gloria" pitcher is the one shown on page 104. As with most Tiffin pitchers of this time, Flanders was sold with or without a cover. Keep in mind that the pitcher top is plain with no pattern etched on it.

An entire new cadre of collectors have discovered Elegant patterns via the Internet. This is influencing prices on already scarce wares and exposing some wares that we thought rare as being more plentiful. More glassware has been distributed into collectors' hands through the Internet than by any other means in the last few years. If you want a pattern, do not postpone getting it. I don't feel the sudden Internet "supply" is going to hold on forever.

Flanders stems are customarily found on Tiffin's #17024 blank. Frequently these have a crystal foot and stem with tops of crystal, pink, or yellow. Color blending that is seen infrequently includes green foot with pink stems, and pink tumblers as well as pitchers with crystal handle and foot. One green Flanders vase was found a couple of years ago and is pictured here. Round plates are Tiffin's line #8800 and each size plate has a different number. Scalloped plates are line #5831. I see more of the round plates than I do the scalloped ones with dinners rarely seen in either style.

Shakers are being found in crystal once in a while, but seldom in pink. I have had a few reports of yellow, but I have never seen one. Lamps are found only in crystal. That cylindrical shade is occasionally found over a candlestick and designated as a Chinese hurricane lamp. I have pictured one with an electric insert.

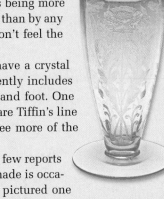

1

	Crystal	Pink	Yellow
29 Almond, ftd., nut, blown	35.00	75.00	55.00
Ashtray, 2¼x3¾", w/cigarette rest	55.00		
Bowl, 2 hdld., bouillon	50.00	135.00	85.00

	Crystal	Pink	Yellow
Bowl, finger, ftd., 8 oz., #185	35.00	95.00	60.00
Bowl, 2 hdld., bonbon	30.00	100.00	65.00
Bowl, 8", ftd., blown	125.00	325.00	
Bowl, 11", ftd., console	75.00	175.00	95.00
Bowl, 12", flanged rim, console	75.00	175.00	95.00
18 Candle, 2 styles, #5831 & #15360 shown	40.00	75.00	50.00

FLANDERS

	Crystal	Pink	Yellow
25 Candy box, w/cover, flat, #329	135.00	350.00	250.00
Candy jar, w/cover, ftd.	100.00	250.00	185.00
Celery, 11"	40.00	95.00	60.00
Cheese & cracker	55.00	130.00	100.00
Comport, 3½"	40.00	95.00	60.00
Comport, 6"	65.00	175.00	95.00
Creamer, flat	45.00	135.00	90.00
Creamer, ftd.	40.00	120.00	70.00
16 Cup, 2 styles, #8869 shown	50.00	100.00	65.00
Decanter	195.00	395.00	295.00
4 Electric lamp w/Chinese style shade	325.00		
Grapefruit, w/liner	75.00	195.00	135.00
Hurricane lamp, Chinese style	295.00		
Mayonnaise, w/liner	50.00	125.00	80.00
Oil bottle & stopper	150.00	350.00	250.00
Parfait, 5⅝", hdld.	75.00	195.00	125.00
21 Pitcher & cover, 54 oz., #194	250.00	395.00	295.00
Plate, 6"	7.00	18.00	12.00
20 Plate, 8", #8833	12.00	26.00	15.50
3 Plate, 10¼", dinner, #8818	65.00	135.00	80.00
Relish, 3 pt.	60.00	125.00	80.00
13 Salt & pepper, pr., #2 (rare)	200.00	450.00	300.00
24 Sandwich server, center hdld., octagon, #337		165.00	
16 Saucer, #8869 shown	8.00	15.00	10.00
Stem, 4½", oyster cocktail	20.00	55.00	25.00
Stem, 4½", sherbet/sundae, 6 oz.	15.00	40.00	17.50
27 Stem, 4¾", cocktail, 3½ oz., #15024	22.00	50.00	30.00

	Crystal	Pink	Yellow
15 Stem, 5", cordial, 1½ oz., #15024	60.00	110.00	75.00
7 Stem, 5⅝", parfait, cafe, 4½ oz., #15024	40.00	100.00	75.00
Stem, 6⅛", wine, 3 oz.	35.00	85.00	45.00
Stem, 6¼", saucer champagne, 6 oz.	18.00	40.00	20.00
26 Stem, 7 oz., hndl., parfait		125.00	
8 Stem, claret, 5 oz., #15024	40.00	125.00	75.00
22 Stem, 8¼", water, 9 oz., #15024	35.00	60.00	40.00
9 Stem, cordial, #15047	60.00	110.00	75.00
10 Stem, sundae/sherbet, low ft., #15047	16.00	35.00	25.00
12 Stem, sundae/sherbet, hi ft., #15047	18.00	40.00	28.00
5 Stem, 9 oz., water, #15047	35.00	60.00	40.00
Sugar, flat, #6	45.00	135.00	90.00
28 Sugar, ftd., #185	40.00	120.00	70.00
17 Tumbler, 2¾", 2½ oz., ftd., whiskey, #020	45.00	100.00	60.00
Tumbler, 4¾", 9 oz., ftd., water	22.00	65.00	25.00
11 Tumbler, 4¾", 10 oz., ftd.	22.00	65.00	30.00
6 Tumbler, 5⅞", 12 oz., ftd., tea, #020	35.00	100.00	40.00
23 Tumbler, 12 oz., tea, #14185	32.00	65.00	45.00
14 Tumbler, 12 oz., ftd., tea, #15071	35.00	100.00	45.00
2 Vase, bud, 8" or 10", #14185	50.00	125.00	70.00
1 Vase, ftd., 8", #2	100.00	250.00	175.00
19 Vase, 10½", Dahlia, cupped, ftd., #151	150.00	275.00	200.00
Vase, fan, #15151	100.00	250.00	150.00

Colors: crystal w/green, Twilight, Twilight w/crystal, pink, crystal w/amber

Fontaine is one Tiffin pattern that would appeal to more collectors were they to see some of it. The purple color shown below is Tiffin's earlier Twilight color that does not change colors when placed under different light sources. Tiffin's later Twilight (1949 – 1980) changes from pink to purple depending upon fluorescent or natural light. I am having difficulty finding new pieces to picture. Some Twilight has appeared at shows, but not at a price that beguiled me into owning it.

Several companies (even on earlier carnival glass) used a fountain motif. As with all Tiffin patterns, cups and saucers are rarely glimpsed. I bought the set pictured about 20 years ago, before I even deemed this pattern a candidate for the book. I only knew cups and saucers were hard to find in Tiffin patterns. I have never found cups and saucers in any other Fontaine colors.

The cordial was from my collection. I once saw one in pink, but passed on it due to price. Water goblets seem to be easier to find than sherbets as I now have three different colors. I favor the crystal tops with colored stems over the single colored pieces, but that's a personal preference.

I have only seen a couple of covered pitchers. Both were Twilight and both sold. If you are lucky enough to spot some Fontaine, buy it no matter the color. Some collector will thank you.

	Amber Green Pink	Twilight
Bowl, 8", deep, ftd., #14194	85.00	175.00
Bowl, 13" ctrpc., #8153	75.00	175.00
Candlestick, low, #9758	35.00	80.00
Creamer, stem. ftd., #4	50.00	75.00
4 Cup, #8869	75.00	135.00
Finger bowl, #022	45.00	85.00
Grape fruit, #251 & footed liner, #881	65.00	195.00
Jug & cover, #194	395.00	1195.00
Plate, 6", #8814	12.50	20.00
Plate, 8", #8833	20.00	35.00
Plate, 10", #8818	75.00	175.00
Plate, 10", cake w/ctr. hdld., oct., #345	65.00	150.00

	Amber Green Pink	Twilight
4 Saucer, #8869	12.50	25.00
Stem, cafe parfait, #033	65.00	150.00
Stem, claret, #033	60.00	135.00
Stem, cocktail, #033	35.00	70.00
3 Stem, cordial, #033	145.00	275.00
6 Stem, saucer champagne, #033	30.00	65.00
2 Stem, sundae, #033	25.00	55.00
1 Stem, water, #033	75.00	125.00
Stem, wine, 2½ oz., #033	65.00	135.00
Sugar, ftd., #4	50.00	75.00
5 Tumbler, 9 oz. table, #032	35.00	65.00
Vase, 8" ftd., #2 (shown in Flanders)	95.00	250.00
Vase, 9¼", bowed top, #7	125.00	250.00

Colors: crystal and crystal w/Wisteria base

Fostoria's Fuchsia was recently included in this book as new pattern. Be sure to look at Tiffin's Fuchsia pattern so you do not confuse these. This Fuchsia pattern is mostly etched on Fostoria's Lafayette mold blank #2244, which can be found on page 137. Stemware line #6044 was also incorporated for Fuchsia.

I know one collector who collects everything Fuchsia, including Fostoria's and Tiffin's as well as Cambridge's Marjorie, which is a Fuchsia design. She also has several pottery designs highlighting Fuchsia. Observe that champagne with the Wisteria stem. Most of those were sold to go with Lafayette Wisteria tableware that was non-etched. I have run into several sets of Lafayette that had Wisteria etched Fuchsia stems, but they all had plain Wisteria cups, saucers, plates, and creamers and sugars.

The large center surface areas of plates are easily scratched from use or from stacking due to the flat, ground bottoms. I have seen some dinner plates that were cloudy looking from all the marks. These will not sell for much, if at all.

Collectors do put a premium on mint condition, and few value shopworn glassware. I have been told a few people around the country are trying their hand at buffing out the scratches from these plates; but I understand it is expensive and not always successful since most of the glassware made at this time is very soft compared to highly polished glass of later years.

		Crystal	Wisteria
	Bonbon, #2470	33.00	
	Bowl, 10", #2395	95.00	
	Bowl, 10½", #2470½	75.00	
	Bowl 11½", "B," #2440	75.00	
	Bowl, 12" #2470	90.00	175.00
	Candlestick, 3", #2375	35.00	
5	Candlestick, 5", #2395½	50.00	
	Candlestick, 5½", #2470½	65.00	
4	Candlestick, 5½", #2470	65.00	195.00
	Comport, 6" low, #2470	40.00	110.00
	Comport, 6" tall, #2470	75.00	150.00
	Creamer, ftd., #2440	30.00	
7	Cup, #2440	20.00	
	Finger bowl, #869	35.00	
	Lemon dish, #2470	32.00	
	Oyster cocktail, 4½ oz., #6004	17.50	40.00
	Plate, 10", cake	60.00	
	Plate, 6", bread & butter, #2440	10.00	
	Plate, 7", salad, #2440	15.00	
1	Plate, 8", luncheon, #2440	22.00	
2	Plate, 9", dinner, #2440	60.00	

		Crystal	Wisteria
7	Saucer, #2440	7.50	
	Stem, ¾ oz., cordial, #6004	70.00	195.00
	Stem, 2½ oz., wine, #6004	35.00	65.00
	Stem, 3 oz., cocktail, #6004	25.00	65.00
	Stem, 4 oz., claret, #6004	45.00	85.00
	Stem, 5 oz., low sherbet, #6004	22.50	40.00
	Stem, 5½ oz., 6" parfait, #6004	37.50	85.00
3	Stem, 5½ oz., 5⅜", saucer champagne, #6004	27.50	55.00
	Stem, 9 oz., water, #6004	38.00	95.00
8	Sugar, ftd., #2440	30.00	
	Sweetmeat, #2470	38.00	
	Tumbler, 2 oz., #833	25.00	
	Tumbler, 2½ oz., ftd. whiskey, #6004	35.00	75.00
	Tumbler, 5 oz., #833	22.50	
	Tumbler, 5 oz., ftd. juice, #6004	20.00	55.00
	Tumbler, 8 oz., #833	22.00	
	Tumbler, 9 oz., ftd., #6004	18.00	55.00
6	Tumbler, 12 oz., #833	30.00	
	Tumbler, 12 oz., ftd., #6004	32.00	75.00

Colors: crystal; a few experimental Twilight pieces which were never marketed

Be sure to check out Fostoria's Fuchsia pattern on page 106. The patterns are comparable, but the shapes are not. You need to be aware that pattern names were not exclusive to any particular company. Remember to state which company made the Fuchsia you collect.

New pieces of Fuchsia continue to be revealed. As with Cambridge's Rose Point that appears etched on almost every line that Cambridge made, Tiffin's Fuchsia seems to have followed this same path. Fuchsia has always attracted collectors; and because of this, dealers are searching every nook and cranny, which explains why so many new pieces are being uncovered.

There are many rarely seen pieces including the bitters bottle, icers with inserts, cocktail shaker, hurricane and electric lamps as well as the tall #17457 stems of all varieties. As with most Tiffin patterns, cups, saucers, and dinner plates are not found often enough to supply every collector's needs. There are footed as well as flat finger bowls; and there are three styles of double candlesticks. The #5831, pointed knob type (pictured below) is the most difficult to find.

You will be able to find diverse serving bowls in Fuchsia unlike most other Tiffin patterns where serving pieces come at a premium. The large handled urn vase must have found favor with customers for years as I see that one vase more than any other Tiffin vase made. I also see some eye-popping high prices on it. My experience has been they have a hard time fetching more than $100.00 on a good day.

		Crystal
	Ashtray, 2¼" x 3¾", w/cigarette rest	40.00
	Bell, 5", #15083	80.00
21	Bitters bottle	495.00
17	Bowl, 4", finger, ftd., #041	60.00
18	Bowl, 4½" finger, w/#8814 liner	75.00
	Bowl, 5³⁄₁₆", 2 hdld., #5831	35.00
	Bowl, 6¼", cream soup, ftd., #5831	55.00
	Bowl, 7¼", salad, #5902	40.00

		Crystal
30	Bowl, 8⅜", 2 hdld., #5831	55.00
	Bowl, 9¾", deep salad	75.00
25	Bowl, 10", salad, #5831	70.00
	Bowl, 10½", console, fan shaped sides, #319	70.00
	Bowl, 11⅞", console, flared, #5902	80.00
28	Bowl, 12", flanged rim, ftd., console, #5831	60.00
	Bowl, 12⅝", console, flared, #5902	90.00
33	Bowl, 13", crimped, #5902	80.00

FUCHSIA

		Crystal
12	Candlestick, 2-lite, w/pointed center, #5831	65.00
	Candlestick, 2-lite, tapered center, #15306	65.00
27	Candlestick, 5", 2-lite, ball center	65.00
	Candlestick, 5⅝", 2-lite, w/fan center, #5902	65.00
	Candlestick, single, #348	35.00
	Celery, 10", oval, #5831	35.00
	Celery, 10½", rectangular, #5902	37.50
	Cigarette box, w/lid, 4" x 2¾", #9305	125.00
	Cocktail shaker, 8", w/metal top	275.00
	Comport, 6¼", #5831	30.00
	Comport, 6½", w/beaded stem, #15082	35.00
	Creamer, 2⅞", individual, #5831	45.00
	Creamer, 3⅜", flat w/beaded handle, #5902	22.00
1	Creamer, 4½", ftd., #5831	22.50
	Creamer, pearl edge	50.00
32	Cup, #5831	95.00
	Electric lamp	350.00
24	Hurricane, 12", Chinese style	250.00
16	Icer, with insert	165.00
	Mayonnaise, flat, w/6¼" liner, #5902 w/ladle	50.00
	Mayonnaise, ftd., w/ladle, #5831	50.00
	Nut dish, 6¼"	40.00
	Pickle, 7⅜", #5831	40.00
	Pitcher & cover, #194	395.00
6	Pitcher, flat	395.00
	Plate, 6¼", bread and butter, #5902	8.00
	Plate, 6¼", sherbet, #8814	9.00
	Plate, 6⅜", 2 hdld., #5831	11.00
29	Plate, 7", marmalade, 3-ftd., #310½	27.50
	Plate, 7½", salad, #5831	15.00
	Plate, 7⅞", cream soup or mayo liner, #5831	12.50
5	Plate, 7⅞", salad, #8814	15.00
	Plate, 8⅛", luncheon, #8833	22.50
	Plate, 8¼", luncheon, #5902	17.50
	Plate, 8⅜", bonbon, pearl edge	27.50
	Plate, 9½", dinner, #5902	85.00
31	Plate, 10½", 2 hdld., cake, #5831	75.00
	Plate, muffin tray, pearl edge	55.00
	Plate, 13", lily rolled and crimped edge	65.00
2	Plate, 14¼", sandwich, #8833	60.00
	Relish, 6⅜", 3 pt., #5902	30.00
	Relish, 9¼", sq., 3 pt.	40.00
34	Relish, 10½" x 12½", hdld., 3 pt., #5902	55.00

		Crystal
23	Relish, 10½" x 12½", hdld., 5 pt.	70.00
	Salt and pepper, pr., #2	155.00
32	Saucer, #5831	15.00
	Stem, 4 1/16", cordial, #15083	30.00
15	Stem, 4⅛", sherbet, #15083	11.00
14	Stem, 4¼", cocktail, #15083	15.00
	Stem, 4⅝", 3½ oz., cocktail, #17453	33.00
	Stem, 4⅞", saucer champagne, hollow stem	125.00
	Stem, 5 1/16", wine, #15083	30.00
	Stem, 5¼", claret, #15083	35.00
	Stem, 5⅜", cocktail, "C" stem, #17457	55.00
	Stem, 5⅜", cordial, "C" stem, #17457	135.00
	Stem, 5⅜", 7 oz., saucer champagne, #17453	30.00
13	Stem, 5⅜", saucer champagne, #15083	15.00
	Stem, 5⅜", saucer champagne, "C" stem, #17457	50.00
9	Stem, 5 15/16", parfait, #15083	40.00
	Stem, 6¼", low water, #15083	25.00
4	Stem, 7⅜", 9 oz., water, #17453, cupped bowl	40.00
3	Stem, 7½", water, high, #15083	25.00
	Stem, 7⅝", water, "C" stem, #17457	75.00
	Sugar, 2⅞", individual, #5831	40.00
	Sugar, 3⅜", flat, w/beaded handle, #5902	22.00
	Sugar, 4½", ftd., #5831	22.50
	Sugar, pearl edge	50.00
35	Tray, sugar/creamer, ind.	55.00
	Tray, 9½", 2 hdld. for cream/sugar	45.00
19	Tumbler, 2 7/16", 2 oz., bar, flat, #506	65.00
20	Tumbler, 3 5/16", oyster cocktail, #14196	14.00
	Tumbler, 3⅜", old-fashioned, flat, #580	55.00
	Tumbler, 4 13/16" flat, juice	35.00
10	Tumbler, 4 5/16", 5 oz., ftd., juice, #15083	25.00
	Tumbler, 5⅛", water, flat, #517	35.00
11	Tumbler, 5 5/16", 9 oz., ftd., water, #15083	25.00
8	Tumbler, 6 5/16", 12 oz., ftd., tea, #15083	35.00
7	Vase, 6½", bud, #14185	32.00
	Vase, 8 13/16", flared, crimped	110.00
	Vase, 8¼", bud, #14185	40.00
	Vase, 10½", bud, #14185	50.00
	Vase, 10¾", bulbous bottom, #5872	195.00
	Vase, 10⅞", beaded stem, #15082	75.00
22	Vase, 11¾", urn, 2 hdld., trophy.	110.00
26	Whipped cream, 3-ftd., #310	35.00

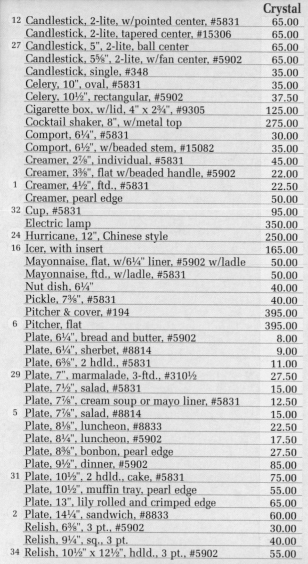

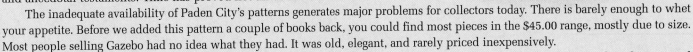

Colors: black, blue, crystal, green, red, and yellow

Gazebo and another Paden City pattern, Utopia, are two very analogous designs, which we are combining for the time being. In the pattern shot at right, Utopia is on the left and Gazebo on the right. The images on Utopia are larger and more detailed than those of Gazebo. Utopia may have been converted from Gazebo for use on larger items or Gazebo downsized from Utopia. Conjecturing today is just that, as no one knows why the glass companies did some of the things they did. Over 30 years ago when I first started researching, I believed all of the interviews from retired workers' reminiscences and anecdotal testaments. Time has proved not all of those held true.

The inadequate availability of Paden City's patterns generates major problems for collectors today. There is barely enough to whet your appetite. Before we added this pattern a couple of books back, you could find most pieces in the $45.00 range, mostly due to size. Most people selling Gazebo had no idea what they had. It was old, elegant, and rarely priced inexpensively.

Several different Paden City mold lines were used for this etching. All measurements in our listing are taken from actual pieces. We have not yet found a punch bowl to go with our punch cups. However, it was the fashion of the day to include "custard" cups with a set, so there may be no punch bowl, though Cathy feels certain she saw one in the 555 line very early in our Depression glass hunts.

		Crystal	Blue
	Bowl, 9", fan handles	42.00	
	Bowl, 9", bead handles	42.00	75.00
	Bowl, 13", flat edge	50.00	
	Bowl, 14", low flat	50.00	
	Cake stand	55.00	
	Candlestick, 5¼"	40.00	
	Candlestick, double, 2 styles, #555	50.00	50.00
	Candy dish, flat, clover	85.00	
	Candy dish, flat, square	85.00	
1	Candy dish w/lid, "heart"	110.00	250.00
4	Candy w/lid, 10¼", small, ftd., #444	65.00	125.00
5	Candy w/lid, 11", large, ftd.	75.00	
3	Cheese dish and cover, #555	85.00	265.00
	Cocktail shaker, w/glass stopper	135.00	

		Crystal	Blue
	Creamer	20.00	
	Mayonnaise liner	15.00	225.00
	Mayonnaise, bead handles	25.00	
	Plate, 10¾"	40.00	
	Plate, 12½", bead handles	45.00	85.00
	Plate, 13", fan handles	50.00	
2	Plate, 16", beaded edge, #555		90.00
6	Relish, 9¾", three part, #555	30.00	65.00
	Server, 10", swan handle	50.00	
5	Server, 11", center handle, #555	40.00	85.00
	Sugar	20.00	
	Tumbler, ftd. juice	22.00	
	Vase, 10¼"	95.00	350.00*
	Vase, 12"	95.00	450.00

*Black or yellow

Color: crystal with Silver Mist ribbing

	Item	Price
	Ash tray, individual	20.00
	Ash tray, square	15.00
	Bowl, 5" fruit	15.00
9	Bowl, 5" hdld. round or square	18.00
	Bowl, 5" hdld. triangular	16.00
	Bowl, 10" hdld.	35.00
	Bowl, 12", salad	40.00
	Bowl, 13" rolled edge	40.00
	Bowl, custard or frozen dessert	15.00
	Butter w/lid, ¼ lb.	40.00
	Candelabra. 2-light w/prisms	95.00
4	Candlestick, 3"	20.00
	Candlestick, 5½"	32.50
	Candlestick, duo	55.00
	Candy w/lid	65.00
5	Celery, 10", hdld.	32.50
	Cigarette & cover	60.00
	Comport, 5" w. x 4" h.	32.50
1	Cream soup	20.00
	Creamer, ftd.	15.00
	Creamer, ind., ftd.	15.00
	Cup	10.00
	Decanter, rectangular	100.00
2	Ice bucket	65.00
	Jelly w/cover, 7¼"	50.00
	Mayonnaise, 3-pc. Set	50.00
	Mustard w/cover and ladle	40.00
	Oil bottle w/stopper, 3 oz.	50.00
	Onion soup w/cover	50.00
8	Pickle, 6"	20.00
	Pitcher, 2-quart	75.00
	Plate, 6"	7.00
7	Plate, 6½", hndl.	55.00
	Plate, 7½"	10.00
	Plate, 8½"	10.00

	Item	Price
	Plate, 9½"	20.00
	Plate 11", torte	35.00
	Plate 12", sandwich	35.00
	Plate, 15", torte	42.50
	Plate, 16"	42.50
	Relish, 6½", 3-part	27.50
	Relish, 8", 4-part	35.00
	Relish, 10", 2-part	25.00
	Salt dip	18.00
	Saucer	3.00
	Shaker, pr.	37.50
	Stem, 3½", 5½ oz., sherbet	11.00
	Stem, 3¼", 3½", fruit cocktail	12.00
	Stem, 4&/8", 4½ oz., claret	15.00
	Stem, 5¾", 9 oz. water	17.50
	Sugar, ftd.	15.00
	Sugar, ind., ftd.	15.00
	Sweetmeat, 6", divided	25.00
	Tray, 6½" for cr/sug.	22.50
	Tray, 7", oval hdld.	27.50
	Tray, 8½", condiment	60.00
	Tray, 10", square	55.00
	Tray, 10½", oblong	50.00
	Tumbler, 2¼", 2 oz. whiskey	10.00
	Tumbler, 3½", 5 oz., juice	12.00
	Tumbler, 3½", 6 oz., old fashioned	12.00
	Tumbler, 3", 4 oz., ftd. cocktail	12.50
	Tumbler, 4⅛", 9 oz., water	10.00
6	Tumbler, 4¾", 9 oz., ftd. water	12.50
	Tumbler, 4⅝", 5 oz., ftd. juice	15.00
	Tumbler, 5¼", 13 oz. ftd. ice tea	15.00
	Tumbler, 5⅛", 13 oz. ice tea	15.00
	Vase, 3½, rose bowl	33.00
	Vase, 5", rose bowl	40.00

Colors: crystal, yellow, Peach-Blo, green, Emerald green (light and dark), amber, blue, Heatherbloom, Ebony with white gold

Cambridge's wonderful Gloria pattern is consistently confused with Tiffin's Flanders. Look closely at these and notice that the flower on Gloria bends the stem. Both are renderings of poppies, a flower identified with WWI and European poppy fields.

Notice the seven colors of ice buckets pictured compliments of a collector who made the effort to show them to you. The blue and Ebony with white gold ones are rare. Gloria can be gathered in large sets of yellow or crystal; any other color will exasperate you. Yellow Gloria is more obtainable than is crystal, so if you like that color, buy it when you can. A luncheon set in blue or Peach-Blo (pink) is found occasionally, but larger sets seem impossible to assemble. For some inexplicable reason, I have always been drawn to the dark Emerald green, but I have only owned a dozen or so pieces in that color as it is rarely found; no ice bucket has yet appeared in that though I keep expecting one.

Gold encrusted items bring 20% to 25% more than those without gold. However, pieces with worn gold are not easy to sell at present. That may possibly change with all the touting of the "shabby" look. Who knows? Shabby-chic glass may soon be the thing.

Gloria might make an ideal candidate for blending of colors, since there are so many from which to choose.

As with other Cambridge patterns in this book, not all Gloria pieces are listed. A more complete listing of Cambridge etched pieces is found under Rose Point. Prices for crystal Gloria will run 30% to 40% less than the prices listed for Rose Point, an exceedingly popular Cambridge pattern.

	Crystal	Green Pink Yellow
Basket, 6", 2 hdld. (sides up)	35.00	60.00
Bowl, 3", indiv. nut, 4 ftd.	65.00	85.00
Bowl, 3½", cranberry	40.00	75.00
Bowl, 5", ftd., crimped edge, bonbon	30.00	50.00
Bowl, 5", sq., fruit, "saucer"	22.00	38.00
Bowl, 5½", bonbon, 2 hdld.	25.00	40.00
Bowl, 5½", bonbon, ftd.	25.00	35.00
Bowl, 5½", flattened, ftd., bonbon	25.00	35.00
Bowl, 5½", fruit, "saucer"	22.00	35.00
Bowl, 6", rnd., cereal	35.00	55.00
Bowl, 6", sq., cereal	35.00	55.00
Bowl, 8", 2 pt., 2 hdld., relish	35.00	45.00
Bowl, 8", 3 pt., 3 hdld., relish	38.00	50.00
Bowl, 8¾", 2 hdld., figure, "8" pickle	30.00	50.00
Bowl, 8¾", 2 pt., 2 hdld., figure "8" relish	30.00	50.00
Bowl, 9", salad, tab hdld.	50.00	100.00
Bowl, 9½", 2 hdld., veg.	75.00	125.00
Bowl, 10", oblong, tab hdld., "baker"	65.00	110.00
Bowl, 10", 2 hdld.	55.00	90.00
Bowl, 11", 2 hdld., fruit	65.00	110.00
14 Bowl, 11", ped. ft., #3400/3	70.00	115.00
Bowl, 12", 4 ftd., console	65.00	110.00
Bowl, 12", 4 ftd., flared rim	65.00	110.00
Bowl, 12", 4 ftd., oval	85.00	150.00
Bowl, 12", 5 pt., celery & relish	60.00	90.00
Bowl, 13", flared rim	70.00	115.00
Bowl, cream soup, w/rnd. liner	55.00	85.00
Bowl, cream soup, w/sq. liner	55.00	85.00
Bowl, finger, flared edge, w/rnd. plate	35.00	65.00
Bowl, finger, ftd.	35.00	60.00
Bowl, finger, w/rnd. plate	40.00	65.00
Butter, w/cover, 2 hdld.	225.00	450.00
8 Candlestick, 6", ea., keyhole	45.00	75.00
17 Candlelabra, 3 lite, keyhole, #638	45.00	75.00

	Crystal	Green Pink Yellow
Candy box, w/cover, 4 ftd., w/tab hdld.	145.00	225.00
Cheese compote w/11½" cracker plate, tab hdld.	60.00	95.00
Cocktail shaker, grnd. stopper, spout (like pitcher)	150.00	250.00
Comport, 4", fruit cocktail	18.00	33.00
Comport, 5", 4 ftd.	25.00	75.00
Comport, 6", 4 ftd.	30.00	80.00
Comport, 7", low	40.00	100.00
Comport, 7", tall	45.00	125.00
Comport, 9½", tall, 2 hdld., ftd. bowl	80.00	195.00
22 Creamer, 6 oz., ftd., #3400/16	20.00	30.00
Creamer, tall, ftd.	20.00	35.00
11 Cup, rnd. or sq.	20.00	35.00
Cup, 4 ftd., sq.	50.00	100.00
Cup, after dinner (demitasse), rnd. or sq.	80.00	125.00
10 Fruit cocktail, 6 oz., ftd. (3 styles), #3135 shown	15.00	25.00
1 Ice pail, metal handle w/tongs, #3400/851	90.00	195.00
Icer, w/insert	65.00	110.00
Mayonnaise, w/liner & ladle (4 ftd. bowl)	45.00	95.00
Oil, w/stopper, tall, ftd., hdld.	110.00	250.00
Oyster cocktail, #3035, 4½ oz.	20.00	30.00
Oyster cocktail, 4½ oz., low stem	20.00	30.00
Pitcher, 67 oz., middle indent	225.00	395.00
Pitcher, 80 oz., ball	295.00	495.00

		Crystal	Green Pink Yellow
	Pitcher, w/cover, 64 oz.	295.00	695.00
	Plate, 6", 2 hdld.	15.00	20.00
6	Plate, 6", bread/butter	12.00	15.00
	Plate, 7½", tea, #3400/60	14.00	18.00
	Plate, 8½", salad, #3400/62	16.00	25.00
2	Plate, 9½", dinner	65.00	100.00
	Plate, 10", tab hdld., salad	45.00	65.00
	Plate, 11", 2 hdld.	50.00	70.00
	Plate, 11", sq., ftd. cake	110.00	265.00
	Plate, 11½", tab hdld., sandwich	60.00	80.00
	Plate, 14", chop or salad	65.00	100.00
	Plate, sq., bread/butter	12.00	15.00
	Plate, sq., dinner	65.00	100.00
	Plate, sq., salad	14.00	20.00
	Plate, sq., service	50.00	90.00
	Platter, 11½"	75.00	150.00
	Salt & pepper, pr., short	45.00	125.00
	Salt & pepper, pr., w/glass top, tall	70.00	150.00
	Salt & pepper, ftd., metal tops	60.00	150.00
	Saucer, rnd.	4.00	6.00
	Saucer, rnd. after dinner	12.00	20.00
	Saucer, sq., after dinner (demitasse)	15.00	25.00
	Saucer, sq.	4.00	6.00

		Crystal	Green Pink Yellow
	Stem, #3035, 2½ oz., wine	30.00	60.00
	Stem, #3035, 3 oz., cocktail	20.00	35.00
5	Stem, #3035, 3½ oz., cocktail, #1066 shown	20.00	35.00
	Stem, #3035, 4½ oz., claret	45.00	85.00
7	Stem, #3035, 6 oz., low sherbet, 17 oz., #1066	18.00	26.00
	Stem, #3035, 6 oz., tall sherbet	22.00	30.00
	Stem, #3035, 9 oz., water	28.00	55.00
	Stem, #3035, 3½ oz., cocktail	20.00	35.00
	Stem, #3115, 9 oz., goblet	28.00	55.00
	Stem, #3120, 1 oz., cordial	70.00	175.00
	Stem, #3120, 4½ oz., claret	45.00	85.00
	Stem, #3120, 6 oz., low sherbet	18.00	26.00
	Stem, #3120, 6 oz., tall sherbet	20.00	30.00
	Stem, #3120, 9 oz., water	28.00	50.00
	Stem, #3130, 1 oz., cordial	70.00	145.00
	Stem, #3130, 2½ oz., wine	30.00	62.50
	Stem, #3130, 6 oz., low sherbet	18.00	26.00
20	Stem, #3130, 6 oz., tall sherbet	20.00	30.00
18	Stem, #3130, 8 oz., water	28.00	55.00
	Stem, #3135, 6 oz., low sherbet	18.00	26.00
	Stem, #3135, 6 oz., tall sherbet	20.00	30.00
	Stem, #3135, 8 oz., water	28.00	55.00
21	Sugar, ftd., #3400/16	20.00	30.00
	Sugar, tall, ftd.	25.00	35.00

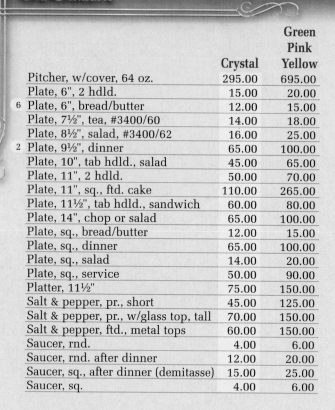

		Crystal	Green Pink Yellow
	Sugar shaker, w/glass top	195.00	395.00
	Syrup, tall, ftd.	95.00	195.00
	Tray, 11", ctr. hdld., sandwich	35.00	75.00
	Tray, 2 pt., ctr. hdld., relish	30.00	50.00
	Tray, 4 pt., ctr. hdld., relish	35.00	65.00
	Tray, 9", pickle, tab hdld.	35.00	70.00
12	Tumbler, #3035, 5 oz., high ftd.	20.00	32.00
	Tumbler, #3035, 10 oz., high ftd.	22.00	42.50
15	Tumbler, #3035, 12 oz., high ftd.	30.00	55.00
	Tumbler, #3115, 5 oz., ftd., juice	22.00	38.00
	Tumbler, #3115, 8 oz., ftd.	22.00	40.00
13	Tumbler, #3115, 10 oz., ftd., #1066 shown	25.00	45.00
	Tumbler, #3115, 12 oz., ftd.	30.00	50.00
9	Tumbler, #3120, 2½ oz., ftd. (used w/cocktail shaker), flat, #1070, 2 oz. shown	30.00	65.00
	Tumbler, #3120, 5 oz., ftd.	22.00	38.00
	Tumbler, #3120, 10 oz., ftd.	25.00	42.00
	Tumbler, #3120, 12 oz., ftd.	30.00	50.00
	Tumbler, #3130, 5 oz., ftd.	22.00	38.00
19	Tumbler, #3130, 10 oz., ftd.	30.00	50.00
16	Tumbler, #3130, 12 oz., ftd.	30.00	50.00
	Tumbler, #3135, 5 oz., juice	22.00	40.00
	Tumbler, #3135, 10 oz., water	25.00	45.00
3	Tumbler, #3135, 12 oz., tea	32.00	55.00

		Crystal	Green Pink Yellow
	Tumbler, 12 oz., flat (2 styles), one indent side to match 67 oz. pitcher	25.00	45.00
23	Tumbler, #3120, 2 oz., whiskey, #3400/92	30.00	65.00
4	Vase, 6", #1308	50.00	85.00
	Vase, 9", oval, 4 indent	115.00	235.00
	Vase, 10", keyhole base	95.00	165.00
	Vase, 10", squarish top	150.00	295.00
	Vase, 11"	125.00	210.00
	Vase, 11", neck indent	145.00	225.00
	Vase, 12", keyhole base, flared rim	165.00	275.00
	Vase, 12", squarish top	195.00	325.00
	Vase, 14", keyhole base, flared rim	175.00	275.00

Note: See pages 252 – 253 for stem identification.

Colors: crystal, Spanish red, Ritz blue, Stiegel green, 14K Topaz, Anna Rose, Old Amethyst, India Black, Venetian (shamrock) green, Azure blue, Aquamarine, Peach, Caramel, Meadow green, Copen blue, Smoke, Light amethyst, Mission gold, Milk

Morgantown's Golf Ball line is the most recognized and assembled design of this company. It is often misidentified as Cambridge's #1066, which is similar to Golf Ball at first glance; Cambridge's #1066 has cut, indented "dimples" at intervals around the stem. I bought a Ritz blue (cobalt) 6" torch candle as well as the 4" Jacobi candle at an outside antique show in Ohio. Both were labeled "hard to find" Cambridge and priced as Cambridge, not Morgantown. Morgantown's Golf Ball has crosshatched bumps symmetrically overlaid all over the ball of the stem.

The Spanish red item between the two Jacobi candles in the top row of page 115 was a damaged candlestick that someone "cut down" to make it usable. I found it intriguing.

As a rule, all pieces of Golf Ball are hard to find except for stems, most vases, and candles. Prices for stems have lowered from previous levels due both to quantities found and saturation of collections with stems. The Dupont (inverted two tiers) candle is not easily found. You should note the Irish coffee (row 2 #5 page 115). It became a creamer when a spout was added. Some square-footed stems can be found.

The Harlequin pastel colors, often marketed in sets of eight, include Amethyst, Copen blue, Gloria blue, Peach, Smoke, Topaz Mist, Shamrock green, and iridized yellow. Other Harlequin sets include Coral and Pink Champagne colors.

Row 3 on page 115 shows ivy balls with and without a rim. They are 4" in diameter but stand a little less than 6" without rim and a little over 7" with rim. The one with the ruffled top is the most difficult to find and few of them have been seen.

To be consistent in terminology for collectors, my listings have used name designations found in *Gallagher's Handbook of Old Morgantown Glass* that unfortunately is no longer in print.

	Steigel Green / Spanish Red / *Ritz Blue	Other colors
Amherst water lamp, super rare	1,000.00+	
Bell	125.00	60.00
Candle, pr., 4⅝", Dupont (inverted 2 tier)	250.00	150.00
14 Candle, 6" torch	175.00	100.00
3 Candlestick, 4" Jacobi (top flat rim)	150.00	100.00
Candy, flat w/golf ball knob cover, 6"x 5½" (Alexandra)	1,000.00	750.00
Creamer	175.00	
Compote, 10" diam., 7½" high, w/14 crimp rim (Truman)	475.00	375.00
Compote w/cover, 6" diam. (Celeste)	750.00	550.00
2 Compote, 6" diam. (Celeste)	450.00	300.00
9 Irish coffee, 5¼", 6 oz.	175.00	125.00
Pilsner, 9⅛", 11 oz.	165.00	110.00
Schooner, 8½", 32 oz.	295.00	195.00
Stem, brandy snifter, 6½", 21 oz.	155.00	125.00
15 Stem, cafe parfait, 6¼", 4 oz.	100.00	55.00
8 Stem, champagne, 5", 5½ oz.	32.00	22.00
10 Stem, champagne, "Old English"	33.00	23.00
Stem, claret, 5¼", 4½ oz.	65.00	38.00
Stem, cocktail, 4⅛",	22.00	18.00

	Steigel Green / Spanish Red / *Ritz Blue	Other colors
5 Stem, cordial, 3½", 1½ oz.	45.00	30.00
Stem, oyster cocktail, 4⅜", 4½ oz.	50.00	28.00
Stem, oyster cocktail, 4¼", 4 oz., flared	40.00	25.00
Stem, sherbet/sundae, 4⅛", 3½ oz.	22.00	16.00
Stem, sherry, 4⅝", 2½ oz.	50.00	30.00
6 Stem, water, 6¾", 9 oz.	38.00	25.00
7 Stem, water, 10 oz., "Old English"	35.00	22.00
Stem, wine, 4¾", 3 oz.	38.00	25.00
Sugar, no handles, cone	175.00	
Tumbler, 4⅜", ftd., wine	35.00	20.00
18 Tumbler, 5", 5 oz., ftd., juice	30.00	18.00
4 Tumbler, 6⅛", 9 oz., ftd., water	33.00	20.00
16 Tumbler, 6¾", 12 oz., ftd., tea	38.00	28.00
17 Urn, 6½" high.	125.00	65.00
12 Vase, 4", Ivy ball, ruffled top	300.00	150.00
11 Vase, 4", Ivy ball w/rim (Kimball)	70.00	50.00
13 Vase, 4", Ivy ball, no rim (Kennon)	70.00	45.00
Vase, 8" high, Charlotte w/crimped rim	275.00	175.00
1 Vase, 8" high, flair rim flute (Charlotte)	265.00	175.00
Vase, 10½", #78 Lancaster (cupped w/tiny stand up rim)	425.00	250.00
Vase, 11", #79 Montague (flair rim)	450.00	300.00

*Add 10% for Ritz Blue.

Colors: crystal; Flamingo pink punch bowl and cups only

Greek Key is an older Heisey pattern that is loved and easily recognized by collectors. Other companies made similar patterns but most Heisey pieces are marked. Stemware in all sizes is troublesome to find and the prices indicate that reality.

1

	Crystal
Bowl, finger	40.00
Bowl, jelly, w/cover, 2 hdld., ftd	145.00
26 Bowl, indiv., ftd., almond	45.00
11 Bowl, 4", nappy	25.00
Bowl, 4", shallow, low ft., jelly	40.00
Bowl, 4½", nappy	25.00
Bowl, 4½", scalloped, nappy	25.00
Bowl, 4½", shallow, low ft., jelly	40.00
Bowl, 5", ftd., almond	40.00
Bowl, 5", ftd., almond, w/cover	110.00
7 Bowl, 5", hdld., jelly	95.00
Bowl, 5", low ft., jelly, w/cover	110.00
Bowl, 5", nappy	30.00
Bowl, 5½", nappy	40.00
Bowl, 5½", shallow nappy, ftd.	65.00
Bowl, 6", nappy	30.00
Bowl, 6", shallow nappy	30.00
Bowl, 6½", nappy	35.00
Bowl, 7", low ft., straight side	90.00
Bowl, 7", nappy	80.00
Bowl, 8", low ft., straight side	70.00
Bowl, 8", nappy	70.00
Bowl, 8", scalloped nappy	65.00
Bowl, 8", shallow, low ft.	75.00
Bowl, 8½", shallow nappy	75.00
Bowl, 9", flat, banana split	45.00
10 Bowl, 9", ftd., banana split	40.00
Bowl, 9", low ft., straight side	65.00
9 Bowl, 9", nappy	70.00
Bowl, 9", shallow, low ft.	70.00
Bowl, 9½", shallow nappy	70.00
Bowl, 10", shallow, low ft.	85.00
Bowl, 11", shallow nappy	70.00
Bowl, 12", orange bowl	500.00
Bowl, 12", punch, ftd., Flamingo	750.00
Bowl, 12", orange, flared rim	450.00
Bowl, 14½", orange, flared rim	500.00
Bowl, 15", punch, ftd.	400.00
Bowl, 18", punch, shallow	400.00
Butter, indiv. (plate)	35.00
Butter/jelly, 2 hdld., w/cover	200.00
6 Candy, w/cover, ½ lb.	140.00
Candy, w/cover, 1 lb.	170.00
Candy, w/cover, 2 lb.	210.00
Cheese & cracker set, 10"	150.00
Compote, 5"	90.00
Compote, 5", w/cover	130.00
Creamer	50.00
Creamer, oval, hotel	55.00
Creamer, rnd., hotel	50.00
12 Cup, 4½ oz., punch	20.00
Cup, punch, Flamingo	40.00

	Crystal
Coaster	20.00
Egg cup, 5 oz.	80.00
Hair receiver	170.00
Ice tub, lg., tab hdld.	150.00
Ice tub, sm., tab hdld.	130.00
1 Ice tub, w/cover, hotel	235.00
Ice tub, w/cover, 5", individual, w/5" plate	200.00
27 Jar, 1 qt., crushed fruit, w/cover	400.00
3 Jar, 2 qt., crushed fruit, w/cover	450.00
Jar, lg. cover, horseradish	140.00
4 Jar, sm. cover, horseradish	130.00
Jar, tall celery	140.00
Jar, w/knob cover, pickle	160.00
Pitcher, 1 pint (jug)	130.00
13 Pitcher, 1 quart (jug)	210.00
15 Pitcher, 3 pint (jug)	250.00
Pitcher, ½ gal. (tankard)	240.00
Oil bottle, 2 oz., squat, w/#8 stopper	90.00
Oil bottle, 2 oz., w/#6 stopper	100.00
24 Oil bottle, 4 oz., squat, w/#8 stopper	90.00
20 Oil bottle, 4 oz., w/#6 stopper	80.00
21 Oil bottle, 6 oz., w/#6 stopper	80.00
Oil bottle, 6 oz., squat, w/#8 stopper	80.00
Plate, 4½"	20.00
Plate, 5"	25.00
Plate, 5½"	25.00
Plate, 6"	35.00
Plate, 6½"	35.00
Plate, 7"	50.00
Plate, 8"	70.00
Plate, 9"	90.00
Plate, 10"	110.00
Plate, 16", orange bowl liner	180.00
Puff box, #1, w/cover	175.00
Puff box, #3, w/cover	175.00
Salt & pepper, pr.	125.00
2 Sherbet, 4½ oz., ftd., straight rim	25.00
8 Sherbet, 4½ oz., ftd., flared rim	25.00
Sherbet, 4½ oz., high ft., shallow	25.00
Sherbet, 4½ oz., ftd., shallow	25.00
Sherbet, 4½ oz., ftd., cupped rim	25.00
Sherbet, 6 oz., low ft.	30.00
Spooner, lg.	110.00
Spooner, 4½" (or straw jar)	110.00
Stem, ¾ oz., cordial	225.00
Stem, 2 oz., wine	100.00
Stem, 2 oz., sherry	200.00
Stem, 3 oz., cocktail	50.00

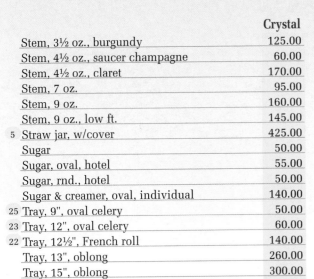

		Crystal
	Stem, 3½ oz., burgundy	125.00
	Stem, 4½ oz., saucer champagne	60.00
	Stem, 4½ oz., claret	170.00
	Stem, 7 oz.	95.00
	Stem, 9 oz.	160.00
	Stem, 9 oz., low ft.	145.00
5	Straw jar, w/cover	425.00
	Sugar	50.00
	Sugar, oval, hotel	55.00
	Sugar, rnd., hotel	50.00
	Sugar & creamer, oval, individual	140.00
25	Tray, 9", oval celery	50.00
23	Tray, 12", oval celery	60.00
22	Tray, 12½", French roll	140.00
	Tray, 13", oblong	260.00
	Tray, 15", oblong	300.00
	Tumbler, 2½ oz. (or toothpick)	600.00
	Tumbler, 5 oz., flared rim	50.00
	Tumbler, 5 oz., straight side	50.00
	Tumbler, 5½ oz., water	50.00

		Crystal
19	Tumbler, 7 oz., flared rim	60.00
18	Tumbler, 7 oz., straight side	60.00
	Tumbler, 8 oz., w/straight, flared, cupped, shallow	60.00
17	Tumbler, 10 oz., flared rim	90.00
16	Tumbler, 10 oz., straight wide	90.00
	Tumbler, 12 oz., flared rim	100.00
	Tumbler, 12 oz., straight side	100.00
	Tumbler, 13 oz., straight side	100.00
	Tumbler, 13 oz., flared rim	100.00
14	Water bottle	220.00

Colors: amber, amethyst, green, pink, crystal, crystal with black, gold, and green trim

Central's No. 401 etch was given the name "Harding" when President and Mrs. Harding selected a set of this "Dragon" design consisting of over 300 pieces; it was etched with gold. Thereafter, Central advertised it as glass "for America's first families." There are few pieces available today, but well worth your search. We have bought all the "Harding" pictured here over the last seven years if that is an indication of scarcity. You must remember, though, we are discussing 80 year old glassware which nobody dreamed would be worth anything 80 years down the pike. They used it, broke it, or gave it away and bought something more modern. It was "cheap glass" then. The prevailing attitude then was that china had worth, but the glass dishes did not.

		*All colors
	Bowl, 12", console, octagon	85.00
	Bowl, finger, #800	35.00
	Bowl, soup, flat	65.00
	Bowl, soup, 2 hdld. cream	45.00
	Candlestick, octagon collar	55.00
	Candlestick, rnd. collar	50.00
	Candy, ftd. cone w/etched lid	110.00
5	Cheese & cracker (plate shown)	35.00
2	Comport, 4½", short stem	35.00
	Comport, 6", short stem	35.00
	Comport, 6", 10 oz., tall stem	50.00
6	Creamer, ftd.	40.00
	Cup, handled custard	22.00
	Decanter, qt. w/cut stop	325.00
	Ice tub, 2 hdld.	425.00
1	Jug, tall, flat bottom	395.00
	Oil & vinegar bottle	195.00
	Plate, 5" sherbet	12.00
	Plate, 6" finger bowl liner	15.00
3	Plate, dinner	75.00

		*All colors
	Plate, lunch	25.00
4	Server, center handle	65.00
	Shaker, ftd. indiv.	85.00
	Stem style, indiv., almond	25.00
	Stem, 5½ oz. sherbet	20.00
	Stem, 6 oz., saucer champagne, #780	25.00
	Stem, 9 oz., water, #780	30.00
	Stem, cordial	75.00
	Stem, oyster cocktail	20.00
	Stem, wine	30.00
	Sugar, ftd.	40.00
	Tumbler, 5 oz	22.00
	Tumbler, 8 oz.	25.00
	Tumbler, 10 oz., #530	30.00
	Tumbler, 12 oz.	30.00
	Tumbler, ftd., hdld., tea	50.00
	Vase, 8"	175.00
	Vase, 10", ruffled top	225.00

* 25% less for crystal

Colors: Amber, Azure (blue), crystal, Ebony, green, Topaz, Wisteria

Hermitage presently has only a small number of devotees; however, a few collectors are beginning to single out the Wisteria. Other Fostoria patterns found in Wisteria are being priced out of sight. Hermitage prices are reasonable right now, so if you like Wisteria this is the time to start buying it. If you put it out to sell in a mall in Florida, tie it down, as it seems to walk away otherwise.

Listings are from a Fostoria catalog that had January 1, 1933, entered on the front page in pencil. Pictured are six different colored ice buckets again compliments of a collector making the effort to get these shown. Enjoy!

10   10   10

		Crystal	Amber/Green/Topaz	Azure	Wisteria
	Ashtray holder, #2449	5.00	8.00	12.00	
	*Ashtray, #2449	3.00	5.00	8.00	
6	Bottle, 3 oz., oil, #2449	20.00	40.00		
	Bottle, 27 oz., bar w/stopper, #2449	45.00			
18	Bowl, 4½", finger, #2449½	4.00	6.00	10.00	22.50
	Bowl, 5", fruit, #2449½	5.00	8.00	15.00	
	Bowl, 6", cereal, #2449½	6.00	10.00	20.00	
	Bowl, 6½", salad, #2449½	6.00	9.00	20.00	
17	Bowl, 7", soup, #2449½	8.00	12.00	22.00	45.00
	Bowl, 7½", salad, #2449½	8.00	12.00	30.00	
19	Bowl, 8", deep, ped., ft., #2449	17.50	35.00	60.00	
14	Bowl, 10", ftd., #2449	20.00	35.00		125.00
	Bowl, grapefruit, w/crystal liner, #2449	20.00	40.00		
20	Candle, 6", #2449	12.50	22.00	35.00	
	Coaster, 5⅝", #2449	5.00	7.50	11.00	
7	Comport, 6", #2449	12.00	17.50	27.50	40.00
	Creamer, ftd., #2449	4.00	6.00	10.00	30.00
	Cup, ftd., #2449	6.00	10.00	15.00	22.00
21	Decanter, 28 oz., w/stopper, #2449	40.00	100.00	165.00	
8	Fruit cocktail, 2⅜", 5 oz., ftd., #2449	5.00	7.50	12.00	
10	Ice tub, 6", #2449	17.50	60.00	85.00	225.00
12	Icer, #2449	10.00	18.00	30.00	50.00
13	Icer, insert	10.00	20.00	25.00	35.00
	Mayonnaise, 5⅝" w/7" plate, #2449	20.00	35.00		
4	Mug, 9 oz., ftd., #2449	15.00			

1   2   3   4   1

5   6   7   8   9

10

HERMITAGE

	Crystal	Amber/Green/Topaz	Azure	Wisteria
Mug, 12 oz., ftd., #2449	17.50			
Mustard w/cover & spoon, #2449	17.50	35.00		
Pitcher, pint, #2449	22.50	40.00	60.00	
1 Pitcher, 3 pint, #2449	75.00	100.00	150.00	595.00
Plate, 6", #2449½	3.00	5.00	8.00	
Plate, 7", ice dish liner	4.00	6.00	10.00	20.00
Plate, 7", #2449½	4.00	6.00	10.00	
Plate, 7⅜", crescent salad, #2449	10.00	17.50	35.00	70.00
Plate, 8", #2449½	6.00	10.00	15.00	25.00
Plate, 9", #2449½	12.50	20.00	30.00	
Plate, 12", sandwich, #2449		12.50	20.00	
Relish, 6", 2 pt., #2449	6.00	10.00	15.00	25.00
16 Relish, 7¼", 3 pt., #2449	8.00	11.00	17.50	50.00
Relish, 8", pickle, #2449	8.00	11.00	17.50	
Relish, 11", celery, #2449	10.00	15.00	25.00	50.00
9 Salt & pepper, 3⅜", #2449	25.00	50.00	75.00	100.00
Salt, indiv., #2449	4.00	6.00	10.00	
Saucer, #2449	2.00	3.50	5.00	8.00
Sherbet, 3", 7 oz., low, ftd., #2449	6.00	8.00	12.50	15.00
Stem, 3¼", 5½ oz., high sherbet, #2449	8.00	11.00	17.50	20.00
Stem, 4⅝", 4 oz., claret, #2449	10.00	15.00		
Stem, 5¼", 9 oz., water goblet, #2449	10.00	15.00	25.00	30.00
5 Sugar, ftd., #2449	4.00	6.00	10.00	30.00
Tray, 6½", condiment, #2449	6.00	12.00	20.00	30.00
2 Tumbler, 2½", 2 oz., #2449½	8.00	10.00	20.00	40.00
Tumbler, 2½", 2 oz., ftd., #2449	5.00	10.00		
11 Tumbler, 3", 4 oz., cocktail, ftd., #2449	5.00	7.50	14.00	25.00
15 Tumbler, 3¼", 6 oz. old-fashion, #2449½	6.00	10.00	18.00	30.00
Tumbler, 3⅞", 5 oz., #2449½	5.00	8.00	12.00	25.00
Tumbler, 4", 5 oz., ftd., #2449	5.00	8.00	12.00	25.00
Tumbler, 4⅛", 9 oz., ftd., #2449	6.00	10.00	15.00	30.00
Tumbler, 4¾", 9 oz., #2449½	6.00	10.00	15.00	32.50
22 Tumbler, 5¼", 12 oz., ftd., iced tea, #2449	10.00	16.00	28.00	
Tumbler, 5⅞", 13 oz., #2449½	10.00	16.00	28.00	40.00
3 Vase, 6", ftd.	22.00	30.00		

* Ebony – $15.00

Colors: amber, black, crystal, Emerald green, Peach Blo, Willow blue

Imperial Hunt Scene photographs favorably when the design is gold encrusted. Gold decoration adds 10% to 20% to the price listed. Be cautious of worn gold; it is not as appealing for collectors.

The Internet has distorted prices on this pattern. Today a piece will fetch a tidy sum and tomorrow the same item will receive no bids. That makes for interesting buying and selling.

Collectors seem to seek glassware that depicts animals, but particularly horses. On Imperial Hunt Scene, you get the bonus of a fox. Cups, saucers, creamers, sugars, and shakers have always been scarce, but currently more collectors are searching for them. Sets can be put together in pink (Peach Blo) and perhaps Emerald green.

Has anyone found a pink creamer to match the sugar and lid I have been picturing? None of Cambridge's catalogs show either a sugar or creamer with this etching, but I'd be highly surprised if they made a sugar without a creamer. Stems are plentiful in most sizes other than cordials and clarets. That is, plentiful in comparison to serving pieces rather than plentiful in comparison to other patterns. I did not say inexpensive! You will find bi-colored Hunt Scene stemware. Pink bowl with a green stem or foot is the typical form — and the choice of most collectors.

Ebony and Emerald green (dark) with gold decorations sell 25% to 50% higher than prices listed if you should stumble upon any.

		Crystal	Colors
	Bowl, 6", cereal	20.00	40.00
	Bowl, 8"	40.00	95.00
	Bowl, 8½", 3 pt.	45.00	100.00
	Candlestick, 2-lite, keyhole	35.00	75.00
21	Candle 3-lite, keyhole, #638	45.00	100.00
	Comport, 5½", #3085		60.00
	Creamer, flat	15.00	60.00
	Creamer, ftd.	20.00	75.00
12	Cup, #933/481	50.00	65.00
	Decanter		295.00
16	Finger bowl, w/plate, #3085		85.00
	Humidor, tobacco		595.00
2	Ice bucket, #851 scallop edge	100.00	210.00
3	Ice bucket, #2978 plain edge	95.00	200.00
	Ice tub	65.00	165.00

* with gold overlay add 00%
** with bi color add 00%

		Crystal	Colors
	Mayonnaise, w/liner	40.00	95.00
	Pitcher, w/cover, 63 oz., #3085		495.00
	Pitcher, w/cover, 76 oz., #711	195.00	395.00
	Plate, 6", #668	20.00	22.50
14	Plate, 7", #554	20.00	22.50
	Plate, 8", #556	20.00	22.50
4	Plate, 8½", #559	20.00	22.50
1	Plate, 9½", #810	20.00	22.50
	Plate, 10½", #244	20.00	22.50
7	Salt & pepper, pr., #396	100.00	295.00
12	Saucer, #1481	10.00	15.00
	Stem, 1 oz., cordial, #1402	100.00	
	Stem, 2½ oz., wine, #1402	65.00	
	Stem, 3 oz., cocktail, #1402	50.00	
	Stem, 6 oz., tomato, #1402	45.00	
	Stem, 6½ oz., sherbet, #1402	40.00	
	Stem, 7½ oz., sherbet, #1402	45.00	
	Stem, 10 oz., water, #1402	50.00	
	Stem, 14 oz., #1402	55.00	
	Stem, 18 oz., #1402	65.00	
13	Stem, 1 oz., cordial, #3075		175.00
20	Stem, 2½ oz., cocktail, #3075		50.00
9	**Stem, 2½ oz., wine, #3085		55.00
8	Stem, 4½ oz., claret, #3075		67.50
	Stem, 5½ oz., parfait, #3085		75.00
	Stem, 6 oz., low sherbet, #3085		22.50
5	Stem, 6 oz., high sherbet, #3075		35.00
19	Stem, 9 oz., water, #3085		60.00
6	Sugar, flat w/ lid, #842	50.00	150.00
	Sugar, ftd.	20.00	80.00
15	Tumbler, 2½ oz., 2⅞", flat, #1402	25.00	
17	Tumbler, 5 oz., flat, #3085	20.00	
	Tumbler, 7 oz., flat, #1402	20.00	
22	Tumbler, 10 oz., flat, #3075, cupped rim	23.00	
	Tumbler, 10 oz., flat, tall, #1402	25.00	
	Tumbler, 15 oz., flat, #1402	35.00	
	Tumbler, 2½ oz., ftd., #3085		65.00
10	Tumbler, 5 oz., 3⅞", ftd., #3085 (cone w/flare rim)		50.00
	Tumbler, 8 oz., ftd., #3085		50.00
18	Tumbler, 10 oz., ftd., #3075 (cone w/cupped rim)		55.00
11	Tumbler, 12 oz., 5⅜", ftd., #3075		55.00

Colors: crystal, Flamingo pink, Sahara yellow, Moongleam green, cobalt, and Alexandrite

I cannot emphasize enough that if you find any colored piece of Ipswich, other than those listed, it was made at Imperial and not Heisey. It may possibly be marked Heisey, but it was created at Imperial from purchased Heisey moulds and, as such, is pretty much disregarded at this point by true Heisey collectors. Mostly, I get letters on (Alexandrite) candy jars that are actually Imperial's Heather (purple) color. Imperial is now out of business; their wares are collectible; but, so far, not the Heisey patterns they made in their own colors. That, of course, could change.

Moongleam is preferred by collectors of Ipswich, and there are collectors who would love a pitcher in that color.

		Crystal	Flamingo	Sahara	Moongleam	Cobalt	Alexandrite
1	Bowl, finger, w/underplate	40.00	90.00	80.00	120.00		
	Bowl, 11", ftd., floral	80.00		300.00	500.00	450.00	
	Candlestick, 6", 1-lite	150.00	275.00	200.00	300.00	400.00	
5	Candlestick centerpiece, ftd., vase, "A"						
	prisms, complete w/inserts	160.00	300.00	350.00	450.00	550.00	
9	Candy jar, ¼ lb., w/cover	175.00			450.00		
	Candy jar, ½ lb., w/cover	175.00	325.00	400.00	500.00		
	Cocktail shaker, 1 quart, strainer, #86 stopper	225.00	600.00	700.00	800.00		
4	Creamer	35.00	70.00	90.00	125.00		
8	Stem, 4 oz., oyster cocktail, ftd.	25.00	60.00	50.00	70.00		
10	Stem, 5 oz., saucer champagne (knob in stem)	25.00	60.00	50.00	70.00		
	Stem, 10 oz., goblet (knob in stem)	35.00	85.00	70.00	90.00		750.00
	Stem, 12 oz., schoppen, flat bottom	100.00					
11	Pitcher, ½ gal.	350.00	600.00	550.00	850.00		
	Oil bottle, 2 oz., ftd., #86 stopper	125.00	285.00	275.00	300.00		
	Plate, 7", sq.	30.00	60.00	50.00	70.00		
7	Plate, 8", sq.	35.00	65.00	55.00	75.00		
3	Sherbet, 4 oz., ftd. (knob in stem)	15.00	35.00	30.00	45.00		
2	Sugar	35.00	70.00	90.00	125.00		
	Tumbler, 5 oz., ftd. (soda)	30.00	45.00	40.00	85.00		
	Tumbler, 8 oz., ftd. (soda)	30.00	45.00	40.00	90.00		
	Tumbler, 10 oz., cupped rim, flat bottom	70.00	110.00	100.00	140.00		
	Tumbler, 10 oz., straight rim, flat bottom	70.00	110.00	100.00	140.00		
6	Tumbler, 12 oz., ftd. (soda)	40.00	80.00	70.00	95.00		

Colors: crystal, Cobalt, Ruby, Light Blue, Emerald, Amethyst

There are many collectors seeking Janice. I reported that Dalzell Viking had recently made both candlesticks pictured on the ends of the top row on page 125. These were made in crystal, cobalt blue, and red that I can confirm. Dalzell Viking has now gone out of business, but they made a bunch of Janice candles. The light blue was not made to my knowledge, but be wary of paying high prices for other colors. The only significant difference is that the newer ones are slightly heavier and not as fire polished as the old. The reissued ones have an oily feel, as does much of the newly made glass.

Ice buckets are rare in Janice, but you couldn't prove it from our photo. The uncommon one is the glass handled one that looks like a basket rather than a bucket. I have been guaranteed it is listed as an ice bucket in the catalogs of New Martinsville; but I haven't seen that information yet. In any case, the handle remaining intact all these years is a marvel.

There is a separate line of swan handled items with the Janice pattern that are not listed, but do note the covered candy on page 126 that I found fascinating.

1

	Item	Crystal	Blue Red
27	Basket, 6½", 9" high, 4 toe	75.00	155.00
18	Basket, 11", #4552	75.00	225.00
	Basket, 12", oval, 10" high	85.00	265.00
14	Bonbon, 5½", 2 hdld., 4½" high	18.00	30.00
13	Bonbon, 6", 2 hdld., 4" high	20.00	33.00
	Bonbon, 7", 2 hdld., 4¾" high	25.00	40.00
	Bowl, 5½", flower, w/eight crimps	22.00	35.00
	Bowl, 6", 2 hdld., crimped	20.00	33.00
	Bowl, 9½", cupped	35.00	65.00
	Bowl, 9½", flared	35.00	65.00
	Bowl, 9", 2 hdld., #4591	37.50	75.00
	Bowl, 10"	37.50	75.00
	Bowl, 10½", cupped, 3 toed, #4512	45.00	75.00
	Bowl, 10½", flared, 3 toed, #4511	45.00	85.00
	Bowl, 11", oval	40.00	95.00
	Bowl, 11", cupped, ftd.	45.00	85.00
	Bowl, 11", flared	40.00	65.00
8	Bowl, 12", flared, #4513	42.50	90.00
	Bowl, 12", fruit, ruffled top	50.00	110.00
	Bowl, 12", oval, #4551	42.50	70.00
	Bowl, 12", salad, scalloped top	50.00	85.00
	Bowl, 12", six crimps, 3½"t, #4515	52.50	125.00
	Bowl, 13", flared	50.00	100.00
	Canape set: tray w/ftd. juice	30.00	
5	Candelbra, 5", 2-lt., 5" wide, #4536	40.00	
2	Candlestick, 5½", 1-lt., 5" wide, #4554	35.00	50.00
	Candlestick, 6", 1-lt., 4½" wide, "flame"	37.50	60.00
	Candy box w/cover, 5½", #4541-SJ Swan	65.00	155.00
	Celery, 11", oblong, #4521	20.00	45.00
	Comport, cracker for cheese plate	14.00	25.00
	Condiment set: tray and 2 cov. jars	55.00	125.00
24	Creamer, 6 oz.	12.00	20.00
	Creamer, individual, flat, 6 oz., #4532	12.00	22.00
11	Creamer, individual, ftd.	12.50	25.00
20	Creamer, tall, #4549	15.00	45.00
6	Cup, #4580	8.00	23.00
	Guest set: bottle w/tumbler	95.00	
20	Ice pail, 10", hdld., #4589	295.00	595.00
19	Ice tub, 6", ftd., #4584	115.00	275.00

	Item	Crystal	Blue Red
1	Jam jar w/cover, 6", #4577	20.00	45.00
	Mayonnaise liner, 7", 2 hdld.	9.00	14.00
	Mayonnaise plate, 6"	7.50	12.50
	Mayonnaise, 6", 2 hdld.	18.00	30.00
9	Mayonnaise, round, #4522	15.00	27.50
4	Oil, 5 oz., w/stopper, #4583	40.00	100.00
12	Pitcher, 15 oz., berry cream, #4576	50.00	165.00
15	Plate, 7", 2 hdld., #4520	9.00	14.00
3	Plate, 8½", salad, #4579	10.00	17.50
26	Plate, 11", cheese, swan hdl., #4528-25J	22.50	40.00
	Plate, 11", ftd., rolled edge	27.50	50.00
	Plate, 12", 2 hdld.	30.00	55.00
	Plate, 13"	30.00	60.00
16	Plate, 13", 2 hdld., #4529	32.50	65.00
	Plate, 14", ftd., rolled edge	40.00	85.00
	Plate, 15"		40.00
	Plate, 15", rolled edge torte		50.00
	Platter, 13", oval, #4588	35.00	90.00
	Relish, 6", 2 part, 2 hdld.	15.00	37.50
	Salt and pepper, pr.	40.00	85.00
6	Saucer, #4580	2.00	4.50
22	Sherbet, #4582, low ft.	12.00	26.00
	Stem, cordial	100.00	
25	Sugar, 6 oz.	12.00	20.00
	Sugar, individual, flat, #4532	10.00	22.00
7	Sugar, individual, ftd., #4586	12.50	25.00
21	Sugar, tall, #4549	15.00	45.00
	Syrup, w/dripcut top	85.00	
10	Tray, oval, 2 hdld., ind. sug/cr	12.00	20.00
23	Tray, oval, 2 hdld., cr/sug	15.00	25.00
17	Tumbler, #4551/23 luncheon	14.00	30.00
	Vase, 4", ivy, 3½" high, #4575	22.00	50.00
	Vase, 4", ivy, 4½" high, w/base peg, #4575	25.00	60.00
	Vase, 7", ftd.	35.00	75.00
	Vase, 8", ball, 7½" high, #4565	45.00	115.00
	Vase, 8", cupped, 3 toed	50.00	135.00
	Vase, 8", flared, 3 toed, #4527	50.00	135.00
	Vase, 9", ball	55.00	135.00

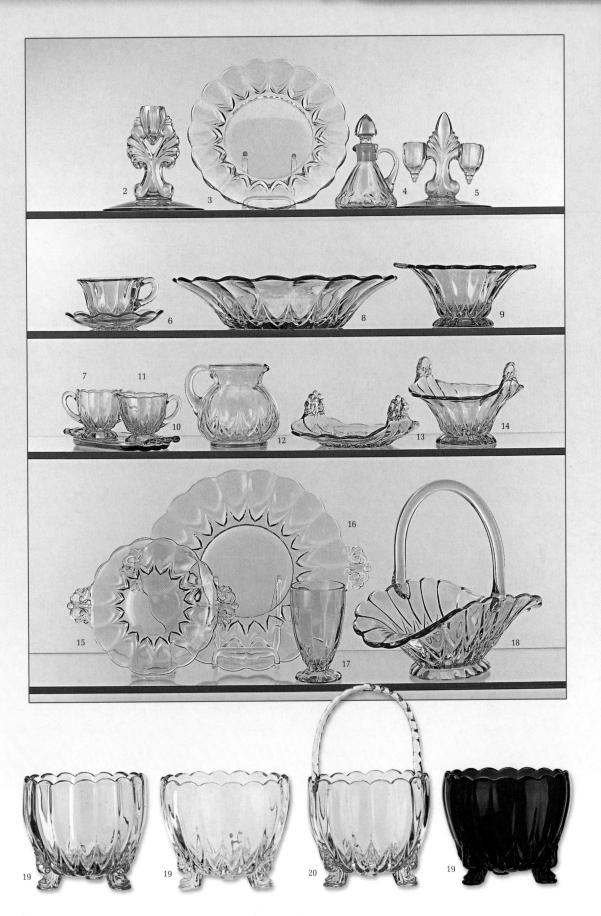

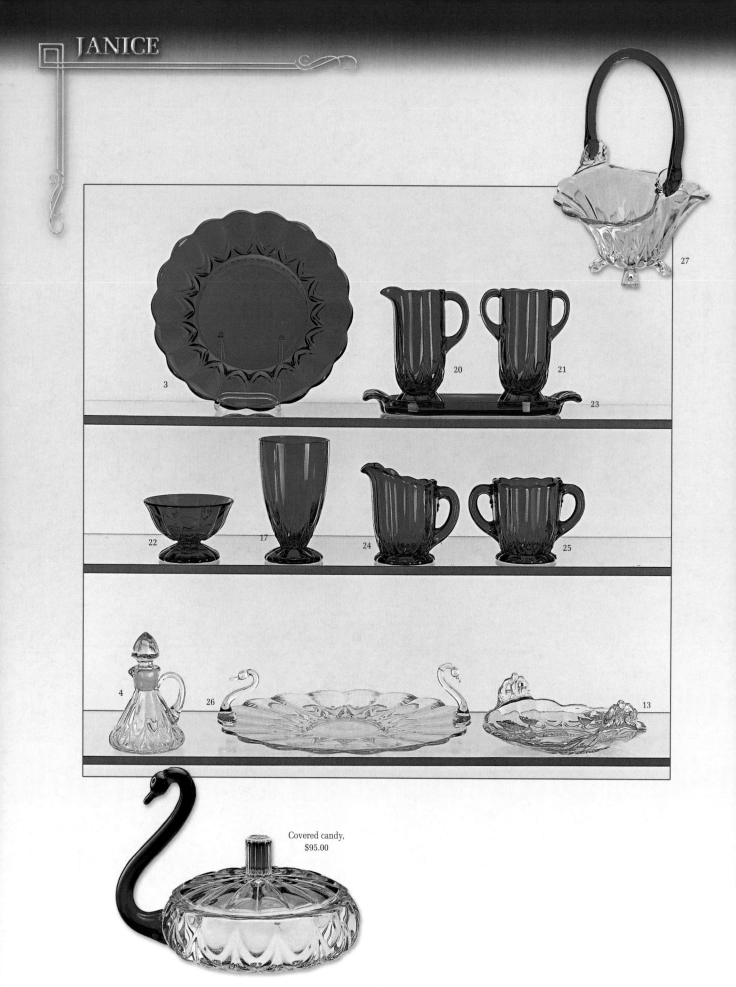

3

20 21

23

27

22 17 24 25

4 26 13

Covered candy,
$95.00

Color: crystal w/amber trim, wide optic

Julia is a Tiffin pattern that is presently being sought. A long-time collector told us that it was only manufactured for about five years. Notice that the plates are totally amber while stems and other pieces are crystal with amber stems, feet, or handles. Unfortunately, the pattern does not show as well on those amber flat pieces. When flat, the design practically vanishes. However, it really zings against the crystal. Amber seems to be the only color in which Julia was made.

It was the trend in the late twenties and early thirties to make bi-colored glass. This is an excellent example of that tradition. You can probably gather this pattern without immediate rivalry, but I would not count on that lasting too long. Few Tiffin patterns can be collected in amber; so, if you like Tiffin's color and design, as a growing number of collectors do, this would be an ideal pattern to seek. There is a growing group of collectors whose focus is bi-colored glass.

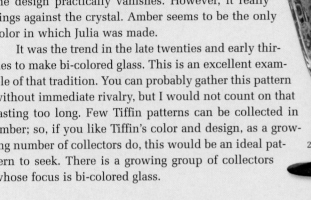

	Amber
Bowl, finger	25.00
Candy jar and cover, ftd., #9557	135.00
9 Creamer, #6	35.00
Jug and cover, ftd., #194	350.00
1 Plate, 8", luncheon, #8833	20.00
12 Plate, dessert, #8814	12.00
13 Plate, dinner, #8818	14.00
4 Stem, cafe parfait, #15011	35.00
Stem, claret, #15011	40.00
Stem, cocktail, #15011	22.00

	Amber
5 Stem, cordial, #15011	65.00
7 Stem, saucer champagne, #15011	20.00
6 Stem, sundae, #15011	16.00
2 Stem, water, #15011	33.00
3 Stem, wine, #15011	38.00
Sugar, #6	35.00
10 Tumbler, ftd., seltzer, #14185	22.00
8 Tumbler, ftd., table, #14185	25.00
11 Tumbler, ftd., tea, #14185	30.00

JUNE, Etch #279, Fostoria Glass Company, 1928 – 1944

Colors: crystal, Azure blue, Topaz yellow, Rose pink

June is the most sought Fostoria etched pattern. Azure and Rose have continued to rise in price, albeit slowly. Prices for crystal and Topaz have remained stable, but a few more collectors have a penchant for crystal of late. If you have been putting off buying crystal or yellow, better start filling your cabinet before the prices catch blue and pink.

Shakers came with both glass and metal tops. Collectors prefer the glass ones first used. In later years, only metal tops were made and all replacement tops were metal; so if you are seeking tops for shakers, you will have to settle for metal.

If you will refer to Versailles (page 236), I have listed all the Fostoria line numbers for each piece. Since these are fundamentally the same listings as June, you can use the ware number listings from Versailles should you need them. Be sure to see the stemware illustrations on page 99. You would not want to pay for a 6" claret and receive a 6" high sherbet simply because you didn't realize they were shaped differently.

		Crystal	Rose Blue	Topaz
	Ashtray	25.00	55.00	40.00
	Bottle, salad dressing,			
	#2083 or #2375	300.00	995.00	495.00
	Bowl, baker, 9", oval	50.00	150.00	90.00
	Bowl, baker, 10", oval	40.00	135.00	75.00
	Bowl, bonbon	12.50	30.00	23.00
25	Bowl, bouillon, ftd., #2375	18.00	50.00	27.00
26	Bowl, finger, w/liner	35.00	75.00	50.00
	Bowl, mint, 3 ftd., 4½"	15.00	45.00	30.00
	Bowl, 6", nappy, 3 ftd., jelly	15.00	45.00	25.00
	Bowl, 6½", cereal	25.00	95.00	45.00
	Bowl, 7", soup	65.00	210.00	165.00
	Bowl, lg., dessert, hdld.	35.00	150.00	95.00
	Bowl, 10"	35.00	150.00	85.00
	Bowl, 10", Grecian	50.00	175.00	95.00
	Bowl, 11", centerpiece	35.00	110.00	75.00
9	Bowl, 12", centerpiece, three types, #2394 shown	55.00	125.00	75.00

		Crystal	Rose Blue	Topaz
	Bowl, 13", oval centerpiece, w/flower frog	90.00	275.00	150.00
15	Candlestick, 2", #2394	14.00	30.00	20.00
	Candlestick, 3", #2394	20.00	45.00	26.00
21	Candlestick, 3", Grecian "Scroll"	20.00	60.00	30.00
	Candlestick, 5", Grecian "Scroll"	30.00	75.00	40.00
22	Candy, w/cover, 3 pt.		350.00	
	Candy, w/cover, ½ lb., ¼ lb.			210.00
17	Celery, 11½"	35.00	110.00	65.00
19	Cheese & cracker set, #2368 or #2375	50.00	135.00	95.00
6	Comport, 5", #2400	30.00	75.00	50.00
	Comport, 6", #5298 or #5299	30.00	95.00	55.00
	Comport, 7", #2375	35.00	125.00	70.00
	Comport, 8", #2400	50.00	165.00	80.00
	Cream soup, ftd.	25.00	60.00	35.00
14	Creamer, ftd., #2375½	15.00	28.00	18.00

		Crystal	Rose Blue	Topaz
	Creamer, tea	30.00	70.00	40.00
	Cup, after dinner	25.00	100.00	50.00
13	Cup, ftd. #2375½	15.00	33.00	25.00
	Decanter	425.00	2,000.00	695.00
	Goblet, claret, 6", 4 oz.	50.00	165.00	90.00
5	Goblet, cocktail, 5¼", 3 oz.	24.00	48.00	35.00
	Goblet, cordial, 4", ¾ oz.	60.00	155.00	80.00
18	Goblet, water, 8¼", 10 oz., #5298	35.00	80.00	50.00
	Goblet, wine, 5½", 3 oz.	25.00	110.00	50.00
8	Grapefruit	40.00	110.00	70.00
11	Grapefruit liner	35.00	90.00	45.00
1	Ice bucket	75.00	155.00	90.00
	Ice dish	35.00	75.00	45.00
	Ice dish liner (tomato, crab, fruit)	8.00	22.00	12.00
12	Mayonnaise, w/liner	30.00	90.00	55.00
	Oil, ftd.	250.00	750.00	350.00
	Oyster cocktail, 5½ oz.	20.00	40.00	28.00
	Parfait, 5¼"	40.00	115.00	70.00
16	Pitcher, ftd., #5000	275.00	695.00	395.00
	Plate, canape	20.00	55.00	30.00
	Plate, lemon	16.00	30.00	25.00
	Plate, 6", bread/butter	7.00	15.00	9.00
	Plate, 6", finger bowl liner	4.50	15.00	10.00
	Plate, 7½", salad	10.00	18.00	13.00
	Plate, 7½, cream soup	7.00	18.00	12.00
3	Plate, 8¾", luncheon, #2375	6.00	25.00	18.00
4	Plate, 9½", sm. dinner	15.00	50.00	30.00
	Plate, 10", cake, hdld. (no indent)	35.00	75.00	45.00
	Plate, 10", cheese with indent, hdld.	35.00	75.00	45.00
	Plate, 10¼", dinner	40.00	125.00	75.00

		Crystal	Rose Blue	Topaz
	Plate, 10¼", grill	40.00	125.00	75.00
	Plate, 13", chop	25.00	90.00	65.00
	Plate, 14", torte		135.00	75.00
	Platter, 12", #2375	40.00	125.00	75.00
	Platter, 15"	75.00	250.00	125.00
20	Relish, 8½", 2 part	35.00		60.00
	Sauce boat	40.00	295.00	110.00
	Sauce boat liner	15.00	90.00	40.00
	Saucer, after dinner	6.00	20.00	10.00
13	Saucer, #2375	4.00	8.00	5.00
27	Shaker, ftd., pr., #2375	60.00	225.00	140.00
2	Sherbet, high, 6", 6 oz., #5298	20.00	40.00	25.00
10	Sherbet, low, 4¼", 6 oz., #5298	18.00	33.00	22.00
24	Sugar, ftd., straight or scalloped top	15.00	30.00	22.00
24	Sugar cover	55.00	250.00	135.00
	Sugar pail	70.00	250.00	150.00
	Sugar, tea	25.00	70.00	40.00
	Sweetmeat	25.00	40.00	25.00
	Tray, service and lemon		350.00	300.00
	Tray, 11", ctr. hdld.	25.00	50.00	40.00
	Tumbler, 2½ oz., ftd.	20.00	100.00	65.00
	Tumbler, 5 oz., 4½", ftd.	15.00	50.00	30.00
7	Tumbler, 6 oz., 5¼", ftd., #5098	15.00	50.00	30.00
	Tumbler, 9 oz., 5¼", water	18.00	45.00	25.00
23	Tumbler, 12 oz., 6", ftd., tea	25.00	70.00	40.00
	Vase, 8", 2 styles	80.00	325.00	225.00
	Vase, 8½", fan, ftd.	90.00	300.00	195.00
	Whipped cream bowl	12.00	30.00	20.00
	Whipped cream pail	95.00	225.00	175.00

Note: See stemware identification on page 99.

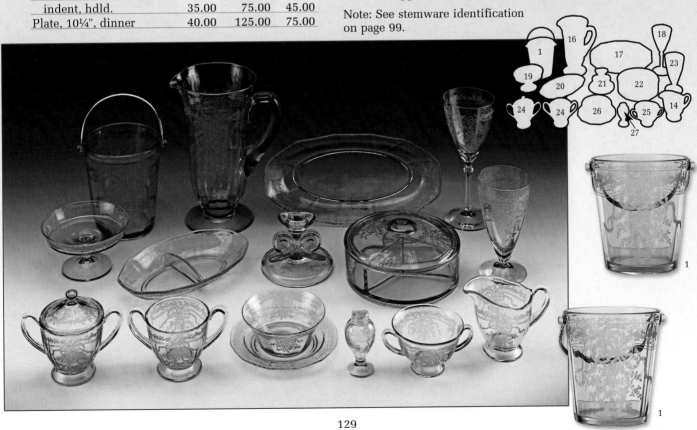

129

Color: crystal

June Night stemware is available. Evidently, Tiffin advertised this rival of Cambridge's Rose Point for consumers to use with their china. I see dozens of stems for every bowl or serving piece. June Night was etched on several stemware lines, but the one most often encountered is Tiffin's #17392 that is shown below. You will also find stem line #17378 (prism stem with pearl edge top), #17441 (quadrangle flowing to hexagonal cut), and #17471. That latter line has a bow tie stem, but I have never witnessed June Night on it. I need one for photography if you should see one. More of this pattern is being displayed at shows, but again mostly stems. I've noticed that comparable pieces in Cherokee Rose have caused identity confusion with many novices and part-time dealers. There is a *flower* encircled on June Night and an *urn* on Cherokee Rose. Shapes are important, but it is the design that makes the pattern. Since both of these patterns are on the same Tiffin mould blank, pay attention to which one it is before buying or selling it.

Shakers and the pitcher seem to be the most difficult components of a set to obtain. I have finally found a pitcher to show you along with the elusive shakers. The pitcher has the encircled flower below the ice lip even though the photographer chose to show the flowers on the side of it.

Gold-trimmed June Night stemware was christened Cherry Laurel by Tiffin. Name altering within same patterns is another glass company attention-grabber. Any different treatment done to a pattern often resulted in a separate name. In the case of gold trim, often they would just add "golden" to the pattern name. Remember that gold trim did not and still does not hold up well with frequent use. Never put gold-trimmed items in the dishwasher especially if you use any soap with lemon in it. Lemon will remove gold trim extremely well.

21	Bowl, 5", finger.	25.00
	Bowl, 6", fruit or nut	30.00
20	Bowl, 7", salad	35.00
	Bowl, 10", deep salad	70.00
	Bowl, 12", crimped	75.00
	Bowl, 12½" centerpiece, flared	75.00
4	Bowl, 13", centerpiece, #5902, cone	75.00
14	Candlestick, double branch, #5902	50.00
18	Candlestick, 9", 2-lite	55.00
22	Celery, 10½", oblong	40.00
12	Creamer	20.00
11	Mayonnaise, liner and ladle	45.00
1	Pitcher, #5859	595.00
6	Plate, 6", sherbet	8.00
	Plate, 8", luncheon	12.50
2	Plate, 13½", turned-up edge, lily, #5902	45.00
	Plate, 14", sandwich	45.00
24	Relish, 6½", 3 pt.	35.00
3	Relish, 12½", 3 pt., #5902	65.00

23	Shaker, pr., #2	225.00
15	Stem, 1 oz., cordial	40.00
9 10	Stem, 2 oz., sherry, 10 is Cherry Laurel	30.00
17	Stem, 3½ oz., cocktail	16.00
	Stem, 3½ oz., wine	25.00
	Stem, 4 oz., claret	33.00
	Stem, 4½ oz., parfait	38.00
7	Stem, 5½ oz., sherbet/champagne, #17441	16.00
8	Stem, 9 oz., water, #17441	25.00
13	Sugar	20.00
26	Table bell, #9742	85.00
16	Tumbler, 4½ oz., oyster cocktail	20.00
25	Tumbler, 5 oz., ftd., juice	16.00
	Tumbler, 8 oz., ftd., water	17.50
19	Tumbler, 10½ oz., ftd., ice tea	22.50
	Vase, 6", bud	25.00
5	Vase, 8", bud, #14185	35.00
	Vase, 10", bud	45.00

JUNGLE ASSORTMENT. Satin Decorated #14 Parrot.

Tiffin Glass Company, et.al., c. 1922 – 1934

Colors: green, pink and crystal satin; various flashed colors

Jungle Assortment is a Tiffin pattern that has charmed collectors over the last few years. There is a possibility that the shiny flashed items are from another company — possibly Lancaster. Cathy started a menagerie of pieces for display in Florida until she found enough to photograph for the book.

We have arranged the photos into assorted groups. The bottom of page 132 shows "Bird on a Bar," the top of page 133 is "Bird on a Branch," and the bottom of page 133 illustrates "Bird on a Perch."

I prefer the flashed colors to the satinized, but each treatment has evidence of problems keeping those hand-painted parrots from leaving wares. This is one pattern where you might like to pick up some slightly worn pieces until mint condition ones appear. You will not find these birds every day.

The basket, lamp, and candle in metal holder are recent additions. We have found three styles of candles. You will certainly find additional items not listed, so let me know what you discover and I will list them.

We found a night set pictured in a 1928 Sears catalog. They called the bird a cockatoo.

		All Colors
1	Basket, 6", #151	95.00
	Bonbon & cover, 5½" high ftd., #330	60.00
	Bonbon and cover, 5", low ftd., #330	60.00
	Bowl, centerpiece, #320	55.00
12	Candle, hdld., #330	40.00
22	Candle, hdld. tall, octagonal base	75.00
16	Candle, low, #10	30.00
5	Candy and cover, ftd., #15179	75.00
9	Candy box & cover, flat, 5½"	55.00
7	Candy box & cover, flat, 6", #329	65.00
15	Candy jar and cover, ftd., cone, #330	75.00
20	Candy jar and cover, ftd., #179	65.00
27	Candy jar and cover, ftd.	65.00
10	Cologne bottle, #5722	125.00
19	Decanter & stopper	135.00
26	Jug and cover, 2 quart, #127	210.00
24	Lamp	110.00
	Marmalade & cover, 2 hdld., #330	45.00
2	Night cap set, #6712	115.00
14	Puff box and cover, hexagonal, #6772	95.00
21	Puff box	45.00

		All Colors
8	Shaker, ftd., #6205	40.00
	Smoking set, 3 pc., #188	40.00
25	Tumbler, 12 oz., #444	32.00
3	Vase, 5½", ftd., rose bowl	75.00
6	Vase, 6", 2 hdld., #151	45.00
17	Vase, 6⅜", flat	45.00
13	Vase, 7" ftd., flair from base, #330	65.00
11	Vase, 7" ftd., flair rim, #151	65.00
4	Vase, 7" sweet pea, #151	80.00
18	Vase, 8", flat	65.00
	Vase, wall, #320	85.00
23	Vase in metal stand	75.00

Color: crystal

This pattern was produced in crystal; however, some pieces with ruby stain have surfaced which was an old technique used to get "color" on the glass. It is generally marked with the Heisey logo, consisting of an H enclosed in a diamond. Because of its pattern number (1776), it became extremely popular with collectors in 1976, during the bicentennial year and it has remained popular since that time.

	Bottle, hdld., molasses, 13 oz.	185.00
	Bottle, hdld., oil, 2 oz.	175.00
	Bottle, hdld., oil, 4 oz.	150.00
	Bottle, hdld., oil, 6 oz.	150.00
	Bottle, water	175.00
	Bowl, 4½", deep	30.00
	Bowl, 5", deep	35.00
8	Bowl, 5", flared	35.00
	Bowl, 5", hdld.	38.00
	Bowl, 5", crimped	35.00
	Bowl, 6", shallow	35.00
	Bowl, 7", deep, straight sided	45.00
	Bowl, 7", deep, flared	45.00
	Bowl, 8", flared	65.00
	Bowl, 9", shallow	65.00
9	Bowl, 10", shallow	70.00
	Bowl, 11", shallow	70.00
	Bowl, 12", punch and stand	275.00
	Butter and cover, domed	150.00
1	Cake plate, 9", ftd.	275.00
2	Celery, tall	90.00
	Celery tray, 12"	65.00
	Comport, deep ftd. jelly, 5"	110.00
	Comport, shallow ftd. jelly, 5½"	110.00
	Comport, deep or shallow, 8", ftd.	225.00
	Comport, deep or shallow, 9", ftd.	225.00
3	Comport, deep or shallow, 10", ftd.	300.00
	Creamer, tall	90.00

	Creamer, hotel	70.00
	Cup, punch, 3 oz.	26.00
	Cup, punch, 3½ oz.	26.00
	Mug, hdld., 8 oz.	175.00
	Mustard and cover	235.00
	Pickle jar and cover	195.00
	Pickle tray	65.00
5	Pitcher, ½ gallon	350.00
	Plate, 5½"	30.00
	Plate, 6"	35.00
	Plate, 8", fruit	55.00
	Shaker, salt & pepper, 3 styles, pr.	180.00
	Shaker, sugar	145.00
	Spoon tray	60.00
	Spooner, tall	65.00
	Stem, egg cup, 9½ oz.	75.00
6	Stem, goblet, 9 oz.	150.00
	Stem, champagne, 6½ oz.	65.00
	Stem, sherbet, 6 oz.	40.00
	Stem, sherbet, 5½ oz., straight sided or scalloped	40.00
	Stem, claret, 5 oz.	100.00
	Stem, sherbet, 4½ oz., scalloped	40.00
	Stem, sherbet, 3½ oz., scalloped	40.00
4	Stem, burgundy, 3 oz.	100.00
11	Stem, wine, 2 oz.	110.00
10	Stem, cordial, 1¼ oz.	300.00
	Sugar and cover, tall	95.00
	Sugar, hotel (no cover)	70.00
7	Toothpick	425.00
	Tumbler, 8 oz.	95.00

Colors: Topaz yellow, Azure blue, some green

Kashmir was not as broadly dispersed as other Fostoria patterns, so accumulating it will probably take longer unless you fortunately live in one of those areas where it was retailed. Blue Kashmir would be the Fostoria pattern to collect if you like that Fostoria color. Other Azure Fostoria etched patterns have thousands of collectors searching for them; but few collectors pay attention to Kashmir. Of course, finding Azure Kashmir is a quandary.

I find more Kashmir in the Midwest than anywhere else; you can see from my pictures how well green Kashmir has been eluding me, and I have been looking for it. Supposedly, there are some 6", 7", and 8" plates to be had along with the two styles of cups and saucers, but I have never found any plates.

Unfortunately, what little Kashmir is offered for sale does not immediately disappear, as do some other Fostoria patterns. Demand always wins over scarcity. You could complete a set of yellow Kashmir more economically than any other etched, yellow Fostoria pattern.

The stemware and tumbler line is #5099, which is the same line on which Trojan is found. This is the cascading "waterfall" stem.

Both styles of after dinner cups are shown in the picture at the bottom of page 136. The square #2419 (Mayfair blank) saucer set is more difficult to find than the round; but I have only found that in green, though it was supposedly made in Azure and Topaz.

1

		Yellow Green	Blue
	Ashtray	25.00	30.00
13	Bowl, cream soup	25.00	33.00
	Bowl, finger	15.00	40.00
	Bowl, 5", fruit	13.00	25.00
12	Bowl, 6", cereal	30.00	40.00
	Bowl, 7", soup	35.00	95.00
27	Bowl, 2 hndl., sweetmeat	40.00	
	Bowl, 8½", pickle	20.00	30.00
	Bowl, 9", baker	37.50	85.00
11	Bowl, 10", 2 hdld.	40.00	65.00
9	Bowl, 12", centerpiece	40.00	50.00
	Candlestick, 2"	15.00	20.00
	Candlestick, 3"	20.00	28.00
14	Candlestick, 5", Grecian "Scroll"	22.50	33.00
	Candlestick, 9½"	40.00	75.00
25	Candy, w/cover, #2430	90.00	165.00
	Cheese and cracker set	65.00	85.00
	Comport, 6"	35.00	45.00
19	Creamer, ftd.	17.50	23.00
15	Cup, #2375½	15.00	20.00
24	Cup, #2350½	15.00	20.00
16	Cup, after dinner, flat, #2350	40.00	
28	Cup, after dinner, ftd., #2375	40.00	55.00
	Grapefruit	60.00	
	Grapefruit liner	50.00	
1	Ice bucket, #2375	95.00	125.00
10	Mayo & liner w/spoon	95.00	125.00
	Oil, ftd.	295.00	495.00
	Pitcher, ftd.	395.00	495.00
21	Plate, cream soup or mayo liner	8.00	10.00
	Plate, 6", bread & butter	5.00	6.00
23	Plate, 7", salad, rnd.	6.00	7.00
	Plate, 7", salad, sq.	6.00	7.00
2	Plate, 8", salad	8.00	10.00

		Yellow Green	Blue
4	Plate, 9", luncheon	9.00	15.00
3	Plate, 10", dinner	45.00	75.00
22	Plate, 10", grill	35.00	55.00
	Plate, cake, 10"	38.00	
	Salt & pepper, pr.	120.00	175.00
26	Sandwich, 11", center hdld., #2375	35.00	40.00
	Sauce boat, w/liner	125.00	165.00
15	Saucer, rnd., #2375	5.00	10.00
24	Saucer, sq., #2419	5.00	10.00
16	Saucer, after dinner, sq.	8.00	
28	Saucer, after dinner, rnd., #2375	8.00	15.00
	Stem, ¾ oz., cordial	85.00	125.00
	Stem, 2½ oz., ftd.	30.00	45.00
	Stem, 2 oz., ftd., whiskey	30.00	50.00
	Stem, 2½ oz., wine	32.00	60.00
	Stem, 3 oz., cocktail	22.00	25.00
17	Stem, 3½ oz., ftd., cocktail	22.00	25.00
	Stem, 4 oz., claret	40.00	65.00
	Stem, 4½ oz., oyster cocktail	16.00	18.00
8	Stem, 5 oz., low sherbet	13.00	20.00
6	Stem, 5½ oz., parfait	30.00	40.00
5	Stem, 6 oz., high sherbet, #5099	17.50	30.00
20	Stem, 9 oz., water, 8½", #5099	25.00	40.00
	Sugar, ftd.	15.00	20.00
	Sugar lid	50.00	85.00
18	Tumbler, 5 oz., 4½", ftd., juice	15.00	25.00
	Tumbler, 9 oz., 5⅜", ftd., water	18.00	30.00
	Tumbler, 10 oz., ftd., water	22.00	35.00
	Tumbler, 11 oz.	22.50	
7	Tumbler, 12 oz., ftd.	25.00	35.00
	Tumbler, 13 oz., ftd., tea	25.00	
	Tumbler, 16 oz., ftd., tea	35.00	
	Vase, 8"	125.00	195.00

Note: See stemware identification on page 99.

135

Colors: crystal, Topaz/Gold Tint (every piece of pattern); at least 12 pieces of Regal Blue, Empire Green, Burgundy; 6 pieces of Ruby & Silver Mist; some amber, green, Wisteria, and Rose

Crystal Lafayette is the mould line used for many of Fostoria's later etchings, with Navarre being the most renown. Colored pieces of Lafayette are collected for themselves. The favored color is Wisteria, but yellow can also be gathered into a large set. I finally found a Regal blue piece. You might blend some of the colors with crystal in order to achieve a larger set, but finding crystal without an etching may be a chore.

	Crystal/Amber	Rose/Green/Topaz	Wisteria	Regal Blue	Burgundy	Empire Green
Almond, indiv.	12.00	15.00	25.00			
Bonbon, 5", 2 hdld.	15.00	22.50	40.00	35.00	30.00	33.00
Bowl, 4½", sweetmeat	18.00	22.50	40.00	35.00	35.00	33.00
Bowl, cream soup	22.50	35.00	85.00			
Bowl, 5", fruit		22.50	35.00			
Bowl, 6", cereal	20.00	25.00	45.00			
Bowl, 6½", olive	18.00	25.00	50.00			
Bowl, 6½", 2-pt. relish	22.50	30.00	55.00	55.00	45.00	45.00
Ruby 50.00; Silver Mist 25.00						
Bowl, 6½", oval sauce	25.00	35.00	125.00	55.00	50.00	45.00
Ruby 65.00; Silver Mist 27.50						
Bowl, 7", "D" cupped	30.00	40.00	135.00			
Bowl, 7½", 3-pt. relish	25.00	35.00	110.00	55.00	45.00	45.00
Ruby 55.00; Silver Mist 30.00						
Bowl, 8", nappy	30.00	40.00	85.00			
Bowl, 8½", pickle	18.00	30.00	60.00			
Bowl, 10", oval baker	35.00		75.00	75.00		
Bowl, 10", "B," flair	35.00	45.00				
Bowl, 12", salad, flair	38.00	50.00	155.00			
Cake, 10½", oval, 2 hdld.	40.00	50.00		65.00	65.00	65.00
Celery, 11½"	30.00	32.00	135.00			
Creamer, 4½", ftd.	15.00	22.00	50.00	40.00	40.00	40.00
Cup	15.00	18.00	20.00	35.00	35.00	35.00
Cup, demi	17.50	45.00	75.00			
Tray, 5", 2-hdld., lemon	17.50	22.50	40.00	35.00	30.00	33.00
Tray, 8½", oval, 2-hdld.	22.50	30.00	135.00	55.00	45.00	45.00
Ruby 55.00; Silver Mist 25.00						
Mayonnaise, 6½", 2 pt.	24.00	30.00	155.00	55.00	55.00	55.00
Ruby 55.00; Silver Mist 30.00						
Plate, 6"	8.00	12.00	14.00			
Plate, 7¼"	8.00	12.00	20.00			
Plate, 8½"	10.00	15.00	22.50			
Plate, 9½"	22.50	27.50	50.00			
Plate, 10¼"	35.00	45.00	95.00			
Plate, 13", torte	40.00	50.00	125.00	115.00	95.00	110.00
Ruby 110.00; Silver Mist 40.00						
Platter, 12"	40.00	52.50	125.00			
Platter, 15"	50.00	65.00				
Saucer	4.00	6.00	5.00	8.00	8.00	6.00
Saucer, demi	8.00	15.00	20.00			
Sugar, 3⅝", ftd.	15.00	22.00	45.00	40.00	40.00	40.00
Vase, 7", rim ft., flair	45.00	60.00				

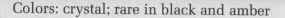
Colors: crystal; rare in black and amber

Lariat prices have remained rather steady except for stems, which have apparently saturated the market in recent years. Uncommon pieces sell well since there are many collectors looking for seldom-found items. Conversely, the horse head candy has softened in price since more have been found than there are collectors willing to pay the price. Common Lariat pieces are still available; you can determine scarce pieces by their prices in my listing.

The cutting most often seen on Lariat is Moonglo. Many non-Lariat collectors adore this cut; strangely, few Lariat collectors try to rope it. We have tried to entice you with the abundance of pieces shown. Enjoy! The ads that I have shown in the past are becoming collectible in their own right. Keep an eye out for them in women's magazines of the 1940s and 1950s.

Amber and black pieces of Lariat are rarely seen; note that in case you should find a piece or two in those colors in your travels.

		Crystal
	Ashtray, 4"	15.00
	Basket, 7½", bonbon	100.00
	Basket, 8½", ftd.	165.00
	Basket, 10", ftd.	195.00
	Bowl, 2 hdld., cream soup	50.00
	Bowl, 7 quart, punch	130.00
25	Bowl, 4", nut, individual	32.00
	Bowl, 7", 2 pt., mayonnaise	24.00
17	Bowl, 7", nappy	20.00
	Bowl, 8", flat, nougat	24.00
	Bowl, 9½", camellia	28.00
	Bowl, 10", hdld., celery	35.00
	Bowl, 10½", 2 hdld., salad	38.00
	Bowl, 10½", salad	40.00
	Bowl, 11", 2 hdld., oblong, relish	30.00
	Bowl, 12", floral or fruit	40.00
	Bowl, 13", celery	50.00
	Bowl, 13", gardenia	35.00
	Bowl, 13", oval, floral	35.00
	Candlestick, 1-lite, individual	28.00
8	Candlestick, 2-lite	35.00
22	Candlestick, 3-lite	40.00
	Candy box, w/cover, caramel	75.00
	Candy, w/cover, 7"	90.00
	Candy, w/cover, 8", w/horse head finial (rare)	1,400.00
	Cheese, 5", ftd., w/cover	50.00
	Cheese dish, w/cover, 8"	60.00
	Cigarette box	55.00
	Coaster, 4"	10.00
	Cologne	85.00
19	Compote, 10", w/cover	100.00
6	Creamer	18.00
	Creamer & sugar, w/tray, indiv.	45.00
11	Cup	20.00
	Cup, punch	8.00

		Crystal
23	Ice tub	75.00
	Jar, w/cover, 12", urn	175.00
12	Lamp & globe, 7", black-out	120.00
21	Lamp & globe, 8", candle, hdld.	95.00
	Mayonnaise, 5" bowl, 7" plate w/ladle set	60.00
24	Oil bottle, 2 oz., hdld., w/#133 stopper	120.00
18	Oil bottle, 4 oz., hdld., w/#133 stopper	180.00
26	Oil bottle, 6 oz., oval	85.00
	Plate, 6", finger bowl liner	8.00
2	Plate, 7", salad	14.00
4	Plate, 8", salad	22.00
3	Plate, 10½", dinner	125.00
	Plate, 11", cookie	35.00
	Plate, 12", demi-torte, rolled edge	40.00
	Plate, 13", deviled egg, round	290.00
	Plate, 14", 2 hdld., sandwich	50.00
	Plate, 15", deviled egg, oval	290.00
	Plate, 21", buffet	70.00
	Platter, 15", oval	60.00
16	Salt & pepper, pr.	200.00
11	Saucer	5.00
14	Stem, 1 oz., cordial, double loop	195.00
15	Stem, 1 oz., cordial blown, single loop	135.00
	Stem, 2½ oz., wine, blown	22.00
	Stem, 3½ oz., cocktail, pressed	18.00
	Stem, 3½ oz., cocktail, blown	18.00
	Stem, 3½ oz., wine, pressed	22.00
	Stem, 4 oz., claret, blown	25.00
13	Stem, 4¼ oz., oyster cocktail or fruit	15.00
	Stem, 4½ oz., oyster cocktail, blown	15.00
	Stem, 5½ oz., sherbet/saucer champagne, blown	12.00
	Stem, 6 oz., low sherbet	8.00
10	Stem, 6 oz., sherbet/saucer champagne, pressed	14.00
	Stem, 9 oz., pressed	20.00
9	Stem, 10 oz., blown	20.00
5	Sugar	18.00
	Tray, rnd., center hdld., w/ball finial	165.00
7	Tray for sugar & creamer, 8", 2 hdld.	24.00
	Tumbler, 5 oz., ftd., juice	22.00
	Tumbler, 5 oz., ftd., juice, blown	22.00
	Tumbler, 12 oz., ftd., ice tea	28.00
	Tumbler, 12 oz., ftd., ice tea, blown	28.00
20	Urn jar & cover, 12"	150.00
1	Vase, 7", ftd., fan	30.00
	Vase, swung	135.00

CORDIAL, YET CAREFREE ··· *that's Heisey* *Lariat*

Heisey
HAND-WROUGHT CRYSTAL

Lariat carries an air of matchless charm, expressed in its lighthearted loop design. Cordial, yet carefree, it will be esteemed by you as highly as any of your treasures. Rare as the western air, this hand-cast crystal gaily blends your own good taste with the trend that is today. Your Heisey dealer will be pleased to show you the complete selection of LARIAT stemware and table accessories.

Lariat is one of several patterns pictured in "CHOOSING YOUR CRYSTAL PATTERN," an informal, streamlined guide to proper crystal, china and silver. Send 10c to Department HB, A. H. HEISEY & CO., NEWARK, OHIO

THE FINEST IN GLASSWARE, MADE IN AMERICA BY HAND

Color: crystal

Duncan's Lily of the Valley is a pattern that even non-collectors appreciate. I first became aware of it from seeing a cordial when I began collecting them in the mid-1970s. I had to be told what it was, but bought it for my cordial collection without hesitation because of its wonderful patterned stem.

Canterbury #115 and Pall Mall #30 blanks were used for this cutting. The mayonnaise pictured is #30 and the bowl and plate are #115. I have not found a cup or saucer in this cut.

Stemware has the Lily of the Valley cut into the stem itself, but the bowls atop said stem are found with or without the cutting. The cutting on the bowl is the icing on the cake for me. Duncan's designation for this stem was D-4 and the cut variety was DC-4. Prices below are for cut (DC-4) bowl items; deduct about a third (or more) for plain bowl stems. Once you see this pattern, you will understand why collectors want the cut version.

One question I have been asked more often than any other is "Where can I find more of this beautiful pattern?" When we were unpacking some glassware at an antique mall, there was a cordial sitting in the glass case next to ours. It does appear sporadically; so keep a keen eye open.

8 Ashtray, 3"	25.00
Ashtray, 6"	35.00
11 Bowl, 12"	60.00
3 Candlestick, double, 5"	60.00
Candy, w/lid	95.00
10 Celery, 10½"	40.00
Cheese and cracker	75.00
Creamer	25.00
12 Mayonnaise	30.00
12 Mayonnaise ladle	8.00

12 Mayonnaise liner	15.00
1 Plate, 8"	30.00
Plate, 9"	45.00
Relish, 3-part	25.00
2 Stem, cocktail	25.00
7 Stem, cordial	80.00
9 Stem, high sherbet	25.00
4 Stem, water goblet	40.00
6 Stem, wine	40.00
Sugar	25.00
5 Tumbler, ftd. water	25.00

Colors: amber, black, crystal, green, pink

I have identified this New Martinsville "coat of arms style" etch as "Lions." I almost called it "Lions Rampant"; but not being a heraldry expert, I was not quite sure they were in the correct stance to be so categorized. I will be more than happy to convert to the original name if one can be determined.

I can already tell you, hunting "Lions" will be a test. Nearly all "Lions" etch is found on New Martinsville's Line #34 as pictured in color below. The only crystal items shown are on Line #37 known as "Moondrops" to collectors. I have not seen this etch on colored pieces of Line #37 or crystal pieces of Line #34, but it would not be startling if those materialize.

You can round up a luncheon set in color, but adding serving pieces may be another matter. I have found two styles of sugar bowls, but no creamer yet. I still need a lid to the pink candy dish we pictured in the last edition,

I am optimistic that additional pieces not in the list exist; so let me know what else you have seen.

	Amber Crystal	Pink Green	Black
4 Bowl, creme soup, ftd., 2 hndl., #34	20.00		
3 Candleholder, #37	25.00		
Candlestick, #34		35.00	
Candy w/lid		75.00	110.00
Center handle server		45.00	
Comport, cheese		25.00	35.00
Creamer, #34		25.00	35.00

	Amber Crystal	Pink Green	Black
Creamer, #37	15.00		
6 Cup, #34		25.00	35.00
2 Plate, 8"		20.00	30.00
Plate, 12", cracker		30.00	40.00
6 Saucer, #34		7.50	10.00
1 Sugar, #34		25.00	35.00
5 Sugar, #37	15.00		

Colors: crystal regular optic w/black and crystal wide optic w/green trim

The Internet has placed Luciana in the consciousness of collectors. The three dancing nymphs caught the eyes of several bidders on an Internet auction and the race was on to accumulate this marvelously decorated Tiffin pattern. I have bought two groupings recently. In Cincinnati, I found a set with black pieces from an estate sale, and in Florida, an antique dealer found a setting with green pieces. The green plates were well worn, so the original owners obviously enjoyed using it. The plates in the black set are frosted and cut into the plate. Surprisingly, they are not as pleasing to the eye as are the pieces with black with the crystal etched. The pattern disappears into the black rather than being revealed as on the crystal and green.

Prices have steadied for now, but with everyone aware of this pattern, how long that will last is the major question.

	Item	Price
	Bonbon, 5" high	75.00
	Candy w/cover #9557	145.00
	Creamer #6	75.00
	Decanter w/stopper #185	250.00
	Finger bowl, ftd. #002	35.00
	Finger bowl, ftd. #185	35.00
	Pitcher w/cover, 2 qt., ftd. #194	350.00
3	Plate, 6" #8833	15.00
	Plate, 7¼" #8814	20.00
4	Plate, 8" #8833	25.00
1	Plate, 10" #8833	90.00
	Stem, claret #016	85.00
	Stem, cocktail, 3 oz. #016	40.00
	Stem, oyster cocktail #043	25.00
	Stem, parfait #016	55.00
	Stem, parfait #043	40.00
	Stem, saucer champagne #016	30.00
7	Stem, sundae #016	22.50
8	Stem, sundae #043	25.00
10	Stem, water #043	55.00
	Stem, water, 11 oz. #016	70.00
	Stem, wine #043	35.00
9	Stem, wine, 2½ oz. #016	75.00
	Sugar #6	75.00
6	Tumbler, 5 oz., juice ftd. # 194	40.00
5	Tumbler, 9 oz., water ftd. # 194	35.00
2	Tumbler, 12 oz., ice tea, ftd. # 194	45.00
	Vase, 10½", bud #004	110.00

Colors: crystal, crystal with ruby or gold, cobalt

Although Mardi Gras was produced primarily in crystal, it may be found with gold trim or ruby flashing and there have been a few pieces surface in cobalt. The piece in cobalt that I have seen is a small tray, perhaps a pickle tray, which lies on a metal (chrome) base. There seems to be an abundance of this pattern available and one could gather a small collection relatively quickly.

Bottle, bitters		75.00
Bottle, molasses, hdld.		85.00
Bottle, oil, hdld.		40.00
Bottle, water	1	65.00
Bowl, berry, 4"		20.00
Bowl, shallow, 6"		24.00
Bowl, round, 8"	7	55.00
Bowl, fruit, 10"		75.00
Bowl, punch, 13½", and stand		165.00
Box, powder and cover		165.00
Butter and cover, domed	13	75.00
Butter and cover, individual		165.00
Cake plate, ftd.		110.00
Celery, tall		65.00
Cracker jar and cover, tall		145.00
Creamer, regular		35.00
Creamer, individual/child's	6 14	100.00
Cup, punch	9	10.00
Egg cup, ftd.		45.00
Jug, honey, individual		65.00
Mustard and cover	11	75.00
Oil bottle	3	65.00
Pitcher, straight sided	5	150.00
Pitcher, bulbous		175.00
Pitcher, syrup, individual		75.00
Plate, 3", butter	8	26.00
Plate, 5"		8.00

Plate, 6"		9.00
Plate, 7"		9.00
Plate, 8"		20.00
Salt & pepper		55.00
Salt, open, individual	15	12.00
Spooner, tall		65.00
Spooner, child's	12	50.00
Stem, goblet		45.00
Stem, claret		50.00
Stem, champagne/sherbet, 2 styles		22.00
Stem, cocktail		24.00
Stem, wine	2	28.00
Stem, sherry, straight sided and flared		35.00
Stem, cordial		60.00
Sugar and cover, regular	10	50.00
Sugar and cover, individual		150.00
Toothpick		45.00
Tumbler, water		24.00
Tumbler, juice		20.00
Tumbler, bar (2 oz.)		20.00
Vase, ball, individual, 1½"	4	165.00
Vase, ball, 4"		40.00
Vase, tall, footed, 10"		55.00

Colors: amethyst w/gold, crystal, Emerald green

Cambridge's early Marjorie pattern was renamed Fuchsia in the 1930s; do not confuse it with the Tiffin or Fostoria Fuchsia. The #7606 stems were advertised in the 1927 Sears catalog.

		Crystal
3	Bottle, oil & vinegar, 6 oz.	350.00
6	Candle, 3 lite, #1307	125.00
	Comport, #4011	90.00
	Comport, 5", #4004	70.00
	Comport, 5", jelly (sherbet), #2090	70.00
	Cream, flat, curved in side, #1917/10	100.00
10	Cream, flat, straight side, #1917/18	150.00
	Cup	50.00
	Decanter, 28 oz., cut stop, #17	500.00
	Decanter, 28 oz. #7606	400.00
	Finger bowl, #7606	40.00
	Grapefruit w/liner inside, #7606	85.00
	Jug, 30 oz., #104	265.00
	Jug w/cover, 30 oz., #106	325.00
	Jug, 3 pint, #93	255.00
	Jug, 3½ pint, #108 short, flair bottom	295.00
	Jug, 3½ pint, rim bottom, bulbous, #111	295.00
	Jug, 54 oz., flat bottom, #51	325.00
	Jug w/cover, 66 oz., #106	350.00
1	Jug, 4 pint, tall, flat bottom, #110	335.00
	Jug, guest room 38 oz. w/tumbler fitting inside, #103	450.00
	Marmalade & cover, #145	95.00
	Nappie, 4", #4111	30.00
	Nappie, 4" ftd., #5000	35.00
	Nappie, 8", #4111	90.00
	Nappie, 8" ftd., #5000	95.00
	Night bottle, 20 oz. w/tumbler, #4002	500.00
2	Oil w/hex cone cut stop, #32	400.00
4	Plate, 7¾", finger bowl liner or salad, #7606	15.00
	Plate, 7¼", finger bowl liner, #7606	15.00

		Crystal
	Saucer	30.00
	Stem, ⅞ oz., cordial, #7606	110.00
	Stem, 1 oz., cordial, #3750	110.00
	Stem, 2½ oz., wine, #7606	65.00
	Stem, 2 oz., creme de menthe, #7606	100.00
	Stem, 3 oz., cocktail, #7606	25.00
	Stem, 3 oz., wine, #3750	35.00
	Stem, 3½ oz., cocktail, #3750	25.00
	Stem, 4½ oz., claret, #3750	55.00
	Stem, 4½ oz., claret, #7606	55.00
	Stem, 5½ oz., cafe parfait, #7606	45.00
	Stem, 6 oz., low sherbet, #3750	15.00
	Stem, 6 oz., low fruit/sherbet, #7606	15.00
	Stem, 6 oz., high sherbet, #3750	18.00
	Stem, 6 oz., high sherbet, #7606	18.00
	Stem, 10 oz., water, #3750	25.00
	Stem, 10 oz., water, #7606	25.00
5	Sugar, flat, curved in side, #1917/10	100.00
11	Sugar, flat, straight side, #1917/18	150.00
	Syrup & cover, 8 oz., #106	300.00
	Tumbler, #8851	20.00
9	Tumbler, 1½ oz. whiskey, #7606	25.00
	Tumbler, 4 oz., 2⁷⁄₁₆"	20.00
	Tumbler, 5 oz., #8858	15.00
	Tumbler, 5 oz., #7606	15.00
	Tumbler, 5 oz. ftd., #3750	18.00
	Tumbler, 6 oz., 3⁷⁄₁₆"	20.00
7	Tumbler, 8 oz., #7606	20.00
	Tumbler, 9 oz., #8858	20.00
	Tumbler, 10 oz., ftd. & hdld., #7606	45.00
	Tumbler, 10 oz., hdld. & ftd., #8023	45.00
8	Tumbler, 10 oz., table, #7606	25.00
	Tumbler, 10 oz., ftd., #3750	25.00
	Tumbler, 12 oz., #8858	22.00
	Tumbler, 12 oz., ftd., #3750	25.00
	Tumbler, 12 oz., tea, #7606	22.00
	Tumbler, 12 oz., hdld., #8858	35.00

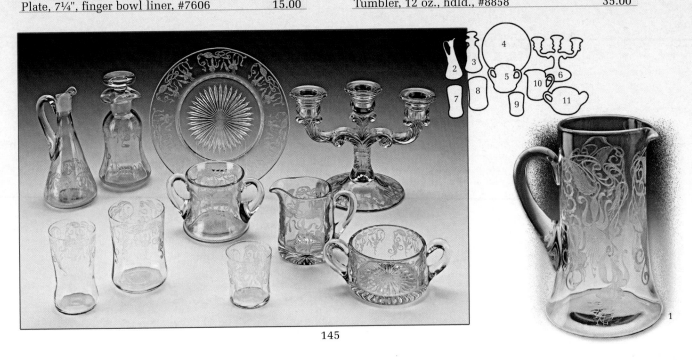

Colors: crystal and some blue

New Martinsville's Meadow Wreath is traditionally found etched on Radiance Line #42, but there are a few exceptions. Meadow Wreath etch sometimes aggravates plain Radiance collectors searching for light blue. I see more blue Meadow Wreath etched candles than I do Radiance ones without an etching. If a collector were willing to mix the etched Meadow Wreath with non-etched wares, a wider range of pieces would be possible.

There is a plethora of bowls and serving pieces available in Meadow Wreath, but essential luncheon items are lacking except for the ubiquitous sugars and creamers. I would recommend using these serving items to balance some of those patterns where serving items are almost imaginary. Blending color is already a trend, so blending patterns does not seem such a long stretch in this day of ever more expensive and hard to find glassware.

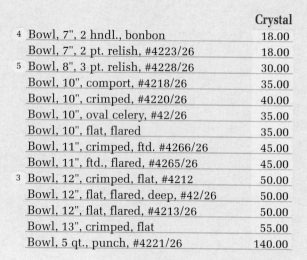

1

	Crystal		Crystal
4 Bowl, 7", 2 hndl., bonbon	18.00	Candle, 2 light, rnd. ft.	42.50
Bowl, 7", 2 pt. relish, #4223/26	18.00	Candy box (3 pt.) & cover, #42/26	55.00
5 Bowl, 8", 3 pt. relish, #4228/26	30.00	Cheese & cracker, 11", #42/26	50.00
Bowl, 10", comport, #4218/26	35.00	Creamer, ftd., tab hdld., #42/26	15.00
Bowl, 10", crimped, #4220/26	40.00	Cup, 4 oz., punch, tab hdld.	9.00
Bowl, 10", oval celery, #42/26	35.00	Ladle, punch, #4226	55.00
Bowl, 10", flat, flared	35.00	2 Mayonnaise set, liner & ladle, #42/26	45.00
Bowl, 11", crimped, ftd. #4266/26	45.00	1 Plate, 11"	35.00
Bowl, 11", ftd., flared, #4265/26	45.00	Plate, 14", #42/26	45.00
3 Bowl, 12", crimped, flat, #4212	50.00	Salver, 12", ftd., #42/26	40.00
Bowl, 12", flat, flared, deep, #42/26	50.00	Sugar, ftd., tab hdld., #42/26	15.00
Bowl, 12", flat, flared, #4213/26	50.00	Tray, oval for sugar & creamer, #42/26	15.00
Bowl, 13", crimped, flat	55.00	Vase, 10", crimped, #4232/26	60.00
Bowl, 5 qt., punch, #4221/26	140.00	Vase, 10", flared, #42/26	55.00

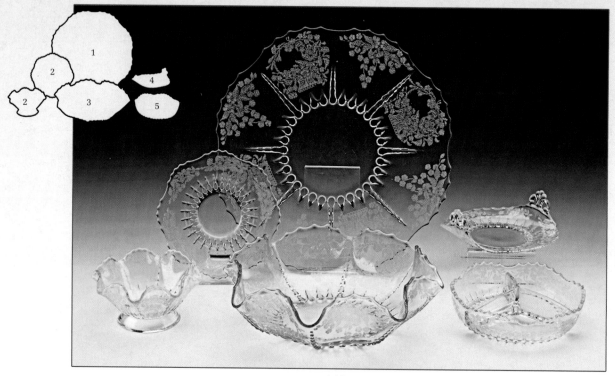

Color: crystal

The manufacture of Minuet began in 1939 making it a fence sitter for relocating it into *Collectible Glassware from the 40s, 50s, and 60s.* This decision will be resolved by how many new patterns I can fit into the allotted pages of the books. There are 13 new patterns in this book after adding 33 the last two editions. Those 46 patterns are really pushing the limits to what we can put into this book, even with 16 additional pages.

Minuet is one Heisey pattern where established prices have prevailed, although a few price modifications have been noted for basic pieces like dinner plates, creamer, and sugars. By the way, dinner plates are listed as service plates in Heisey catalogs. That was generally the case in Cambridge and Fostoria catalogs, also — and explains their dearth today.

Minuet stemware is bountiful as is the case in most Heisey patterns, but most tumblers are elusive. As with many other stemware lines, Minuet was purchased to go with china settings. Serving pieces were rarely bought since china was mostly used for fashionable serving. Only the three-part relish and the three-footed bowl seem to be found with regularity. You will meet staunch competition procuring this pattern.

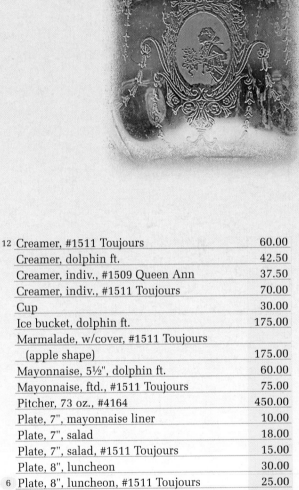

	Bell, dinner, #3408	75.00
11	Bowl, finger, #3309	50.00
	Bowl, 6", ftd., dolphin, mint	45.00
	Bowl, 6", ftd., 2 hdld., jelly	30.00
	Bowl, 6½", salad dressings	35.00
10	Bowl, 7", salad dressings, 2 part	40.00
	Bowl, 7", triplex, relish	60.00
	Bowl, 7½", sauce, ftd.	70.00
	Bowl, 9½", 3 pt., "5 o'clock," relish	70.00
	Bowl, 10", salad, #1511 Toujours	65.00
	Bowl, 11", 3 pt., "5 o'clock," relish	80.00
	Bowl, 11", ftd., dolphin, floral	120.00
	Bowl, 12", oval, floral, #1511 Toujours	65.00
	Bowl, 12", oval, #1514	65.00
	Bowl, 13", floral, #1511 Toujours	60.00
	Bowl, 13", pickle & olive	45.00
5	Bowl, 13½", shallow salad	75.00
	Candelabrum, 1-lite, w/prisms	110.00
	Candelabrum, 2-lite, bobeche & prisms	175.00
	Candlestick, 1-lite, #112	35.00
	Candlestick, 2-lite, #1511 Toujours	150.00
	Candlestick, 3-lite, #142 Cascade	90.00
	Candlestick, 5", 2-lite, #134 Trident	60.00
	Centerpiece vase & prisms, #1511 Toujours	200.00
	Cocktail icer, w/liner, #3304 Universal	125.00
	Comport, 5½", #5010	40.00
	Comport, 7½", #1511 Toujours	60.00

12	Creamer, #1511 Toujours	60.00
	Creamer, dolphin ft.	42.50
	Creamer, indiv., #1509 Queen Ann	37.50
	Creamer, indiv., #1511 Toujours	70.00
	Cup	30.00
	Ice bucket, dolphin ft.	175.00
	Marmalade, w/cover, #1511 Toujours (apple shape)	175.00
	Mayonnaise, 5½", dolphin ft.	60.00
	Mayonnaise, ftd., #1511 Toujours	75.00
	Pitcher, 73 oz., #4164	450.00
	Plate, 7", mayonnaise liner	10.00
	Plate, 7", salad	18.00
	Plate, 7", salad, #1511 Toujours	15.00
	Plate, 8", luncheon	30.00
6	Plate, 8", luncheon, #1511 Toujours	25.00
	Plate, 10½", service	190.00
	Plate, 12", rnd., 2 hdld., sandwich	150.00

	Plate, 13", floral, salver, #1511 Toujours	60.00
	Plate, 14", torte, #1511 Toujours	60.00
	Plate, 15", sandwich, #1511 Toujours	65.00
	Plate, 16", snack rack, w/#1477 center	80.00
	Salt & pepper, pr. (#10)	75.00
	Saucer	10.00
2	Stem, #5010, Symphone, 1 oz., cordial	135.00
	Stem, #5010, 2½ oz., wine	50.00
4	Stem, #5010, 3½ oz., cocktail	35.00
	Stem, #5010, 4 oz., claret	40.00
8	Stem, #5010, 4½ oz., oyster cocktail	25.00
	Stem, #5010, 6 oz., saucer champagne	25.00
	Stem, #5010, 6 oz., sherbet	25.00
	Stem, #5010, 9 oz., water	35.00
	Sugar, indiv., #1511 Toujours	70.00
	Sugar, indiv., #1509 Queen Ann	37.50
7	Sugar, dolphin ftd., #1509 Queen Ann	40.00

1	Sugar, #1511 Toujours	60.00
	Tray, 12", celery, #1511 Toujours	50.00
	Tray, 15", social hour	90.00
	Tray for indiv. sugar & creamer	30.00
3	Tumbler, #5010, 5 oz., fruit juice	34.00
9	Tumbler, #5010, 9 oz., low ftd., water	35.00
	Tumbler, #5010, 12 oz., tea	60.00
	Tumbler, #2351, 12 oz., tea	60.00
	Vase, 5", #5013	50.00
	Vase, 5½", ftd., #1511 Toujours	95.00
	Vase, 6", urn, #5012	75.00
	Vase, 7½", urn, #5012	90.00
	Vase, 8", #4196	95.00
	Vase, 9", urn, #5012	110.00
	Vase, 10", #4192	110.00
	Vase, 10", #4192, Saturn optic	115.00

Colors: amber, amethyst, black, blue, crystal, green, pink, lilac, crystal stems w/color bowls

Joseph Balda designed Morgan for Central in 1920, although he was better known for his designs for Heisey. A family named Morgan allegedly adopted Morgan for use in the West Virginia governor's mansion. Thus, the very masculine pattern name attached to this seated fairy design.

Finally, I was able to find a Morgan pitcher to show you. We have been buying Morgan for about 20 years and this is the first pitcher we had a chance to own. Cathy found the little fairy fascinating and began obtaining every piece she could find. At the time few dealers knew what it was and very little was offered for sale at shows or markets.

After introducing it in my book, many new collectors were intrigued by this sparsely distributed pattern. With all the competition, it has been more difficult to find supplementary pieces to include in the book. Notice the three styles of center handled servers and straight and ruffled 10" vases on page 150. Slender bud vases are being found with straight or ruffled tops also.

There are few pieces of amber turning up, but there are fewer collectors buying it. Pieces of black being found include a candy, 6" bonbon, and a bud vase with a gold encrusted fairy. Does anyone have a gold decorated piece other than a bud vase?

The Morgan pattern is found only on the lid of the covered items; so, do not fret too much about condition of the bottom. Other bottoms will turn up. Cups and saucers in color are the items missing from most collections of this Central Glass Works pattern. I have only heard of crystal and pink cup and saucers, with crystal the primary one found.

Morgan stemware has become more difficult to find, with blue and lilac stems commanding some royal prices. Internet auctions have increased the demand for Morgan tremendously. Note that there are five styles and shapes of stemware. The beaded stems seem to come in solid colors of crystal, pink, or green. The "wafer" stem is found all pink, green stems with crystal tops, and crystal stems with blue tops. All lilac stems are solid lilac, but the bowls are shaped differently than other colors. This is the same mould line as "Balda" shown on page 21.

If you have knowledge of additional pieces not listed, please let us know, so we may list them.

		*All Colors
	Bonbon, 6", two hdld.	65.00
	Bonbon, 9", two hdld.	95.00
6	Bowl, 4¼", ftd., fruit	60.00
5	Bowl, 5", finger	65.00
7	Bowl, 10", console	100.00
	Bowl, 13", console	125.00
	Candlestick, 3"	75.00
	Candy, blown, pattern on top	595.00
	Candy w/lid, diamond shaped, 4 ftd.	595.00
	Cheese & cracker	150.00
	Comport, 6½" tall, 5" wide	85.00
	Comport, 6½" tall, 6" wide	95.00
	Creamer, ftd.	75.00
	Cup	160.00
9	Decanter, w/stopper	495.00
	Ice bucket, 4¾" x7½", 2 hdld.	695.00
	Mayonnaise	75.00
	Mayonnaise liner	20.00
	Oil bottle	295.00
20	Pitcher, 75 oz., flat w/optic, #411	995.00
	Plate, 6½", fruit bowl liner	15.00
3	Plate, 6½", squared	35.00
	Plate, 7¼", salad	25.00
	Plate, 8½", luncheon	35.00
	Plate, 9¼", dinner	125.00
	Salt & pepper, pr.	155.00
	Saucer	25.00
14	Server, 9½", octagonal, center hdld.	125.00

		*All Colors
19	Server, 10⅜", round, center hdld.	100.00
17	Server, 11", octagonal, flat, center hdld.	100.00
	Stem, 3¼", sherbet	35.00
	Stem, 4⅜", sherbet, beaded stem	40.00
	Stem, 5⅛", cocktail, beaded stem	40.00
16	Stem, 5⅜", high, sherbet, beaded stem	45.00
4	Stem, 5⅞", high sherbet	65.00
2	Stem, 5⅞", wine	65.00
	Stem, 6", wine, wafer & straight stem	65.00
1	Stem, 7¼", 10 oz., water	75.00
15	Stem, 8¼", water	75.00
	Sugar, ftd.	75.00
	Tumbler, oyster cocktail	42.50
10	Tumbler, 2⅛", whiskey	100.00
	Tumbler, 10 oz., flat water	40.00
	Tumbler, 4⅜", ftd. juice	40.00
12	Tumbler, 5⅜", ftd., 10 oz., water	40.00
18	Tumbler, 5¾", ftd., water	40.00
11	Tumbler, 5⅞", ftd., 12 oz., tea	65.00
	Vase, fan shaped	450.00
	Vase, 8", drape optic	295.00
	Vase, 9⅞", straight w/flared top	395.00
	**Vase, 10", bud, straight or ruffled top	225.00
8	Vase, 10", flared top	350.00
13	Vase, 10", ruffled top	595.00

*Crystal 10% to 20% lower. Blue, lilac 25% to 30% higher.

**Gold decorated $300.00.

MORGAN

Colors: amber, crystal, Carmen, Royal Blue, Heatherbloom, Emerald green (light and dark); rare in Violet

Large sets of Mt. Vernon can only be assembled in amber or crystal. You could acquire small luncheon sets in red, cobalt blue, or Heatherbloom; but only a few extra pieces are available in those colors. However, prices for any of those colors can more than double the prices listed for amber and crystal. Many collectors are mingling their crystal Mt. Vernon with a splash of color. Indiana's Diamond Point is often confused with Mt. Vernon. See #12 for an example of Diamond Point for comparison.

	Amber Crystal		Amber Crystal
Ashtray, 3½", #63	8.00	Bowl, 12½", flared, #121	35.00
Ashtray, 4", #68	12.00	Bowl, 12½", flared, #44	35.00
Ashtray, 6" x 4½", oval, #71	12.00	Bowl, 13", shallow, crimped, #116	35.00
Bonbon, 7", ftd., #10	12.50	Box, 3", w/cover, round, #16	30.00
Bottle, bitters, 2½ oz., #62	65.00	Box, 4", w/cover, sq., #17	32.50
Bottle, 7 oz., sq., toilet, #18	75.00	9 Box, 4½", w/cover, ftd., round, #15	37.50
Bowl, finger, #23	10.00	5 Butter tub, w/cover, #73	65.00
Bowl, 4½", ivy ball or rose, ftd., #12	27.50	Cake stand, 10½" ftd., #150	35.00
Bowl, 5¼", fruit, #6	10.00	Candelabrum, 13½", #38	150.00
Bowl, 6", cereal, #32	12.50	Candlestick, 4", #130	10.00
Bowl, 6", preserve, #76	12.00	Candlestick, 5", 2-lite, #110	25.00
Bowl, 6½", rose, #106	18.00	Candlestick, 8", #35	27.50
Bowl, 8", pickle, #65	17.50	Candy, w/cover, 1 lb., ftd., #9	90.00
Bowl, 8½", 4 pt., 2 hdld., sweetmeat, #105	32.00	Celery, 10½", #79	15.00
Bowl, 10", 2 hdld., #39	20.00	Celery, 11", #98	17.50
Bowl, 10½", deep, #43	30.00	Celery, 12", #79	20.00
Bowl, 10½", salad, #120	25.00	Cigarette box, 6", w/cover, oval, #69	32.00
Bowl, 11", oval, 4 ftd., #136	27.50	Cigarette holder, #66	15.00
Bowl, 11", oval, #135	25.00	Coaster, 3", plain, #60	5.00
2 Bowl, 11½", belled, #128	30.00	Coaster, 3", ribbed, #70	5.00
Bowl, 11½", shallow, #126	30.00	Cocktail icer, 2 pc., #85	30.00
Bowl, 11½", shallow cupped, #61	30.00	Cologne, 2½ oz., w/stopper, #1340	45.00
Bowl, 12", flanged, rolled edge, #129	32.50	Comport, 4½", #33	12.00
Bowl, 12", oblong, crimped, #118	32.50	Comport, 5½", 2 hdld., #77	15.00
Bowl, 12", rolled edge, crimped, #117	32.50	Comport, 6", #34	15.00
Bowl, 12½", flanged, rolled edge, #45	35.00	Comport, 6½", #97	17.50

		Amber Crystal
	Comport, 6½", belled, #96	22.50
	Comport, 7½" #11	25.00
	Comport, 8", #81	25.00
	Comport, 9", oval, 2 hdld., #100	35.00
	Comport, 9½", #99	30.00
	Creamer, ftd., #8	10.00
	Creamer, indiv., #4	10.00
	Creamer, #86	10.00
1	Cup, #7	6.00
	Decanter, 11 oz., #47	60.00
	Decanter, 40 oz., w/stopper, #52	85.00
4	Honey jar, w/cover (marmalade), #74	35.00
	Ice bucket, w/tongs, #92	40.00
	Lamp, 9" hurricane, #1607	95.00
	Mayonnaise, divided, 2 spoons, #107	25.00
6	Mug, 14 oz., stein, #84	30.00
	Mustard, w/cover, 2½ oz., #28	25.00
	Pickle, 6", 1 hdld., #78	12.00
	Pitcher, 50 oz., #90	90.00
	Pitcher, 66 oz., #13	95.00
	Pitcher, 80 oz., ball, #95	110.00
	Pitcher, 86 oz., #91	130.00
	Plate, finger bowl liner, #23	4.00
	Plate, 6", bread & butter, #4	3.00
	Plate, 6⅜", bread & butter, #19	4.00
	Plate, 8½", salad, #5	7.00
	Plate, 10½", dinner, #40	38.00
7	Plate, 11½", hdld., #37	20.00
	Relish, 6", 2 pt., 2 hdld., #106	12.00
	Relish, 8", 2 pt., hdld., #101	17.50
	Relish, 8", 3 pt., 3 hdld., #103	20.00
	Relish, 11", 3 part, #200	25.00
	Relish, 12", 2 part, #80	30.00
11	Relish, 12", 5 part, #104	30.00
	Salt, indiv., #24	7.00
	Salt, oval, 2 hdld., #102	12.00
	Salt & pepper, pr., #28	22.50
	Salt & pepper, pr., short, #88	20.00

		Amber Crystal
	Salt & pepper, tall, #89	25.00
17	Salt dip, #24	9.00
	Sauce boat & ladle, tab hdld., #30-445	65.00
1	Saucer, #7	7.50
14	Stem, 3 oz., wine, #27	15.00
	Stem, 3½ oz., cocktail, #26	9.00
	Stem, 4 oz., oyster cocktail, #41	9.00
16	Stem, 4½ oz., claret, #25	13.50
	Stem, 4½ oz., low sherbet, #42	7.50
13	Stem, 6½ oz., tall sherbet, #2	10.00
15	Stem, 10 oz., water, #1	16.00
	Sugar, ftd., #8	10.00
	Sugar, indiv., #4	12.00
	Sugar, #86	10.00
18	Tray, 8½", 4 pt., 2 hndl., sweetmeat	8.00
	Tray, for indiv., sugar & creamer, #4	10.00
	Tumbler, 1 oz., ftd., cordial, #87	20.00
8	Tumbler, 2 oz., whiskey, #55	9.00
3	Tumbler, 3 oz., ftd., juice, #22	8.00
	Tumbler, 5 oz., #56	10.00
	Tumbler, 5 oz., ftd., #21	10.00
	Tumbler, 7 oz., old-fashion, #57	14.00
10	Tumbler, 10 oz., ftd., water, #3	15.00
	Tumbler, 10 oz., table, #51	12.00
	Tumbler, 10 oz., tall, #58	12.00
	Tumbler, 12 oz., barrel shape, #13	15.00
	Tumbler, 12 oz., ftd., tea, #20	17.00
	Tumbler, 14 oz., barrel shape, #14	20.00
	Tumbler, 14 oz., tall, #59	22.00
	Urn, w/cover (same as candy), #9	90.00
	Vase, 5", #42	15.00
	Vase, 6", crimped, #119	20.00
	Vase, 6", ftd., #50	25.00
	Vase, 6½", squat, #107	27.50
	Vase, 7", #58	30.00
	Vase, 7", ftd., #54	35.00
	Vase, 10", ftd., #46	65.00

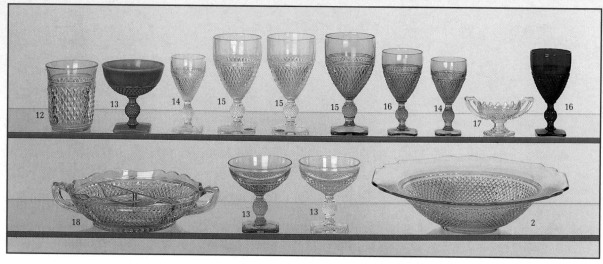

Color: crystal

Narcissus was a cutting applied to glassware by the A.H. Heisey Company, Newark, Ohio, from the early 1940s until 1957. Narcissus, Heisey cutting number 965, was applied to a number of Heisey blanks but more often on the Jamestown stemware line (#3408) and the Waverly general line blanks (#1519). This cutting was very popular because of its beauty, ease of identity and the wide production, which allows for a complete set of glassware.

	Item	Price
9	Bell (made from goblet)	55.00
	Bottle, oil (#1519)	175.00
	Bowl, floral, ftd., 11" (#1519)	65.00
	Bowl, floral, 13" (#1519)	60.00
	Bowl, gardenia, 13 (#1519)	50.00
	Candlestick, 2-light (#134)	35.00
	Candlestick, 3-light (#1519)	65.00
	Candy and cover, ftd., 5" (#1519)	185.00
	Celery tray, 12" (#1519)	35.00
	Comport, low ftd., 6" (#1519)	35.00
	Comport, ftd. honey, 7" (#1519)	40.00
	Comport, ftd., nut, 7" (#1519)	70.00
	Creamer, ftd. (#1519)	30.00
8	Cup (#1519)	30.00
6	Mayonnaise, ftd. and underplate (#1519)	55.00
	Relish, oval, 3-part, 11" (#1519)	40.00
	Relish, round, 3-part, 8" (#1519)	35.00
5	Plate, 7" (#1519)	12.00
4	Plate luncheon, 8" (#1519)	16.00
	Plate, party, 14" (#1519)	45.00
	Salt & pepper (#1519)	75.00
8	Saucer (#1519)	10.00
	Stem, goblet, 9 oz. (#3408)	28.00
7	Stem, sherbet/saucer-champ., 6 oz. (#3408)	16.00
	Stem, claret, 4½ oz. (#3408)	32.00
3	Stem, cocktail, 3 oz. (#3408)	18.00
	Stem, wine, 2-oz. (#3408)	26.00
	Stem, cordial, 1 oz. (#3408)	85.00
	Sugar (#1519)	30.00
2	Tumbler, ice tea, ftd., 12 oz. (#3408)	26.00
1	Tumbler, juice, ftd., 5 oz. (#3408)	24.00
	Vase, round, ftd., 7" (#1519)	85.00

Color: crystal, blue, blue and pink opalescent

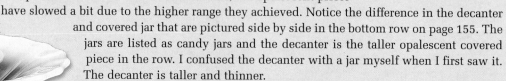

Nautical surprises still occur. Last year, I received an e-mail from someone who said he had a pair of Nautical shakers on a stand. I had heard of shakers and stands, but usually the stand was the one used in Caribbean. This stand had an anchor in the center. (See #5 below.)

Most Nautical is easily recognized; but various pieces slip through the cracks. It is hard to miss items with anchors and rope; however, some pieces do not have the anchor, which means they can elude you unless you are attentive. Blue, and particularly the opalescent, is the most sought color; but collectors are inclined to mix blue with crystal in order to have more pieces. Prices for blue continue to rise, but opalescent prices have slowed a bit due to the higher range they achieved. Notice the difference in the decanter and covered jar that are pictured side by side in the bottom row on page 155. The jars are listed as candy jars and the decanter is the taller opalescent covered piece in the row. I confused the decanter with a jar myself when I first saw it. The decanter is taller and thinner.

That 7" comport with an anchor for the stem can be found with two different tops. The opalescent one has a pointed edge top while the other style has a plain edge.

154

		*Blue	Crystal	Opalescent
6	Ashtray, 3"	30.00	8.00	
	Ashtray, 6"	40.00	12.50	
	Candy jar, w/lid	550.00	295.00	695.00
	Cigarette holder	55.00	15.00	
12	Cigarette jar	75.00	25.00	
17	Cocktail shaker (fish design)	195.00	65.00	
1	Comport, 7"	295.00	110.00	595.00
15	Creamer	45.00	15.00	
18	Decanter	550.00	225.00	695.00
2	Ice bucket	195.00	95.00	300.00
8	Marmalade	75.00	25.00	
9	Plate, 6"	25.00	10.00	
10	Plate, 6½", 2 hdld., cake	35.00	12.00	
3	Plate, 8"	40.00	10.00	
16	Plate, 10"	100.00	25.00	
	Relish, 12", 7 part	75.00	35.00	
11	Relish, 3-part, 2 hdld., tray	45.00	22.50	
4	Shakers, pr., w/tray	200.00	65.00	
	Sugar	45.00	15.00	
14	Tumbler, 2 oz., bar	30.00	12.50	
13	Tumbler, 8 oz., whiskey & soda	30.00	12.00	
	Tumbler, 9 oz., water, ftd.	30.00	15.00	
	Tumbler, cocktail	25.00	12.00	
	Tumbler, ftd., orange juice	30.00	15.00	
	Tumbler, high ball	33.00	18.00	
5	Tray for shakers	100.00		

*Add 10% for satinized.

7 Duncan sailfish added for ambiance

Colors: crystal; all other colors found made very late

Fostoria's Navarre pattern is the most collected patterns of the crystal etchings made by Fostoria. (American is the most widely collected pressed Fostoria crystal pattern; but it was made for about 70 years and several generations came to know it.) Navarre was made for over 40 years; and the thin delicate stems even enhance modern day china patterns. Navarre was distributed nationally, but prices on the West Coast were always more expensive due to shipping costs. With the price of gasoline and postage increasing, transportation costs may have to factor into dealers' prices of glassware once again.

Only older crystal pieces of Navarre are priced in this book. Pink and blue were made in the 1970s and 1980s as were additional crystal pieces not originally made in the late 1930s and 1940s. These later pieces include carafes, Roemer wines, continental champagnes, and brandies. You can find these later pieces in my *Collectible Glassware from the 40s, 50s, and 60s....* Most of these pieces are acid signed on the base "Fostoria" although some carried only a sticker. I am telling you this to make you aware of the colors made in Navarre. You will even find a few pieces of Navarre that are signed Lenox. These were made after Fostoria closed. Some collectors shy away from the colored Lenox pieces since the color is lighter than the original; but it does not seem to make much difference to most Navarre collectors. A few Depression era glass shows have not allowed these pieces or colors to be sold since they were of so recent manufacture. However, most shows are changing these stricter rules to allow patterns to be included as long as production began earlier.

Note the footed shakers in the photo below. They came with both glass and metal lids. Glass tops were used in the early production years, but were changed to metal after the 1940s. Metal lids were the ones most often shipped as replacements when customers ordered new lids.

		Crystal				Crystal
	Bell, dinner	75.00		8	Bowl, #2545, 12½", oval, "Flame"	95.00
	Bowl, #2496, 4", sq., hdld.	18.00			Candlestick, #2496, 4"	25.00
15	Bowl, #2496, 4⅜", hdld.	16.00			Candlestick, #2496, 4½", double	40.00
23	Bowl, #869, 4½", finger	75.00			Candlestick, #2472, 5", double	50.00
	Bowl, #2496, 4⅝", tri-cornered	22.00			Candlestick, #2496, 5½"	42.00
10	Bowl, #2496, 5", hdld., ftd.	20.00			Candlestick, #2496, 6", triple	55.00
	Bowl, #2496, 6", square, sweetmeat	30.00			Candlestick, #2545, 6¾", double, "Flame"	85.00
	Bowl, #2496, 6¼", 3 ftd., nut	25.00		22	Candlestick, #2482, 6¾", triple	85.00
	Bowl, #2496, 7⅜", ftd., bonbon	30.00			Candy, w/cover, #2496, 3 part	130.00
	Bowl, #2496, 10", oval, floating garden	65.00				
	Bowl, #2496, 10½", hdld., ftd.	95.00				
21	Bowl, #2470½, 10½", ftd.	70.00				
	Bowl, #2496, 12", flared	75.00				

		Crystal
29	Celery, #2440, 9"	35.00
	Celery, #2496, 11"	50.00
	Comport, #2496, 3¼", cheese	33.00
4	Comport, #2400, 4½"	35.00
	Comport, #2496, 4¾"	37.50
	Cracker, #2496, 11", plate	45.00
28	Creamer, #2440, 4¼", ftd.	18.00
6	Creamer, #2496, individual	18.00
27	Cup, #2440	20.00
	Ice bucket, #2496, 4⅜" high	125.00
	Ice bucket, #2375, 6" high	145.00
	Mayonnaise, #2375, 3 piece	65.00
	Mayonnaise, #2496½, 3 piece	65.00
	Pickle, #2496, 8"	27.50
24	Pickle, #2440, 8½"	32.50
	Pitcher, #5000, 48 oz., ftd.	375.00
	Plate, #2440, 6", bread/butter	10.00
	Plate, #2440, 7½", salad	14.00
20	Plate, #2440, 8½", luncheon	22.00
19	Plate, #2440, 9½", dinner	50.00
	Plate, #2496, 10", hdld., cake	60.00
	Plate, #2440, 10½", oval cake	65.00
	Plate, #2496, 14", torte	75.00
	Plate, #2464, 16", torte	135.00
13	Relish, #2496, 6", 2 part, sq.	30.00
9	Relish, #2496, 10" x 7½", 3 part	50.00
	Relish, #2496, 10", 4 part	60.00
3	Relish, #2419, 13¼", 5 part	90.00
12	Salt & pepper, #2364, 3¼", flat, pr.	80.00
7	Salt & pepper, #2375, 3½", ftd., pr.	120.00

		Crystal
	Salad dressing bottle, #2083, 6½"	495.00
	Sauce dish, #2496, div. mayonnaise, 6½"	45.00
	Sauce dish, #2496, 6½" x 5¼"	120.00
	Sauce dish liner, #2496, 8", oval	25.00
	Saucer, #2440	4.00
25	Stem, #6016, 1 oz., cordial, 3⅞"	55.00
26	Stem, #6106, 3¼ oz., wine, 5½"	33.00
	Stem, #6106, 3½ oz., cocktail, 6"	25.00
11	Stem, #6106, 4 oz., oyster cocktail, 3⅝"	25.00
	Stem, #6106, 4½ oz., claret, 6½"	40.00
16	Stem, #6106, 6 oz., low sherbet, 4⅜"	20.00
17	Stem, #6106, 6 oz., saucer champagne, 5⅝"	22.00
18	Stem, #6106, 10 oz., water, 7⅝"	35.00
30	Sugar, #2440, 3⅝", ftd.	18.00
5	Sugar, #2496, individual	18.00
	Syrup, #2586, metal cut-off top, 5½"	450.00
	Tid bit, #2496, 8¼", 3 ftd., turned up edge	28.00
	Tray, #2496½", for ind. sugar/creamer	22.00
14	Tumbler, #6106, 5 oz., ftd., juice, 4⅝"	22.00
1	Tumbler, #6106, 10 oz., ftd., water, 5⅜"	25.00
2	Tumbler, #6106, 13 oz., ftd., tea, 5⅞"	33.00
	Vase, #4128, 5"	135.00
	Vase, #4121, 5"	120.00
	Vase, #4128, 5"	100.00
	Vase, #2470, 10", ftd.	185.00

Colors: crystal, frosted crystal, some cobalt with crystal stem and foot

Except for stems, the celery tray, and candlesticks, the production of New Era falls outside production dates of this book; so, be warned, New Era will be transferred into my *Collectible Glassware from the 40s, 50s, and 60s* book in the future. The New Era double-branched candelabrum with bobeches is probably the most recognized Heisey candle. Stemware abounds; but keep your eye peeled for flat pieces of New Era that often goes unrecognized as Heisey.

16

		Crystal
12	Ashtray or indiv. nut	35.00
	Bottle, rye, w/stopper	140.00
1	Bowl, 11", floral	35.00
3	Candelabra, 2-lite, w/2 #4044 bobeche	
	& prisms	140.00
	Creamer	37.50
15	Cup	15.00
	Cup, after dinner	62.50
	Pilsner, 8 oz.	40.00
	Pilsner, 12 oz.	45.00
	Plate, 5½" x 4½", bread & butter	20.00
2	Plate, 9" x 7"	25.00
14	Plate, 10" x 8"	75.00
	Relish, 13", 3 part	35.00
15	Saucer	8.00
	Saucer, after dinner	12.50

		Crystal
9	Stem, 1 oz. cordial	40.00
4	Stem, 3 oz. wine	25.00
16	Stem, 3½ oz., high, cocktail	14.00
11	Stem, 3½ oz., oyster cocktail	12.00
6	Stem, 4 oz., claret	20.00
10	Stem, 6 oz., champagne	15.00
13	Stem, 6 oz., sherbet, low	12.00
8	Stem, 10 oz., goblet	20.00
	Sugar	37.50
	Tray, 13", celery	30.00
	Tumbler, 5 oz., ftd., soda	10.00
	Tumbler, 8 oz., ftd., soda	14.00
	Tumbler, 10 oz., low, ftd.	14.00
7	Tumbler, 12 oz., ftd., soda	20.00
5	Tumbler, 14 oz., ftd., soda	24.00

Colors: Amber, Rose, and Topaz

New Garland is a Fostoria pattern that is seriously being considered by new collectors. These collectors have been attracted to the older, squared mould shape of Fostoria's #2419 Mayfair line. This, by the way, was designed by George Sakier, the man behind many of Fostoria's more avant-garde designs of that era. Notice the ice buckets, which are not often found.

Pink appears to be the color of choice, but we are getting a few requests for Topaz recently. Our problem has been finding some for sale.

		Amber Topaz	Rose
	Bonbon, 2 hdld.	15.00	20.00
	Bottle, salad dressing	195.00	250.00
	Bowl, 5", fruit	10.00	15.00
	Bowl, 6", cereal	12.00	20.00
8	Bowl, 7", soup	22.00	30.00
	Bowl, 7½"	25.00	40.00
10	Bowl, 10", baker	35.00	50.00
	Bowl, 11", ftd.	50.00	70.00
	Bowl, 12"	55.00	70.00
	Candlestick, 2"	15.00	20.00
	Candlestick, 3"	17.50	22.50
	Candlestick, 9½"	30.00	40.00
	Candy jar, cover, ½ lb.	55.00	85.00
	Celery, 11"	22.00	30.00
	Comport, 6"	20.00	28.00
	Comport, tall	30.00	40.00
11	Cream soup	18.00	22.50
	Creamer	12.50	15.00
	Creamer, ftd.	15.00	17.50
	Creamer, tea	17.50	20.00
7	Cup, after dinner, #2419	20.00	25.00
4	Cup, ftd., #2419	14.00	17.50
	Decanter	145.00	210.00
	Finger bowl, #4121	12.00	15.00
	Finger bowl, #6002, ftd.	15.00	18.00
3	Ice bucket, #2375	75.00	120.00
	Ice dish	20.00	25.00
	Jelly, 7"	18.00	22.50
	Lemon dish, 2 hdld.	15.00	18.00
	Mayonnaise, 2 hdld.	18.00	22.50
	Mint, 5½"	12.50	16.00
	Nut, individual	10.00	13.00
	Oil, ftd.	135.00	210.00
	Pickle, 8½"	16.00	20.00
	Pitcher, ftd.	250.00	335.00
6	Plate, 6", #2419	4.00	6.00
	Plate, 7"	7.00	10.00
	Plate, 8"	12.00	15.00

		Amber Topaz	Rose
1	Plate, 9", #2419	25.00	35.00
	Plate, 10" cake, 2 hdld.	27.50	35.00
2	Platter, 12"	35.00	50.00
	Platter. 15"	50.00	80.00
	Relish, 4 part	20.00	27.50
	Relish, 8½"	14.00	18.00
	Sauce boat	50.00	75.00
	Sauce boat liner	20.00	25.00
4	Saucer, #2419	3.00	4.00
	Saucer, after dinner	8.00	10.00
	Shaker, pr.	40.00	60.00
	Shaker, pr., ftd.	75.00	100.00
	Stem, #4120, 2 oz., whiskey	20.00	30.00
	Stem, #4120, 3½ oz., cocktail	20.00	24.00
	Stem, #4120, 5 oz., low sherbet	14.00	16.00
	Stem, #4120, 7 oz., low sherbet	15.00	18.00
	Stem, #4120, high sherbet	18.00	20.00
	Stem, #4120, water goblet	22.00	28.00
	Stem, #6002, claret	25.00	35.00
	Stem, #6002, cordial	30.00	40.00
	Stem, #6002, goblet	22.00	28.00
	Stem, #6002, high sherbet	18.00	20.00
	Stem, #6002, low sherbet	14.00	16.00
	Stem, #6002, oyster cocktail	16.00	20.00
9	Stem, #6002, wine	22.00	28.00
	Sugar	12.50	15.00
	Sugar, ftd.	15.00	17.50
	Sugar, tea	17.50	20.00
	Tumbler, #4120, 5 oz.	12.00	18.00
	Tumbler, #4120, 10 oz.	14.00	20.00
	Tumbler, #4120, 13 oz.	15.00	22.00
	Tumbler, #4120, 16 oz.	20.00	28.00
	Tumbler, #6002, ftd., 2 oz.	18.00	25.00
5	Tumbler, #6002, ftd., 5 oz.	12.00	18.00
	Tumbler, #6002, ftd., 10 oz.	14.00	20.00
	Tumbler, #6002, ftd., 13 oz.	15.00	22.00
	Vase, 8"	75.00	95.00

Colors: amber, Emerald green, Peach Blo; #3095 colored Peach-blo w/ribbed bowl, crystal stem & foot, optic, amber

Cambridge's Number 520 and Numbers 703 and 704, which follow on the next pages, are usually referred to as "one of those Cambridge numbered patterns," but few members of the public take the trouble to learn which one. There are some avid collectors of these lines, and hopefully adding names "Byzantine," "Florentine," and "Windows Border" may help identify the patterns as did "Rosalie" for Number 731. Collectors like names. Since no factory name has been forthcoming, let's adopt one collector's idea. She told me it reminded her of the elaborate designs seen in her travels. "It's very Byzantine," she said.

I see equal amounts of Peach Blo (pink) and Emerald (green), but apparently, there are more admirers of the Emerald. I found some amber pieces that I had never seen before. Enjoy seeing those this time.

		Peach Blo Green Amber				Peach Blo Green Amber
	Bouillon, 2 hdld. soup cup, #934	25.00		Plate, 10", grill		35.00
	Bowl, 5¼", fruit, #928	22.50	3	Plate, 11", club luncheon, grill		30.00
	Bowl, 6½", cereal or grapefruit, #466	33.00		Plate, finger bowl liner, #3060		12.50
1	Bowl, 12", oval, #914	45.00	4	Platter for gravy boat, #917		40.00
	Bowl, cream soup	25.00	2	Platter, 14½", oval/service, #903		75.00
	Bowl, finger, #3060	28.00		Saucer, #933		7.00
	Butter w/cover	195.00		Saucer, cupped, liner for bouillon		12.00
	Candy box, #300	125.00		Stem, 2½ oz., cocktail, #3060		22.50
	Comport, 7¼" h., #531	40.00		Stem, 2½ oz., wine, #3060		35.00
	Comport, jelly, #2900	35.00		Stem, 6 oz., hi sherbet, #3060		22.50
	Comport, #3095 (twist stem)	40.00		Stem, 7 oz., sherbet, #3060		22.50
	Creamer, rim ft., #138	20.00		Stem, 9 oz., water, #3060		30.00
	Cup, #933	18.00		Stem, cocktail, #3095		22.50
4	Gravy or sauce boat, double, #917	95.00		Stem, high sherbet, #3095		20.00
	Oil bottle, #193	195.00		Stem, low sherbet, #3095		18.00
	Oil bottle w/cut flattened stop, 6 oz., #197	210.00		Sugar, rim ft., #138		20.00
	Plate, 6", sherbet	10.00		Tumbler, 3 oz., ftd., #3060		20.00
	Plate, 8", luncheon	18.00		Tumbler, 5 oz., ftd., #3060		22.50
	Plate, 9½" dinner, #810	60.00		Tumbler, 10 oz., ftd., #3060		25.00
				Tumbler, 12 oz., low ft., #3095		30.00

Colors: green, green w/gold

Cambridge's No. 703 is another of the numbered lines that collectors can never remember what the number is. Maybe the name "Florentine" may stick. Still, even seasoned dealers often have to sneak a look at the book to identify many of these numbered lines. I have only found "Florentine" in green or green with gold, but I suspect it was made in other colors. We bought a large set last year and sold most of it the first couple of shows where we had it displayed. You may find additional pieces and colors so keep us informed.

		Green
2	Bouillon liner, 6", #934	5.00
3	Bouillon, 2-hdld., #934	15.00
	Bowl, 5¼", fruit, #928	12.50
	Bowl, 6½", cereal, #466	17.50
	Bowl, 8", #1004	55.00
4	Bowl, 8½" soup, #381	25.00
	Candlestick, #625	30.00
6	Creamer, #138	15.00
5	Cup, ftd., #494	12.00
	Finger bowl liner, #3060	6.00
	Finger bowl, #3060	12.50
	Fruit salad, 7 oz., #3060	15.00
	Platter, 12½", oval, #901	75.00
	Platter, 16", oval, #901	95.00
	Sandwich tray, 12" oval, center handle, #173	37.50
5	Saucer, #494	3.00
	Stem, 1 oz., cordial, #3060	45.00
	Stem, 2½ oz., cocktail, #3060	20.00

		Green
	Stem, 2½ oz., wine, #3060	25.00
	Stem, 4½ oz., claret, #3060	27.50
	Stem, 5 oz., low sherbet, #3060	10.00
	Stem, 5½ oz., tall sherbet, #3060	12.50
	Stem, 6 oz., café parfait, #3060	25.00
	Stem, 9 oz., water, #3060	22.50
1	Sugar, #138	15.00
	Tumbler, 2 oz., bar, #3060	10.00
	Tumbler, 3 oz., ftd., #3060	12.00
7	Tumbler, 4 oz., oyster cocktail, #3060	12.00
	Tumbler, 5 oz., juice, #3060	12.00
	Tumbler, 5 oz., ftd. juice, #3060	14.00
	Tumbler, 8 oz., table, #3060	15.00
	Tumbler, 8 oz., ftd, #3060	17.50
	Tumbler, 10 oz., ftd., water, #3060	20.00
	Tumbler, 10 oz., water, #3060	17.50
	Tumbler, 12 oz., tea, #3060	20.00
	Tumbler, 12 oz., ftd., tea, #3060	22.50

Colors: amber, Bluebell, crystal, Emerald, Peach-blo

Number 704 is another Cambridge numbered line that has been referred to by a collector as "Windows Border" and that might be recalled better than Number 704, which typically is forgotten once it has been looked up.

"Windows Border" is often displayed in sets in malls without an identifying name, but labeled Cambridge since most pieces are marked with that revealing C in a triangle signifying Cambridge. I am hoping this exposure will enhance its appeal to collectors and bring it the acknowledgment it justly warrants. Look at it! It's a magnificent etching and most of all, it can still be found with searching.

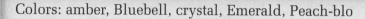

1

		All Colors
	Bottle, decanter, #0315	210.00
	Bottle, decanter, #3075	235.00
	Bowl, 5¼", fruit	18.00
8	Bowl, 6", cereal	25.00
7	Bowl, 7", 3 ftd.	35.00
10	Bowl, 8", rolled edge, #460	35.00
	Bowl, 8½", soup	33.00
	Bowl, 8¾", oval	33.00
	Bowl, 10½", #912 casserole and cover	175.00
	Bowl, 12", oval, #914	50.00
	Bowl, 12", oval w/cover, #915	125.00
	Bowl, 2 hdld. cream soup, #922	20.00
	Bowl, finger, #3060	35.00
	Bowl, finger, #3075	35.00
	Butter and cover, #920	125.00
	Candlestick, 2", #227½	22.50
	Candlestick, 3½", #628	27.50
	Candlestick, 7½", #439	35.00
	Candlestick, 8½", #438	40.00
	Candlestick, 9½", #437	45.00
	Candy box and cover, 5", #98, 3-part, flat	95.00

	All Colors
Candy box and cover, 5", #299, 3-ftd.	95.00
Candy box and cover, 6", #300, 3-ftd.	110.00
Celery, 11", #908	35.00
Celery tray, 11", #652	45.00
Cheese plate, #468	35.00
Cheese plate & cover, #3075	125.00
Cigarette box, #430	50.00
Cigarette box, #616	50.00
Cologne, 1 oz., #198 or #199	125.00
Comport, 5", #3075	30.00
Creamer, flat, #137	22.50
Creamer, flat, #942	22.50
Creamer, flat, #943	22.50
Creamer, flat, #944	22.50
Cup, #933	12.00
Cup, demi, #925	35.00
Gravy boat, double and stand, #917	125.00
Ice bucket w/bail, short, #970	110.00

		All Colors
	Ice bucket w/bail, tall, #957	125.00
	Ice tub, straight up tab hdlds., #394	100.00
	Jug, nite set, #103, 38 oz. w/tumbler	295.00
	Jug, #107	195.00
	Jug, #124, 68 oz., w/lid	295.00
	Jug, 62 oz., flat, #955	225.00
	Jug, #3077 w/lid	395.00
	Mayonnaise, 3 pc., #169	75.00
	Mayonnaise, 3 pc., #533	65.00
	Oil, 6 oz., #193	75.00
	Oyster cocktail, 4½ oz., ftd., #3060	14.00
	Pickle tray, 9", #907	30.00
	Plate, 6"	6.00
2	Plate, 7"	8.00
	Plate, 8"	15.00
	Plate, 8½"	20.00
11	Plate, 9½", dinner	65.00
4	Plate, 10½", service	75.00
12	Plate, 12", oval/cracker, #487	30.00
	Plate,13½"	75.00
	Plate, cupped, liner for creme soup, #922	8.00
	Plate, liner for finger bowl, #3060	8.00
	Plate, liner for finger bowl, #3075	8.00
	Platter, 12½", oval service, #901	75.00
	Platter, 16", oval, #904	95.00
	Puff & cover, 3" or 4", #578, blown	85.00
	Puff & cover, 4", #582	55.00
	Saucer, #933	5.00
	Saucer, demi, #925	10.00
5	Stem, 1 oz., cordial, #3075	60.00
9	Stem, 2½ oz., cocktail (wide bowl), #3075	16.00
	Stem, 2½ oz., wine (slender bowl), #3075	30.00
	Stem, 4½ oz., claret, #3075	35.00

		All Colors
	Stem, 5 oz., parfait, #3060	35.00
	Stem, 5½ oz., cafe parfait, #3075	35.00
3	Stem, 6 oz., high sherbet, #3060	18.00
	Stem, 9 oz., #3060	30.00
	Stem, 9 oz., #3075	30.00
	Stem, low sherbet, #3075	14.00
	Stem, hi sherbet, #3075	18.00
	Sugar, flat, #137	20.00
	Sugar, flat, #942	20.00
	Sugar, flat, #943	20.00
	Sugar, flat, #944	20.00
	Syrup, 9 oz., w/metal cover, #170	165.00
	Syrup, tall jug, #814	175.00
	Toast dish and cover, 9", #951	250.00
14	Tray, 10", center handle, #140	45.00
13	Tray, 12", oval, center handle, #173	40.00
	Tumbler, 2 oz., flat, #3060	30.00
	Tumbler, 2 oz., whiskey, #3075	30.00
	Tumbler, 3 oz., ftd., #3075	28.00
	Tumbler, 5 oz., ftd., #3075	20.00
	Tumbler, 5 oz., #3075	20.00
	Tumbler, 6 oz., ftd. fruit salad (sherbet)	14.00
	Tumbler, 8 oz., ftd., #3075	18.00
	Tumbler, 10 oz., #3075	20.00
1	Tumbler, 10 oz., flat, #3060	20.00
	Tumbler, 10 oz., ftd., #3075	22.50
	Tumbler, 12 oz., #3075	25.00
6	Tumbler, 12 oz., flat, #3060	25.00
	Tumbler, 12 oz., ftd., #3060	25.00
	Tumbler, 12 oz., ftd., #3075	27.00
	Vase, 6½", ftd., #1005	100.00
	Vase, 9½", ftd., #787	150.00

Colors: crystal, Flamingo pink, Sahara yellow, Moongleam green, Hawthorne orchid, Marigold deep amber/yellow, and Dawn

Octagon was frequently marked by Heisey's trademark H within a diamond; so, it is one pattern that every one can enthusiastically conclude is Heisey. Not many collectors search for this plainer pattern, but it does come in a rainbow of colors. In the price list below, the only pieces that stick out are the basket, ice tub, and the 12" four-part tray. Note ice tubs were sometimes cut or etched as shown here. That tray can be found in the rare gray/black color called Dawn. Octagon is prudently priced.

Marigold pieces are found occasionally in Octagon. This is a seldom seen Heisey color; but be cautious when buying it because the color is subject to peeling and crazing which cannot be undone. If that should happen, it becomes uninviting to collectors.

		Crystal	Flamingo	Sahara	Moongleam	Hawthorne	Marigold
3	Basket, 5", #500	500.00	300.00	300.00	425.00	450.00	350.00
	Bonbon, 6", sides up, #1229	10.00	40.00	25.00	25.00	40.00	
	Bowl, cream soup, 2 hdld.	10.00	20.00	25.00	30.00	40.00	
	Bowl, 2 hdld, ind. nut bowl	15.00	25.00	25.00	25.00	60.00	65.00
	Bowl, 5½", jelly, #1229	15.00	30.00	25.00	25.00	50.00	
	Bowl, 6", mint, #1229	10.00	20.00	25.00	25.00	45.00	30.00
	Bowl, 6", #500	14.00	20.00	22.00	25.00	35.00	
	Bowl, 6½", grapefruit	10.00	20.00	22.00	25.00	35.00	
	Bowl, 8", ftd., #1229 comport	15.00	25.00	35.00	45.00	55.00	
	Bowl, 9", flat soup	10.00	15.00	20.00	27.50	30.00	
	Bowl, 9", vegetable	15.00	32.00	25.00	30.00	50.00	
	Candlestick, 3", 1-lite	15.00	30.00	30.00	40.00	50.00	
	Cheese dish, 6", 2 hdld., #1229	7.00	15.00	10.00	15.00	15.00	
7	Creamer, #500	10.00	30.00	35.00	35.00	50.00	
	Creamer, hotel	10.00	30.00	30.00	35.00	50.00	
5	Cup, after dinner	10.00	20.00	20.00	25.00	42.00	
4	Cup, #1231	5.00	15.00	20.00	20.00	35.00	
	Dish, frozen dessert, #500	15.00	30.00	20.00	30.00	35.00	50.00
1	Ice tub, #500	30.00	75.00	80.00	85.00	129.00	150.00
	Mayonnaise, 5½", ftd., #1229	10.00	25.00	30.00	35.00	55.00	
8	Nut, two hdld.	10.00	25.00	20.00	25.00	65.00	70.00
	Plate, cream soup liner	3.00	5.00	7.00	9.00	12.00	
	Plate, 6"	4.00	8.00	8.00	10.00	15.00	
	Plate, 7", bread	5.00	10.00	10.00	15.00	20.00	
	Plate, 8", luncheon	7.00	10.00	10.00	15.00	25.00	
	Plate, 10", sand., #1229	15.00	20.00	25.00	30.00	80.00	

	Crystal	Flamingo	Sahara	Moongleam	Hawthorne	Marigold
Plate, 10", muffin, #1229, sides up	15.00	25.00	30.00	35.00	40.00	
Plate, 10½"	17.00	25.00	30.00	35.00	45.00	
Plate, 10½", ctr. hdld., sandwich	25.00	40.00	40.00	45.00	70.00	
Plate, 12", muffin, #1229, sides up	20.00	27.00	30.00	35.00	45.00	
2 Plate, 13", hors d'oeuvre, #1229	20.00	35.00	35.00	45.00	60.00	
Plate, 14"	22.00	25.00	30.00	35.00	50.00	
Platter, 12¾", oval	20.00	25.00	30.00	40.00	50.00	
5 Saucer, after dinner	5.00	8.00	10.00	10.00	12.00	
4 Saucer, #1231	5.00	8.00	10.00	10.00	12.00	
6 Sugar, #500	10.00	25.00	35.00	35.00	50.00	
Sugar, hotel	10.00	30.00	30.00	35.00	50.00	
Tray, 6", oblong, #500	8.00	15.00	15.00	15.00	30.00	
Tray, 9", celery	10.00	20.00	20.00	25.00	45.00	
Tray, 12", celery	10.00	25.00	25.00	30.00	50.00	
Tray, 12", 4 pt., #500 variety	60.00	120.00	140.00	160.00	250.00	*350.00

*Dawn

Colors: crystal, Flamingo pink, Sahara yellow, Moongleam green, Marigold deep amber/yellow

Due to the abundance of Sahara (yellow), Old Colony pricing will be based on Sahara as follows: crystal, subtract 50%; Flamingo, subtract 10%; Moongleam, add 10%; Marigold, add 20%. Space does not permit pricing each color separately. If you like Heisey's Sahara, this would be the ideal pattern to collect due to its availability.

		Sahara
	Bouillon cup, 2 hdld., ftd.	25.00
	Bowl, finger, #4075	15.00
	Bowl, ftd., finger, #3390	25.00
	Bowl, 4½", nappy	14.00
	Bowl, 5", ftd., 2 hdld.	24.00
	Bowl, 6", ftd., 2 hdld., jelly	30.00
	Bowl, 6", dolphin ftd., mint	35.00
	Bowl, 7", triplex, dish	35.00
	Bowl, 7½", dolphin ftd., nappy	70.00
	Bowl, 8", nappy	40.00
	Bowl, 8½", ftd., floral, 2 hdld.	60.00
	Bowl, 9", 3 hdld.	90.00
	Bowl, 10", rnd., 2 hdld., salad	60.00
	Bowl, 10", sq., salad, 2 hdld.	55.00
	Bowl, 10", oval, dessert, 2 hdld.	50.00
	Bowl, 10", oval, veg.	42.00
	Bowl, 11", floral, dolphin ft.	80.00
	Bowl, 13", ftd., flared	40.00
	Bowl, 13", 2 pt., pickle & olive	24.00
	Cigarette holder, #3390	44.00
	Comport, 7", oval, ftd.	80.00
	Comport, 7", ftd., #3368	70.00
	Cream soup, 2 hdld.	22.00
1	Creamer, dolphin ft.	45.00
	Creamer, indiv.	40.00
	Cup, after dinner	40.00
9	Cup	32.00
	Decanter, 1 pt.	325.00
	Flagon, 12 oz., #3390	100.00
	Grapefruit, 6"	30.00
	Grapefruit, ftd., #3380	20.00
	Ice tub, dolphin ft.	115.00
	Mayonnaise, 5½", dolphin ft.	70.00
6	Nut dish, individual, dolphin ft.	60.00

		Sahara
	Oil, 4 oz., ftd.	105.00
	Pitcher, 3 pt., #3390	230.00
	Pitcher, 3 pt., dolphin ft.	240.00
	Plate, bouillon	15.00
	Plate, cream soup	12.00
	Plate, 4½", rnd.	7.00
	Plate, 6", rnd.	15.00
	Plate, 6", sq.	15.00
	Plate, 7", rnd.	22.00
8	Plate, 7", sq.	22.00
	Plate, 8", rnd.	28.00
2	Plate, 8", sq.	28.00
	Plate, 9", rnd.	28.00
	Plate, 10½", rnd.	80.00
	Plate, 10½", sq.	70.00
	Plate, 12", rnd.	75.00
	Plate, 12", 2 hdld., rnd., muffin	75.00
	Plate, 12", 2 hdld., rnd., sand.	70.00
	Plate, 13", 2 hdld., sq., sand.	50.00
	Plate, 13", 2 hdld., sq., muffin	50.00
	Platter, 14", oval	45.00
	Salt & pepper, pr.	125.00
9	Saucer, sq.	10.00
	Saucer, rnd.	10.00
5	Stem, #3380, 1 oz., cordial	125.00
	Stem, #3380, 2½ oz., wine	32.00
	Stem, #3380, 3 oz., cocktail	22.00
	Stem, #3380, 4 oz., oyster/cocktail	18.00
	Stem, #3380, 4 oz., claret	38.00
	Stem, #3380, 5 oz., parfait	20.00
	Stem, #3380, 6 oz., champagne	18.00
	Stem, #3380, 6 oz., sherbet	18.00
	Stem, #3380, 10 oz., short soda	18.00
	Stem, #3380, 10 oz., tall soda	22.00
	Stem, #3390, 1 oz., cordial	110.00
	Stem, #3390, 2½ oz., wine	33.00
	Stem, #3390, 3 oz., cocktail	18.00

		Sahara			Sahara
	Stem, #3390, 3 oz., oyster/cocktail	18.00	Tumbler, dolphin ft.		165.00
	Stem, #3390, 4 oz., claret	28.00	Tumbler, #3380, 1 oz., ftd., bar		40.00
4	Stem, #3390, 6 oz., champagne	22.00	Tumbler, #3380, 2 oz., ftd., bar		20.00
	Stem, #3390, 6 oz., sherbet	22.00	Tumbler, #3380, 5 oz., ftd., bar		16.00
	Stem, #3390, 11 oz., low water	22.00	Tumbler, #3380, 8 oz., ftd., soda		18.00
	Stem, #3390, 11 oz., tall water	25.00	Tumbler, #3380, 10 oz., ftd., soda		18.00
7	Sugar, dolphin ft.	45.00	3 Tumbler, #3380, 12 oz., ftd., tea		20.00
	Sugar, indiv.	40.00	Tumbler, #3390, 2 oz., ftd.		22.00
	Tray, 10", celery	30.00	Tumbler, #3390, 5 oz., ftd., juice		20.00
	Tray, 12", ctr. hdld., sandwich	75.00	Tumbler, #3390, 8 oz., ftd., soda		25.00
	Tray, 12", ctr. hdld., sq.	75.00	Tumbler, #3390, 12 oz., ftd., tea		27.00
	Tray, 13", celery	40.00	Vase, 9", dolphin ftd.		150.00
	Tray, 13", 2 hdld., hors d'oeuvre	75.00			

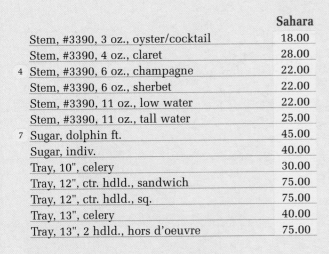

OLD SANDWICH, Blank #1404, A.H. Hesiey & Co.

Colors: crystal, Flamingo pink, Sahara yellow, Moongleam green, cobalt, amber

Moongleam is the most desirable Old Sandwich color as with its sister pattern Ipswich. However, we are showing you Flamingo pink and Sahara yellow this time. Sets can be gathered in crystal, but colored sets are more scarce and costly. Notice there are four sizes of creamers, but only one sugar. Cobalt blue pieces of Old Sandwich are rare and usually expensive as you can see by the price listing.

	Crystal	Flamingo	Sahara	Moongleam	Cobalt
15 Ashtray, individual	9.00	60.00	35.00	60.00	45.00
Beer mug, 12 oz.	50.00	300.00	210.00	400.00	240.00
6 Beer mug, 14 oz.*	55.00	325.00	225.00	425.00	250.00
Beer mug, 18 oz.	65.00	400.00	270.00	475.00	380.00
17 Bottle, catsup, w/#3 stopper (like large cruet)	70.00	200.00	175.00	225.00	
Bowl, finger	12.00	50.00	60.00	60.00	
2 Bowl, ftd., popcorn, cupped	80.00	110.00	110.00	135.00	
19 Bowl, 11", rnd., ftd., floral	50.00	85.00	65.00	100.00	
20 Bowl, 12", oval, ftd., floral	50.00	80.00	70.00	80.00	
1 Candlestick, 6"	60.00	120.00	110.00	150.00	250.00
Cigarette holder	50.00	65.00	60.00	65.00	
7 Comport, 6"	60.00	95.00	90.00	100.00	
Creamer, oval	25.00	90.00	85.00	50.00	
Creamer, 12 oz.	32.00	185.00	170.00	175.00	575.00
Creamer, 14 oz.	35.00	175.00	180.00	185.00	
Creamer, 18 oz.	40.00	185.00	190.00	195.00	
16 Cup	40.00	65.00	65.00	125.00	
Decanter, 1 pint, w/#98 stopper	75.00	185.00	200.00	225.00	500.00
Floral block, #22	15.00	25.00	30.00	35.00	
14 Oil bottle, 2½ oz., #85 stopper	65.00	250.00	170.00	180.00	
Parfait, 4½ oz.	15.00	50.00	50.00	60.00	
Pilsner, 8 oz.	14.00	28.00	32.00	38.00	

		Crystal	Flamingo	Sahara	Moongleam	Cobalt
	Pilsner, 10 oz.	16.00	32.00	37.00	42.00	
	Pitcher, ½ gallon, ice lip	100.00	175.00	165.00	185.00	
4	Pitcher, ½ gallon, reg.	100.00	175.00	165.00	185.00	
	Plate, 6", sq., ground bottom	10.00	20.00	17.00	22.00	
	Plate, 7", sq.	10.00	27.00	25.00	30.00	
3	Plate, 8", sq.	15.00	30.00	27.00	32.00	
5	Salt & pepper, pr.	40.00	65.00	75.00	85.00	
16	Saucer	10.00	15.00	15.00	25.00	
18	Stem, 2½ oz., wine	18.00	45.00	45.00	55.00	
	Stem, 3 oz., cocktail	20.00	30.00	32.00	40.00	
	Stem, 4 oz., claret	17.00	35.00	35.00	50.00	150.00
13	Stem, 4 oz., oyster cocktail	12.00	27.00	27.00	32.00	
12	Stem, 4 oz., sherbet	7.00	17.00	17.00	20.00	
	Stem, 5 oz., saucer champagne	12.00	32.00	32.00	35.00	
21	Stem, 10 oz., low ft.	20.00	30.00	35.00	40.00	
	Sugar, oval	25.00	90.00	55.00	60.00	
	Sundae, 6 oz.	18.00	30.00	30.00	35.00	
9	Tumbler, 1½ oz., bar, ground bottom	20.00	130.00	120.00	135.00	100.00
	Tumbler, 5 oz., juice	7.00	15.00	15.00	25.00	
	Tumbler, 6½ oz., toddy	20.00	35.00	40.00	40.00	
	Tumbler, 8 oz., ground bottom, cupped & straight rim	20.00	35.00	35.00	40.00	
11	Tumbler, 10 oz.	20.00	40.00	40.00	45.00	
	Tumbler, 10 oz., low ft.	15.00	40.00	42.00	45.00	
8	Tumbler, 12 oz., ftd., iced tea	20.00	45.00	45.00	55.00	
10	Tumbler, 12 oz., iced tea	20.00	45.00	45.00	55.00	

*Amber; $300.00.

22 Whimsey crystal basket made from footed soda, $725.00.

PIONEER, #2350, Fostoria Glass Company, c. 1926

Colors: amber, Blue, crystal, green, Rose, Ebony, Topaz, Azure, Orchid

Fostoria's Pioneer is the mould blank on which Seville and Vesper are etched. There are collectors of #2350 Pioneer who search for the less expensive non-etched blank. Blue, as the color pictured here was called, can be bought at prices well below those of Vesper. The Blue butter dish pictured could be bought for $125.00, but one etched Vesper would be exceedingly costly. Gathering non-etched glassware can augment etched settings. Numerous collectors have informed me that it is better to have an undecorated piece in their set than nothing at all.

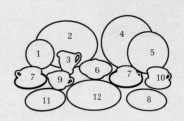

	Crystal/Amber Green	Ebony	Rose Topaz	Azure Orchid	Blue
Ashtray, 3¾"	16.00	18.00	20.00	24.00	
Ashtray, lg., deep	18.00	18.00	22.00	25.00	
Bouillon, flat	12.00				14.00
Bouillon, ftd., #2350½	10.00				
8 Bowl, 5", fruit (shallow)	8.00				15.00
Bowl, 6", cereal	12.00				18.00
12 Bowl, 7", rnd. soup	15.00				25.00
Bowl, 8", nappy	20.00				25.00
Bowl, 8", oval pickle	17.50				22.50
Bowl, 9", nappy	17.50				25.00
Bowl, 9", oval baker	32.00				42.00
Bowl, 10", oval baker	40.00				50.00
Bowl, 10", salad	25.00				40.00
Bowl, creme soup, flat	15.00				27.50
Bowl, creme soup, ftd., #2350½	18.00				
6 Butter & cover	75.00				125.00
Celery, 11", oval narrow	20.00				24.00
Comport, 8"	27.50		30.00	40.00	
9 Creamer, flat	9.00				15.00
3 Creamer, ftd., #2350½ (Ruby 17.50)	9.00	10.00	12.00		15.00
Cup, after dinner	10.00	14.00			16.00
7 Cup, flat	12.00				15.00
10 Cup, ftd., #2350½	10.00	12.50			15.00

	Crystal/Amber Green	Ebony	Rose Topaz	Azure Orchid	Blue
Egg cup	20.00		25.00		
Grapefruit liner (looks like straight crystal glass)	6.00				
Grapefruit, strt. side	25.00				33.00
1 Plate, 5", bouillon liner	4.00				8.00
11 Plate, 6"	5.00	8.00			
5 Plate, 7", salad	6.00	9.00			9.00
Plate, 8"	8.00	10.00			15.00
4 Plate, 9"	12.50	14.00			20.00
Plate, 10"	17.50	20.00			30.00
Plate, 12", chop	18.00				35.00
Plate, 15", service	25.00				40.00
Plate, bouillon liner	5.00				
Plate, creme soup	6.00				7.00
Plate, oval sauce boat	10.00				12.50
2 Platter, 10½"	22.50				30.00
Platter, 12"	20.00				35.00
Platter, 15"	25.00				35.00
Relish, rnd., 3 pt.	12.50		15.00	20.00	
Sauce boat, flat	22.50				35.00
7 Saucer	3.00	4.00			5.00
10 Saucer, after dinner	3.00	4.00			4.00
Sugar cover	14.00				30.00
Sugar, flat	9.00				15.00
Sugar, ftd., #2350½ (Ruby 17.50)	9.00	10.00	12.00		15.00
Tumbler, ftd., water					25.00

Colors: amber, crystal, green, pink, cobalt blue, red

Plaza was Duncan & Miller's pattern #21, which was made in an array of colors. I find more amber in my travels as indicated by my photograph. You buy what you find when you are laboring to add a new example to a book.

Pink and green are sought more than other colors. Were blue and red more available, those would be the preferred colors. I see very little of those colors except in the Pittsburgh area; and in that part of the country, everyone knows Duncan and it is valued for the knowledgeable determined collector. Let me know what you find, as I am sure my listing is not complete at this juncture of including Plaza.

		Amber/Crystal	*Pink/Green			Amber/Crystal	*Pink/Green
8	Bowl, 4⅜", finger	6.00	15.00		Salt and pepper, pr.	35.00	
10	Bowl, 6¼", cereal	8.00	20.00	11	Saucer	1.00	4.00
	Bowl, 9", oval vegetable	28.00	60.00	6	Stem, cocktail	10.00	20.00
	Bowl, 10", deep vegetable	30.00	55.00		Stem, cordial	20.00	40.00
	Bowl, 14", flared, console	35.00	95.00	4	Stem, saucer champagne	8.00	17.50
	Candle, 4¾"h. x 7"w. double	22.00	52.50		Stem, 3¾, sherbet	6.00	15.00
1	Candy and lid, 4½", round	18.00	40.00		Stem, water	14.00	25.00
11	Cup	5.00	12.00		Stem, wine	14.00	25.00
9	Mustard, w/slotted lid	17.50	30.00		Tumbler, flat juice	6.00	15.00
	Oil bottle	27.50	60.00		Tumbler, flat tea	10.00	20.00
	Parfait	12.00	30.00		Tumbler, flat water	9.00	17.50
	Pitcher, flat	40.00	125.00		Tumbler, flat whiskey	8.00	15.00
	Plate, 5¼", finger bowl liner	4.00	10.00	2	Tumbler, 3½", ftd., juice	7.00	15.00
	Plate, 6½", bread and butter	3.00	9.00		Tumbler, ftd., tea	12.00	25.00
	Plate, 7½", salad	4.00	12.00	5	Tumbler, ftd., water	10.00	18.00
3	Plate, 8½", luncheon	6.00	15.00		Vase, 8"	30.00	65.00
	Plate, 10½", hdld.	18.00	37.50				

*Add 50% for any cobalt blue or red

7 Cup, not Plaza

Colors: crystal, Flamingo pink, Moongleam green, and amber

Many novices call this Depression glass; and elite Heisey dealers I know would rather put Pleat and Panel in that category.

There are color variations in the pink. Pink was not an easy color to manage in the days before precise temperature controls on glass vats. Only inexpensively made Depression glass companies were supposed to have color deviations. Yes, even Heisey had difficulty maintaining color. Although avid Heisey connoisseurs will not admit it, not all Heisey was first quality. They had their glass rejects. However, it does echo a starting Deco influence in its design.

Most Pleat & Panel pieces carry the well-known H in a diamond mark. Stems are marked on the stem itself and not the foot, so look there if you are searching for a mark. Remember, it does not have to be marked to be Heisey.

		Crystal	Flamingo	Moongleam
	Bowl, 4", chow chow	6.00	11.00	14.00
	Bowl, 4½", nappy	6.00	11.00	14.00
	Bowl, 5", 2 hdld., bouillon	7.00	14.00	17.50
	Bowl, 5", 2 hdld., jelly	9.00	14.00	17.50
	Bowl, 5", lemon, w/cover	20.00	60.00	65.00
	Bowl, 6½", grapefruit/cereal	5.00	14.00	17.50
	Bowl, 8", nappy	10.00	32.50	40.00
	Bowl, 9", oval, vegetable	12.50	35.00	40.00
	Cheese & cracker set, 10½", tray, w/compote	25.00	75.00	80.00
1	Compotier, w/cover, 5", high ftd.	35.00	75.00	80.00
	Creamer, hotel	10.00	25.00	30.00
	Cup	7.00	15.00	17.50
	Marmalade, 4¾"	10.00	30.00	35.00
	*Oil bottle, 3 oz., w/pressed stopper	30.00	75.00	110.00
	Pitcher, 3 pint, ice lip	45.00	140.00	165.00
3	Pitcher, 3 pint	45.00	140.00	165.00

		Crystal	Flamingo	Moongleam
	Plate, 6"	4.00	8.00	8.00
	Plate, 6¾", bouillon underliner	4.00	8.00	8.00
	Plate, 7", bread	4.00	8.00	10.00
4	Plate, 8", luncheon	5.00	12.50	15.00
	Plate, 10¾", dinner	15.00	48.00	52.00
	Plate, 14", sandwich	15.00	32.50	40.00
	Platter, 12", oval	15.00	42.50	47.50
	Saucer	3.00	5.00	5.00
6	Sherbet, 5 oz., footed	4.00	10.00	12.00
	Stem, 5 oz., saucer champagne	5.00	14.00	18.00
5	Stem, 7½ oz., low foot	12.00	30.00	35.00
7	Stem, 8 oz.	15.00	35.00	40.00
	Sugar w/lid, hotel	10.00	30.00	35.00
	Tray, 10", compartmented spice	10.00	25.00	30.00
	Tumbler, 8 oz., ground bottom	5.00	17.50	22.50
	Tumbler, 12 oz., tea, ground bottom	7.00	25.00	30.00
2	Vase, 8"	30.00	80.00	100.00

*Amber 175.00

Colors: crystal, yellow, Heatherbloom, green, amber, Carmen, and Crown Tuscan w/gold

Portia crystal items not listed here may be found under Rose Point, which has a more detailed listing of Cambridge pieces. Prices for the Portia items will run 20% to 30% less than the same item in Rose Point.

	Crystal
Basket, 2 hdld. (upturned sides)	30.00
Basket, 7", 1 hdld.	350.00
Bowl, 3", indiv. nut, 4 ftd.	60.00
Bowl, 3½", cranberry	45.00
Bowl, 3½", sq., cranberry	45.00
Bowl, 5¼", 2 hdld., bonbon, #3400/180	30.00
Bowl, 6", 2 pt., relish	27.50
Bowl, 6", ftd., 2 hdld., bonbon	30.00
Bowl, 6", grapefruit or oyster	35.00
Bowl, 6½", 3 pt., relish	30.00
Bowl, 7", 2 pt., relish	35.00

	Crystal
Bowl, 7", ftd., bonbon, tab hdld.	32.00
Bowl, 7", pickle or relish	38.00
Bowl, 9", 3 pt., celery & relish, tab hdld.	48.00
Bowl, 9½", ftd., pickle (like corn bowl)	35.00
Bowl, 10", flared, 4 ftd.	50.00
Bowl, 11", 2 pt., 2 hdld., "figure 8" relish	35.00
Bowl, 11", 2 hdld.	60.00
Bowl, 12", 3 pt., celery & relish, tab hdld.	55.00
Bowl, 12", 5 pt., celery & relish	55.00
Bowl, 12", flared, 4 ftd.	60.00
Bowl, 12", oval, 4 ftd., "ears" handles	85.00

PORTIA

		Crystal
	Bowl, finger, w/liner, #3124	50.00
28	Bowl, 10", hndl., #3500/28	65.00
	Bowl, seafood (fruit cocktail w/liner)	35.00
9	Candlestick, 5", keyhole, #3400/646	35.00
24	Candlestick, 5½", double, #502	75.00
	Candlestick, 6", 2-lite, keyhole, #3400/647	45.00
	Candlestick, 6", 3-lite, keyhole, #3400/648	55.00
	Candy box, w/cover, rnd.	135.00
2	Candy box, w/cover, 6", Ram's head, #3500/78	195.00
	Cigarette holder, urn shape	60.00
	Cocktail icer, 2 pt.	75.00
	Cocktail shaker, w/glass stopper	195.00
	Cocktail shaker, 80 oz., hdld. ball w/chrome top	235.00
15	Cologne, 2 oz., hdld. ball w/stopper, #3400/97	195.00
	Comport, 5½"	50.00
	Comport, 5⅜", blown	65.00
11	Creamer, ftd., #3400/68	20.00
	Creamer, hdld. ball	45.00
	Creamer, indiv.	20.00
	Cup, ftd., sq.	25.00
17	Cup, rd., #3400/54	18.00
20	Cup, after dinner, #3400/69	100.00
	Decanter, 29 oz., ftd., sherry, w/stopper	265.00
1	Decanter, 35 oz., flat, hdld, #3400/113	200.00
	Hurricane lamp, candlestick base	195.00
	Hurricane lamp, keyhole base, w/prisms	250.00
	Ice bucket, w/chrome handle	125.00
	Ivy ball, 5¼"	95.00
	Mayonnaise, div. bowl, w/liner & 2 ladles	60.00
23	Mayonnaise, w/liner & ladle, #3400/11	60.00
	Oil, 6 oz., loop hdld., w/stopper	125.00
	Oil, 6 oz., hdld. ball, w/stopper	110.00
	Pitcher, ball, 80 oz., #3400/38	275.00
	Pitcher, Doulton, 76 oz., #3400/152	395.00
6	Pitcher, 76 oz., #3400/100	195.00

		Crystal
	Plate, 6", 2 hdld.	15.00
4	Plate, 6½", bread/butter	7.50
26	Plate, 7", tab hndl., mayonnaise/liner, #3400/15	15.00
	Plate, 8", salad	15.00
	Plate, 8", ftd., 2 hdld.	20.00
	Plate, 8", ftd., bonbon, tab hdld.	22.00
	Plate, 8½", sq.	18.00
25	Plate, 10½", dinner	95.00
	Plate, 13", 4 ftd., torte	65.00
	Plate, 13½", 2 hdld., cake	65.00
	Plate, 14", torte	75.00
	Puff box, 3½", ball shape, w/lid	225.00
16	Salt & pepper, pr., ftd., #3400/77	45.00
17	Saucer, rnd., #3400/54	5.00
20	Saucer, after dinner, #3400/69	25.00
	Set: 3 pc. frappe (bowl, 2 plain inserts)	65.00
13	Stem, #3121, 1 oz., cordial	65.00
	Stem, #3121, 1 oz., low ftd., brandy	60.00
	Stem, #3121, 2½ oz., wine	40.00
	Stem, #3121, 3 oz., cocktail	28.00
	Stem, #3121, 4½ oz., claret	45.00
	Stem, #3121, 4½ oz., oyster cocktail	18.00
	Stem, #3121, 5 oz., parfait	40.00
	Stem, #3121, 6 oz., low sherbet	18.00
	Stem, #3121, 6 oz., tall sherbet	20.00
	Stem, #3121, 10 oz., goblet	30.00
7	Stem, #3122, 1 oz., cordial	60.00
18	Stem, #3122, 5oz., ftd., juice	25.00
	Stem, #3124, 3 oz., cocktail	18.00
	Stem, #3124, 3 oz., wine	30.00
	Stem, #3124, 4½ oz., claret	40.00
	Stem, #3124, 7 oz., low sherbet	18.00
	Stem, #3124, 7 oz., tall sherbet	20.00
	Stem, #3124, 10 oz., goblet	30.00
14	Stem, #3126, 1 oz., cordial	60.00
	Stem, #3126, 1 oz., low ft., brandy	60.00

		Crystal
22	Stem, #3126, 2½ oz., wine	38.00
	Stem, #3126, 3 oz., cocktail	20.00
	Stem, #3126, 4½ oz., claret	40.00
	Stem, #3126, 4½ oz., low ft., oyster cocktail	18.00
	Stem, #3126, 7 oz., low sherbet	16.00
3	Stem, #3126, 7 oz., tall sherbet	18.00
	Stem, #3126, 9 oz., goblet	30.00
12	Stem, #3130, 1 oz., cordial	60.00
	Stem, #3130, 2½ oz., wine	38.00
	Stem, #3130, 3 oz., cocktail	18.00
	Stem, #3130, 4½ oz., claret	40.00
27	Stem, #3130, 4½ oz., fruit/oyster cocktail	18.00
	Stem, #3130, 7 oz., low sherbet	16.00
	Stem, #3130, 7 oz., tall sherbet	18.00
	Stem, #3130, 9 oz., goblet	30.00
	Sugar, ftd., hdld. ball	45.00
10	Sugar, ftd., #3400/68	20.00
	Sugar, indiv.	20.00
	Tray, 11", celery	40.00
8	Tray, 11", hndl., sandwich	40.00
19	Tumbler, 1 oz., cordial, #1344	45.00
	Tumbler, #3121, 2½ oz., bar	40.00
	Tumbler, #3121, 5 oz., ftd., juice	20.00
	Tumbler, #3121, 10 oz., ftd., water	25.00
	Tumbler, #3121, 12 oz., ftd., tea	28.00

		Crystal
	Tumbler, #3124, 3 oz.	18.00
	Tumbler, #3124, 5 oz., juice	20.00
	Tumbler, #3124, 10 oz., water	25.00
	Tumbler, #3124, 12 oz., tea	30.00
	Tumbler, #3126, 2½ oz.	38.00
	Tumbler, #3126, 5 oz., juice	20.00
	Tumbler, #3126, 10 oz., water	24.00
	Tumbler, #3126, 12 oz., tea	28.00
	Tumbler, #3130, 5 oz., juice	24.00
	Tumbler, #3130, 10 oz., water	24.00
	Tumbler, #3130, 12 oz., tea	28.00
29	Tumbler, #3400/38, 12 oz.	30.00
	Vase, 5", globe	65.00
	Vase, 6", ftd.	75.00
	Vase, 8", ftd.	100.00
	Vase, 9", keyhole ft.	85.00
5	Vase, 10", #1242	70.00
	Vase, 11", flower	100.00
	Vase, 11", pedestal ft.	110.00
	Vase, 12", keyhole ft.	130.00
	Vase, 13", flower	165.00

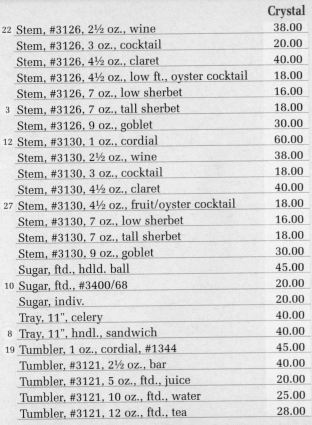

PRINCESS FEATHER, #201 Westmoreland Glass Company,

late 1924 – early 1950s; reissued as Golden Sunset (amber) in 1960s

Colors: blue, crystal, crystal w/black base, crystal w/lavender or red flash, green, pink

Princess Feather is frequently misidentified with other companies' Sandwich patterns. Note the end-to-end quarter moons tied together in the pattern. If that visual is kept in mind, you will never confuse this with any Sandwich pattern again.

The color most often found is Golden Sunset (amber) which was not made until the 1960s. Initially made in crystal in the mid-1920s, this long-lasting pattern can be gathered in crystal more easily than any color.

Pink or green catch the eye of more collectors. Sets can be collected in either color with work and patience. I have seen little of the lavender or red flashed.

		Amber/Crystal	*Pink/Green			Amber/Crystal	*Pink/Green
	Basket, 8", hdld.	50.00		5	Plate, 8"	8.00	17.50
	Bonbon, 6", hdld.	20.00			Plate, 10½", dinner	35.00	75.00
	Bonbon, 7½", crimped	25.00			Plate, 13", service	38.00	80.00
	Bowl, finger	8.00	15.00		Plate, 18"	75.00	
11	Bowl, 5", nappy	8.00	15.00		Relish, 5 part, 2 hdld.	40.00	
	Bowl, 6½", nappy	12.50	20.00		Salt and pepper	25.00	55.00
	Bowl, 6½", grapefruit	12.00	20.00	12	Saucer	3.00	4.00
	Bowl, 9½", bell, ftd.	40.00			Stem, 2 oz., cordial	18.00	
	Bowl, 10", banana, ftd.	60.00		1	Stem, 2½ oz., wine	12.00	22.50
	Bowl, 10", crimped, ftd.	55.00		3	Stem, 3 oz., cocktail	10.00	20.00
	Bowl, 11" x 8", oval, hdld.	50.00			Stem, 5 oz., high sherbet	10.00	20.00
	Bowl, 12" nappy	35.00	60.00	4	Stem, 5 oz.. saucer champagne	10.00	20.00
	Cake salver, 10"	40.00		10	Stem, 6 oz., sherbet	8.00	16.00
	Candle, one lite	15.00	25.00	2	Stem, 8 oz., water	12.50	25.00
	Candle, double	25.00	37.50	8	Sugar	10.00	20.00
9	Creamer	10.00	20.00		Tray, creamer/sugar	12.00	
12	Cup	8.00	5.00		Tumbler, 6 oz., juice	8.00	16.00
	Decanter w/stopper	50.00		6	Tumbler, 9 oz., ftd.	10.00	22.00
	Jelly w/lid, 5"	30.00		7	Tumbler, 10 oz., water, flat	12.50	25.00
	Pitcher, 54 oz.	95.00			Tumbler, 12 oz., ice tea, flat	15.00	30.00
	Plate, 6", #3400/60	5.00	10.00		Vase, 14", flat	70.00	
	Plate, 6½", liner finger bowl	5.00	10.00				
	Plate, 7"	6.00	12.50				

*Add 25% for blue or ruby/lavender flash.

Colors: amber, black, Blue, crystal, green, pink

Priscilla is an early Fostoria pattern that does not have a variety of pieces, but is collected for its colors and simplistic lines. The blue shown was called Blue by Fostoria. Not much imagination is shown, but is does get the job done.

There are differing viewpoints as to whether the handled custard or sherbet goes on the canapé plate, but the handled custard base fits that ring quite well. You will find more amber than any other color, but collecting this pattern will save you enough money for gasoline to search for it.

6

		Amber Green	Blue
	Ashtray, 3", sq.		12.50
2	Bouillon	10.00	17.50
	Cream soup	15.00	20.00
1	Creamer	9.00	15.00
	Cup	9.00	15.00
3	Custard, ftd., hdld.	8.00	15.00
	Pitcher, 48 oz., ftd.	125.00	250.00
	Plate, 8"	8.00	15.00
4	Plate, 8" w/indent (Mah Jongg)	8.00	12.00
	Saucer	2.00	4.50
	Stem, 7 oz.	10.00	22.50
	Stem, 9 oz., water	12.00	25.00
	Stem, saucer champagne	10.00	20.00
5	Sugar	9.00	15.00
6	Tumbler, ftd.	12.00	22.50
	Tumbler, ftd., hdld.	15.00	25.00

1930s – 1957

Colors: crystal, Limelight green

This pattern was first called Whirlpool in the 1930s; but Heisey changed its name to Provincial for the 1952 reissue. Limelight colored Provincial was Heisey's attempt at revitalizing the earlier, popular Zircon color.

		Crystal	Limelight Green
	Ashtray, 3", sq.	12.50	
	Bonbon dish, 7", 2 hdld., upturned sides	12.00	45.00
	Bowl, 5 quart, punch	120.00	
	Bowl, individual, nut/jelly	20.00	40.00
9	Bowl, 4½", nappy	15.00	70.00
	Bowl, 5", 2 hdld., nut/jelly	20.00	
	Bowl, 5½", nappy	20.00	40.00
	Bowl, 5½", round, hdld., nappy	20.00	
11	Bowl, 5½", tri-corner, hdld., nappy, mayo	30.00	80.00
10	Bowl, 10", 4 part, relish	40.00	150.00
16	Bowl, 12", floral	40.00	
	Bowl, 13", gardenia	40.00	
4	Box, 5½", footed, candy, w/cover	85.00	550.00
	Butter dish, w/cover	80.00	
	Candle, 1-lite, block	35.00	
	Candle, 2-lite	80.00	
	Candle, 3-lite, #4233, 5", vase	95.00	
	Cigarette box w/cover	65.00	
	Cigarette lighter	30.00	

		Crystal	Limelight Green
	Coaster, 4"	15.00	
7	Creamer, ftd.	25.00	95.00
	Creamer & sugar, w/tray, individual	80.00	
19	Cup, punch	10.00	
14	Marmalade	45.00	
	Mayonnaise, 7" (plate, ladle, bowl)	40.00	150.00
	Mustard	140.00	
	Oil bottle, 4 oz., #1 stopper	45.00	
12	Oil & vinegar bottle (french dressing)	65.00	
	Plate, 5", footed, cheese	20.00	
	Plate, 7", 2 hdld., snack	25.00	
15	Plate, 7", bread	10.00	
3	Plate, 8", luncheon	15.00	50.00
17	Plate, 14", torte	45.00	
	Plate, 18", buffet	70.00	175.00
	Salt & pepper, pr.	40.00	
	Stem, 3½ oz., oyster cocktail	20.00	
	Stem, 3½ oz., wine	20.00	
18	Stem, 5 oz., sherbet/champagne	10.00	
	Stem, 10 oz.	20.00	
8	Sugar, footed	25.00	95.00
	Tray, 13", oval, celery	22.00	
2	Tumbler, 5 oz., ftd., juice	14.00	60.00
13	Tumbler, 8 oz.	17.00	
6	Tumbler, 9 oz., ftd.	17.00	80.00
1	Tumbler, 12 oz., ftd., iced tea	20.00	80.00
	Tumbler, 13", flat, ice tea	20.00	
5	Vase, 3½", violet	30.00	95.00
	Vase, 4", pansy	35.00	
	Vase, 6", sweet pea	45.00	

Color: crystal and crystal w/green

Psyche is a Tiffin pattern that has attracted collectors for years. The design speaks of style and quality. It is not a profuse pattern, but enough can be found to whet your appetite.

As with most Tiffin patterns from this era, you can find tumblers and stems, but basic serving pieces are elusive. I found a creamer, but no sugar to go with it. The green stem and handled pieces are found more than the all crystal pieces, but finding plates or bowls is a chore.

The cordial shown is one from a set of Tiffin cordials displayed at the national Heisey show about 20 years ago. A dealer had a large set of Tiffin with a floral cutting on the same stemware line as Psyche. It was priced as a set, not individually. Most observers of the set marveled at the outrageous price, but one vigilant dealer noticed that several of the cordials were Psyche and not the floral design. He persuaded the dealer to sell those cordials since they did not match the rest of the set. I was able to acquire my cordial that way. The price of that set may now have caught up with prices on it at that time — but I doubt it. What something "ought to be" worth because of its age and beauty and what it "actually" will bring in the marketplace are often two very different things. *Demand* stimulates price — not age or beauty.

	Item	Price
	Bonbon	65.00
	Bowl, 13", centerpiece	125.00
	Bowl, finger, ftd.	45.00
	Candleholder, #9758	85.00
6	Creamer	65.00
	Cup	85.00
	Pitcher	495.00
	Pitcher w/cover	595.00
3	Plate, 6"	20.00
	Plate, 8"	30.00
	Plate, 10"	150.00
	Saucer	20.00

	Item	Price
	Stem, café parfait	60.00
	Stem, claret	60.00
4	Stem, cocktail	38.00
7	Stem, cordial	150.00
	Stem, grapefruit w/liner	95.00
2	Stem, saucer champagne	35.00
	Stem, sherbet	30.00
	Stem, water goblet	55.00
	Stem, wine	60.00
	Sugar	65.00
1	Tumbler, iced tea	50.00
5	Tumbler, juice	40.00
	Tumbler, oyster cocktail	35.00
	Tumbler, water	40.00
	Vase, bud	125.00

Colors: crystal, green, pink

Puritan has taken a lot of work to get enough pieces to photograph. Last spring, I finally ran into a large amount of green in a mall in Florida. I bought one of each piece, so green will be the theme next time.

Notice that several pieces have cuttings or etches on them. I have not been able to determine if these are Duncan factory accoutrements or if they were added by a decorating or cutting company afterwards. If you know, I'd appreciate being enlightened.

		*All colors
	Bowl, cream soup, 2-hdld.	20.00
3	Bowl, 5"	12.50
	Bowl, 9", oval vegetable	55.00
6	Bowl, 9¼"	55.00
5	Bowl, 12", rolled console	65.00
7	Candlestick	26.00
	Comport	35.00
	Creamer	17.50
4	Cup	12.50
	Cup, demi	17.50
1	Ice bucket	110.00
	Pitcher	135.00

		*All colors
	Plate, 7½", salad	8.00
2	Plate, 10", dinner	20.00
	Plate, cream soup liner	6.00
4	Saucer	2.00
	Saucer, demi	5.00
	Server, center hdld.	35.00
	Stem, water goblet	20.00
	Sugar	17.50
	Tumbler, flat tea	22.00
	Vase	65.00

* Crystal 25% less.

Color: crystal

When Empress (#1401) was produced later (a second time) in crystal, it was renamed Queen Ann (c. 1938). According to Heisey experts, there supposedly is a slight difference between the later Queen Ann and the earlier Empress; most collectors and dealers cannot distinguish a difference, so there is no difference in pricing.

Queen Ann's mould blank was utilized for several of Heisey's most popular etched patterns including Orchid, Rose, Minuet, etc. This plainer, non-etched line has been easy to find and inexpensive in the past; however, the prices are now adjusting to demand, particularly for rarely found pieces.

6

Ashtray		30.00
Bonbon, 6"		12.00
Bowl, cream soup		18.00
Bowl, cream soup, w/sq. liner		25.00
Bowl, frappe, w/center		25.00
Bowl, nut, dolphin ftd., indiv.		35.00
Bowl, 4½", nappy		8.00
Bowl, 5", preserve, 2 hdld.		15.00
Bowl, 6", ftd., jelly, 2 hdld.		15.00
7	Bowl, 6", dolphin ftd., mint	20.00
	Bowl, 6", grapefruit, sq. top, ground bottom	12.00
16	Bowl, 6½", oval, lemon, w/cover	45.00
	Bowl, 7", 3 pt., relish, triplex	18.00
	Bowl, 7", 3 pt., relish, ctr. hand.	25.00
13	Bowl, 7½", dolphin ftd., nappy	28.00
	Bowl, 7½", dolphin ftd., nasturtium	35.00
	Bowl, 8", nappy	25.00
	Bowl, 8½", ftd., floral, 2 hdld	32.00
	Bowl, 9", floral, rolled edge	25.00
	Bowl, 9", floral, flared	32.00
	Bowl, 10", 2 hdld., oval dessert	30.00
	Bowl, 10", lion head, floral	250.00
	Bowl, 10", oval, veg.	30.00
	Bowl, 10", square, salad, 2 hdld.	35.00
	Bowl, 10", triplex, relish	25.00

	Bowl, 11", dolphin ftd., floral	38.00
8	Bowl, 13", pickle/olive, 2 pt.	20.00
	Bowl, 15", dolphin ftd., punch	400.00
12	Candlestick, 3", 3 ftd	60.00
	Candlestick, low, 4 ftd., w/2 hdld.	40.00
	Candlestick, 6", dolphin ftd.	70.00
4	Candy, w/cover, 6", dolphin ftd.	50.00
	Comport, 6", ftd.	25.00
	Comport, 6", square	40.00
	Comport, 7", oval	35.00
	Compotier, 6", dolphin ftd.	70.00
11	Creamer, dolphin ftd.	30.00
	Creamer, indiv.	20.00
18	Cup	15.00
15	Cup, after dinner	20.00
	Cup, bouillon, 2 hdld.	20.00
	Cup, 4 oz., custard or punch	12.00
	Cup, #1401½, has rim as demi-cup	20.00
	Grapefruit, w/sq. liner	20.00
6	Ice tub, w/metal handles	60.00
	Jug, 3 pint, ftd.	100.00
	Marmalade, w/cover, dolphin ftd.	60.00
9	Mayonnaise, 5½", ftd., w/ladle	30.00
	Mustard, w/cover	60.00
	Oil bottle, 4 oz.	40.00
	Plate, bouillon liner	8.00
	Plate, cream soup liner	8.00
	Plate, 4½"	5.00
	Plate, 6"	5.00
	Plate, 6", sq.	5.00

	Plate, 7"	8.00
5	Plate, 7", sq.	7.00
	Plate, 8", sq.	10.00
	Plate, 8"	9.00
	Plate, 9"	12.00
1	Plate, 10½"	60.00
2	Plate, 10½", sq.	60.00
	Plate, 12"	25.00
14	Plate, 12", muffin, sides upturned	35.00
	Plate, 12", sandwich, 2 hdld.	30.00
	Plate, 13", hors d'oeuvre, 2 hdld.	60.00
	Plate, 13", sq., 2 hdld.	35.00
3	Platter, 14"	30.00
10	Salt & pepper, pr.	50.00
	Saucer, sq.	5.00

15	Saucer, after dinner	5.00
18	Saucer	5.00
	Stem, 2½ oz., oyster cocktail	15.00
	Stem, 4 oz., saucer champagne	20.00
	Stem, 4 oz., sherbet	15.00
	Stem, 9 oz., Empress stemware, unusual	40.00
	Sugar, indiv.	20.00
17	Sugar, dolphin ftd., 3 hdld.	30.00
	Tray, condiment & liner for indiv. sugar/creamer	20.00
	Tray, pickle & olive	15.00
	Tray, 10", 3 pt., relish	20.00
	Tray, 10", 7 pt., hors d'oeuvre	60.00
	Tray, 10", celery	12.00
	Tray, 12", ctr. hdld., sand.	30.00
	Tray, 12", sq. ctr. hdld., sand.	32.50
	Tray, 13", celery	20.00
	Tray, 16", 4 pt., buffet relish	35.00
	Tumbler, 8 oz., dolphin ftd., unusual	75.00
	Tumbler, 8 oz., ground bottom	20.00
	Tumbler, 12 oz., tea, ground bottom	20.00
	Vase, 8", flared	55.00

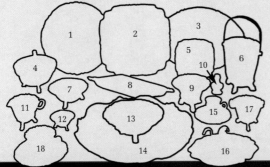

Color: crystal bowl w/Anna Rose (pink) stem and foot

Queen Louise is one of my favorite Elegant patterns. It is absolutely magnificent with that silkscreen process that must have cost a fortune when originally sold. If I were going to collect a set of any pattern in this book, this is the pattern I would choose.

Queen Louise still commands a significant price, but may be under valued taking into consideration its scarcity today. The only new item I was able to find we used as a close-up pattern shot. I paid dearly just to have a footed tumbler to show you.

Looking for this has been an adventure of almost twelve years. Apparently, Queen Louise was distributed in the Chicago and St. Louis areas since that is where it is being found today. Even the Internet auctions have been void of offerings of this pattern recently.

Personal observation shows that all stems sell in the same price range with waters being found the most often. Champagnes and parfaits may be the most difficult stems to find. Plates are rare and the footed bowl is seldom seen.

	Item	Price		Item	Price
8	Bowl, finger, ftd.	250.00	7	Stem, 7 oz., parfait	465.00
	Plate, 6", finger bowl liner	125.00	3	Stem, 9 oz., water	495.00
4	Plate, salad	150.00	1	Tumbler, 9 oz., ftd.	395.00
6	Stem, 2½ oz., wine	400.00			
5	Stem, 3 oz., cocktail	400.00			
2	Stem, 5½ oz., saucer champagne	395.00			
	Stem, 5½ oz., sherbet	325.00			

Colors: crystal, Sahara, Zircon, rare

		Crystal
	Ashtray, rnd.	14.00
10	Ashtray, sq.	10.00
	Ashtray, 4", rnd.	22.00
	Ashtray, 6", sq.	35.00
15	Ashtray, 6", sq. w/oval cig. holder	95.00
	Ashtrays, bridge set (heart, diamond, spade, club)	85.00
	Basket, bonbon, metal handle	25.00
	Bottle, rock & rye, w/#104 stopper	240.00
14	Bottle, 4 oz., cologne	130.00
	Bottle, 5 oz., bitters, w/tube	130.00
19	Bowl, indiv., nut	15.00
13	Bowl, oval, indiv., jelly	20.00
	Bowl, indiv., nut, 2 part	20.00
	Bowl, 4½", nappy, bell or cupped	20.00
	Bowl, 4½", nappy, scalloped	20.00
	Bowl, 5", lemon, w/cover	65.00
	Bowl, 5", nappy, straight	18.00
	Bowl, 5", nappy, sq.	25.00
	Bowl, 6", 2 hdld., div., jelly	40.00
	Bowl, 6", 2 hdld., jelly	30.00
	Bowl, 7", 2 part, oval, relish	30.00
	Bowl, 8", centerpiece	55.00
	Bowl, 8", nappy, sq.	55.00
	Bowl, 9", nappy, sq.	65.00
	Bowl, 9", salad	50.00
	Bowl, 10", flared, fruit	45.00
	Bowl, 10", floral	45.00
	Bowl, 11", centerpiece	50.00
4	Bowl, 11", cone beverage	195.00
	Bowl, 11", punch	175.00
	Bowl, 11½", floral	50.00
8	Bowl, 12", oval, floral	55.00
	Bowl, 12", flared, fruit	50.00
	Bowl, 13", cone, floral	65.00
	Bowl, 14", oblong, floral	70.00
	Bowl, 14", oblong, swan hdld., floral	280.00
	Box, 8", floral	70.00
16	Candle block, 3", #1469½	30.00
	Candle vase, 6"	35.00
	Candlestick, 2", 1-lite	35.00
	Candlestick, 2-lite, bobeche & "A" prisms	80.00
	Candlestick, 7", w/bobeche & "A" prisms	120.00
12	Cheese, 6", 2 hdld.	22.00
	Cigarette box, w/cover, oval	90.00
	Cigarette box, w/cover, 6"	35.00
	Cigarette holder, oval, w/2 comp. ashtrays	70.00
18	Cigarette holder, rnd.	18.00
	Cigarette holder, sq.	18.00
	Cigarette holder, w/cover	30.00
	Coaster or cocktail rest	15.00
	Cocktail shaker, 1 qt., w/#1 strainer & #86 stopper	300.00
	Comport, 6", low ft., flared	25.00
	Comport, 6", low ft., w/cover	40.00
	Creamer	30.00
	Creamer, indiv.	20.00
	Cup	16.00
5	Cup, beverage	24.00
	Cup, punch	12.00
	Decanter, 1 pint, w/#95 stopper	210.00
	Ice tub, 2 hdld.	100.00
	Marmalade, w/cover (scarce)	90.00
	Mayonnaise and under plate	55.00

		Crystal
	Mustard, w/cover	80.00
	Oil bottle, 3 oz., w/#103 stopper	50.00
	Pitcher, ½ gallon, ball shape	380.00
	Pitcher, ½ gallon, ice lip, ball shape	380.00
11	Plate, oval, hors d'oeuvres	500.00
	Plate, 2 hdld., ice tub liner	50.00
	Plate, 6", rnd.	12.00
	Plate, 6", sq.	24.00
	Plate, 7", sq.	28.00
	Plate, 8", rnd.	20.00
	Plate, 8", sq.	32.00
	Plate, 13½", sandwich	45.00
	Plate, 13½", ftd., torte	45.00
	Plate, 14", salver	50.00
6	Plate, 20", punch bowl underplate	140.00
	Puff box, 5", and cover	90.00
	Salt & pepper, pr.	45.00
	Salt dip, indiv.	13.00
	Saucer	5.00
	Soda, 12 oz., ftd., no knob in stem (rare)	50.00
1	Stem, cocktail, pressed	25.00
	Stem, claret, pressed	45.00
	Stem, oyster cocktail, pressed	30.00
	Stem, sherbet, pressed	20.00
2	Stem, saucer champagne, pressed	25.00
	Stem, wine, pressed	40.00
	Stem, 1 oz., cordial, blown	160.00
	Stem, 2 oz., sherry, blown	90.00
	Stem, 2½ oz., wine, blown	80.00
	Stem, 3½ oz., cocktail, blown	35.00
	Stem, 4 oz., claret, blown	55.00
	Stem, 4 oz., oyster cocktail, blown	30.00
	Stem, 5 oz., saucer champagne, blown	25.00
	Stem, 5 oz., sherbet, blown	20.00
	Stem, 8 oz., luncheon, low stem	30.00
3	Stem, 9 oz., goblet, pressed	35.00
	Sugar	30.00
	Sugar, indiv.	20.00
	Tray, for indiv. sugar & creamer	20.00
	Tray, 10½", oblong	40.00
	Tray, 11", 3 part, relish	50.00
	Tray, 12", celery & olive, divided	50.00
	Tray, 12", celery	40.00
17	Tumbler, 2½ oz., bar, pressed	45.00
	Tumbler, 5 oz., juice, blown	30.00
	Tumbler, 5 oz., soda, ftd., pressed	30.00
	Tumbler, 8 oz., #1469¾, pressed	35.00
	Tumbler, 8 oz., old-fashion, pressed	40.00
	Tumbler, 8 oz., soda, blown	40.00
	Tumbler, 10 oz., #1469½, pressed	45.00
	Tumbler, 12 oz., ftd., soda, pressed	50.00

185

	Crystal
Tumbler, 12 oz., soda, #1469½, pressed	50.00
Tumbler, 13 oz., iced tea, blown	40.00
Vase, #1 indiv., cuspidor shape	40.00
Vase, #2 indiv., cupped top	45.00
Vase, #3 indiv., flared rim	30.00
Vase, #4 indiv., fan out top	55.00

	Crystal
Vase, #5 indiv., scalloped top	55.00
Vase, 3½"	25.00
9 Vase, 6" (also flared)	35.00
7 Vase, 8"	75.00
Vase, 8", triangular, #1469¾	110.00

Color: crystal

Rogene is an early Fostoria pattern that has recently been noticed by collectors searching for something different to collect. There are multitudes of pieces that are reasonably priced for their age and beauty, judging by standards of other Fostoria patterns. After introducing Rogene to this book, there have been some slight price hikes observed.

	Item	Price
	Almond, ftd., #4095	11.00
	Comport, 5" tall, #5078	30.00
	Comport, 6", #5078	30.00
9	Creamer, flat, #1851	30.00
	Decanter, qt., cut neck, #300	90.00
	Finger bowl, #766	22.00
	Jelly, #825	22.50
	Jelly & cover, #825	40.00
	Jug 4, ftd., #4095	100.00
	Jug 7, #318	150.00
	Jug 7, #2270	165.00
	Jug 7, #4095	195.00
	Jug 7, covered, #2270	250.00
	Marmalade & cover, #1968	45.00
	Mayonnaise bowl, #766	30.00
	Mayonnaise ladle	22.50
5	Mayonnaise set, 3 pc., #2138 (ftd. compote, ladle, liner)	60.00
	Nappy, 5" ftd. (comport/sherbet), #5078	17.50
	Nappy, 6" ftd., #5078	25.00
	Nappy, 7" ftd., #5078	30.00
	Night set, 2 pc., #1697 (carafe & tumbler)	135.00
	Oil bottle w/cut stop, 5 oz., #1495	65.00
	Oyster cocktail, ftd., #837	12.50
	Plate, 5"	6.00
	Plate, 6"	7.50
	Plate, 6", #2283	7.00
	Plate, 7" salad, #2283	10.00
4	Plate, 8"	15.00
	Plate, 11"	25.00
	Plate, 11", w/cut star	27.50
	Plate, finger bowl liner	7.50
	Plate, mayonnaise liner, #766	12.50
	Shaker, pr., glass (pearl) top, #2283	60.00
	Stem, ¾ oz., cordial, #5082	40.00
	Stem, 2½ oz., wine, #5082	22.00
10	Stem, 3 oz., cocktail, #5082	16.00
	Stem, 4½ oz., claret, #5082	27.00
	Stem, 5 oz., fruit, #5082	12.50
	Stem, 5 oz., saucer champagne, #5082	15.00
	Stem, 6 oz., parfait, #5082	22.50
1	Stem, 9 oz., #5082	22.50
	Stem, grapefruit, #945½	30.00
	Stem, grapefruit liner, #945½	15.00
6	Sugar, flat, #1851	30.00
	Tumbler, 2½ oz., whiskey, #887	17.50
	Tumbler, 2½ oz., ftd., #4095	17.50
8	Tumbler, 5 oz., flat, #889	12.50
	Tumbler, 5 oz., ftd., #4095	12.50
	Tumbler, 8 oz., flat,, #889	14.00
3	Tumbler, 10 oz., ftd., #4095	15.00
	Tumbler, 12 oz., flat, hdld., #837	25.00
7	Tumbler, 13 oz., flat, #889	17.50
2	Tumbler, 13 oz., ftd., #4095	20.00
	Tumbler, flat, table, #4076	14.00
	Vase, 8½" rolled edge	100.00

Colors: Amber, Bluebell, Carmen, crystal, Emerald green, Heatherbloom, Peach-Blo, Topaz, Willow blue

Rosalie, Cambridge's #731 line, is a pattern that can be collected in a variety of colors; but completing an entire set might take years of searching unless you are exceptionally fortunate. The good news is that Rosalie is one of Cambridge's least expensive colored wares principally in pink and green. Perhaps a small set of Willow Blue is possible; but Carmen, Bluebell, or Heatherbloom are colors that are too seldom seen to be assembled into sets. Note how well the pattern shows on the green and blue pieces that have been highlighted with enamel. These were factory made; and for photography purposes, I wish all patterns were emphasized that way.

The Ebony vase at right has Rosalie decoration on black with an additional gold decoration along the rim. Rosalie decoration on black is highly unusual.

	Blue Pink Green	Amber/ Crystal
Bottle, French dressing	210.00	125.00
Bowl, bouillon, 2 hdld.	30.00	15.00
Bowl, cream soup	30.00	20.00
Bowl, finger, w/liner	70.00	55.00
Bowl, finger, ftd., w/liner	75.00	60.00
Bowl, 3½", cranberry	50.00	35.00
Bowl, 5½", fruit	22.00	15.00
Bowl, 5½", 2 hdld., bonbon	25.00	15.00
Bowl, 6¼", 2 hdld., bonbon	25.00	18.00
Bowl, 7", basket, 2 hdld.	35.00	22.00
Bowl, 8½", soup	65.00	35.00
Bowl, 8½", 2 hdld.	75.00	35.00
Bowl, 8½", w/cover, 3 pt.	150.00	75.00
Bowl, 10"	75.00	40.00
9 Bowl, 10", 2 hdld., #984	75.00	40.00

	Blue Pink Green	Amber/ Crystal
Bowl, 11"	80.00	40.00
Bowl, 11", basket, 2 hdld.	85.00	45.00
Bowl, 11½"	90.00	55.00
Bowl, 12", decagon	125.00	85.00
15 Bowl, 13", console	125.00	
Bowl, 14", decagon, deep	245.00	195.00
Bowl, 15", oval console	135.00	75.00
Bowl, 15", oval, flanged	145.00	75.00
Bowl, 15½", oval	150.00	85.00
12 Candlestick, 4", #627	40.00	25.00
Candlestick, 5", keyhole	45.00	30.00
Candlestick, 6", 3-lite keyhole	80.00	45.00
16 Candy and cover, 6", #864	150.00	75.00

		Blue Pink Green	Amber/ Crystal
	Celery, 11"	40.00	25.00
4	Cheese & cracker, 11", plate	80.00	50.00
	Cigarette jar & cover	100.00	60.00
	Comport, 5½", 2 hdld.	30.00	15.00
3	Comport, 5¾"	30.00	15.00
	Comport, 6", ftd., almond	45.00	30.00
	Comport, 6½", low ft.	45.00	30.00
	Comport, 6½", high ft.	45.00	30.00
	Comport, 6¾"	55.00	35.00
18	Creamer, ftd., #867	22.00	15.00
	Creamer, ftd., tall, ewer	65.00	35.00
11	Cup	35.00	25.00
7	Gravy, double, w/platter, #1147	175.00	100.00
14	Ice bucket or pail	125.00	75.00
8	Icer, w/liner	85.00	50.00
	Ice tub	110.00	70.00
	Mayonnaise, ftd., w/liner	75.00	35.00
	Nut, 2½", ftd.	65.00	50.00
	Pitcher, 62 oz., #955	295.00	195.00
	Plate, 6¾", bread/butter	10.00	7.00
	Plate, 7", 2 hdld.	16.00	10.00
	Plate, 7½", salad	15.00	8.00
	Plate, 8⅜"	20.00	10.00
	Plate, 9½", dinner	70.00	45.00
	Plate, 11", 2 hdld.	45.00	25.00
	Platter, 12"	95.00	55.00
	Platter, 15"	150.00	100.00
	Relish, 9", 2 pt.	45.00	20.00
	Relish, 11", 2 pt.	50.00	30.00
	Salt dip, 1½", ftd.	65.00	40.00
11	Saucer	5.00	4.00

		Blue Pink Green	Amber/ Crystal
	Stem, 1 oz., cordial, #3077	100.00	65.00
10	Stem, 3 oz., cocktail, #7606	30.00	20.00
	Stem, 3½ oz., cocktail, #3077	20.00	14.00
	Stem, 4½ oz., claret, #7606	35.00	25.00
6	Stem, 6 oz., saucer/champagne, #7606	35.00	25.00
	Stem, 6 oz., low sherbet, #3077	16.00	12.00
	Stem, 6 oz., high sherbet, #3077	18.00	14.00
	Stem, 9 oz., water goblet, #3077	30.00	23.00
	Stem, 10 oz., goblet, #801	35.00	22.00
5	Stem, 10 oz., water goblet, #7606	40.00	30.00
17	Sugar, ftd., #867	22.00	13.00
	Sugar shaker	325.00	225.00
	Tray for sugar shaker/creamer	30.00	20.00
	Tray, ctr. hdld., for sugar/creamer	20.00	14.00
	Tray, 11", ctr. hdld.	38.00	28.00
	Tumbler, 2½ oz., ftd., #3077	45.00	25.00
	Tumbler, 5 oz., ftd., #3077	32.00	22.00
	Tumbler, 8 oz., ftd., #3077	20.00	16.00
	Tumbler, 10 oz., ftd., #3077	30.00	20.00
2	Tumbler, 12 oz., ftd., #3077	40.00	25.00
	Vase, 5½", ftd.	85.00	50.00
	Vase, 6"	90.00	55.00
	Vase, 6½", ftd.	125.00	60.00
1	Vase, 12", w/rim (black), #402	195.00	
13	Wafer tray	140.00	90.00

Colors: crystal; some crystal with gold; Ebony, Carmen, and amber, all with gold

Unquestionably, Rose Point is the most collected pattern of Cambridge and most likely the most collected pattern in this book. Only Fostoria American might approximate the collecting numbers of Rose Point; but American has the advantage of being made for over 70 years.

There were so many mould lines used to make Rose Point that individual collectors can choose what they prefer. Consequently, not all are always looking for the same pieces. Variety spreads the supply.

Take note of the two gold encrusted nude stem goblets pictured on page 193. These were the first Rose Point Statuesque table stems to be found gold decorated. Notice the amber, gold decorated ice bucket pictured as a pattern shot. Some collectors are paying particular attention to gold "encrusted" items of late.

Pages 190 and 191 show a Rose Point brochure with a listing where pieces are identified by number and that should aid you in distinguishing pieces. There are limitations to how much catalog information we can do and still show you the actual glass. An uncertainty confronting new collectors is identifying different blanks on which Rose Point is found. Be sure to examine the brochure to see the different line numbers of #3400, #3500, and #3900. These are the major mould lines upon which Rose Point was etched. Item #3 is an ice bucket that is a cross of line #3400 and #3900 and was never cataloged by Cambridge. It sells in the $200.00 range.

LIST OF ROSE POINT ITEMS

3500	10 oz.	Goblet
3500	7 oz.	Tall Sherbet
3500	7 oz.	Low Sherbet
3500	3 oz.	Cocktail
3500	2½ oz.	Wine
3500	4½ oz.	Claret
3500	4½ oz.	Oyster Cocktail
3500	1 oz.	Cordial
3500	5 oz.	Cafe Parfait
3500	12 oz.	Ftd. Ice Tea
3500	10 oz.	Ftd. Tumbler
3500	5 oz.	Ftd. Tumbler
477	9½ in.	Pickle
3400/1180	5¼ in.	2 Hdl. Bonbon
3400/1181	6 in.	2 Hdl. Plate
3400/90	6 in.	2 part Relish
3500/15		Ind. Sugar & Cream
3500/54	6 in.	2 Hdl. Ftd. Bonbon
3500/55	6 in.	2 Hdl. Ftd. Basket
3500/69	6½ in.	3 part Relish
3500/161	8 in.	2 Hdl. Ftd. Plate
3400/91	8 in.	3 part Relish
3500/57	8 in.	3 part Candy Box & Cover
3500/101	5¾ in.	Tall Comport
3900/17		Cup & Saucer
3900/19		2 pc. Mayonnaise Set
3900/20	6½ in.	Bread & Butter Plate
3900/22	8 in.	Salad Plate
3900/24	10½ in.	Dinner Plate
3900/26	12 in.	4 Ftd. Plate
3900/28	11½ in.	Ftd. Bowl
3900/33	13 in.	4 Ftd. Torte Plate, R. E.
3900/34	11 in.	2 Handled Bowl
3900/35	13½ in.	2 Handled Cake Plate
3900/40		Ind. Sugar & Cream
3900/41		Sugar & Cream
3900/54	10 in.	4 Ftd. Bowl, flared
3900/62	12 in.	4 Ftd. Bowl, flared
3900/65	12 in.	4 Ftd. Oval Bowl
3900/67	5 in.	Candlestick
3900/72	6 in.	2 lite Candlestick
3900/74	6 in.	3 lite Candlestick
3900/100	6 oz.	Oil, g. s.
3900/111		4 pc. Mayonnaise Set
3900/115	13 oz.	Tumbler
3900/120	12 in.	5 part Celery & Relish
3900/123	7 in.	Relish or Pickle
3900/124	7 in.	2 part Relish
3900/125	9 in.	3 part Celery & Relish
3900/126	12 in.	3 part Celery & Relish
3900/129		2 pc. Mayonnaise Set
3900/130	7 in.	2 handled Ftd. Bonbon
3900/131	8 in.	2 handled Ftd. Bonbon Plate
3900/136	5½ in.	Comport
3900/165		Candy Box & Cover
3900/166	14 in.	Plate, r. e.
3900/671		Ice Bucket
3900/671		Ice Bucket with chrome Handle
		Chrome Ice Tongs (long)
3900/1177		Salt & Pepper Shaker (doz. pr.)
274	10 in.	Bud Flower Holder
278	11 in.	Ftd. Flower Holder
279	13 in.	Ftd. Flower Holder
968		2 pc. Cocktail Icer
1237	9 in.	Ftd. Flower Holder
1238	12 in.	Ftd. Flower Holder
1299	11 in.	Ftd. Flower Holder
1309	5 in.	Glode Flower Holder
1603		Hurricane Lamp (Etch. Chimney only)
1617		Hurricane Lamp (Etch. Chimney only)
6004	6 in.	Ftd. Flower Holder
6004	8 in.	Ftd. Flower Holder
P. 101		Cocktail Shaker (Patent—D133,198)

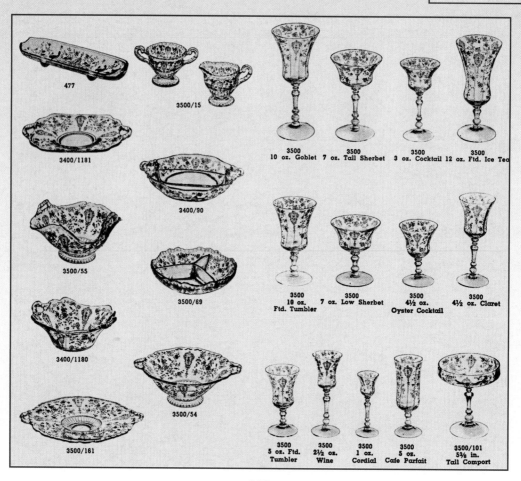

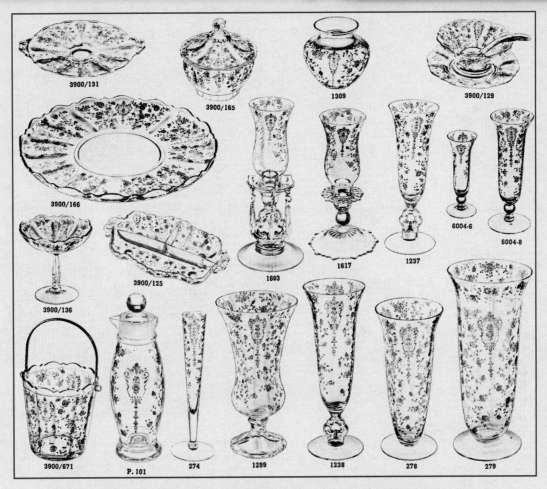

3900/131

3900/165

1309

3900/129

3900/166

3900/136

3900/125

1603

1617

1237

6004-6

6004-8

3900/671

P. 101

274

1299

1238

278

279

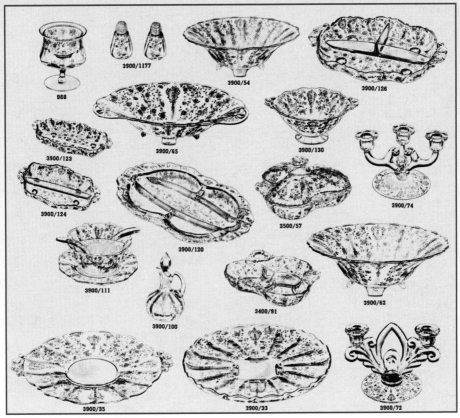

968

3900/1177

3900/54

3900/126

3900/123

3900/65

3900/130

3900/124

3900/120

3500/57

3900/74

3900/111

3900/100

3400/91

3900/62

3900/35

3900/33

3900/72

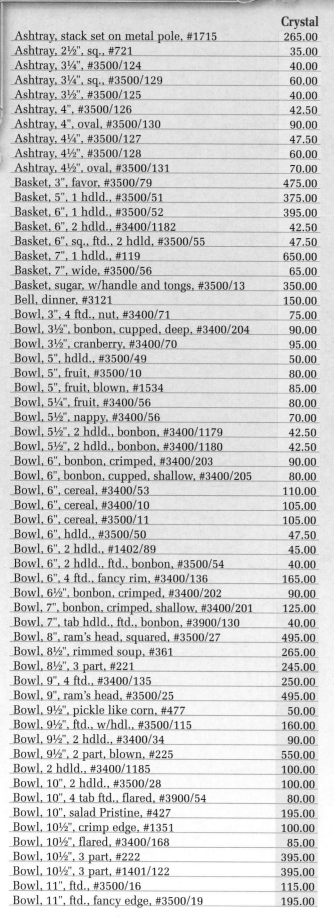

	Crystal
Ashtray, stack set on metal pole, #1715	265.00
Ashtray, 2½", sq., #721	35.00
Ashtray, 3¼", #3500/124	40.00
Ashtray, 3¼", sq., #3500/129	60.00
Ashtray, 3½", #3500/125	40.00
Ashtray, 4", #3500/126	42.50
Ashtray, 4", oval, #3500/130	90.00
Ashtray, 4¼", #3500/127	47.50
Ashtray, 4½", #3500/128	60.00
Ashtray, 4½", oval, #3500/131	70.00
Basket, 3", favor, #3500/79	475.00
Basket, 5", 1 hdld., #3500/51	375.00
Basket, 6", 1 hdld., #3500/52	395.00
Basket, 6", 2 hdld., #3400/1182	42.50
Basket, 6", sq., ftd., 2 hdld, #3500/55	47.50
Basket, 7", 1 hdld., #119	650.00
Basket, 7", wide, #3500/56	65.00
Basket, sugar, w/handle and tongs, #3500/13	350.00
Bell, dinner, #3121	150.00
Bowl, 3", 4 ftd., nut, #3400/71	75.00
Bowl, 3½", bonbon, cupped, deep, #3400/204	90.00
Bowl, 3½", cranberry, #3400/70	95.00
Bowl, 5", hdld., #3500/49	50.00
Bowl, 5", fruit, #3500/10	80.00
Bowl, 5", fruit, blown, #1534	85.00
Bowl, 5¼", fruit, #3400/56	80.00
Bowl, 5½", nappy, #3400/56	70.00
Bowl, 5½", 2 hdld., bonbon, #3400/1179	42.50
Bowl, 5½", 2 hdld., bonbon, #3400/1180	42.50
Bowl, 6", bonbon, crimped, #3400/203	90.00
Bowl, 6", bonbon, cupped, shallow, #3400/205	80.00
Bowl, 6", cereal, #3400/53	110.00
Bowl, 6", cereal, #3400/10	105.00
Bowl, 6", cereal, #3500/11	105.00
Bowl, 6", hdld., #3500/50	47.50
Bowl, 6", 2 hdld., #1402/89	45.00
Bowl, 6", 2 hdld., ftd., bonbon, #3500/54	40.00
Bowl, 6", 4 ftd., fancy rim, #3400/136	165.00
Bowl, 6½", bonbon, crimped, #3400/202	90.00
Bowl, 7", bonbon, crimped, shallow, #3400/201	125.00
Bowl, 7", tab hdld., ftd., bonbon, #3900/130	40.00
Bowl, 8", ram's head, squared, #3500/27	495.00
Bowl, 8½", rimmed soup, #361	265.00
Bowl, 8½", 3 part, #221	245.00
Bowl, 9", 4 ftd., #3400/135	250.00
Bowl, 9", ram's head, #3500/25	495.00
Bowl, 9½", pickle like corn, #477	50.00
Bowl, 9½", ftd., w/hdl., #3500/115	160.00
Bowl, 9½", 2 hdld., #3400/34	90.00
Bowl, 9½", 2 part, blown, #225	550.00
Bowl, 2 hdld., #3400/1185	100.00
Bowl, 10", 2 hdld., #3500/28	100.00
Bowl, 10", 4 tab ftd., flared, #3900/54	80.00
Bowl, 10", salad Pristine, #427	195.00
Bowl, 10½", crimp edge, #1351	100.00
Bowl, 10½", flared, #3400/168	85.00
Bowl, 10½", 3 part, #222	395.00
Bowl, 10½", 3 part, #1401/122	395.00
Bowl, 11", ftd., #3500/16	115.00
Bowl, 11", ftd., fancy edge, #3500/19	195.00

	Crystal
Bowl, 11", 4 ftd., oval, #3500/109	395.00
Bowl, 11", 4 ftd., shallow, fancy edge, #3400/48	120.00
Bowl, 11", fruit, #3400/1188	120.00
Bowl, 11", low foot, #3400/3	175.00
Bowl, 11", tab hdld., #3900/34	90.00
Bowl, 11½", ftd., w/tab hdl., #3900/28	90.00
Bowl, 12", crimped, pan Pristine, #136	395.00
Bowl, 12", 4 ftd., oval, #3400/1240	145.00
Bowl, 12", 4 ftd., oval, w/"ears" hdl., #3900/65	110.00
Bowl, 12", 4 ftd., fancy rim oblong, #3400/160	100.00
Bowl, 12", 4 ftd., flared, #3400/4	90.00
Bowl, 12", 4 tab ftd., flared, #3900/62	90.00
Bowl, 12", ftd., #3500/17	150.00
Bowl, 12", ftd., oblong, #3500/118	190.00
Bowl, 12", ftd., oval w/hdld., #3500/21	245.00
Bowl, 12½", flared, rolled edge, #3400/2	185.00
Bowl, 12½", 4 ftd., #993	110.00
Bowl, 13", #1398	150.00
Bowl, 13", 4 ftd., narrow, crimped, #3400/47	150.00
Bowl, 13", flared, #3400/1	90.00
Bowl, 14", 4 ftd., crimp edge, oblong, #1247	165.00
Bowl, 18", crimped, pan Pristine, #136	695.00
Bowl, cream soup, w/liner, #3400	195.00
Bowl, cream soup, w/liner, #3500/2	195.00
Bowl, finger, w/liner, #3106	110.00
Bowl, finger, w/liner, #3121	110.00
Butter, w/cover, round, #506	210.00
Butter, w/cover, 5", #3400/52	210.00
Butter dish, ¼ lb., #3900/52	495.00
Candelabrum, 2-lite w/bobeches & prisms, #1268	225.00
Candelabrum, 2-lite, #3500/94	150.00
Candelabrum, 3-lite, #1338	95.00
Candelabrum, 5½", 3-lite w/#19 bobeche & #1 prisms, #1545	175.00
Candelabrum, 6½", 2-lite, w/bobeches & prisms Martha, #496	195.00
Candle, torchere, cup ft., #3500/90	275.00
Candle, torchere, flat ft., #3500/88	250.00
Candlestick Pristine, #500	150.00
Candlestick, sq. base & lites, #1700/501	225.00
Candlestick, 2½", #3500/108	40.00
Candlestick, 3½", #628	45.00
Candlestick, 4", #627	75.00
Candlestick, 4", ram's head, #3500/74	125.00
Candlestick, 5", 1-lite keyhole, #3400/646	55.00
Candlestick, 5", inverts to comport, #3900/68	85.00
Candlestick, 5½", 2-lite Martha, #495	125.00
Candlestick, 6", #3500/31	150.00
Candlestick, 6", 2-lite keyhole, #3400/647	55.00
Candlestick, 6", 2-lite, #3900/72	65.00
Candlestick, 6", 3-lite, #3900/74	75.00
Candlestick, 6", 3-lite keyhole, #3400/638	80.00
Candlestick, 6", 3-tiered lite, #1338	95.00
Candlestick, 6½", Calla Lily, #499	135.00
Candlestick, 7", #3121	110.00
Candlestick, 7½", w/prism Martha, #497	145.00
Candy box, w/cover, 5", apple shape, #316	1,250.00
Candy box, w/cover, 5⅜", #1066 stem	225.00
Candy box, w/cover, 5⅜", tall stem, #3121/3	185.00
Candy box, w/cover, 5⅜", short stem, #3121/4	175.00

1 2

	Crystal
Candy box, w/cover, blown, 5⅜", #3500/103	210.00
Candy box, w/cover, 6", ram's head, #3500/78	325.00
Candy box, w/rose finial, 6", 3 ftd., #300	395.00
Candy box, w/cover, 7", #3400/9	175.00
Candy box, w/cover, 7", rnd., 3 pt., #103	195.00
Candy box, w/cover, 8", 3 pt., #3500/57	120.00
Candy box, w/cover, rnd., #3900/165	150.00
Celery, 12", #3400/652	60.00
Celery, 12", #3500/652	65.00
Celery, 12", 5 pt., #3400/67	85.00
Celery, 14", 4 pt., 2 hdld., #3500/97	185.00
Celery & relish, 9", 3 pt., #3900/125	65.00
Celery & relish, 12", 3 pt., #3900/126	75.00
Celery & relish, 12", 5 pt., #3900/120	90.00
Cheese, 5", comport & cracker, 13", plate, #3900/135	145.00
Cheese, 5½", comport & cracker, 11½", plate, #3400/6	145.00
Cheese, 6", comport & cracker, 12", plate, #3500/162	165.00
Cheese dish, w/cover, 5", #980	625.00
Cigarette box, w/cover, #615	175.00
Cigarette box, w/cover, #747	195.00
Cigarette holder, oval, w/ashtray ft., #1066	185.00
Cigarette holder, rnd., w/ashtray ft., #1337	165.00
Coaster, 3½", #1628	65.00
Cocktail icer, 2 pc., #3600	80.00
Cocktail shaker, metal top, #3400/157	210.00
Cocktail shaker, metal top, #3400/175	200.00
Cocktail shaker, 12 oz., metal top, #97	400.00
Cocktail shaker, 32 oz., w/glass stopper, #101	295.00
Cocktail shaker, 46 oz., metal top, #98	225.00
Cocktail shaker, 48 oz., glass stopper, #102	225.00
Comport, 5", #3900/135	50.00
Comport, 5", 4 ftd., #3400/74	70.00
Comport, 5½", scalloped edge, #3900/136	80.00
Comport, 5⅜", blown, #3500/101	90.00
Comport, 5⅜", blown, #3121 stem	95.00
Comport, 5⅜", blown, #1066 stem	85.00
Comport, 6", #3500/36	160.00
Comport, 6", #3500/111	195.00
Comport, 6", 4 ftd., #3400/13	65.00
Comport, 7", 2 hdld., #3500/37	150.00

	Crystal
Comport, 7", keyhole, #3400/29	155.00
Comport, 7", keyhole, low, #3400/28	110.00
Creamer, #3400/68	25.00
Creamer, #3500/14	30.00
Creamer, flat, #137	150.00
Creamer, flat, #944	165.00
Creamer, ftd., #3400/16	100.00
Creamer, ftd., #3900/41	25.00
Creamer, indiv., #3500/15 pie crust edge	27.50
Creamer, indiv., #3900/40 scalloped edge	25.00
Cup, 3 styles, #3400/54, #3500/1, #3900/17	32.50
Cup, 5 oz., punch, #488	40.00
Cup, after dinner, #3400/69	300.00
Decanter, 12 oz., ball, w/stopper, #3400/119	395.00
Decanter, 14 oz., ftd., #1320	500.00
Decanter, 26 oz., sq., #1380	695.00
Decanter, 28 oz., tall, #1372	795.00
Decanter, 28 oz., w/stopper, #1321	425.00
Decanter, 32 oz., ball, w/stopper, #3400/92	495.00
Dressing bottle, flat, #1263	425.00
Dressing bottle, ftd., #1261	395.00
Epergne candle w/vases, #3900/75	295.00
Grapefruit, w/liner, #187	125.00
Hat, 5", #1704	500.00
Hat, 6", #1703	535.00
Hat, 8", #1702	695.00
Hat, 9", #1701	900.00
Honey dish, w/cover, #3500/139	425.00
Hot plate or trivet	125.00
Hurricane lamp, w/prisms, #1613	400.00
Hurricane lamp, candlestick base, #1617	300.00
Hurricane lamp, keyhole base, w/prisms, #1603	300.00
Hurricane lamp, 8", etched chimney, #1601	300.00
Hurricane lamp, 10", etched chimney & base, #1604	400.00
Ice bucket, #1402/52	210.00
8 Ice bucket, w/chrome hand., #3900/671	195.00
6 Ice bucket, P.672	195.00
3 Ice bucket, #3400 & #3900	200.00
5 Ice pail, P.1705	275.00
7 Ice pail, #3400/851	185.00
4 Ice tub, Pristine, P.671	335.00
Icer, cocktail, #968 or, #18	80.00
Marmalade, 8 oz., #147	195.00
Marmalade, w/cover, 7 oz., ftd., #157	215.00
Mayonnaise sherbet type w/ladle, #19	85.00
Mayonnaise, div., w/liner & 2 ladles, #3900/111	95.00
Mayonnaise, 3 pc., #3400/11	85.00
Mayonnaise, 3 pc., #3900/129	85.00
Mayonnaise, w/liner & ladle, #3500/59	85.00
Mustard, 3 oz., #151	185.00
Mustard, 4½ oz., ftd., #1329	400.00
Oil, 2 oz., ball, w/stopper, #3400/96	130.00
Oil, 6 oz., ball, w/stopper, #3400/99	185.00
Oil, 6 oz., hdld., #3400/193	140.00
Oil, 6 oz., loop hdld., w/stopper, #3900/100	185.00
Oil, 6 oz., w/stopper, ftd., hdld., #3400/161	295.00
Pickle, 9", #3400/59	70.00
Pickle or relish, 7", #3900/123	45.00
Pitcher, 20 oz., #3900/117	395.00
Pitcher, 20 oz., w/ice lip, #70	395.00
Pitcher, 32 oz., #3900/118	400.00

ROSE POINT

	Crystal
Pitcher, 32 oz., martini slender, w/metal insert, #3900/114	579.00
Pitcher, 60 oz., martini, #1408	1,995.00
Pitcher, 76 oz., #3900/115	325.00
Pitcher, 76 oz., ice lip, #3400/100	250.00
Pitcher, 76 oz., ice lip, #3400/152	400.00
Pitcher, 80 oz., ball, #3400/38	300.00
Pitcher, 80 oz., ball, #3900/116	300.00
Pitcher, 80 oz., Doulton, #3400/141	395.00
Pitcher, nite set, 2 pc., w/tumbler insert top, #103	995.00
Plate, 6", bread/butter, #3400/60	14.00
Plate, 6", bread/butter, #3500/3	14.00
Plate, 6", 2 hdld., #3400/1181	20.00
Plate, 6⅛", canape, #693	195.00
Plate, 6½", bread/butter, #3900/20	14.00
Plate, 7½", #3500/4	18.00
Plate, 7½", salad, #3400/176	18.00
Plate, 8", salad, #3900/22	20.00
Plate, 8", 2 hdld., ftd., #3500/161	45.00
Plate, 8", tab hdld., ftd., bonbon, #3900/131	42.00
Plate, 8½", breakfast, #3400/62	22.00
Plate, 8½", salad, #3500/5	22.00
Plate, 9½", crescent salad, #485	275.00
Plate, 9½", luncheon, #3400/63	36.00
Plate, 10½", dinner, #3400/64	175.00
Plate, 10½", dinner, #3900/24	175.00
Plate, 11", 2 hdld., #3400/35	65.00
Plate, 12", 4 ftd., service, #3900/26	75.00
Plate, 12", ftd., #3500/39	92.00
Plate, 12½", 2 hdld., #3400/1186	75.00
Plate, 13", rolled edge, ftd., #3900/33	75.00
Plate, 13", 4 ftd., torte, #3500/110	130.00
Plate, 13", ftd., cake Martha, #170	250.00
Plate, 13", torte, #3500/38	185.00
Plate, 13½", #242	165.00
Plate, 13½", rolled edge, #1397	80.00
Plate, 13½", tab hdld., cake, #3900/35	75.00
Plate, 14", rolled edge, #3900/166	85.00
Plate, 14", service, #3900/167	85.00
Plate, 14", torte, #3400/65	155.00
Plate, 18", punch bowl liner, Martha, #129	695.00
Punch bowl, 15", Martha, #478	4,300.00
Punch set, 15-pc., Martha	5,600.00
Relish, 5½", 2 pt., #3500/68	30.00
Relish, 5½", 2 pt., hdld., #3500/60	40.00
Relish, 6", 2 pt., #3400/90	40.00
Relish, 6", 2 pt., 1 hdl., #3400/1093	100.00
Relish, 6½", 3 pt., #3500/69	60.00
Relish, 6½", 3 pt., hdld., #3500/61	65.00
Relish, 7", 2 pt., #3900/124	42.50
Relish, 7½", 3 pt., center hdld., #3500/71	150.00
Relish, 7½", 4 pt., #3500/70	65.00
Relish, 7½", 4 pt., 2 hdld., #3500/62	90.00
Relish, 8", 3 pt., 3 hdld., #3400/91	40.00
Relish, 10", 2 hdld., #3500/85	100.00
Relish, 10", 3 pt., 2 hdld., #3500/86	90.00
Relish, 10", 3 pt., 4 ftd., 2 hdld., #3500/64	75.00
Relish, 10", 4 pt., 4 ftd., #3500/65	90.00
Relish, 10", 4 pt., 2 hdld., #3500/87	90.00
Relish, 11", 2 pt., 2 hdld., #3400/89	100.00
Relish, 11", 3 pt., #3400/200	70.00

	Crystal
Relish, 12", 5 pt., #3400/67	90.00
Relish, 12", 5 pt., Pristine, #419	295.00
Relish, 12", 6 pc., #3500/67	285.00
Relish, 14", w/cover, 4 pt., 2 hdld., #3500/142	1,200.00
Relish, 15", 4 pt., hdld., #3500/113	250.00
Salt & pepper, egg shape, pr., #1468	135.00
Salt & pepper, individual, rnd., glass base, pr., #1470	135.00
Salt & pepper, individual, w/chrome tops, pr., #360	95.00
Salt & pepper, lg., rnd., glass base, pr., #1471	135.00
Salt & pepper, w/chrome tops, pr., ftd. #3400/77	60.00
Salt & pepper w/chrome tops, pr., flat, #3900/1177	60.00
Sandwich tray, 11", center handled, #3400/10	145.00
Saucer, after dinner, #3400/69	75.00
Saucer, 3 styles, #3400, #3500, #3900	7.00
1 Statusque, cocktail	3,000.00
2 Statusque, banquet goblet	4,000.00
Stem, #3104, 3½ oz., cocktail	325.00
Stem, #3106, ¾ oz., brandy	140.00
Stem, #3106, 1 oz., cordial	140.00
Stem, #3106, 1 oz., pousse cafe	140.00
Stem, #3106, 2 oz., sherry	65.00
Stem, #3106, 2½ oz., wine	60.00
Stem, #3106, 3 oz., cocktail	35.00
Stem, #3106, 4½ oz., claret	55.00
Stem, #3106, 5 oz., oyster cocktail	30.00
Stem, #3106, 7 oz., high sherbet	30.00
Stem, #3106, 7 oz., low sherbet	22.00
Stem, #3106, 10 oz., water goblet	42.00
Stem, #3121, 1 oz., brandy	135.00
Stem, #3121, 1 oz., cordial	75.00
Stem, #3121, 3 oz., cocktail	32.00
Stem, #3121, 3½ oz., wine	60.00
Stem, #3121, 4½ oz., claret	90.00
Stem, #3121, 4½ oz., low oyster cocktail	35.00
Stem, #3121, 5 oz., low ft. parfait	90.00
Stem, #3121, 6 oz., low sherbet	20.00
Stem, #3121, 6 oz., tall sherbet	22.00
Stem, #3121, 10 oz., water	42.00
Stem, #3500, 1 oz., cordial	75.00
Stem, #3500, 2½ oz., wine	65.00
Stem, #3500, 3 oz., cocktail	35.00
Stem, #3500, 4½ oz., claret	95.00
Stem, #3500, 4½ oz., low oyster cocktail	35.00
Stem, #3500, 5 oz., low ft. parfait	100.00
Stem, #3500, 7 oz., low ft. sherbet	22.00
Stem, #3500, 7 oz., tall sherbet	28.00
Stem, #3500, 10 oz., water	45.00
Stem, #7801, 4 oz., cocktail, plain stem	40.00
Stem, #7966, 1 oz., cordial, plain ft.	150.00
Stem, #7966, 2 oz., sherry, plain ft.	125.00
Sugar, #3400/68	22.00
Sugar, #3500/14	25.00
Sugar, flat, #137	150.00
Sugar, flat, #944	165.00
Sugar, ftd., #3400/16	100.00
Sugar, ftd., #3900/41	25.00
Sugar, indiv., #3500/15, pie crust edge	27.50
Sugar, indiv., #3900/40, scalloped edge	22.00

	Crystal		Crystal
Syrup, w/drip stop top, #1670	395.00	Tumbler, #3400/115, 13 oz.	60.00
Tray, 6", 2 hdld., sq., #3500/91	195.00	Urn, 10", w/cover, #3500/41	695.00
Tray, 12", 2 hdld., oval, service, #3500/99	275.00	Urn, 12", w/cover, #3500/42	795.00
Tray, 12", rnd., #3500/67	210.00	Vase, 5", #1309	125.00
Tray, 13", 2 hdld., rnd., #3500/72	210.00	Vase, 5", globe, #3400/102	110.00
Tray, sugar/creamer, #3900/37	35.00	Vase, 5", ftd., #6004	70.00
Tumbler, #498, 2 oz., straight side	130.00	Vase, 6", high ftd., flower, #6004	75.00
Tumbler, #498, 5 oz., straight side	50.00	Vase, 6", #572	180.00
Tumbler, #498, 8 oz., straight side	50.00	Vase, 6½", globe, #3400/103	130.00
Tumbler, #498, 10 oz., straight side	50.00	Vase, 7", ivy, ftd., ball, #1066	325.00
Tumbler, #498, 12 oz., straight side	90.00	Vase, 8", #1430	295.00
Tumbler, #3000, 3½ oz., cone, ftd.	120.00	Vase, 8", flat, flared, #797	210.00
Tumbler, #3000, 5 oz., cone, ftd.	135.00	Vase, 8", ftd., #3500/44	195.00
Tumbler, #3106, 3 oz., ftd.	40.00	Vase, 8", high ftd., flower, #6004	90.00
Tumbler, #3106, 5 oz., ftd.	37.50	Vase, 9", ftd., keyhole, #1237	125.00
Tumbler, #3106, 9 oz., ftd.	40.00	Vase, 9", ftd., #1620	195.00
Tumbler, #3106, 12 oz., ftd.	45.00	Vase, 9½" ftd., keyhole, #1233	145.00
Tumbler, #3121, 2½ oz., ftd.	75.00	Vase, 10", ball bottom, #400	265.00
Tumbler, #3121, 5 oz., low ft., juice	40.00	Vase, 10", bud, #1528	150.00
Tumbler, #3121, 10 oz., low ft., water	35.00	Vase, 10", cornucopia, #3900/575	265.00
Tumbler, #3121, 12 oz., low ft., ice tea	45.00	Vase, 10", flat, #1242	185.00
Tumbler, #3400/1341, 1 oz., cordial	125.00	Vase, 10", ftd., #1301	120.00
Tumbler, #3400/92, 2½ oz.	125.00	Vase, 10", ftd., #6004	125.00
Tumbler, #3400/38, 5 oz.	110.00	Vase, 10", ftd., #3500/45	225.00
Tumbler, #3400/38, 12 oz.	70.00	Vase, 10", slender, #274	75.00
Tumbler, #3900/115, 13 oz.	65.00	Vase, 11", ftd., flower, #278	165.00
Tumbler, #3500, 2½ oz., ftd.	75.00	Vase, 11", ped. ftd., flower, #1299	225.00
Tumbler, #3500, 5 oz., low ft., juice	42.00	Vase, 12", ftd., #6004	150.00
Tumbler, #3500, 10 oz., low ft., water	32.00	Vase, 12", ftd., keyhole, #1234	185.00
Tumbler, #3500, 13 oz., low ftd.	42.00	Vase, 12", ftd., keyhole, #1238	195.00
Tumbler, #3500, 12 oz., tall ft., ice tea	42.00	Vase, 13", ftd., flower, #279	295.00
Tumbler, #7801, 5 oz., ftd.	50.00	Vase 18", #1336	2,500.00
Tumbler, #7801, 12 oz., ftd., ice tea	75.00	Vase, sweet pea, #629	395.00
Tumbler, #3900/117, 5 oz.	70.00		

Colors: amber, Ebony, blue, green

Fostoria's Royal is intermittently (inaccurately) identified as Vesper, since both etchings are similar. Both designs are found on the #2350 blank and both were distributed in the same colors. Royal does not lure as many collectors as Vesper, possibly due to a limited dispersal. New collectors should find Royal pricing more to their liking since there is less demand. Remember that demand raises prices more than scarcity.

Adequate amber or green is around to acquire a set; but only a minuscule number of pieces can be found in blue or black. Fostoria's blue color found with Royal etching was called blue as opposed to the Azure blue which is a lighter hue found etched with June or other patterns.

I have added a few unusual pieces in green, but they are marked in the listings. We hope you appreciate everyone's efforts to enhance this book by labeling every piece. It was time consuming, tedious work and added several weeks to the production; readers have been requesting this.

Unusual and hard to find pieces of Royal include both styles of pitchers, covered cheese and butter dishes, cologne bottle, and sugar lid. The cologne bottle is a combination powder jar and cologne. The dauber is the hardest part of the three-piece set to find.

Published material indicates production of Royal continued until 1934, although the January 1, 1933, Fostoria catalog no longer listed Royal as being for sale. I have changed my cutoff date of production to 1932. If you can find a May 1928 copy of *House and Garden*, there is a charming Fostoria Royal advertisement displayed.

		*Amber/Green			*Amber/Green
14	Almond, #4095	30.00		Bowl, #2350, 9", nappy	32.00
	Ashtray, #2350, 3½"	22.50		Bowl, #2350, 9", oval, baker	45.00
	Bowl, #2350, bouillon, flat	15.00	24	Bowl, #2324, 10", ftd.	45.00
	Bowl, #2350½, bouillon, ftd.	18.00		Bowl, #2350, 10", salad	35.00
	Bowl, #2350, cream soup, flat	18.00		Bowl, #2350, 10½", oval, baker	55.00
11	Bowl, #2350½, cream soup, ftd.	20.00		Bowl, #2315, 10½", ftd.	45.00
10	Bowl, #869, 4½", finger	22.00		Bowl, #2329, 11", console	22.00
13	Bowl, #2350, 5½", fruit	15.00		Bowl, #2297, 12", deep	22.00
	Bowl, #2350, 6½", cereal	26.00		Bowl, #2329, 13", console	30.00
	Bowl, #2267, 7", ftd.	35.00		Bowl, #2324, 13", ftd.	50.00
	Bowl, #2350, 7¾", soup	32.00		Bowl, #2371, 13", oval, w/flower frog	160.00
	Bowl, #2350, 8", nappy	30.00		Butter, w/cover, #2350	325.00
				Candlestick, #2324, 4"	22.00

		*Amber/Green
	Candlestick, #2324, 9"	75.00
	Candy, w/cover, #2331, 3 part	85.00
	Candy, w/cover, ftd., ½ lb.	165.00
	Celery, #2350, 11"	25.00
	Cheese, w/cover/plate, #2276 (plate 11")	175.00
	Cologne, #2322, tall	135.00
	Cologne, #2323, short	110.00
	Cologne/powder jar combination	295.00
	Comport, #1861½, 6", jelly	25.00
	Comport, #2327, 7"	28.00
	Comport, #2358, 8" wide	30.00
16	Creamer, flat	18.00
	Creamer, #2315½, ftd., fat	18.00
17	Creamer, #2350½, ftd.	15.00
4	Cup, #2350, flat	10.00
20	Cup, #2350½, ftd.	11.00
	Cup, #2350, demi	25.00
	Egg cup, #2350	28.00
	Grapefruit, w/insert	90.00
15	Grapefruit, #2315	30.00
12	Grapefruit, #2350	40.00
	Ice bucket, #2378	65.00
	Mayonnaise, #2315	25.00
	Pickle, 8", #2350	20.00
	Pitcher, #1236	395.00
	Pitcher, #5000, 48 oz.	325.00
	Plate, 8½", deep soup/underplate	37.50
9	Plate, #2350, 6", bread/butter	3.00
	Plate, #2350, 7½", salad	4.00
18	Plate, #2350, 8½", luncheon	8.00
21	Plate, #2321, 8¾, Maj Jongg (canape)	35.00

		*Amber/Green
	Plate, #2350, 9½", small dinner	12.00
	Plate, #2350, 10½", dinner	28.00
3	Plate, #2350, 13", chop	33.00
	Plate, #2350, 15", chop	50.00
	Platter, #2350, 10½"	28.00
	Platter, #2350, 12"	55.00
	Platter, #2350, 15½"	100.00
	Salt and pepper, #5100, pr.	75.00
	Sauce boat, w/liner	150.00
5	Saucer, #2350/#2350½	3.00
	Saucer, #2350, demi	8.00
	Server, #2287, 11", center hdld.	25.00
	Stem, #869, ¾ oz., cordial	65.00
	Stem, #869, 2¾ oz., wine	30.00
	Stem, #869, 3 oz., cocktail	20.00
25	Stem, #869, 5½ oz., oyster cocktail	18.00
1	Stem, #869, 5½ oz., parfait	30.00
6	Stem, #869, 6 oz., low sherbet	12.00
8	Stem, #869, 6 oz., high sherbet	15.00
22	Stem, #869, 9 oz., water	25.00
	Sugar, flat, w/lid	175.00
	Sugar, #2315, ftd., fat	18.00
19	Sugar, #2350½, ftd.	15.00
	Sugar lid, #2350½	135.00
	Tumbler, #869, 5 oz., flat	20.00
	Tumbler, #859, 9 oz., flat	22.00
7	Tumbler, #859, 12 oz., flat	28.00
2	Tumbler, #5000, 2½ oz., ftd.	33.00
	Tumbler, #5000, 5 oz., ftd.	12.00
23	Tumbler, #5000, 9 oz., ftd.	15.00
	Tumbler, #5000, 12 oz., ftd.	22.00
	Vase, #2324, urn, ftd.	100.00
	Vase, #2292, flared	110.00

Colors: Smokey Topaz, Jungle Green, French Crystal, Silver Gray, Lilac, Sunshine, Jade; some milk glass, Apple Green, black, French Opalescent

Ruba Rombic has seen a few price corrections, and surprisingly not on the descending side as has happened to some patterns. Mostly prices have held firm, but firm prices for Ruba Rombic is way beyond the expenditure by most collectors of glass. There are collectors who feel this is the most wonderful pattern in the book, while others scoff at anyone who thinks it is. If you see a piece, inexpensively priced, buy it regardless of your feelings. Someone will love it.

The color shown in the larger photo here is Smokey Topaz, priced below with the Jungle Green. Both of these colors are transparent as opposed to the other colors that are cased (layered). Smokey Topaz will be the color you are most likely to find if you are lucky enough to spot a piece.

The cased color column below includes three colors. They are Lilac (lavender), Sunshine (yellow), and Jade (green). French crystal is a white, applied color except that the raised edges are crystal with no white coloring at all. Silver is sometimes called Gray Silver.

Once a piece of glass attains four digit prices, there are a limited number of collectors willing to stand that cost. Once five digit prices are attained, there is only a handful. You can get a good used car or a new import in that range.

Ruba Rombic has always sold in a specialized market that eluded most dealers who did not have a special outlet. The Internet is changing that.

There were three bowls marketed recently — all with chunks, chips and cracks. The owner wanted hundreds of dollars for quite damaged wares. It was interesting to note he packed them at market's end.

	Smokey Topaz, Jungle Green	Cased Colors	French Opal, French Crystal, Silver
Ashtray, 3½"	600.00	750.00	850.00
Bonbon, flat, 3 part	250.00	350.00	400.00
2 Bottle, decanter, 9"	1,800.00	2,200.00	2,500.00
Bottle, perfume, 4¾"	1,800.00	1,500.00	1,950.00
Bottle, toilet, 7½"	1,200.00	1,500.00	1,800.00
Bowl, 3", almond	275.00	300.00	375.00
9 Bowl, 8", cupped	975.00	1,200.00	1,300.00
8 Bowl, 9", flared	950.00	1,200.00	1,300.00
5 Bowl, 12", oval	1,500.00	1,800.00	1,800.00
Bowl, bouillon	175.00	250.00	275.00
4 Bowl, finger	110.00	135.00	145.00
Box, cigarette, 3½" x 4¼"	850.00	1,250.00	1,500.00
Box, powder, 5", round	850.00	1,250.00	1,500.00
Candlestick, 2½" high, pr.	500.00	650.00	750.00
Celery, 10", 3 part	850.00	950.00	1,000.00
Comport, 7", wide	850.00	950.00	1,000.00
3 Creamer	200.00	250.00	300.00
Light, ceiling fixture, 10"		1,500.00	1,500.00
Light, ceiling fixture, 16"		2,500.00	2,500.00
Light, table light		1,200.00	1,200.00

	Smokey Topaz, Jungle Green	Cased Colors	French Opal, French Crystal, Silver
Light, wall sconce		1,500.00	1,500.00
Pitcher, 8¼"	2,500.00	3,000.00	4,000.00
Plate, 7"	75.00	100.00	150.00
Plate, 8"	75.00	100.00	150.00
Plate, 10"	250.00	275.00	300.00
Plate, 15"	1,275.00	1,500.00	1,500.00
Relish, 2 part	350.00	450.00	500.00
Sugar	200.00	250.00	300.00
Sundae	100.00	135.00	150.00
Tray for decanter set	2,000.00	2,250.00	2,500.00
1 Tumbler, 2 oz., flat, 2¾"	120.00	140.00	160.00
Tumbler, 3 oz., ftd.	130.00	155.00	175.00
Tumbler, 9 oz., flat	130.00	175.00	200.00
Tumbler, 10 oz., ftd.	170.00	300.00	350.00
Tumbler, 12 oz., flat	195.00	300.00	350.00
Tumbler, 15 oz., ftd., 7"	350.00	450.00	500.00
7 Vase, 6"	850.00	1,000.00	1,500.00
6 Vase, 9½"	1,500.00	2,500.00	3,000.00
Vase, 16"	10,000.00	12,000.00	12,000.00

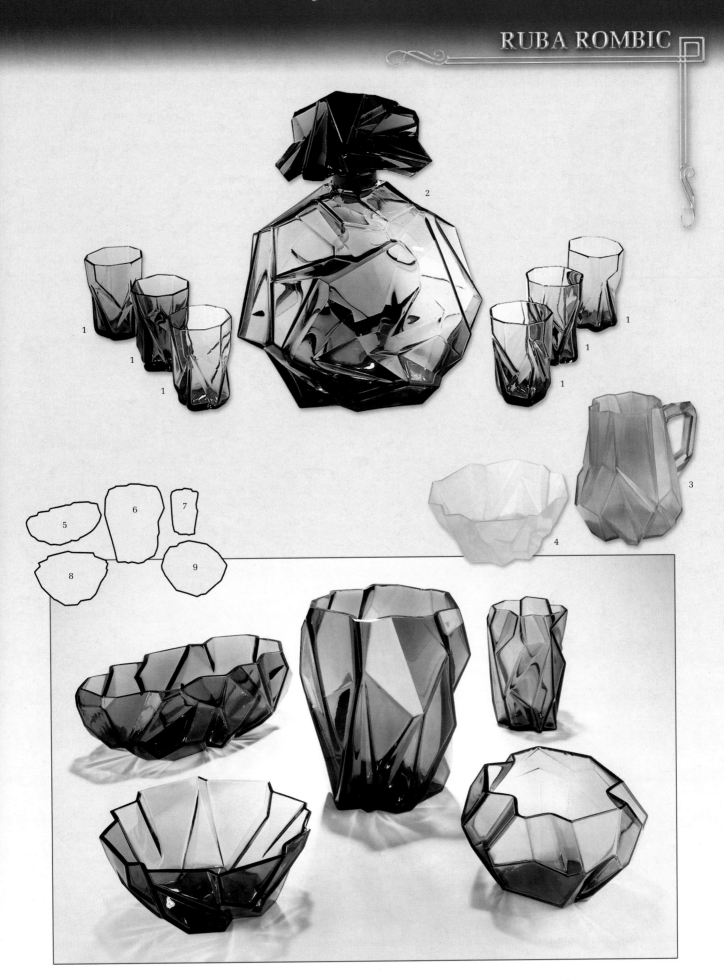

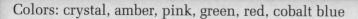

Colors: crystal, amber, pink, green, red, cobalt blue

Lancaster Colony continues to produce some Sandwich pieces in their lines today. The bright blue, green, or amberina color combinations were made by Indiana from Duncan moulds and were sold by Montgomery Ward in the early 1970s. There are a few collectors beginning to ask for these colors, but most Depression glass shows do not allow 1970s glass, so the Internet and antique malls are where these colors are being sold.

I just saw a Sunset (amberina) bowl priced for $95.00, labeled rare Sandwich glass, at an antique market. Cobalt blue and true red pieces seem to invigorate a few Duncan collectors. Tiffin also made a few Sandwich pieces in milk glass and Chartreuse out of Duncan moulds before they were turned over to Lancaster Colony.

I have eliminated the factory catalog pages of Sandwich from this book. If those interest you, an older copy of this book will have to be located on the secondary market.

An abundance of crystal Sandwich stemware makes it as inexpensive to buy as nearly all currently made imported stemware sold in department stores. If you enjoy this design, now would be a good time to start picking it up while you can still afford the gasoline to search for it.

	Crystal			Crystal
Ashtray, 2½" x 3¾", rect.	10.00		Cake stand, 13", ftd., plain pedestal	80.00
Ashtray, 2¾", sq.	8.00		Candelabra, 10", 1-lite, w/bobeche & prisms	85.00
Basket, 6½", w/loop hdl.	135.00		Candelabra, 10", 3-lite, w/bobeche & prisms	225.00
Basket, 10", crimped, w/loop hdl.	225.00		Candelabra, 16", 3-lite, w/bobeche & prisms	275.00
Basket, 10", oval, w/loop hdl.	275.00		Candlestick, 4", 1-lite	15.00
Basket, 11½", w/loop hdl.	250.00		Candlestick, 4", 1-lite, w/bobeche & stub.	
Bonbon, 5", heart shape, w/ring hdl.	15.00		prisms	35.00
Bonbon, 5½", heart shape, hdld.	15.00		Candlestick, 5", 3-lite	45.00
Bonbon, 6", heart shape, w/ring hdl.	20.00		Candlestick, 5", 3-lite, w/bobeche & stub.	
Bonbon, 7½", ftd., w/cover	45.00		prisms	125.00
Bowl, 2½", salted almond	11.00		Candlestick, 5", 2-lite, w/bobeche & stub.	
Bowl, 3½", nut	10.00		prisms	110.00
Bowl, 4", finger	12.50		Candlestick, 5", 2-lite	38.00
Bowl, 5½", hdld.	15.00		Candy, 6", sq.	395.00
Bowl, 5½", ftd., grapefruit, w/rim liner	17.50		Candy box, w/cover, 5", flat	55.00
Bowl, 5½", ftd., grapefruit, w/fruit cup liner	17.50		Candy jar, w/cover, 8½", ftd.	80.00
Bowl, 5", 2 pt., nappy	12.00		Cheese, w/cover (cover 4¾", plate 8")	135.00
Bowl, 5", ftd., crimped ivy	40.00		Cheese/cracker (3" compote, 13" plate)	55.00
Bowl, 5", fruit	10.00		Cigarette box, w/cover, 3½"	22.00
Bowl, 5", nappy, w/ring hdl.	13.00		Cigarette holder, 3", ftd.	27.50
Bowl, 6", 2 pt., nappy	15.00	5	Coaster, 5"	12.00
Bowl, 6", fruit salad	12.00		Comport, 2¼"	15.00
Bowl, 6", grapefruit, rimmed edge	17.50		Comport, 3¼", low ft., crimped candy	22.00
Bowl, 6", nappy, w/ring hdl.	18.00		Comport, 3¼", low ft., flared candy	17.50
Bowl, 10", salad, deep	75.00		Comport, 4¼", ftd.	25.00
Bowl, 10", 3 pt., fruit	90.00		Comport, 5", low ft.	25.00
Bowl, 10", lily, vertical edge	52.50		Comport, 5½", ftd., low crimped	30.00
Bowl, 11", cupped nut	55.00		Comport, 6", low ft., flared	27.50
Bowl, 11½", crimped flower	55.00		Condiment set (2 cruets, 3¾" salt & pepper,	
Bowl, 11½", gardenia	45.00		4 pt. tray)	125.00
Bowl, 11½", ftd., crimped fruit	60.00		Creamer, 4", 7 oz., ftd.	10.00
Bowl, 12", fruit, flared edge	45.00		Cup, 6 oz., tea	10.00
Bowl, 12", shallow salad	40.00		Epergne, 9", garden	150.00
Bowl, 12", oblong console	40.00		Epergne, 12", 3 pt., fruit or flower	275.00
Bowl, 12", epergne, w/ctr. hole	100.00		Jelly, 3", indiv.	9.00
Butter, w/cover, ¼ lb.	55.00	4	Mayonnaise set, 3 pc.: ladle, 5" bowl, 7" plate	32.00
Cake stand, 11½", ftd., rolled edge	95.00		Oil bottle, 5¾"	35.00
Cake stand, 12", ftd., rolled edge, plain			Pan, 6¾" x 10½", oblong, camelia	65.00
pedestal	80.00			

	Crystal
Pitcher, 13 oz., syrup top	55.00
Pitcher, w/ice lip, 8", 64 oz.	145.00
Plate, 3", indiv. jelly	6.00
Plate, 6", bread/butter	7.00
Plate, 6½", finger bowl liner	9.00
Plate, 7", dessert	9.00
Plate, 8", mayonnaise liner, w/ring	10.00
Plate, 8", salad	10.00
Plate, 9½", dinner	38.00
Plate, 11½", hdld., service	40.00
Plate, 12", torte	45.00
Plate, 12", ice cream, rolled edge	60.00
Plate, 12", deviled egg	75.00
Plate, 13", salad dressing, w/ring	50.00
Plate, 13", service	45.00
Plate, 13", service, rolled edge	45.00
Plate, 13", cracker, w/ring	35.00
Plate, 16", lazy susan, w/turntable	115.00
Plate, 16", hostess	100.00
Relish, 5½", 2 pt., rnd., ring hdl.	18.00
Relish, 6", 2 pt., rnd., ring hdl.	20.00
Relish, 7", 2 pt., oval	22.00
Relish, 10", 4 pt., hdld.	30.00
Relish, 10", 3 pt., oblong	32.50
Relish, 10½", 3 pt., oblong	32.50
Relish, 12", 3 pt.	45.00
Salad dressing set:	
(2 ladles, 5" ftd. mayonnaise,	
13" plate w/ring)	75.00
Salad dressing set:	
(2 ladles, 6" ftd. div. bowl,	
8" plate w/ring)	85.00
Salt & pepper, 2½", w/glass tops, pr.	20.00
Salt & pepper, 2½", w/metal tops, pr.	20.00
Salt & pepper, 3¾", w/metal top (on 6" tray), 3 pc.	30.00
Saucer, 6", w/ring	4.00

		Crystal
	Stem, 2½", 6 oz., ftd., fruit cup/jello	10.00
	Stem, 2¾", 5 oz., ftd., oyster cocktail	12.00
8	Stem, 3½", 5 oz., sundae (flared rim)	10.00
2	Stem, 4¼", 3 oz., cocktail	12.00
	Stem, 4¼", 5 oz., ice cream	10.00
7	Stem, 4¼", 3 oz., wine	18.00
	Stem, 5¼", 4 oz., ftd., parfait	28.00
9	Stem, 5¼", 5 oz., champagne	18.00
10	Stem, 6", 9 oz., goblet	20.00
	Sugar, 3¼", ftd., 9 oz.	9.00
	Sugar, 5 oz.	8.00
	Sugar (cheese) shaker, 13 oz., metal top	65.00
	Tray, oval (for sugar/creamer)	10.00
	Tray, 6" mint, rolled edge, w/ring hdl.	17.50
	Tray, 7", oval, pickle	15.00
	Tray, 7", mint, rolled edge, w/ring hdl.	22.00
	Tray, 8", oval	18.00
	Tray, 8", for oil/vinegar	22.00
	Tray, 10", oval, celery	18.00
	Tray, 12", fruit epergne	55.00
	Tray, 12", ice cream, rolled edge	55.00
1	Tumbler, 3¾", 5 oz., ftd., juice	12.00
3	Tumbler, 4½", 9 oz., flat, water	10.00
	Tumbler, 4¾", 9 oz., ftd., water	16.00
6	Tumbler, 5¼", 13 oz., flat, iced tea	20.00
11	Tumbler, 5¼", 12 oz., ftd., iced tea	20.00
	Urn, w/cover, 12", ftd.	175.00
	Vase, 3", ftd., crimped	22.50
	Vase, 3", ftd., flared rim	18.00
	Vase, 4", hat shape	25.00
	Vase, 4½", flat base, crimped	30.00
	Vase, 5", ftd., flared rim	25.00
	Vase, 5", ftd., crimped	45.00
	Vase, 5", ftd., fan	55.00
	Vase, 7½", epergne, threaded base	70.00
	Vase, 10", ftd.	80.00

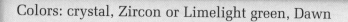

Colors: crystal, Zircon or Limelight green, Dawn

Limelight and Zircon are the same color. Zircon was originally made in 1937. In the 1950s, it was made again by Heisey, but called Limelight. Zircon prices are steadily rising, especially all sizes of plates, pitchers, and shakers. I have been watching one Zircon comport for at least eight years making long journeys across the country and back. Either the dealer likes to display it at an outrageous price or doesn't understand that a reduction in price might be a smart move in order to sell it and buy something else.

Crystal Saturn prices are remaining steady.

		Crystal	Zircon Limelight
	Ashtray	10.00	150.00
	Bitters bottle, w/short tube, blown	75.00	
12	Bowl, baked apple	25.00	100.00
	Bowl, finger	15.00	90.00
	Bowl, rose, lg.	40.00	
	Bowl, 4½", nappy	15.00	
	Bowl, 5", nappy	15.00	90.00
	Bowl, 5", whipped cream	25.00	120.00
	Bowl, 7", pickle	35.00	
	Bowl, 9", 3 part, relish	20.00	
	Bowl, 10", celery	15.00	
13	Bowl, 11", salad	40.00	140.00
	Bowl, 12", fruit, flared rim	35.00	100.00
	Bowl, 13", floral, rolled edge	37.00	
	Bowl, 13", floral	37.00	
11	Candelabrum, w/"e" ball drops, 2-lite	175.00	500.00
8	Candle block, 2-lite	95.00	350.00
	Candlestick, 3", ftd., 1-lite	30.00	500.00
	Comport, 7"	50.00	550.00
10	Creamer	25.00	180.00
	Cup	10.00	160.00
	Hostess Set, 8 pc. (low bowl w/ftd. ctr. bowl, 3 toothpick holders & clips)	65.00	300.00
	Marmalade, w/cover	45.00	500.00
6	Mayonnaise	8.00	80.00
	Mustard, w/cover and paddle	60.00	450.00*

*Zircon $800.00 at 1998 **auction**.

	Crystal	Zircon Limelight
7 Oil bottle, 3 oz.	55.00	650.00
3 Pitcher, 70 oz., w/ice lip, blown	65.00	550.00
Pitcher, juice	40.00	500.00
Plate, 6"	5.00	50.00
Plate, 7", bread	5.00	55.00
Plate, 8", luncheon	10.00	50.00
Plate, 13", torte	25.00	
Plate, 15", torte	30.00	
5 Salt & pepper, pr.	45.00	600.00
Saucer	5.00	40.00
Stem, 3 oz., cocktail	15.00	75.00
Stem, 4 oz., fruit cocktail or oyster cocktail, no ball in stem, ftd.	10.00	75.00
Stem, 4½ oz., sherbet	8.00	70.00
Stem, 5 oz., parfait	10.00	110.00
Stem, 6 oz., saucer champagne	10.00	95.00
Stem, 10 oz.	20.00	100.00
9 Sugar	25.00	180.00
Sugar shaker (pourer)	80.00	
Sugar, w/cover, no handles	25.00	
Tray, tidbit, 2 sides turned as fan	25.00	110.00
Tumbler, 5 oz., juice	8.00	80.00
2 Tumbler, 7 oz., old-fashion	10.00	
Tumbler, 8 oz., old-fashion	10.00	
Tumbler, 9 oz., luncheon	15.00	
4 Tumbler, 10 oz.	20.00	80.00
Tumbler, 12 oz., soda	20.00	85.00
Vase, violet	35.00	160.00
1 Vase, 8½", flared	55.00	225.00
Vase, 8½", straight	55.00	225.00
Vase, 10½"		260.00

Colors: amber, green

Seville continues to be an ignored Fostoria pattern. I have never understood why it has never caught on with collectors in either green or amber. It is attractive, 70 to 80 years old, and made by Fostoria, one of the major glass companies of the time — a winning scenario; and, Fostoria is no longer in business.

Seville would be an economical Elegant pattern to collect in spite of there not being huge displays at shows. You might have to ask for it if it is not out for sale. It might surprise you what dealers have in inventory that often is not displayed at shows. Green would be easier to obtain than amber as you may note by the lack of amber in my photos. The butter dish, pitcher, grapefruit and liner, and sugar lid are all challenging to find, but oh, so heartwarming when you do run across them. Those pieces are costly items, but not as dear as those same pieces in other Fostoria patterns such as June or Versailles.

		Amber	Green
	Ashtray, #2350, 4"	17.50	22.50
20	Bowl, #2350, fruit, 5½"	10.00	12.00
	Bowl, #2350, cereal, 6½"	18.00	25.00
	Bowl, #2350, soup, 7¾"	20.00	30.00
	Bowl, #2315, low foot, 7"	18.00	22.00
	Bowl, #2350, vegetable	22.00	27.50
	Bowl, #2350, nappy, 9"	30.00	37.50
	Bowl, #2350, oval, baker, 9"	25.00	30.00
	Bowl, #2315, flared, 10½", ftd.	25.00	30.00
	Bowl, #2350, oval, baker, 10½"	35.00	40.00
	Bowl, 10", ftd.	35.00	42.50
	Bowl, #2350, salad, 10"	30.00	35.00
15	Bowl, #2329, rolled edge, console, 11"	27.50	37.50
	Bowl, #2297, deep, flared, 12"	30.00	35.00
	Bowl, #2371, oval, console, 13"	35.00	38.00
	Bowl, #2329, rolled edge, console, 13"	32.00	40.00
	Bowl, #2350, bouillon, flat	13.50	18.00
19	Bowl, #2350½, bouillon, ftd.	14.00	18.00
	Bowl, #2350, cream soup, flat	14.50	20.00
12	Bowl, #2350½, cream soup, ftd.	15.50	20.00
	Bowl, #869/2283, finger, w/6" liner	22.00	30.00
11	Butter, w/cover, #2350, round	210.00	295.00
	Candlestick, #2324, 2"	18.00	22.00
10	Candlestick, #2324, 4"	16.00	22.00
	Candlestick, #2324, 9"	45.00	50.00
	Candy jar, w/cover, #2250, ½ lb., ftd.	100.00	145.00
	Candy jar, w/cover, #2331, 3 pt., flat	75.00	95.00
	Celery, #2350, 11"	15.00	17.50
	Cheese and cracker, #2368 (11" plate)	40.00	45.00
3	Comport, #2327, 7½", (twisted stem)	20.00	25.00
	Comport, #2350, 8"	27.50	35.00
	Creamer, #2315½, flat, ftd.	13.50	15.00
16	Creamer, #2350½, ftd.	12.50	13.50
	Cup, #2350, after dinner	25.00	30.00
	Cup, #2350, flat	10.00	12.50
18	Cup, #2350½, ftd.	10.00	12.50
	Egg cup, #2350	30.00	35.00

		Amber	Green
	Grapefruit, #945½, blown	45.00	50.00
1	Grapefruit, #945½, liner, blown	35.00	40.00
	Grapefruit, #2315, molded	25.00	32.00
	Ice bucket, #2378	55.00	65.00
	Pickle, #2350, 8"	13.50	15.00
4	Pitcher, #5084, ftd.	250.00	295.00
21	Plate, #2350, bread and butter, 6"	3.50	4.00
22	Plate, #2350, salad, 7½"	5.00	5.50
	Plate, #2350, luncheon, 8½"	6.00	6.50
	Plate, #2321, Maj Jongg (canape), 8¾"	30.00	35.00
5	Plate, #2350, sm. dinner, 9½"	12.00	13.50
	Plate, #2350, dinner, 10½"	35.00	45.00
	Plate, #2350, chop, 13¾"	30.00	35.00
	Plate, #2350, round, 15"	45.00	50.00
13	Plate, #2350, cream soup liner	5.00	6.00
	Platter, #2350, 10½"	30.00	35.00
23	Platter, #2350, 12"	40.00	50.00
	Platter, #2350, 15"	85.00	110.00
	Salt and pepper shaker, #5100, pr.	65.00	75.00
	Sauce boat liner, #2350	25.00	30.00
	Sauce boat, #2350	55.00	75.00
18	Saucer, #2350	3.00	3.00
	Saucer, after dinner, #2350	5.00	5.00
	Stem, #870, cocktail	14.00	15.00
7	Stem, #870, cordial	55.00	60.00
8	Stem, #870, high sherbet	15.00	15.00
6	Stem, #870, low sherbet	12.00	12.00
	Stem, #870, oyster cocktail	15.00	15.00
	Stem, #870, parfait	25.00	30.00
2	Stem, #870, water	22.00	24.00
9	Stem, #870, wine	22.00	24.00
14	Sugar cover, #2350½	80.00	110.00
	Sugar, fat, ftd., #2315	13.50	14.50
14	Sugar, ftd., #2350½	12.50	13.50
17	Tray, 11", center hdld., #2287	27.50	30.00
	Tumbler, #5084, ftd., 2 oz.	30.00	35.00
	Tumbler, #5084, ftd., 5 oz.	12.00	13.00
	Tumbler, #5084, ftd., 9 oz.	14.00	15.00
	Tumbler, #5084, ftd., 12 oz.	16.00	18.00
	Urn, small, #2324	75.00	110.00
	Vase, #2292, 8"	75.00	95.00

Colors: amber, green, pink, crystal

"Spiral Flutes" is a Duncan & Miller pattern that is easily spotted by collectors because it has the look of several well-known Depression glass patterns. Numerous Duncan & Miller patterns have suffered due to limited information on that company's wares. For some reason, most Duncan collectors seem to want to keep their knowledge to themselves. Thankfully, that attitude is changing, albeit slowly. The more people aware of Duncan patterns, the more Duncan glass will be exposed to those who root it out of basements, garages, and attics.

"Spiral Flutes" pattern has pieces that are rarely seen. However, the three smaller plates, 5" and 6¾" bowls, and the seven ounce footed tumbler proliferate. After that, there is little easily found. Green can be accumulated more quickly than amber and crystal, but few collectors are presently attempting to collect those.

	Amber Green Pink
Candle, 3½"	25.00
Candle, 7½"	65.00
Candle, 9½"	90.00
Candle, 11½"	110.00
8 Candy w/cover	45.00
Celery, 10¾" x 4¾"	17.50
*Chocolate jar, w/cover	250.00
9 Cigarette holder, 4"	35.00
Comport, 4⅜"	15.00
17 Comport, 6⅝"	17.50
Comport, 9", low ft., flared	55.00
Console stand, 1½" h. x 4⅝" w.	12.00
16 Creamer, oval	8.00
18 Cup	9.00
12 Cup, demi	25.00
*Fernery, 10" x 5½", 4 ftd., flower box	350.00
Grapefruit, ftd.	20.00
Ice tub, handled	95.00
Lamp, 10½", countess	295.00
Mug, 6½", 9 oz., handled	28.00
Mug, 7", 9 oz., handled	30.00
Oil, w/stopper, 6 oz.	195.00
Pickle, 8⅝"	12.00
Pitcher, ½ gal.	175.00
10 Plate, 6", pie	3.00
Plate, 7½", salad	4.00
Plate, 8⅜", luncheon	4.00
Plate, 10⅜", dinner	22.50
Plate, 13⅝", torte	27.50
Plate, w/star, 6" (fingerbowl item)	6.00
Platter, 11"	35.00
Platter, 13"	55.00

	Amber Green Pink
Bowl, 2", almond	12.00
15 Bowl, 3¾", bouillon	15.00
Bowl, 4⅜", finger	7.00
Bowl, 4¾", ftd., cream soup	14.00
Bowl, 4" w., mayonnaise	17.50
13 Bowl, 5", nappy	6.00
Bowl, 6½", cereal, sm. flange	30.00
Bowl, 6¾", grapefruit	7.50
Bowl, 6", hdld. nappy	20.00
Bowl, 6", hdld. nappy, w/cover	75.00
Bowl, 7", nappy	15.00
Bowl, 7½", flanged (baked apple)	22.50
Bowl, 8", nappy	17.50
Bowl, 8½", flanged (oyster plate)	22.50
Bowl, 9", nappy	27.50
19 Bowl, 10", oval, veg., two styles	45.00
Bowl, 10½", lily pond	40.00
Bowl, 11¾" w. x 3¾" t., console, flared	28.00
4 Bowl, 11", nappy	28.00
Bowl, 12", cupped console	30.00

*Crystal, $135.00

		Amber Green Pink			Amber Green Pink
	Relish, 10" x 7⅜", oval, 3 pc. (2 inserts)	100.00	11	Tumbler, 3⅜", ftd., 2½ oz., cocktail (no stem)	7.00
	Saucer	3.00		Tumbler, 4¼", 8 oz., flat	25.00
12	Saucer, demi	5.00	1	Tumbler, 4⅜", ftd., 5½ oz., juice (no stem)	14.00
	Seafood sauce cup, 3" w. x 2½" h.	22.00		Tumbler, 4¾", 7 oz., flat, soda	30.00
	Stem, 3¾", 3½ oz., wine	17.50		Tumbler, 5⅛", ftd., 7 oz., water (1 knob)	8.00
	Stem, 3¾", 5 oz., low sherbet	8.00	7	Tumbler, 5⅛", ftd., 9 oz., water (no stem)	20.00
3	Stem, 4¾", 6 oz., tall sherbet	12.00	2	Tumbler, 5½", 11 oz., ginger ale	55.00
	Stem, 5⅝", 4½ oz., parfait	16.00		Vase, 6½"	20.00
6	Stem, 6¼", 7 oz., water	18.00		Vase, 8½"	30.00
14	Sugar, oval	8.00	5	Vase, 10½"	40.00
	Sweetmeat, w/cover, 7½"	110.00			

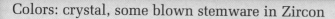

Colors: crystal, some blown stemware in Zircon

Heisey's Stanhope is a Deco pattern that more collectors than just Heisey ones are hunting. Deco people seem to have a high regard for the red or black "T" knobs, which were inserted in all the open round handles of Stanhope. "T" knobs, in the price listings, are insert handles (black or red, round, wooden knobs) which are like wooden dowel rods that act as horizontal handles. The insert handles are capricious to some; but others think them magnificent. Although items are listed with or without the knobs, you can expect items to fetch 20% to 25% less when they are missing. I had a challenging time of marketing that rarely seen candy in the photo below since it was missing the insert on the top. If you ever see these inserts for sale, buy them.

Notice that prices have held their own except for the omnipresent stemware. Some people mistake the 11" salad bowl shown at the bottom of page 208 for a punch bowl; it would not hold much punch, but enough salad for a small dinner party.

		Crystal
	Ashtray, indiv.	25.00
19	Bottle, oil, 3 oz., w or w/o rd. knob	325.00
	Bowl, 6", mint, 2 hdld., w or w/o rd. knobs	35.00
	Bowl, 6", mint, 2 pt., 2 hdld., w or w/o rd. knobs	35.00
2	Bowl, 11", salad	90.00
15	Bowl, 11", floral, 2 hdld.	75.00
	Bowl, finger, #4080 (blown, plain)	10.00
	Bowl, floral, 11", 2 hdld., w or w/o "T" knobs	80.00
1	Candelabra, 2-lite, w bobeche & prisms	225.00
12	Candy box & lid, rnd., w or w/o rd. knob	180.00
	Cigarette box & lid, w or w/o rd. knob	95.00
13	Creamer, 2 hdld., w or w/o rd. knobs	45.00
6	Cup, w or w/o rd. knob.	25.00
17	Ice tub, 2 hdld., w or w/o "T" knobs	70.00
	Jelly, 6", 1 hdld., w or w/o rd. knobs	30.00
7	Jelly, 6", 3 pt., 1 hdld., w or w/o rd. knobs	30.00
20	Mayonnaise, 2 hdld.	35.00
	Nappy, 4½", 1 hdld., w or w/o rd. knob	30.00
	Nut, indiv., 1 hdld., w or w/o rd. knob	40.00
11	Plate, 7"	25.00

		Crystal
16	Plate, 12", torte, 2 hdld., w or w/o "T" knobs	45.00
3	Plate, 15", torte, rnd. or salad liner	65.00
21	Relish, 11", triplex buffet, 2 hdld., w or w/o "T" knobs	45.00
	Relish, 12", 4 pt., 2 hdld., w or w/o "T" knobs	55.00
	Relish, 12", 5 pt., 2 hdld., w or w/o "T" knobs	55.00
	Salt & pepper, #60 top	125.00
6	Saucer	10.00
	Stem, 1 oz., cordial, #4083 (blown)	70.00
	Stem, 2½ oz., pressed wine	35.00
9	Stem, 2½ oz., wine, #4083	25.00
10	Stem, 3½ oz., cocktail, #4083	20.00
	Stem, 3½ oz., pressed cocktail	25.00
	Stem, 4 oz., claret, #4083	25.00
	Stem, 4 oz., oyster cocktail, #4083	10.00
	Stem, 5½ oz., pressed saucer champagne	20.00
	Stem, 5½ oz., saucer champagne, #4083	15.00
	Stem, 9 oz., pressed goblet	45.00
5	Stem, 10 oz., goblet, #4083	22.50*
	Stem, 12 oz., pressed soda	45.00
14	Sugar, 2 hdld., w or w/o rd. knobs	45.00
	Tray, 12" celery, 2 hdld., w or w/o "T" knobs	55.00
8	Tumbler, 5 oz., soda, #4083	20.00
	Tumbler, 8 oz., soda, #4083	22.50
18	Tumbler, 12 oz., soda, #4083	25.00**
	Vase, 7", ball	100.00
4	Vase, 9", 2 hdld., w or w/o "T" knobs	85.00

*Limelight – $125.00

**Limelight – $95.00

Color: crystal

This early Heisey pattern was produced in crystal only. Sunburst items may have a variant in the pattern consisting of punties (thumbprints) around the item just above the sunburst. This is not considered a separate pattern.

	Bottle, molasses, 13 oz.	175.00
	Bottle, oil, 2 oz.	85.00
	Bottle, oil, 4 oz.	85.00
	Bottle, oil, 6 oz.	85.00
2	Bottle, water	90.00
	Bridge Set: Approx. 5" each.	
	Club	65.00
	Diamond	75.00
	Heart	75.00
	Spade	65.00
	Bowl, 4", round, scalloped top	22.00
18	Bowl, 4½", round, scalloped top	22.00
6	Bowl, 5", round, scalloped top, flared	25.00
15	Bowl, 5", finger	25.00
	Bowl, 5", hdld.	25.00
	Bowl, 5", three corner, hdld.	30.00
	Bowl, 6", round	30.00
	Bowl, 7", round	35.00

9	Bowl, 7", oblong	35.00
	Bowl, 8", round	40.00
	Bowl, 8", round, ftd.	40.00
	Bowl, 9", round	40.00
	Bowl, 9", round, ftd.	65.00
	Bowl, 9", oblong	45.00
	Bowl, 10", round	50.00
	Bowl, 10", round, ftd.	85.00
	Bowl, 10", oblong	45.00
13	Bowl, 10", round punch, pegged bottom & stand	350.00
	Bowl, 12", round, punch & stand	225.00
	Bowl, 12", oblong	55.00
	Bowl, 14", round, punch & stand	250.00
	Bowl, 15", round, punch & stand	275.00
8	Butter and domed cover	125.00
	Cake plate 9", ftd.	165.00
	Cake plate, 10, ftd.	165.00

	Celery tray, 12"	65.00
	Comport, 5", ftd.	45.00
1	Comport, 6", ftd.	45.00
	Creamer, lg.	45.00
	Creamer, hotel	40.00
	Creamer, individual	45.00
14	Cup, punch, two styles	15.00
11	Egg cup, ftd.	65.00
4	Goblet, water	150.00
	Mayonnaise and underplate	55.00
16	Pickle jar and stopper	145.00
	Pickle tray, 6"	35.00
	Pitcher, 1 qt., upright	145.00
	Pitcher, 1 qt., bulbous	145.00
	Pitcher, 3 pt., upright	150.00
	Pitcher, 3 pt., bulbous	150.00

	Pitcher, ½ gal., upright	175.00
	Pitcher, ½ gal., straight sided	175.00
12	Pitcher, ½ gal., bulbous	185.00
	Pitcher, 3 qt. upright	225.00
	Plate, torte, 13"	35.00
	Pitcher, 3 qt., bulbous	235.00
10	Plate, 9", oval-underliner	30.00
3	Rose bowl, 3", footed	195.00
	Salt & pepper, 3 styles	125.00
	Spooner	90.00
	Sugar, lg.	45.00
	Sugar, hotel	40.00
	Sugar, individual	45.00
7	Toothpick holder	135.00
17	Tumbler, 2 styles	40.00
5	Vase, orchid, 6"	125.00

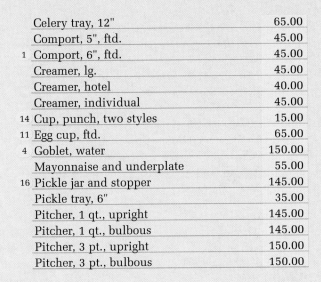

Colors: crystal, red, blue, green, yellow

New listings of Fostoria's Sunray are included after several collectors have been kind enough to supply them. Pricing is still tricky due to the disparity of prices I am finding. Be sure to see Glacier (page 110) which is Sunray with frosted panels added by Fostoria. Some Sunray enthusiasts are willing to mix the two, but most gather one or the other. Both patterns sell in the same price range, although Glacier is more limited in supply.

We price only crystal; but be aware of pieces that are found in red, blue, green, and yellow. I rarely see colored Sunray; so I doubt that you could assemble a set in color. A few colored pieces placed among your crystal would most likely add to its appeal.

The cream soup is tab handled, but by placing a lid on the cream soup, it becomes an onion soup according to Fostoria's catalogs. The condiment tray with cruets and mustards is fashioned like a cloverleaf similar to the one in Fostoria's American. It is obviously scarcer than the American one, but not as many collectors are in quest of it.

If you are a beginner, you might know that Duncan & Miller made a similar pattern, and if you see a punch set that you think is Sunray, as I once did when I first started buying this pattern, it is not. The item pictured as #23 is also a Duncan piece, and often confused with Sunray.

#	Item	Crystal
24	Almond, ftd., ind.	12.00
	Ashtray, ind., 2510½	8.00
	Ashtray, sq.	12.00
	Bonbon, 6½", hdld.	16.00
	Bonbon, 7", 3 toed	17.50
	Bowl, 5", fruit	10.00
	Bowl, 9½", flared	30.00
	Bowl, 12", salad	35.00
	Bowl, 13", rolled edge	40.00
	Bowl, custard, 2¼", high	10.00
12	Bowl, 10", hdld.	35.00
	Butter, w/lid, ¼ lb.	35.00
	Candelabra, 2-lite, bobeche & prisms	85.00
	Candlestick, 3"	20.00
4	Candlestick, 5½"	27.50
8	Candlestick, duo	40.00
16	Candy jar, w/cover	55.00
	Celery, hdld.	25.00
15	Cigarette and cover	20.00
	Cigarette box, oblong	25.00
	Coaster, 4"	8.00
9	Comport	22.00
	Cream soup	27.50
	Cream soup liner	6.00
	Cream, ftd.	10.00
	Cream, individual	10.00
14	Cup	12.00
	Decanter, w/stopper, 18 oz.	70.00
	Decanter, w/stopper, oblong, 26 oz.	85.00
	Ice bucket, no handle	55.00
3	Ice bucket, w/handle	65.00
	Jelly	16.00
7	Jelly, w/cover	45.00
11	Mayonnaise, w/liner, ladle	35.00
19	Mustard, w/cover, spoon	45.00
	Nappy, hdld., flared	13.00
	Nappy, hdld., reg.	12.00
	Nappy, hdld., sq.	14.00
	Nappy, hdld., tri-corner	15.00
10	Oil bottle, w/stopper, 3 oz.	35.00
21	Onion soup, w/cover	45.00
	Pickle, hdld.	20.00
	Pitcher, 16 oz., cereal	50.00
	Pitcher, 64 oz.	80.00

#	Item	Crystal
5	Pitcher, 64 oz., ice lip	105.00
	Plate, 6"	6.00
6	Plate, 7½"	8.00
17	Plate, 8½"	12.00
	Plate, 9½"	25.00
	Plate, 11", torte	30.00
	Plate, 12", sandwich	32.00
	Plate, 15", torte	50.00
	Plate, 16"	60.00
13	Relish, 6½", 3 part	22.00
	Relish, 8", 4 part	24.00
	Relish, 10", 2 part	18.00
	Salt dip	12.50
14	Saucer	3.00
22	Shaker, 4", pr.	45.00
	Shaker, individual, 2¼", #2510½, pr.	40.00
	Stem, 3½", 5½ oz., sherbet, low	10.00
	Stem, 3¼", 3½ oz., fruit cocktail	10.00
	Stem, 3", 4 oz., cocktail, ftd.	10.00
	Stem, 4⅞", 4½ oz., claret	22.00
1	Stem, 5¾", 9 oz., goblet	17.50
	Sugar, ftd.	10.00
	Sugar, individual	10.00
	Sweetmeat, hdld., divided, 6"	25.00
	Tray, 6½", ind. sugar/cream	10.00
	Tray, 10½", oblong	38.00
	Tray, 10", sq.	40.00
18	Tray, condiment, 8½", cloverleaf	45.00
	Tray, oval hdld.	25.00
	Tumbler, 2¼", 2 oz., whiskey, #2510½	10.00
	Tumbler, 3½", 5 oz., juice, #2510½	10.00
20	Tumbler, 3½", 6 oz., old fashion, #2510½	12.00
	Tumbler, 4⅛", 9 oz., table, #2510½	12.00
2	Tumbler, 4¾", 9 oz., ftd., table	12.00
	Tumbler, 4⅝", 5 oz., ftd., juice	13.00
	Tumbler, 5¼", 13 oz., ftd., tea	16.00
	Tumbler, 5⅛", 13 oz., tea, #2510½	18.00
	Vase, 3½", rose bowl	25.00
	Vase, 5", rose bowl	32.50
	Vase, 6", crimped	40.00
	Vase, 7"	50.00
	Vase, 9", sq. ftd.	60.00
	Vase, sweet pea	75.00

Works, late 1920s – early 1930s

Colors: pink, green, blue, crystal

Collectors traditionally had identified Sunrise Medallion (Morgantown's etching #758) as "Dancing Girl." Recent collectors are more willing to use the accurate Sunrise Medallion name.

Catalog measurements were steadfastly written in ounces, not heights. Measurements for height in this book came from measuring the items.

Those twisted stem wares (#7642½) are slightly taller than their plain stem counterparts (#7630, called "lady leg" stems). Measurements listed here are mainly from the #7630 line that I acquire more often than twisted one. Twisted blue and crystal champagnes, sherbets, and waters are the only #7642½ stems I have owned. If you have others, I would appreciate having measurements (height and capacity to top rim).

Blue is the preferred color of collectors, something true in almost all patterns. Pink and crystal turn up infrequently and are not as highly priced. Green appears to be rare with only a few pieces emerging. I have only owned a green sugar and 10" vase, but I have seen a picture of a creamer. It was not for sale. Speaking of creamers and sugars, they are the most difficult to find pieces. I had the blue creamer and sugar for over 15 years until a collector in California convinced me he wanted to own them more than I did. For such a highly priced pitcher, the blue one turns up repeatedly in the Northwest. There are two different styled oyster cocktails, which look something like a bar tumbler to me. I had six and their capacities varied from a little over to a little under four ounces.

The cordials are found in crystal, but only a few blue ones have appeared. I have never found a twisted stem cordial in any color.

	Crystal	Blue	Pink Green
10 Bowl, finger, ftd.		85.00	
12 Creamer		325.00	295.00
Cup	40.00	100.00	80.00
Parfait, 5 oz.	55.00	135.00	100.00
Pitcher		625.00	
11 Plate, 5⅞", sherbet	6.00	15.00	10.00
6 Plate, 7½", salad	15.00	25.00	25.00
4 Plate, 8⅜"	12.50	25.00	22.50
Saucer	15.00	22.50	17.50
Sherbet, cone	20.00		
3 Stem, 1½ oz., cordial	110.00	375.00	225.00
Stem, 2½ oz., wine	35.00	85.00	55.00
1 Stem, 6 oz., low sherbet	24.00	40.00	35.00
Stem, 6¼", 7 oz., champagne	25.00	50.00	40.00
2 Stem, 6¾", 7 oz., champagne, twist stem	25.00	50.00	40.00
9 Stem, 6⅛", cocktail	30.00	55.00	40.00
8 Stem, 7¾", 9 oz., water	35.00	75.00	55.00
17 Stem, 8¼", 9 oz., water, twist stem	35.00	75.00	55.00
13 Sugar		325.00	275.00
Tumbler, 2½", 4 oz., ftd.	25.00	150.00	
Tumbler, 3½", 4 oz., ftd.			35.00
14 Tumbler, 4¼", 5 oz., ftd.	45.00	65.00	50.00
Tumbler, 4¼", flat	20.00		
7 Tumbler, 4¾", 9 oz., ftd.	20.00	55.00	45.00
Tumbler, 5½", 11 oz., ftd.	35.00	80.00	65.00
5 Tumbler, 5½", flat	25.00		75.00
15 Vase, 6" tall, 5" wide			395.00
16 Vase, 10", slender, bud	65.00	450.00	375.00
Vase, 10", bulbous bottom			400.00

Colors: amber, Carmen, crystal, Forest Green, Royal Blue

Tally Ho is a massive Cambridge pattern in both production and the size of many of its pieces. It has been previously represented in this book in various patterns from Elaine to Valencia. For purposes of identification, the heavy pressed one-color stems are listed as goblets in the listing below and the blown, thin, tall crystal stems with colored bowls are listed as stems. We have tried to show you as many of these as we could find.

Ice buckets seem to be plentiful in all colors and etched crystal ones are a prize catch. Crystal punch bowl sets can be found with cups and ladles with colored handles as well as all crystal. The ones with colored handles are preferred.

	Amber Crystal	Carmen Royal	Forest Green		Amber Crystal	Carmen Royal	Forest Green
Ashtray, 4"	12.50	22.50	18.00	Bowl, 10", pan	30.00	60.00	45.00
Ashtray, 4" w/ctr. hdld.	17.50	27.50	25.00	Bowl, 10½", belled	35.00	65.00	50.00
Ash well, 2 pc., ctr. hdld.	20.00	35.00	30.00	Bowl, 10½", 2 comp. salad	30.00	65.00	45.00
Bowl, 4½", ftd., fruit/sherbet	12.50	22.50	20.00	Bowl, 10½", 2 hdld.	40.00	55.00	45.00
Bowl, 5", frappe cocktail, 10 side rim	17.50	27.50	25.00	Bowl, 10½", 3 comp.	40.00	85.00	65.00
Bowl, 6", iced fruit, 10 side rim	25.00	40.00	35.00	Bowl, 10½", low ft.	40.00	90.00	65.00
Bowl, 6", 2 hdld.	17.50	27.50	25.00	Bowl, 11", flat, flared	35.00	75.00	50.00
Bowl, 6", 2 hdld. nappy	17.50	27.50	25.00	Bowl, 12", oval celery	25.00	40.00	35.00
Bowl, 6½", grapefruit, flat rim	20.00	35.00	30.00	Bowl, 12", pan	35.00	80.00	65.00
Bowl, 6½", 2 hdld.	20.00	35.00	30.00	Bowl, 12½", flat rim	35.00	90.00	60.00
Bowl, 7", fruit, 10 side rim	20.00	35.00	30.00	Bowl, 12½", belled	35.00	85.00	60.00
Bowl, 8"	25.00	40.00	35.00	Bowl, 13", ftd., punch	195.00	350.00	250.00
Bowl, 8½", 3 comp.	45.00	75.00	65.00	Bowl, 13½", salad, flared	30.00	85.00	70.00
Bowl, 9"	30.00	60.00	40.00	Bowl, 17", pan	35.00	95.00	75.00
Bowl, 9", pan	30.00	60.00	40.00	Bowl, 2 comp., 2 ladle, salad dressing, flared	30.00	75.00	65.00

17 Bowl, 13", ftd., punch

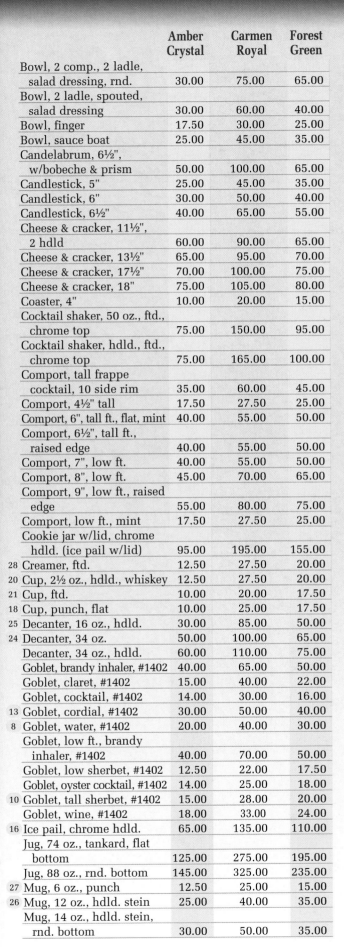

Item	Amber Crystal	Carmen Royal	Forest Green
Bowl, 2 comp., 2 ladle, salad dressing, rnd.	30.00	75.00	65.00
Bowl, 2 ladle, spouted, salad dressing	30.00	60.00	40.00
Bowl, finger	17.50	30.00	25.00
Bowl, sauce boat	25.00	45.00	35.00
Candelabrum, 6½", w/bobeche & prism	50.00	100.00	65.00
Candlestick, 5"	25.00	45.00	35.00
Candlestick, 6"	30.00	50.00	40.00
Candlestick, 6½"	40.00	65.00	55.00
Cheese & cracker, 11½", 2 hdld	60.00	90.00	65.00
Cheese & cracker, 13½"	65.00	95.00	70.00
Cheese & cracker, 17½"	70.00	100.00	75.00
Cheese & cracker, 18"	75.00	105.00	80.00
Coaster, 4"	10.00	20.00	15.00
Cocktail shaker, 50 oz., ftd., chrome top	75.00	150.00	95.00
Cocktail shaker, hdld., ftd., chrome top	75.00	165.00	100.00
Comport, tall frappe cocktail, 10 side rim	35.00	60.00	45.00
Comport, 4½" tall	17.50	27.50	25.00
Comport, 6", tall ft., flat, mint	40.00	55.00	50.00
Comport, 6½", tall ft., raised edge	40.00	55.00	50.00
Comport, 7", low ft.	40.00	55.00	50.00
Comport, 8", low ft.	45.00	70.00	65.00
Comport, 9", low ft., raised edge	55.00	80.00	75.00
Comport, low ft., mint	17.50	27.50	25.00
Cookie jar w/lid, chrome hdld. (ice pail w/lid)	95.00	195.00	155.00
28 Creamer, ftd.	12.50	27.50	20.00
20 Cup, 2½ oz., hdld., whiskey	12.50	27.50	20.00
21 Cup, ftd.	10.00	20.00	17.50
18 Cup, punch, flat	10.00	25.00	17.50
25 Decanter, 16 oz., hdld.	30.00	85.00	50.00
24 Decanter, 34 oz.	50.00	100.00	65.00
Decanter, 34 oz., hdld.	60.00	110.00	75.00
Goblet, brandy inhaler, #1402	40.00	65.00	50.00
Goblet, claret, #1402	15.00	40.00	22.00
Goblet, cocktail, #1402	14.00	30.00	16.00
13 Goblet, cordial, #1402	30.00	50.00	40.00
8 Goblet, water, #1402	20.00	40.00	30.00
Goblet, low ft., brandy inhaler, #1402	40.00	70.00	50.00
Goblet, low sherbet, #1402	12.50	22.00	17.50
Goblet, oyster cocktail, #1402	14.00	25.00	18.00
10 Goblet, tall sherbet, #1402	15.00	28.00	20.00
Goblet, wine, #1402	18.00	33.00	24.00
16 Ice pail, chrome hdld.	65.00	135.00	110.00
Jug, 74 oz., tankard, flat bottom	125.00	275.00	195.00
Jug, 88 oz., rnd. bottom	145.00	325.00	235.00
27 Mug, 6 oz., punch	12.50	25.00	15.00
26 Mug, 12 oz., hdld. stein	25.00	40.00	35.00
Mug, 14 oz., hdld. stein, rnd. bottom	30.00	50.00	35.00
Plate, 6", bread & butter	10.00	15.00	12.50
Plate, 7", 2 hdld.	20.00	30.00	25.00
Plate, 7½", salad	12.50	20.00	17.50
Plate, 8", salad	15.00	20.00	18.00
Plate, 9½", lunch	35.00	55.00	40.00
Plate, 10½", dinner	45.00	125.00	
Plate, 11½", 2 hdld., sandwich	35.00	60.00	50.00
Plate, 13½", raised edge	35.00	70.00	50.00
Plate, 14", chop	35.00	75.00	50.00
Plate, 14", w/4" seat in center	40.00	75.00	55.00
Plate, 17½", Sunday night supper	40.00	95.00	60.00
Plate, 17½"	40.00	95.00	60.00
Plate, 18", w/4" seat in center	45.00	95.00	65.00
Plate, 18", buffet lunch	45.00	95.00	65.00
Plate, 18", ftd., weekend supper	50.00	95.00	70.00
Plate, finger bowl	10.00	15.00	12.50
Plate, salad dressing liner	12.50	20.00	17.50
Plate, sauce boat liner	12.50	20.00	17.50
Relish, 6", 2 comp., 2 hdld.	20.00	30.00	25.00
Relish, 8", 2 hdld., 3 comp.	25.00	35.00	30.00
Relish, 10", 4 comp.	25.00	40.00	30.00
21 Saucer	3.00	5.00	4.00
23 Shaker, w/glass top	25.00	50.00	35.00
12 Stem, 1 oz., cordial	32.00	75.00	55.00
4 Stem, 2½ oz., high stem wine	20.00	45.00	30.00
Stem, 3 oz., ftd., tumbler	15.00	35.00	25.00
5 Stem, 3 oz., high stem cocktail	15.00	35.00	25.00
Stem, 4 oz., low stem cocktail	15.00	35.00	25.00
Stem, 4½ oz., low sherbet	12.50	20.00	17.50
3 Stem, 4½ oz., high stem claret	20.00	40.00	25.00
Stem, 5 oz., ftd., tumbler	12.50	25.00	17.50
7 Stem, 5 oz., low stem juice	12.50	25.00	18.00
Stem, 6 oz., high stem juice	15.00	25.00	20.00
6 Stem, 6½ oz., low stem sherbet	15.00	25.00	20.00
2 Stem, 7½ oz., high sherb.	18.00	30.00	25.00
1 Stem, 10 oz., high stem	20.00	38.00	25.00
14 Stem, 10 oz., low stem lunch	22.00	38.00	28.00
15 Stem, 12 oz., ftd. tumbler	20.00	38.00	28.00
Stem, 14 oz., high stem	20.00	45.00	30.00
Stem, 16 oz., ftd., tumbler	20.00	45.00	30.00
Stem, 18 oz., tall stem	25.00	60.00	35.00
22 Sugar, ftd.	12.50	27.50	20.00
19 Top hat, 10", vase	125.00	295.00	195.00
11 Tumbler, 2½ oz.	30.00	50.00	40.00
9 Tumbler, 5 oz.	25.00	40.00	35.00
Tumbler, 7 oz., old fashion	25.00	40.00	35.00
Tumbler, 10 oz., short	25.00	42.00	35.00
Tumbler, 10 oz., tall	25.00	45.00	35.00
Tumbler, 14 oz., rnd. bottom	17.50	35.00	27.50
Tumbler, 15 oz.	20.00	40.00	30.00
Vase, 12", ftd.	95.00	225.00	175.00

Colors: crystal, some yellow and cobalt blue

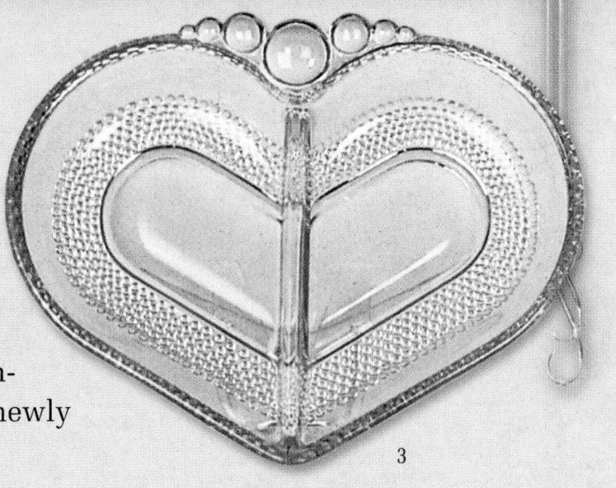

As with Duncan's Sandwich, Tear Drop stemware can be found priced inexpensively enough that you could use it today cheaper than you could buy some current newly made stems. Owners of Tear Drop used it; so, mint condition dinner plates and supplementary serving pieces are not easily located. This is an excellent starting point for those looking for an easily found and reasonably priced crystal Elegant pattern.

Colored pieces discovered may have been produced at Tiffin from Duncan moulds. Reprints of original Duncan catalogs showing Tear Drop stemware and tumblers can be found in previous editions of this book. In order to have room for the newly listed patterns, I had to retire some catalog pages that we used earlier.

	Crystal		Crystal
Ashtray, 3", indiv.	7.00	Coaster/ashtray, 3", rolled edge	7.00
Ashtray, 5"	8.00	Comport, 4¾", ftd.	12.00
Bonbon, 6", 4 hdld.	12.00	Comport, 6", low foot., hdld.	15.00
Bottle, w/stopper, 12", bar	165.00	Condiment set, 5 pc. (salt/pepper, 2	
Bowl, 4¼", finger	7.00	3 oz. cruets, 9", 2 hdld. tray)	125.00
Bowl, 5", fruit nappy	8.00	Creamer, 3 oz.	8.00
Bowl, 5", 2 hdld., nappy	10.00	Creamer, 6 oz.	6.00
Bowl, 6", dessert, nappy	8.00	Creamer, 8 oz.	8.00
Bowl, 6", fruit, nappy	8.00	Cup, 2½ oz., demi	12.00
Bowl, 7", fruit, nappy	9.00	Cup, 6 oz., tea	6.00
Bowl, 7", 2 hdld., nappy	10.00	Flower basket, 12", loop hdl.	110.00
Bowl, 8" x 12", oval, flower	55.00	Ice bucket, 5½"	85.00
Bowl, 9", salad	30.00	Marmalade, w/cover, 4"	40.00
Bowl, 9", 2 hdld., nappy	25.00	Mayonnaise, 4½" (2 hdld. bowl, ladle,	
Bowl, 10", crimped console, 2 hdld.	32.50	6" plate)	40.00
Bowl, 10", flared, fruit	30.00	Mayonnaise set, 3 pc. (4½" bowl, ladle,	
Bowl, 11½", crimped, flower	35.00	8" hdld. plate)	40.00
Bowl, 11½", flared, flower	32.50	Mustard jar, w/cover, 4¼"	40.00
Bowl, 12", salad	40.00	Nut dish, 6", 2 pt.	11.00
Bowl, 12", crimped, low foot	40.00	Oil bottle, 3 oz.	20.00
Bowl, 12", ftd., flower	50.00	Olive dish, 4¼", 2 hdld., oval	15.00
Bowl, 12", sq., 4 hdld.	45.00	Olive dish, 6", 2 pt.	15.00
Bowl, 13", gardenia	35.00	Pickle dish, 6"	15.00
Bowl, 15½", 2½ gal., punch	110.00	Pitcher, 5", 16 oz., milk	55.00
Butter, w/cover, ¼ lb., 2 hdld.	28.00	Pitcher, 8½", 64 oz., w/ice lip	120.00
Cake salver, 13", ftd.	55.00	Plate, 6", bread/butter	4.00
Canape set (6" plate w/ring, 4 oz., ftd.,		Plate, 6", canape	10.00
cocktail)	30.00	Plate, 7", 2 hdld., lemon	12.50
Candlestick, 4"	12.50	Plate, 7½", salad	5.00
Candlestick, 7", 2-lite, ball loop ctr.	30.00	Plate, 8½", luncheon	7.00
Candlestick, 7", lg. ball ctr. w/bobeches,		Plate, 10½", dinner	40.00
prisms	90.00	Plate, 11", 2 hdld.	27.50
Candy basket, 5½" x 7½", 2 hdld., oval	85.00	Plate, 13", 4 hdld.	35.00
Candy box, w/cover, 7", 2 pt., 2 hdld.	65.00	Plate, 13", salad liner, rolled edge	35.00
Candy box, w/cover, 8", 3 pt., 3 hdld.	70.00	Plate, 13", torte, rolled edge	35.00
Candy dish, 7½", heart shape	22.50	Plate, 14", torte	38.00
Celery, 11", 2 hdld.	20.00	Plate, 14", torte, rolled edge	38.00
Celery, 11", 2 pt., 2 hdld.	22.50	Plate, 16", torte, rolled edge	40.00
Celery, 12", 3 pt.	25.00	Plate, 18", lazy susan	65.00
Cheese & cracker (3½" comport, 11"		Plate, 18", punch liner, rolled edge	60.00
2 hdld. plate)	45.00		

TEAR DROP

		Crystal
2	Relish, 7", 2 pt., 2 hdld.	17.50
3	Relish, 7½", 2 pt., heart shape	22.50
	Relish, 9", 3 pt., 3 hdld.	30.00
	Relish, 11", 3 pt., 2 hdld.	32.50
	Relish, 12", 3 pt.	35.00
	Relish, 12", 5 pt., rnd.	38.00
	Relish, 12", 6 pt., rnd.	42.00
	Relish, 12", sq., 4 pt., 4 hdld.	42.00
	Salad set, 6" (compote, 11", hdld. plate)	37.50
	Salad set, 9" (2 pt. bowl, 13" rolled edge plate)	75.00
	Salt & pepper, 5"	25.00
	Saucer, 4½", demi	3.00
	Saucer, 6"	1.50
	Stem, 2½", 5 oz., ftd., sherbet	5.00
	Stem, 2¾", 3½ oz., ftd., oyster cocktail	7.50
	Stem, 3½", 5 oz., sherbet	6.00
	Stem, 4", 1 oz., cordial	30.00
	Stem, 4½", 1¾ oz., sherry	25.00
	Stem, 4½", 3½ oz., cocktail	12.50
	Stem, 4¾", 3 oz., wine	17.50
	Stem, 5", 5 oz., champagne	10.00
	Stem, 5½", 4 oz., claret	20.00
	Stem, 5¾", 9 oz.	12.00
	Stem, 6¼", 8 oz., ale	16.00
	Stem, 7", 9 oz.	16.00
	Sugar, 3 oz.	8.00
	Sugar, 6 oz.	6.00

		Crystal
	Sugar, 8 oz.	8.00
	Sweetmeat, 5½", star shape, 2 hdld.	35.00
	Sweetmeat, 6½", ctr. hdld.	30.00
	Sweetmeat, 7", star shape, 2 hdld.	40.00
	Tray, 5½", ctr. hdld. (for mustard jar)	12.00
	Tray, 6", 2 hdld. (for salt/pepper)	12.00
	Tray, 7¾", ctr. hdld. (for cruets)	12.50
	Tray, 8", 2 hdld. (for oil/vinegar)	12.50
	Tray, 8", 2 hdld. (for sugar/creamer)	12.00
	Tray, 10", 2 hdld (for sugar/creamer)	12.00
	Tumbler, 2¼", 2 oz., flat, whiskey	18.00
	Tumbler, 2¼", 2 oz., ftd., whiskey	14.00
	Tumbler, 3", 3 oz., ftd., whiskey	14.00
	Tumbler, 3¼", 3½ oz., flat, juice	7.00
1	Tumbler, 3¼", 7 oz., flat, old-fashioned	12.00
	Tumbler, 3½", 5 oz., flat, juice	8.00
	Tumbler, 4", 4½ oz., ftd., juice	9.00
	Tumbler, 4¼", 9 oz., flat	10.00
	Tumbler, 4½", 8 oz., flat, split	10.00
	Tumbler, 4½", 9 oz., ftd.	10.00
	Tumbler, 4¾", 10 oz., flat, hi-ball	11.00
	Tumbler, 5", 8 oz., ftd., party	10.00
	Tumbler, 5¼", 12 oz., flat, iced tea	15.00
	Tumbler, 5¾", 14 oz., flat, hi-ball	17.50
	Tumbler, 6", 14 oz., iced tea	17.50
	Urn, w/cover, 9", ftd.	135.00
	Vase, 9", ftd., fan	33.00
	Vase, 9", ftd., round	42.00

1

Colors: crystal, amber, cobalt, red

Terrace is another Duncan pattern that had been pretty much ignored over the years by collectors outside the Pittsburgh area due to limited distribution and lack of information. With the advent of Internet auctions that is no longer as true as it once was. After photographing the red and cobalt shown here, I ran many of the rarer pieces on an Internet auction. I did learn that there are buyers for it. Sugar lids are rarer than anyone thought.

Little amber is available and most of that found has a gold decoration on it. Those yearning for crystal usually look for First Love or some other etching rather than Terrace itself.

Note the crystal bowls and plates with cobalt bases. They also are found with red bases. Learn to identify that base pattern so you do not pass one of these.

		Crystal Amber	Cobalt Red
10	Ashtray, 3½", sq.	17.50	25.00
	Ashtray, 4¾", sq.	20.00	75.00
23	Bowl, 4", crystal top	30.00	
	Bowl, 4¼", finger, #5111½	30.00	75.00
22	Bowl, 4¾", turned up edge	10.00	25.00
26	Bowl, 6", crystal top	25.00	
	Bowl, 6¾" x 4¼", ftd., flared rim	30.00	
	Bowl, 8" sq. x 2½", hdld.	55.00	
	Bowl, 9" x 4½", ftd.	42.00	
	Bowl, 9½" x 2½", hdld.	42.00	
	Bowl, 10" x 3¾", ftd., flared rim	55.00	
	*Bowl, 10¼" x 4¾", ftd.	75.00	145.00
	Bowl, 11" x 3¼", flared rim	32.50	
	Butter or cheese, 7" sq. x 1¼"	120.00	
	Candle, 3", 1-lite	25.00	95.00
	Candle, 4", low	25.00	
14	Candlestick, 1-lite, bobeche & prisms	75.00	
	Candlestick 2-lite, 7" x 9¼", bobeche & prisms	100.00	
7	Candy dish, hdld.	35.00	135.00
	Candy urn, w/lid	135.00	425.00
	Cheese stand, 3" x 5¼"	25.00	40.00
	Cocktail shaker, metal lid	85.00	225.00
	Comport, w/lid, 8¾" x 5½"	150.00	425.00
1	Comport, 3½" x 4¾" w	30.00	80.00
2	Creamer, 3", 10 oz.	18.00	38.00
18	Cup	15.00	40.00
12	Cup, demi	20.00	
3	Ice bucket	65.00	
	Mayonnaise, 5½" x 2½", ftd., hdld., #111	35.00	
	Mayonnaise, 5½" x 3½", crimped,	32.00	
	Mayonnaise, 5¾" x 3", w/dish hdld. tray	35.00	75.00
	Mayonnaise, w/7" tray, hdld	35.00	
	Nappy, 5½" x 2", div., hdld.	18.00	
21	Nappy, 6" x 1¾", hdld.	22.00	35.00
	Pitcher	325.00	995.00
	Plate, 6"	12.00	22.00
25	Plate, 6", hdld., lemon	14.00	30.00
13	Plate, 6", sq.	14.00	30.00
	Plate, 7"	17.50	35.00
	Plate, 7½"	18.00	35.00
16	Plate, 7½", sq.	19.00	38.00
	Plate, 8½"	20.00	25.00

		Crystal Amber	Cobalt Red
15	Plate, 9", sq.	25.00	110.00
6	Plate, 11", sq.	30.00	125.00
	Plate, 11", hdld.	30.00	
	Plate, 11", hdld., cracker w/ring	30.00	110.00
	Plate, 11", hdld., sandwich	30.00	
	Plate, 12", torte, rolled edge	32.50	
24	*Plate, 13", cake, ftd., crystal top		210.00
	Plate, 13", torte, flat edge	35.00	
	Plate, 13", torte, rolled edge	37.50	
	Plate, 13¼", torte	35.00	195.00
11	Relish, 6" x 1¾", hdld., 2 pt.	20.00	50.00
	Relish, 9", 4 pt.	35.00	100.00
	Relish, 10½" x 1½", hdld., 5 pt.	65.00	
20	Relish, 12", 4 pt., hdld.	40.00	100.00
	Relish, 12", 5 pt., hdld.	40.00	
5	Relish, 12", 5 pt., w/lid	100.00	295.00
19	Salad dressing bowl, 2 pt., 5½" x 4¼"	45.00	95.00
18	Saucer, sq.	6.00	12.00
12	Saucer, demi	5.00	
	Stem, 3¾", 1 oz., cordial, #5111½	42.50	
	Stem, 3¾", 4½ oz., oyster cocktail, #5111½	20.00	
	Stem, 4", 5 oz., ice cream, #5111½	14.00	
	Stem, 4½", 3½ oz., cocktail, #5111½	22.50	
9	Stem, 5", 5 oz., saucer champagne, #5111½	15.00	50.00
	Stem, 5¼", 3 oz., wine, #5111½	32.50	
	Stem, 5¼", 5 oz., ftd. juice, #5111½	20.00	
	Stem, 5¾", 10 oz., low luncheon goblet, #5111½	22.00	
	Stem, 6", 4½ oz., claret, #5111½	45.00	
	Stem, 6½", 12 oz., ftd. ice tea, #5111½	32.50	
8	Stem, 6¾", 10 oz., tall water goblet, #5111½	25.00	
	Stem, 6¾", 14 oz., ftd. ice tea, #5111½	32.50	
4	Sugar, 3", 10 oz.	15.00	35.00
4	Sugar lid	12.50	90.00
17	Tumbler, 2 oz., shot	15.00	40.00
27	Tumbler, 4", 9 oz., water	17.50	65.00
	Tray, 8" x 2", hdld., celery	17.50	
	Urn, 4½" x 4½"	27.50	
	Urn, 10½" x 4½"	135.00	425.00
	Vase, 10, ftd.	115.00	

*Colored foot

Color: crystal

Both Tiffin and Central made this particular Thistle etching. The designs are exactly alike so you only have the mould shapes to help you decide which company made a specific piece. The good news is that there should be more of this pattern available with two different makers distributing Thistle.

6

1	Bowl, 14 oz. finger	12.50
	Bowl, 8½", soup	22.50
	Comport, 5" high	22.00
	Comport, 6" high	25.00
	Comport, low, 4½" diameter	15.00
	Comport, low, 6" diameter	18.00
	Comport, low, 7" diameter	22.00
	Cup, 4½ oz. handled custard	12.00
	Decanter, 32 oz., w/stopper	75.00
	Marmalade, 8 oz. w/lid	35.00
	Marmalade liner/coaster, 4½"	4.00
	Night bottle	75.00
	Night set tumbler	12.50
5	Pitcher w/cover. 80 oz.	95.00
6	Plate, 5" sherbet	4.00
	Plate, 6" finger bowl liner	5.00
	Stem, 3 oz. cocktail	12.50
3	Stem, 3 oz. wine	18.00
	Stem, 4 oz. or 5 oz. claret	18.00
	Stem, 4 oz. small sherbet	10.00

	Stem, 6 oz. large sherbet	10.00
	Stem, 6 oz. saucer champagne	12.00
	Stem, 10 oz. water	18.00
	Tea pot with lid	125.00
	Tumbler, 2½ oz., flared shot	10.00
4	Tumbler, 3¼ oz., flared	7.00
	Tumbler, 5 oz., flared	8.00
	Tumbler, 5½ oz., flared	18.00
	Tumbler, 6½ oz. ale (like vase)	25.00
	Tumbler, 7 oz., flared	10.00
	Tumbler, 8 oz., flared	12.00
	Tumbler, 8 oz., narrow, high ball	12.00
2	Tumbler, 9 oz., flared	12.00
	Tumbler, 9 oz., straight	12.00
	Tumbler, 10 oz., flared	12.00
	Tumbler, 11 oz. handled tea	20.00
	Tumbler, 11 oz., flared	14.00
	Tumbler, 12 oz., flared	14.00
	Tumbler, 14 oz., flared	15.00

Colors: blue, green, and pink

Thistle Cut appears on two Fry dinnerware lines, which are both represented in the photo below. Line 3101 is shown by the round pieces; and Line 3104 is the octagon shaped. The stems with the disc connectors (beehive shape) are usually found with the round line. You can find this cutting on pink (Rose), green (Emerald), or blue (Azure). Most collectors have branded the blue "Cornflower" over the years

I bought this set over 25 years ago at Washington Court House, Ohio, because of the blue color, which I found interesting. At that time, no one seemed to know what it was, so it sat in storage anonymously until Cathy was putting together the first *Pattern Identification* book. She rummaged for patterns for the book and uncovered the set and the maker. We took all the extra pieces to a show where a dealer quickly bought it. As with Duncan patterns, I rarely find Fry patterns outside a circle of 100 miles of Pittsburgh.

Over a dozen years ago, I met with the descendants of the Fry factory owners. They have some wonderful Fry glass, including a rare Fry insulator, which I had never seen before. In fact, I didn't even know they made insulators, but it was a beauty and I was told it was extremely rare.

		All colors			All colors
8	Bowl, 9", round, ftd.	65.00		Plate, 10", round, dinner	45.00
4	Candlestick	40.00	6	Saucer	5.00
6	Cup	30.00	1	Stem, high sherbet	22.00
5	Plate, 6", round, bread & butter	10.00		Stem, juice, ftd.	25.00
	Plate, 8", octagonal, luncheon	15.00		Stem, low sherbet	20.00
7	Plate, 8", round, luncheon	15.00	3	Stem, water goblet	33.00
2	Plate, 10½", octagonal, dinner	45.00			

Colors: crystal and crystal w/pale burgundy, champagne (yellow), and green-blue lustre stain; more intense ruby color replaced pale burgundy later; black turtles in 1952

Westmoreland's Thousand Eye is probably that company's most recognized non milk glass pattern and had one of the greatest production runs of any pattern except English Hobnail. It was begun in 1934 and terminated, except for turtles, in 1956. The turtle cigarette box has been copied. Those decorated turtles pictured are an earlier production. Obviously these were one of the favorite advertised pieces as there are so many seen today. Fairy lamps, both footed and flat versions, were produced into the late 1970s.

I continue to run into a 13" bowl on an 18" plate. They are usually crystal, but are seen in other colors as well. They are commonly attributed to Westmoreland's Thousand Eye line, but are actually Canton's Glass Line 100. The colored pieces were evidently Paden City, but Canton did advertise in 1954 that they would make standard colors as well as special colors if the customer so wanted. They used many of Paden City's moulds after that company's demise.

Many Thousand Eye pieces are reminiscent of previous pattern glass items. It seems to be another one of the patterns that collectors really adore or cannot tolerate. Stemware abounds and like some of the Duncan patterns, you can buy these older pieces and use them less expensively than most of today's glassware lines sold in department stores. Thousand Eye is durable, but it was used extensively. You need to check plates and other flat pieces for wear and tear. Mint condition flatware is more challenging to find than any of the stems and tumblers.

		Crystal
11	Ashtray (sm. turtle)	8.00
	Basket, 8", hdld., oval	48.00
8	Bowl, 4½", nappy	8.00
	Bowl, 5½", nappy	12.00
	Bowl, 7½", hdld.	22.50
	Bowl, 10", 2 hdld.	37.50
	Bowl, 11", belled	35.00
	Bowl, 11", crimped, oblong	40.00
	Bowl, 11", triangular	40.00
	Bowl, 11, round	40.00
	Bowl, 12", 2 hdld., flared	45.00
	Candelabra, 2 light	35.00
7	Cigarette box & cover (lg. turtle)	30.00
	Comport, 5", high ft.	22.50
	Creamer, high ft.	12.50
1	Creamer, low rim	10.00
6	Cup, ftd., bead hdld.	6.00
	Fairy lamp, flat.	45.00
	Fairy lamp, ftd.	50.00
	Jug, ½ gal.	95.00
	Mayonnaise, ftd., w/ladle	30.00
	Plate, 6"	5.00
	Plate, 7"	7.50
4	Plate, 8½"	10.00
3	Plate, 10", service	22.00
	Plate, 16"	30.00

		Crystal
	Plate, 18"	45.00
9	Relish, 10", rnd., 6 part	30.00
6	Saucer	2.00
	Shaker, ftd., pr.	30.00
	Stem, 1 oz., cordial	15.00
	Stem, 2 oz., wine	12.00
	Stem, 3 oz., sherry	12.50
	Stem, 3½ oz., cocktail	10.00
	Stem, 5 oz., claret	12.50
	Stem, 8 oz.	12.00
	Stem, high ft., sherbet	8.50
	Stem, low ft., sherbet	7.50
	Stem, parfait, ftd.	12.50
	Sugar, high ft.	12.50
2	Sugar, low rim	10.00
	Tumbler, 1½ oz., whiskey	10.00
	Tumbler, 5 oz., flat ginger ale	8.00
	Tumbler, 5 oz., ftd.	8.00
	Tumbler, 6 oz., old fashion	10.00
10	Tumbler, 7 oz., ftd.	9.00
	Tumbler, 8 oz., flat	9.00
	Tumbler, 9 oz., ftd.	10.00
5	Tumbler, 12 oz., ftd., tea	12.50
	Vase, crimped bowl	30.00
	Vase, flair rim	30.00

Colors: azure, green

Cathy talked me into buying eight water goblets and eight champagnes in the middle 1970s, although we did not have any idea who made them. We called the etch "Tinkerbell," for lack of a better name, and that has stuck all these years. We now know that they are Morgantown's #7631 Jewel stem.

I talked to Jerry Gallagher at the Heisey show about ten years later and told him about "Tinkerbell" etched stems we had found. He said they were indeed Morgantown and "Tinkerbell" was what he was calling them, also. After displaying them, we found they sold very fast. I have only seen the goblets and champagnes in blue. I never did find a "Tinkerbell" cordial for my collection; but that is not the only one that escaped me.

The green bud vase is 10" tall and found in an antique mall near Columbus, Ohio. It remains the only piece of green "Tinkerbell" I have seen. A four-piece water bottle set is one of the most interesting pieces in this pattern. I've seen it "live" in a not-for-sale display.

	Azure Green		Azure Green
Bowl, finger, ftd.	100.00	Stem, 3½ oz., cocktail	125.00
Night or medicine set bottle, 4 pc. (med. bottle w/stop, night glass, w/water bottle)	695.00	4 Stem, 5½ oz., saucer champagne	125.00
		Stem, 5½ oz., sherbet	100.00
Plate, finger bowl liner	30.00	2 Stem, 9 oz., goblet	195.00
Stem, 1½ oz., cordial	225.00	Vase, 10", plain top, ftd., #36 Uranus	395.00
3 Stem, 2½ oz., wine	175.00	1 Vase, 10", ruffled top, ftd., #36 Uranus	495.00

Colors: Rose pink, Topaz, yellow

Supplies of Topaz and Rose Trojan are becoming increasingly slim. Quantities of pink have never caught up to demand. Topaz sells quite well, and has always been more abundant in the market. A few years ago, there was a glut of Topaz being offered for sale due to the dispersal of some large collections. Now collectors are once again having trouble finding pieces other than stems.

Soup and cereal bowl costs have soared further than all other Trojan pieces in the last few years. Soup bowls are rare. If you find either one, be pleased and pull out the checkbook or credit card. There are limited chances to obtain these. Don't be regretting for years that you should've purchased them.

You need to know the following Fostoria facts: liner plates for cream soup and mayonnaise are the same piece; two-handled cake plates come with and without an indent in the center (the indented version also serves as a plate for one of two styles of cheese comports); bonbon, lemon dish, sweetmeat, and whipped cream bowls all come with loop or bow handles; and sugars come with a straight or ruffled edge. Surprisingly, it is the ruffled top sugar that takes a lid.

Trojan stemware can be found except for cordials and clarets in either color. Clarets are nearly impossible to find in most Fostoria patterns. If you need them, you had better buy them whenever you find them. The claret has the same shape as the wine, but holds four ounces as opposed to the three ounces of the wine. Yes, wine glasses in those days held 2 to 3½ ounces of liquid. This confuses today's collector who is used to wine goblets holding eight ounces or more. In those days, that capacity was reserved for water.

The quarter and half-pound candy jars are depicted on page 229. They sell in about the same price range, but the quarter pound is harder to find. On that bottom row are two ice dishes with inserts. The ice dish has to have the Trojan pattern to be the correct one. The inserts themselves are always plain without the pattern. Pictured are the shrimp and tomato juice inserts. The last item in the top row is the grapefruit. It takes a liner with the pattern on it although it is missing in the photo. The inserts are equally valuable in price.

		Rose	Topaz
	Ashtray, #2350, lg.	35.00	28.00
	Ashtray, #2350, sm.	28.00	22.00
	Bottle, salad dressing, #2983	595.00	395.00
7	Bowl, baker, #2375, 9"		75.00
	Bowl, bonbon, #2375		22.50
	Bowl, bouillon, #2375, ftd.		22.00
	Bowl, cream soup, #2375, ftd.	40.00	33.00
	Bowl, finger, #869/2283, w/6¼" liner	55.00	50.00
	Bowl, lemon, #2375	24.00	20.00
	Bowl, #2394, 3 ftd., 4½", mint	25.00	22.00
	Bowl, #2375, fruit, 5"	26.00	22.00
	Bowl, #2354, 3 ftd., 6"	50.00	42.00
	Bowl, cereal, #2375, 6½"	60.00	45.00
	Bowl, soup, #2375, 7"	135.00	115.00
	Bowl, lg. dessert, #2375, 2 hdld.	100.00	85.00
	Bowl, #2395, 10"	115.00	80.00
	Bowl, #2395, scroll, 10"	110.00	90.00
	Bowl, combination #2415, w/candleholder handles	250.00	175.00
	Bowl, #2375, centerpiece, flared optic, 12"	75.00	65.00
	Bowl, #2394, centerpiece, ftd., 12"	85.00	70.00
	Bowl, #2375, centerpiece, mushroom, 12"	95.00	75.00

		Rose	Topaz
6	Candlestick, #2394, 2"	25.00	22.50
	Candlestick, #2375, flared, 3"	30.00	25.00
1	Candlestick, #2395½, scroll, 5"	75.00	65.00
14	Candy, w/cover, #2394, ¼ lb.	325.00	260.00
13	Candy, w/cover, #2394, ½ lb.	225.00	200.00
	Celery, #2375, 11½"	48.00	38.00
9	Cheese & cracker, set, #2375, #2368	85.00	70.00
3	Comport, #5299 or #2400, 6"	65.00	50.00
	Comport, #2375, 7"	65.00	50.00
4	Creamer, #2375, ftd.	22.50	18.00
	Creamer, tea, #2375½	60.00	45.00
	Cup, after dinner, #2375	50.00	35.00
	Cup, #2375½, ftd.	18.00	15.00
	Decanter, #2439, 9"	1,395.00	995.00
	Goblet, claret, #5099, 4 oz., 6"	125.00	75.00
	Goblet, cocktail, #5099, 3 oz., 5¼"	32.50	26.00
	Goblet, cordial, #5099, ¾ oz., 4"	110.00	67.50
	Goblet, water, #5299, 10 oz., 8¼"	45.00	35.00
	Goblet, wine, #5099, 3 oz., 5½"	58.00	42.00
5	Grapefruit, #5282½	60.00	45.00
	Grapefruit liner, #945½	60.00	45.00
15	Ice bucket, #2375	110.00	90.00
10	Ice dish, #2451, #2455	55.00	42.00
11 12	Ice dish liner (tomato, crab, fruit), #2451	20.00	10.00

	Rose	Topaz
Mayonnaise ladle	30.00	20.00
Mayonnaise, w/liner, #2375	60.00	50.00
Oil, ftd., #2375	395.00	310.00
Oyster, cocktail, #5099, ftd.	32.00	25.00
Parfait, #5099	70.00	45.00
Pitcher, #5000	495.00	350.00
Plate, #2375, canape, 6¼"	35.00	25.00
Plate, #2375, bread/butter, 6"	8.00	6.00
Plate, #2375, salad, 7½"	12.00	9.00
Plate, 2375, cream soup or mayo liner, 7½"	15.00	10.00
Plate, #2375, luncheon, 8¾"	20.00	16.00
Plate, #2375, sm., dinner, 9½"	35.00	28.00
Plate, #2375, cake, handled, 10"	65.00	50.00
Plate, #2375, grill, rare, 10¼"	100.00	90.00
Plate, #2375, dinner, 10¼"	85.00	65.00
Plate, #2375, chop, 13"	80.00	65.00
Plate, #2375, round, 14"	80.00	75.00
Platter, #2375, 12"	90.00	70.00
8 Platter, #2375, 15"	175.00	140.00
Relish, #2375, 8½"		45.00
Relish, #2350, 3 pt., rnd., 8¾"	55.00	50.00
Sauce boat, #2375	150.00	100.00

	Rose	Topaz
Sauce plate, #2375	45.00	40.00
Saucer, #2375, after dinner	10.00	10.00
Saucer, #2375	6.00	5.00
Shaker, #2375, pr., ftd.	130.00	100.00
Sherbet, #5099, high, 6"	28.00	22.00
Sherbet, #5099, low, 4¼"	20.00	16.00
2 Sugar, #2375½, ftd.	22.50	18.00
15 Sugar cover, #2375½	150.00	110.00
Sugar pail, #2378	250.00	195.00
Sugar, tea, #2375½	55.00	40.00
Sweetmeat, #2375	25.00	20.00
Tray, 11", ctr. hdld, #2375	60.00	45.00
Tray, #2429, service & lemon insert		265.00
Tumbler, #5099, ftd., 2½ oz.	60.00	45.00
Tumbler, #5099, ftd., 5 oz., 4½"	35.00	28.00
Tumbler, #5099, ftd., 9 oz., 5¼"	25.00	20.00
Tumbler, #5099, ftd., 12 oz., 6"	50.00	35.00
Vase, #2417, 8"	200.00	150.00
Vase, #4105, 8"	275.00	195.00
Vase, #2369, 9"		250.00
Whipped cream bowl, #2375	37.50	26.00
Whipped cream pail, #2378	150.00	115.00

Colors: amber, amber w/green, amber w/red, rose w/green

Turkey Tracks is what this pattern has been called for years. It tends to turn up in quantities when it is found. We know McKee Glass Company made a Turkey Tracks design. Was it this one, patented in 1927? Patent was applied for October 26, 1926, from inventor J.H. Venon and was granted April 19, 1927.

The color combinations are rather striking with the colors fluorescing. Amber is usually not one of my favorite colors, but this amber is quite different from most amber in that it even glows under a black light, not the normal circumstance. I wonder if all the people calling green glass "vaseline" will add this to the mix also. "Vaseline" is canary yellow, not green, which fluoresces because of uranium in its composition. (I did get a big chuckle out of a "dealer" explaining to me that the crystal piece of unmarked Heisey that I was buying was clear "vaseline." He even held up a portable ultra violet light to "prove" it. All I saw was the purple reflection, but bought the piece for the $20 he wanted!)

You will find some highly priced bi-colored stems and footed tumblers in Turkey Tracks, but then, two-tone items have many admirers by themselves — without the added unusual design. Flat tumblers and plates seem to be available in amber, but you could find other colors. If you have additional pieces or colors, please let us know.

	Plate, 6", sherbet	12.50
4	Plate, 7⅞", salad	20.00
3	Plate, 9⅛" dinner	50.00
2	Stem, 1½ oz., 5⅛" cordial	195.00
	Stem, 3 oz., cocktail	150.00
8	Stem, 3 oz., wine	175.00
	Stem, 6 oz., 4", high sherbet	150.00
6	Stem, 6 oz., low sherbet	130.00
7	Tumbler, 3 oz., bar	100.00
	Tumbler, 6 oz., old fashion	125.00
	Tumbler, 6 oz., 4", ftd., juice	90.00
	Tumbler, 9 oz., ftd.	110.00
5	Tumbler, 10 oz., 4¼" ftd. water	110.00
	Tumbler, 12 oz., 5½", ftd. tea	135.00
1	Tumbler, 13 oz., 5⅞" ftd. ice tea	135.00

Colors: crystal, Flamingo pink, Moongleam green, Marigold amber/yellow, Sahara yellow, some Alexandrite (rare)

Few collectors have searched for crystal Twist in the past, but there is a growing force attracted by this Deco influenced pattern. The Moongleam cocktail shaker on the right is one of few to be uncovered, although the mould turned up during the purchase of old moulds by the National Heisey Club several years ago. Cocktail shakers in other colors have never surfaced.

That amber/yellow colored ice bucket below is Marigold; and the pink/purple color is Alexandrite. Both are rare Heisey colors. Be aware that Marigold is tricky to find in mint condition because the applied color has a propensity to flake or peel. Items that are beginning to destabilize will continue to do so. If you have a choice in owning a piece of this rarely seen color that has some problems, pass it unless it is very inexpensive. Nothing can be done to refurbish it, but there have been many who have tried.

Few price adjustments have been seen in colored Twist lately. Most Twist items are marked with the H in diamond. When examining stemmed pieces, check on the stem itself. Of course, this easily recognized pattern doesn't really need a mark to distinguish it as Heisey. Oil bottles, large bowls, and the three-footed utility plates have seen upward price adjustments. The individual sugar and creamer have both disappeared into collections; grab one if a chance presents itself.

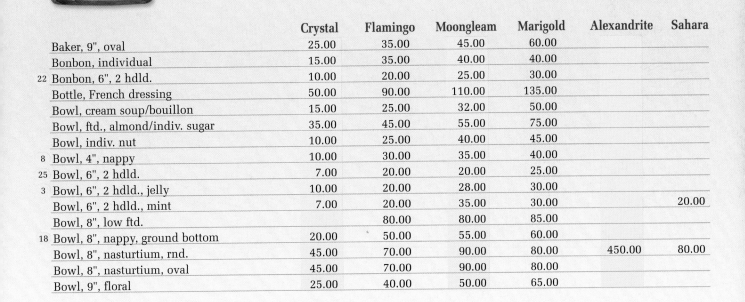

		Crystal	Flamingo	Moongleam	Marigold	Alexandrite	Sahara
	Baker, 9", oval	25.00	35.00	45.00	60.00		
	Bonbon, individual	15.00	35.00	40.00	40.00		
22	Bonbon, 6", 2 hdld.	10.00	20.00	25.00	30.00		
	Bottle, French dressing	50.00	90.00	110.00	135.00		
	Bowl, cream soup/bouillon	15.00	25.00	32.00	50.00		
	Bowl, ftd., almond/indiv. sugar	35.00	45.00	55.00	75.00		
	Bowl, indiv. nut	10.00	25.00	40.00	45.00		
8	Bowl, 4", nappy	10.00	30.00	35.00	40.00		
25	Bowl, 6", 2 hdld.	7.00	20.00	20.00	25.00		
3	Bowl, 6", 2 hdld., jelly	10.00	20.00	28.00	30.00		
	Bowl, 6", 2 hdld., mint	7.00	20.00	35.00	30.00		20.00
	Bowl, 8", low ftd.		80.00	80.00	85.00		
18	Bowl, 8", nappy, ground bottom	20.00	50.00	55.00	60.00		
	Bowl, 8", nasturtium, rnd.	45.00	70.00	90.00	80.00	450.00	80.00
	Bowl, 8", nasturtium, oval	45.00	70.00	90.00	80.00		
	Bowl, 9", floral	25.00	40.00	50.00	65.00		

		Crystal	Flamingo	Moongleam	Marigold	Alexandrite	Sahara
	Bowl, 9", floral, rolled edge	30.00	40.00	45.00	65.00		
6	Bowl, 12", floral, oval, 4 ft.	45.00	100.00	110.00	90.00	550.00	85.00
21	Bowl, 12", floral, rnd., 4 ft.	30.00	40.00	50.00	65.00		
5	Candlestick, 2", 1-lite		40.00	50.00	85.00		
	Cheese dish, 6", 2 hdld.	10.00	20.00	25.00	30.00		
	Claret, 4 oz.	15.00	30.00	40.00	50.00		
2	Cocktail shaker, metal top			400.00			
4	Comport, 7", tall	40.00	90.00	120.00	150.00		
19	Creamer, hotel, oval	25.00	40.00	45.00	50.00		
	Creamer, individual (unusual)	30.00	50.00	60.00	65.00		
	Creamer, zigzag handles, ftd.	20.00	40.00	50.00	70.00		
7	Cup, zigzag handles	10.00	25.00	32.00	35.00		
	Grapefruit, ftd.	15.00	25.00	35.00	60.00		
	Ice bucket w/metal handle	50.00	125.00	115.00	135.00	300.00	125.00
15	Mayonnaise	35.00	65.00	80.00	80.00		
14	Mayonnaise, #1252½	20.00	35.00	45.00	50.00		
26	Mustard, w/cover, spoon	40.00	90.00	140.00	100.00		
	Oil bottle, 2½ oz., w/#78 stopper	50.00	140.00	170.00	200.00		
	Oil bottle, 4 oz., w/#78 stopper	50.00	110.00	120.00	120.00		90.00
16	Pitcher, 3 pint	95.00	175.00	230.00			
	Plate, cream soup liner	5.00	7.00	10.00	15.00		
	Plate, 8", Kraft cheese	20.00	40.00	60.00	50.00		
	Plate, 8", ground bottom	7.00	14.00	20.00	30.00		20.00
9	Plate, 10½", dinner	40.00	80.00	100.00	120.00		90.00
	Plate, 12", 2 hdld., sandwich	30.00	60.00	90.00	80.00		
	Plate, 12", muffin, 2 hdld., turned sides	40.00	80.00	90.00	80.00		
	Plate, 13", 3 part, relish	10.00	17.00	22.00	35.00		
12	Platter, 12"	15.00	50.00	60.00	75.00		
	Salt & pepper, ftd.	100.00	140.00	160.00	200.00		140.00
10	Salt & pepper, flat	50.00	90.00	100.00	60.00		
7	Saucer	3.00	5.00	7.00	10.00	140.00	

	Crystal	Flamingo	Moongleam	Marigold	Alexandrite	Sahara
Stem, 2½ oz., wine, 2 block stem	40.00	90.00	110.00	125.00		
Stem, 3 oz., oyster cocktail, ftd.	10.00	30.00	40.00	50.00		
Stem, 3 oz., cocktail, 2 block stem	10.00	30.00	45.00	50.00		
Stem, 5 oz., saucer champagne, 2 block stem	10.00	35.00	25.00	30.00		
Stem, 5 oz., sherbet, 2 block stem	10.00	18.00	40.00	28.00		
Stem, 9 oz., luncheon (1 block in stem)	40.00	60.00	70.00	75.00		
11 Stem, 9 oz., goblet (2 block in stem)	35.00	55.00	60.00	65.00		
Sugar, ftd.	20.00	30.00	37.50	60.00		
20 Sugar, hotel, oval	25.00	45.00	50.00	50.00		
Sugar, individual (unusual)	30.00	50.00	60.00	65.00		
Sugar, w/cover, zigzag handles	25.00	40.00	60.00	80.00		
Tray, 7", pickle, ground bottom	7.00	35.00	35.00	45.00		
24 Tray, 10", celery	30.00	50.00	50.00	40.00		40.00
Tray, 13", celery	25.00	50.00	60.00	50.00		
17 Tumbler, 5 oz., soda, flat bottom	10.00	25.00	32.00	36.00		
Tumbler, 6 oz., ftd., soda	10.00	25.00	32.00	36.00		
23 Tumbler, 8 oz., flat, ground bottom	15.00	45.00	70.00	40.00		
Tumbler, 8 oz., soda, straight & flared	12.00	35.00	40.00	40.00		
13 Tumbler, 9 oz., ftd., soda	20.00	45.00	50.00	60.00		
Tumbler, 12 oz., iced tea, flat bottom	20.00	50.00	60.00	70.00		
Tumbler, 12 oz., ftd., iced tea	20.00	45.00	50.00	60.00		

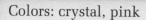

Colors: crystal, pink

Valencia is regularly misidentified with a similar Cambridge pattern, Minerva. Notice in the photo of Valencia that the lines in the pattern are perpendicular to each other (think of a volleyball net). On Minerva, the lines in the pattern meet on a diagonal forming diamonds instead of squares. I have explained that in every book, but have continually been amazed at the number of dealers who have handed me a piece and asked which one is it. Valencia had a limited distribution; dealers are not as familiar with it as with many Cambridge patterns.

Valencia has many pieces that would be sold for sizeable sums in other Cambridge patterns where demand exceeds the supply. However, with Valencia, there are so few collectors that rare pieces often are very under valued. Most pieces shown are enthusiastically pursued in Rose Point, but are only just being noticed in Valencia. Valencia items are, without a doubt, rarer than the enormously fashionable Rose Point. However, rarity is less important in collecting; demand is the driving force.

Some of the more exceptional pieces pictured include the square, covered honey dish, the Doulton pitcher, and that small metal-handled piece that Cambridge called a sugar basket. This is similar to Fostoria's sugar pail, but closer in size to Fostoria's whipped cream pail. Terminology used by glass companies in those days sometimes mystifies collectors today.

	Crystal
16 Ashtray, #3500/16, 3¼", square	12.00
17 Ashtray, #3500/124, 3¼", round	12.00
Ashtray, #3500/126, 4", round	15.00
18 Ashtray, #3500/128, 4½", round	20.00
3 Ashtray/soapdish, #3500/130, 4", oval	65.00
Basket, #3500/55, 6", 2 hdld., ftd.	30.00
Bowl, #3500/49, 5", hdld.	18.00
Bowl, #3500/37, 6", cereal	30.00
Bowl, #1402/89, 6", 2 hdld.	20.00
Bowl, #1402/88, 6", 2 hdld., div.	20.00
Bowl, #3500/115, 9½", 2 hdld., ftd.	38.00
Bowl, #1402/82, 10"	50.00
Bowl, #1402/88, 11"	55.00
Bowl, #1402/95, salad dressing, div.	40.00
Bowl, #1402/100, finger, w/liner	45.00
Bowl, #3500, ftd., finger	35.00
Candy dish, w/cover, #3500/103	165.00
Celery, #1402/94, 12"	32.00
Cigarette holder, #1066, ftd.	65.00
6 Comport, #3500/36, 6"	30.00
Comport, #3500/37, 7"	45.00
Creamer, #3500/14	18.00
Creamer, #3500/15, individual	20.00
21 Cup, #3500/1	20.00
Decanter, #3400/92, 32 oz., ball	235.00
Decanter, #3400/119, 12 oz., ball	195.00
20 Honey dish, w/cover, #3500/139	195.00
12 Ice pail, #1402/52	110.00
Mayonnaise, #3500/59, 3 pc.	45.00
Nut, #3400/71, 3", 4 ftd.	65.00
Perfume, #3400/97, 2 oz., perfume	195.00
8 Plate, #3500/167, 7½", salad	10.00
Plate, #3500/5, 8½", breakfast	12.00
Plate, #1402, 11½", sandwich, hdld.	32.00
4 Plate, #3500/39, 12", ftd.	40.00
Plate, #3500/67, 12"	40.00
1 Plate, #3500/38, 13", torte	50.00
2 Pitcher, 80 oz., Doulton, #3400/141	395.00
Relish, #3500/68, 5½", 2 comp.	30.00
Relish, #3500/69, 6½", 3 comp.	35.00

	Crystal
10 Relish, #3500/71, 7½", 3 part, hdld.	95.00
Relish, #1402/91, 8", 3 comp.	60.00
Relish, #3500/64, 10", 3 comp.	60.00
Relish, #3500/65, 10", 4 comp.	65.00
19 Relish, #3500/67, 12", 6 pc.	225.00
15 Relish, #3500/112, 15", 3 pt., 2 hdld.	95.00
Relish, #3500/13, 15", 4 pt., 2 hdld.	95.00
11 Salt and pepper, #3400/18	65.00
21 Saucer, #3500/1	3.00
Stem, #1402, cordial	65.00
Stem, #1402, wine	38.00
Stem, #1402, cocktail	22.00
Stem, #1402, claret	40.00
Stem, #1402, oyster cocktail	18.00
Stem, #1402, low sherbet	15.00
Stem, #1402, tall sherbet	18.00
Stem, #1402, goblet	33.00
Stem, #3500, cordial	70.00
Stem, #3500, wine, 2½ oz.	40.00
Stem, #3500, cocktail, 3 oz.	20.00
Stem, #3500, claret, 4½ oz.	40.00
Stem, #3500, oyster cocktail, 4½ oz.	18.00
Stem, #3500, low sherbet, 7 oz.	15.00
Stem, #3500, tall sherbet, 7 oz.	18.00
Stem, #3500, goblet, long bowl	33.00
Stem, #3500, goblet, short bowl	33.00
14 Sugar, #3500/14	16.00
Sugar, #3500/15, individual	20.00
13 Sugar basket, #3500/13	175.00
9 Tumbler, #3400/92, 2½ oz.	25.00
7 Tumbler, #3400/100, 13 oz.	25.00
Tumbler, #3400/115, 14 oz.	27.00
Tumbler, #3500, 2½ oz., ftd.	25.00
Tumbler, #3500, 3 oz., ftd.	22.00
Tumbler, #3500, 5 oz., ftd.	20.00
Tumbler, #3500, 10 oz., ftd.	22.00
5 Tumbler, #3500, 12 oz., ftd.	25.00
Tumbler, #3500, 13 oz., ftd.	25.00
Tumbler, #3500, 16 oz., ftd.	30.00

Colors: blue, yellow, pink, green

Fostoria line numbers (which also pertain to June and Fairfax listings) are cataloged for each piece of Versailles. All colors of Versailles are in demand and the increased prices indicate that the numerous buyers are elevating the asking prices.

Blue Versailles no longer stands at the top of the class since green has attracted hordes of new collectors, particularly on the West Coast. I used to avoid buying green Versailles, as it was difficult to sell, but that is no longer true.

All Fostoria soup and cereal bowls are silently vanishing from the market. There is a cereal pictured in front in pink. However, I have never owned soup bowls in any color of Versailles other than yellow. Do you have another color?

Be sure to see page 99 for various types of Fostoria stemware. Confusion reigns because stem heights are similar. Here, shapes and capacities are more important. Yellow Versailles is always found on stem line #5099, which has a cascading stem; all other Versailles is found on stem line #5098, which is shown in both photos.

		Green	Blue	Pink Yellow
33	Ashtray, #2350	30.00	35.00	25.00
	Bottle, #2083, salad dressing, crystal glass top	695.00	995.00	495.00
	Bottle, #2375, salad dressing, w/sterling top or colored top	595.00	895.00	495.00
	Bowl, #2375, baker, 9"	95.00	150.00	85.00
	Bowl, #2375, bonbon	30.00	33.00	22.00
	Bowl, #2375, bouillon, ftd.	28.00	40.00	25.00
	Bowl, #2375, cream soup, ftd.	40.00	55.00	35.00
18	Bowl, #869/2283, finger, w/6" liner	60.00	85.00	50.00
	Bowl, lemon	30.00	22.00	30.00
	Bowl, 4½", mint, 3 ftd.	33.00	45.00	27.50
16	Bowl, #2375, fruit, 5"	30.00	45.00	30.00
	Bowl, #2394, 3 ftd., 6"			40.00
29	Bowl, #2375, cereal, 6½"	55.00	85.00	45.00
	Bowl, #2375, soup, 7"	125.00	160.00	90.00
	Bowl, #2375, lg., dessert, 2 hdld.	100.00	135.00	90.00
1	Bowl, #2375, baker, 10", oval	95.00	135.00	85.00
	Bowl, #2395, centerpiece, scroll, 10"	100.00	145.00	90.00
	Bowl, #2375, centerpiece, flared top, 12"	85.00	110.00	75.00
	Bowl, #2394, ftd., 12"	85.00	110.00	75.00
	Bowl, #2375½, oval, centerpiece, 13"	95.00	135.00	
17	Candlestick, #2394, 2"	35.00	40.00	30.00
	Candlestick, #2395½, 3"	40.00	50.00	35.00
9	Candlestick, #2395½, scroll, 5"	55.00	65.00	45.00
	Candy, w/cover, #2331, 3 pt.	200.00	285.00	
	Candy, w/cover, #2394, ¼ lb.			225.00
	Candy, w/cover, #2394, ½ lb.			175.00
	Celery, #2375, 11½"	85.00	110.00	75.00
12	Cheese & cracker, #2375 or #2368, set	95.00	125.00	85.00
	Comport, #5098, 3"	35.00	50.00	30.00
	Comport, #5099/2400, 6"	75.00	95.00	75.00
24	Comport, #2375, 7½"	50.00	95.00	
	Comport, #2400, 8"	75.00	140.00	
14	Creamer, #2375½, ftd.	25.00	25.00	20.00
31	Creamer, #2375½, tea	60.00	65.00	40.00
27	Cup, #2375, after dinner	60.00	75.00	35.00
10	Cup, #2375½, ftd.	22.00	25.00	18.00
	Decanter, #2439, 9"	1,200.00	2,000.00	895.00
13	Goblet, cordial, #5098 or #5099, ¾ oz., 4"	165.00	150.00	90.00
	Goblet, #5098 or #5099, claret, 4 oz., 6"	110.00	150.00	90.00
6	Goblet, cocktail, #5098 or #5099, 3 oz., 5¼"	35.00	40.00	30.00
20	Goblet, water, #5098 or #5099, 10 oz., 8¼"	100.00	85.00	50.00
	Goblet, wine, #5098 or #5099, 3 oz., 5½"	75.00	90.00	60.00
	Grapefruit, #5082½	60.00	65.00	40.00

		Green	Blue	Pink Yellow
	Grapefruit liner, #945½, etched	60.00	65.00	40.00
25	Ice bucket, #2375	100.00	125.00	80.00
	Ice dish, #2451	50.00	65.00	40.00
	Ice dish liner (tomato, crab, fruit), #2451	20.00	20.00	10.00
	Mayonnaise, w/liner, #2375	70.00	85.00	60.00
	Mayonnaise ladle	20.00	30.00	20.00
26	Oil, #2375, ftd.	495.00	595.00	395.00
8	Oyster cocktail, #5098 or #5099	30.00	40.00	28.00
	Parfait, #5098 or #5099	70.00	95.00	55.00
2	Pitcher, #5000	495.00	595.00	395.00
	Plate, #2375, bread/butter, 6"	9.00	12.00	8.00
	Plate, #2375, canape, 6"	30.00	35.00	30.00
	Plate, #2375, salad, 7½"	15.00	16.00	13.00
	Plate, #2375, cream soup or mayo liner, 7½"	14.00	18.00	12.00
3	Plate, #2375, luncheon, 8¾"	20.00	25.00	15.00
19	Plate, #2375, sm., dinner, 9½"	40.00	50.00	33.00
	Plate, #2375, cake, 2 hdld., 10"	50.00	65.00	40.00
	Plate, #2375, dinner, 10¼"	100.00	120.00	75.00
	Plate, #2375, chop, 13"	90.00	95.00	60.00
	Platter, #2375, 12"	100.00	135.00	85.00
	Platter, #2375, 15"	160.00	225.00	135.00
30	Relish, #2375, 8½", 2-part			38.00
	Sauce boat, #2375	175.00	250.00	125.00
	Sauce boat plate, #2375	35.00	50.00	25.00
	Saucer, #2375, after dinner	15.00	20.00	10.00
11	Saucer, #2375	5.00	6.00	4.00
	Shaker, #2375, pr., ftd.	150.00	175.00	110.00
21	Sherbet, #5098/5099, high, 6"	30.00	35.00	28.00
7	Sherbet, #5098/5099, low, 4¼"	28.00	30.00	22.00
15	Sugar, #2375½, ftd.	25.00	25.00	20.00
15	Sugar cover, #2375½	160.00	200.00	125.00
	Sugar pail, #2378	225.00	295.00	165.00
28	Sugar, #2375½, tea	60.00	65.00	40.00
	Sweetmeat, #2375	22.00	25.00	20.00
	Tray, #2375, ctr. hdld., 11"	55.00	65.00	45.00
	Tray, service & lemon	395.00	450.00	250.00
22	Tumbler, flat, old-fashioned (pink only)			125.00
23	Tumbler, flat, tea (pink only)			135.00
	Tumbler, #5098 or #5099 2½ oz., ftd.	75.00	90.00	55.00
	Tumbler, #5098 or #5099, 5 oz., ftd., 4½"	32.00	38.00	25.00
5	Tumbler, #5098 or #5099, 9 oz., ftd., 5¼"	38.00	42.00	28.00
4	Tumbler, #5098 or #5099 12 oz., ftd., 6"	55.00	65.00	40.00
	Vase, #2417, 8"			235.00
	Vase, #4100, 8"	265.00	350.00	
	Vase, #2385, fan, ftd., 8½"	295.00	395.00	
32	Whipped cream bowl, #2375	30.00	35.00	25.00
	Whipped cream pail, #2378	200.00	250.00	175.00

Note: See page 99 for stem identification.

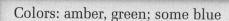

Colors: amber, green; some blue

Amber Vesper is the color most often seen. Today, the popularity of amber is increasing but it wilts a bit when compared to other colors. Obviously, from the abundance of amber glassware made in the late 1920s and 1930s, it was an exceedingly popular color then. I recently sold quite a bit of amber Vesper that had been stored from the late 1970s. As of today, I only have a few pieces left. It wasn't a large dollar volume, but it was quite a quantity to sell in six quick weeks.

There is little blue Vesper to be found for sale at a price collectors are willing to pay. The Fostoria name for the particular blue color of Vesper is simply Blue. Hardly original, I agree; but that does distinguish it from the lighter blue dubbed Azure. Hard to find, attractive, colored glassware often is priced out of the reach of the average collector. Blue Vesper has not reached that point yet, but it is slowly rising in price. Green Vesper is easier to obtain than blue, but it is not capturing many collectors. That lack of collector appeal now over 70 years later makes for more affordable prices for that color than for blue or amber. Difficult to gain are the vanity set (combination perfume and powder jar), moulded and blown grapefruits, egg cup, butter dish, both styles of candy dishes, and the Maj Jongg (8¾" canapé) plate. It is the high sherbet that fits the ring on that plate. All of these have been pictured in earlier editions; but finding them, today, has also been a problem for me. I did manage to round up the two styles of grapefruits and the flat, three-part candy, but that was all for this time.

Vesper comes on stem line #5093 and tumbler line #5100. The shapes are slightly different from those Fostoria etches found on the Fairfax blank (page 99). Cordials, clarets, and parfaits are the most difficult stems to acquire while the footed, 12-ounce iced tea and two-ounce footed bar are the most difficult tumblers.

There will never be a better time to start collecting Vesper, so if this is your cup of tea, better start now.

		Green	Amber	Blue
15	Ashtray, #2350, 4"	25.00	30.00	
	Bowl, #2350, bouillon, ftd.	20.00	25.00	36.00
	Bowl, #2350, cream soup, flat	25.00	30.00	
	Bowl, #2350, cream soup, ftd.	22.00	25.00	36.00
	Bowl, #2350, fruit, 5½"	12.00	18.00	30.00
	Bowl, #2350, cereal, sq. or rnd., 6½"	30.00	35.00	50.00
	Bowl, #2267, low, ftd., 7"	25.00	30.00	
14	Bowl, #2350, soup, shallow, 7¾"	30.00	40.00	65.00
	Bowl, soup, deep, 8¼"		40.00	
	Bowl, 8⅞"	32.00	40.00	
	Bowl, #2350, baker, oval, 9"	65.00	75.00	100.00
	Bowl, #2350, rd.	45.00	55.00	
	Bowl, #2350, baker, oval, 10½"	75.00	85.00	145.00
	Bowl, #2375, flared bowl, 10½"	50.00	55.00	
	Bowl, #2350, ped., ftd., 10½"	55.00	65.00	
	Bowl, #2329, console, rolled edge, 11"	37.50	40.00	
	Bowl, #2375, 3 ftd., 12½"	50.00	55.00	125.00
	Bowl, #2371, oval, 13"	55.00	60.00	
11	Bowl, #2329, rolled edge, 13"	50.00	55.00	
	Bowl, #2329, rolled edge, 14"	55.00	60.00	150.00
	Butter dish, #2350	425.00	850.00	
	Candlestick, #2324, 2"	22.00	25.00	
	Candlestick, #2394, 3"	23.00	25.00	
2	Candlestick, #2324, 4"	24.00	25.00	50.00
	Candlestick, #2394, 9"	85.00	100.00	110.00
10	Candy jar, w/cover, #2331, 3 pt.	135.00	135.00	295.00
	Candy jar, w/cover, #2250, ftd., ½ lb.	295.00	250.00	
	Celery, #2350	26.00	30.00	50.00
	Cheese, #2368, ftd.	22.00	25.00	
	Comport, 6"	26.00	30.00	50.00
1	Comport, #2327 (twisted stem), 7½"	35.00	40.00	75.00
9	Comport, 8"	55.00	60.00	85.00
	Creamer, #2350½, ftd.	16.00	20.00	

	Green	Amber	Blue
Creamer, #2315½, fat, ftd.	20.00	22.00	35.00
Creamer, #2350½, flat		25.00	
16 Cup, #2350	14.00	14.00	40.00
Cup, #2350, after dinner	42.00	40.00	85.00
Cup, #2350½, ftd.	15.00	16.00	35.00
Egg cup, #2350		45.00	
Finger bowl and liner, #869/2283, 6"	32.00	35.00	65.00
12 Grapefruit, #5082½, blown	55.00	50.00	90.00
13 Grapefruit liner, #945½, blown	50.00	50.00	65.00
Grapefruit, #2315, molded	55.00	60.00	
6 Ice bucket, #2378	85.00	95.00	250.00
22 Oyster cocktail, #5100	25.00	30.00	40.00
Pickle, #2350	30.00	30.00	50.00
Pitcher, #5100, ftd.	335.00	395.00	595.00
Plate, #2350, bread/butter, 6"	7.00	6.00	12.00
Plate, #2350, salad, 7½"	10.00	10.00	18.00
Plate, #2350, luncheon, 8½"	14.00	16.00	25.00
Plate, #2321, Maj Jongg (canape), 8¾"		50.00	
Plate, #2350, sm., dinner, 9½"	25.00	30.00	40.00
Plate, dinner, 10½"	50.00	82.00	
Plate, #2287, ctr. hand., 11"	30.00	35.00	65.00
Plate, chop, 13¾"	40.00	45.00	85.00
Plate, #2350, server, 14"	55.00	65.00	110.00
Plate, w/indent for cheese, 11"	25.00	30.00	
Platter, #2350, 10½"	45.00	50.00	
3 Platter, #2350, 12"	65.00	75.00	150.00
Platter, #2350, 15",	110.00	125.00	225.00
Salt & pepper, #5100, pr.	75.00	90.00	
Sauce boat, w/liner, #2350	175.00	195.00	
16 Saucer, #2350, after dinner	10.00	10.00	25.00
Saucer, #2350	4.00	4.00	8.00
18 Stem, #5093, high sherbet	18.00	18.00	35.00
7 Stem, #5093, water goblet	28.00	28.00	60.00
17 Stem, #5093, low sherbet	16.00	16.00	30.00
5 Stem, #5093, parfait	40.00	45.00	75.00
20 Stem, #5093, cordial, ¾ oz.	70.00	70.00	150.00
4 Stem, #5093, wine, 2¾ oz.	38.00	38.00	70.00
8 Stem, #5093, cocktail, 3 oz.	25.00	28.00	50.00
19 Stem, #5093, claret, 4 oz.	65.00	75.00	
Sugar, #2350½, flat		25.00	
Sugar, #2315, fat, ftd.	20.00	22.00	35.00
Sugar, #2350½, ftd.	14.00	16.00	
Sugar, lid	200.00	195.00	
21 Tumbler, #5100, ftd., 2 oz.	35.00	40.00	70.00
23 Tumbler, #5100, ftd., 5 oz.	18.00	20.00	45.00
25 Tumbler, #5100, ftd., 9 oz.	18.00	20.00	50.00
24 Tumbler, #5100, ftd., 12 oz.	30.00	35.00	65.00
Urn, #2324, small	100.00	110.00	
Urn, large	115.00	135.00	
Vase, #2292, 8"	125.00	115.00	225.00
Vanity set, combination cologne/ powder & stopper	265.00	310.00	425.00

Note: See stemware identification on page 99.

Colors: crystal, Sahara, Cobalt, rare in pale Zircon

More Victorian has appeared for sale recently than I have ever seen. There was a large set displayed for sale at a show I attended. All the rarely found items sold early. The rest of the set did not sell well because, I believe, it was offered above market price. The rare pieces sold at high prices to avid collectors who needed them no matter what the price. It may take a longer time to find collectors willing to pay outrageous prices on the more commonly found items.

Notice the two tumblers used as a pattern shot. The taller one is Victorian while the shorter one is Duncan's Block. Block is an older ware often confused with Victorian and you can understand why. Most Victorian pieces are marked with the Heisey H inside a diamond.

Heisey Victorian was only made in the colors listed. If you see pink (Azalea), green (Verde), or amber Victorian in your travels, then you have Imperial's copy of the pattern made in 1964 and 1965. These colors are usually also marked with the H in diamond trademark but were made from Heisey moulds after Heisey was no longer in business; Imperial did not remove Heisey's mark at first.

I saw a set of amber offered rather reasonably at a show a few months ago, with a sign proclaiming rare Heisey amber and $4.00 each. Rare and $4.00 do not seem to belong in the same sentence. Those pieces had been offered so long the sign has faded. Amber Victorian is striking, but understand that it is Imperial and not Heisey; and, right now collectors of older Heisey tend to shun Imperial made wares. I suspect that will change with Imperial now also being closed.

Imperial made a few pieces in crystal Victorian, but there is no magic way to separate that which Heisey made from Imperial. These are not as ignored by Heisey collectors, as are the colored Victorian pieces since they are impossible to distinguish.

		Crystal
17	Bottle, 3 oz., oil	65.00
16	Bottle, 27 oz., rye	160.00
4	Bottle, French dressing	80.00
	Bowl, 10½", floral	50.00
	Bowl, finger	25.00
	Bowl, punch	250.00
	Bowl, rose	90.00
19	Bowl, triplex, w/flared or cupped rim	125.00
12	Butter dish, ¼ lb.	70.00
1	Candlestick, 2-lite	110.00
15	Cigarette box, 4"	80.00
10	Cigarette box, 6"	100.00
	Cigarette holder & ashtray, ind.	30.00
	Comport, 5"	60.00
	Comport, 6", 3 ball stem	120.00
	Compote, cheese (for center sandwich)	40.00
11	Creamer	30.00
	Cup, punch, 5 oz.	10.00
	Decanter and stopper, 32 oz.	70.00
	Jug, 54 oz.	400.00
	Nappy, 8"	40.00
	Plate, 6", liner for finger bowl	10.00
	Plate, 7"	20.00
2	Plate, 8"	35.00
	Plate, 12", cracker	75.00
	Plate, 13", sandwich	90.00

		Crystal
	Plate, 21", buffet or punch bowl liner	200.00
	Relish, 11", 3 pt.	50.00
	Salt & pepper	65.00
7	Stem, 2½ oz., wine	30.00
9	Stem, 3 oz., claret	28.00
21	Stem, 5 oz., oyster cocktail	22.00
20	Stem, 5 oz., saucer champagne	20.00
	Stem, 5 oz., sherbet	18.00
18	Stem, 9 oz., goblet (one ball)*	26.00
	Stem, 9 oz., high goblet (two ball)	30.00
8	Sugar	30.00
	Tray, 12", celery	40.00
14	Tray, condiment (s/p & mustard)	130.00
13	Tumbler, 2 oz., bar	40.00
	Tumbler, 5 oz., soda (straight or curved edge)	25.00
	Tumbler, 8 oz., old fashion	35.00
22	Tumbler, 10 oz., w/rim foot	40.00
	Tumbler, 12 oz., ftd. soda	30.00
6	Tumbler, 12 oz., soda (straight or curved edge)	28.00
	Vase, 4"	50.00
	Vase, 5½"	60.00
5	Vase, 6", ftd.	120.00
3	Vase, 7½" (pitcher mold) rare	600.00+
	Vase, 9", ftd., w/flared rim	140.00

Colors: crystal; rare in amber

Waverly #1519 mould blank is better known for the Orchid and Rose etchings appearing on it than for itself, though it's a wonderful, graceful blank in its own right.

		Crystal
	Bowl, 6", oval, lemon, w/cover	45.00
6	Bowl, 6", relish, 2 part, 3 ftd.	10.00
	Bowl, 6½", 2 hdld., ice	60.00
	Bowl, 7", 3 part, relish, oblong	30.00
	Bowl, 7", salad	20.00
	Bowl, 9", 4 part, relish, round	25.00
	Bowl, 9", fruit	30.00
	Bowl, 9", vegetable	35.00
	Bowl, 10", crimped edge	25.00
	Bowl, 10", gardenia	20.00
7	Bowl, 11", seahorse foot, floral	70.00
	Bowl, 12", crimped edge	35.00
5	Bowl, 13", gardenia, w/candleholder center	75.00
8	Box, 5", chocolate, w/cover	80.00
	Box, 5" tall, ftd., w/cover, seahorse hdl.	90.00
1	Box, 6", candy, w/bow tie knob	45.00
	Box, trinket, lion cover (rare)	600.00
	Butter dish, w/cover, 6", square	65.00
12	Candleholder, 1-lite, block (rare)	100.00
	Candleholder, 2-lite	40.00
	Candleholder, 2-lite, "flame" center	65.00
2	Candleholder, 3-lite	70.00
3	Candle epergnette, 5"	15.00
	Candle epergnette, 6", deep	20.00
	Candle epergnette, 6½"	15.00
	Cheese dish, 5½", ftd.	20.00
	Cigarette holder	60.00
11	Comport, 6", low ftd.	20.00

	Crystal
10 Comport, 6½", jelly	35.00
Comport, 7", low ftd., oval	50.00
Creamer, ftd.	25.00
Creamer & sugar, individual, w/tray	50.00
4 Cruet, 3 oz., w/#122 stopper	75.00
Cup	14.00
Honey dish, 6½", ftd.	50.00
Mayonnaise, w/liner & ladle, 5½"	50.00
Plate, 7", salad	9.00
Plate, 8", luncheon	10.00
Plate, 10½", dinner	50.00
Plate, 11", sandwich	20.00
Plate, 13½", ftd., cake salver	70.00
13 Plate, 14", center handle, sandwich	65.00
Plate, 14", sandwich	35.00
Salt & pepper, pr.	60.00
Saucer	4.00
Stem, #5019, 1 oz., cordial	60.00
Stem, #5019, 3 oz., wine, blown	20.00
Stem, #5019, 3½ oz., cocktail	15.00
Stem, #5019, 5½ oz., sherbet/champagne	9.00
Stem, #5019, 10 oz., blown	20.00
Sugar, ftd.	25.00
Tray, 12", celery	20.00
Tumbler, #5019, 5 oz., ftd., juice, blown	20.00
Tumbler, #5019, 13 oz., ftd., tea, blown	22.00
14 Vase, 3½", violet	60.00
9 Vase, 7", ftd.	35.00
Vase, 7", ftd., fan shape	45.00

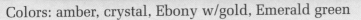

Colors: amber, crystal, Ebony w/gold, Emerald green

Wildflower can be found etched on numerous Cambridge tableware blanks, but is mostly found on #3121 stems. I have attempted to price a portion of the pattern, but the list is extensive. You can rationalize that, like Rose Point, almost any Cambridge blank may have been used to etch Wildflower. Price gold encrusted crystal items up to 25% higher. Price colored items about 50% higher, except for gold-encrusted Ebony, which brings double or triple the prices listed. A majority of collectors are searching for crystal because that can be found.

	Crystal
Basket, #3400/1182, 2 hdld., ftd., 6"	35.00
10 Bowl, #3500/54, 2 hdld., ftd.	33.00
14 Bowl, #3500/69, 3 pt. relish	30.00
28 Bowl, finger, blown, 4½"	30.00
Bowl, #3400/1180, bonbon, 2 hdld., 5¼"	32.50
Bowl, bonbon, 2 hdld., ftd., 6"	33.00
13 Bowl, #3400/90, 2 pt., relish, 6"	30.00
Bowl, #3500/61, 3 pt., relish, hdld., 6½"	50.00
Bowl, #3900/123, relish, 7"	35.00
Bowl, #3900/130, bonbon, 2 hdld., 7"	35.00
32 Bowl, #3400/88, 2 pt., relish, 8"	35.00
27 Bowl, #3400/91, 3 pt., relish, 3 hdld., 8"	37.50
Bowl, #3900/125, 3 pt., celery & relish, 9"	40.00
Bowl, #477, pickle (corn), ftd., 9½"	32.50
3 Bowl, #3900/1185, 10"	60.00
29 Bowl, #3900/34, 2 hdld., 11"	67.50
Bowl, #3900/28, w/tab hand., ftd., 11½"	72.50
15 Bowl, #3900/126, 3 pt., celery & relish, 12"	55.00
Bowl, #3400/4, 4 ft., flared, 12"	70.00
Bowl, #3400/1240, 4 ft., oval, "ears" hdld., 12"	85.00
Bowl, #3900/120, 5 pt., celery & relish, 12"	55.00
Butter dish, #3900/52, ¼ lb.	250.00
11 Butter dish, #3400/52, 5"	165.00
Candlestick, #3400/638, 3-lite, ea.	65.00
Candlestick, #3400/646, 5"	45.00
Candlestick, #3400/647, 2-lite, "keyhole" 6"	50.00
2 Candlestick, #3121, 7"	110.00
1 Candlestick, P.500	50.00
Candy box, w/cover, #3400/9, 4 ftd.	135.00
Candy box, w/cover, #3900/165, rnd.	115.00
19 Candy box, w/cover, #1066, 5½"	125.00
26 Cocktail icer, #968, 2 pc.	75.00
4 Cocktail shaker, P.101, w/top	175.00
20 Cocktail shaker, #3400/175	165.00
Comport, #3900/136, 5½"	50.00
Comport, #3121, blown, 5⅜"	65.00
18 Comport, #3500/148, 6"	40.00
Creamer, #3900/41	20.00
Creamer, #3900/40, individual	25.00
16 Creamer, #3500/15, individual	25.00
Cup, #3900/17 or #3400/54	20.00
Hat, #1704, 5"	295.00
Hat, #1703, 6"	395.00
Hurricane lamp, #1617, candlestick base	195.00
23 Hurricane lamp, #1603, keyhole base & prisms	225.00
Ice bucket, w/chrome hand., #3900/671	135.00
9 Mayonnaise set, 3 pc., #3400/11	60.00
33 Mayonnaise, #3900/19, sherbet style	35.00

	Crystal
8 Oil, w/stopper, #3900/100, 6 oz.	135.00
Pitcher, ball, #3400/38, 80 oz.	235.00
Pitcher, #3900/115, 76 oz.	225.00
Pitcher, Doulton, #3400/141	395.00
Plate, crescent salad	175.00
25 Plate, #3900/20, bread/butter, 6½"	12.00
Plate, #3400/176, 7½"	10.00
Plate, #3900/161, 2 hdld., ftd., 8"	18.00
Plate, #3900/22, salad, 8"	18.00
Plate, #3400/62, 8½"	18.00
Plate, #3900/24, dinner, 10½"	95.00
Plate, #3900/26, service, 4 ftd., 12"	55.00
21 Plate, #3900/35, cake, 2 hdld., 13½"	85.00
Plate, #3900/167, torte, 14"	65.00
Plate, #3900/65, torte, 14"	65.00
Salt & pepper, #3400/77, pr.	50.00
31 Salt & pepper, #3900/1177	50.00
Saucer, #3900/17 or #3400/54	3.50
Set: 2 pc. Mayonnaise, #3900/19 (ftd. sherbet w/ladle)	55.00
Set: 3 pc. Mayonnaise, #3900/129 (bowl, liner, ladle)	60.00
Set: 4 pc. Mayonnaise, #3900/111 (div. bowl, liner, 2 ladles)	65.00
Stem, #3121, cordial, 1 oz.	65.00
Stem, #3121, cocktail, 3 oz.	28.00
Stem, #3121, wine, 3½ oz.	50.00
12 Stem, #3121, claret, 4½ oz.	55.00
Stem, #3121, 4½ oz., low oyster cocktail	18.00
Stem, #3121, 5 oz., low parfait	42.00
24 Stem, #3121, 6 oz., low sherbet	20.00
7 Stem, #3121, 6 oz., tall sherbet	26.00
5 Stem, #3121, 10 oz., water	37.50
6 Stem, #3725, 10 oz., water	30.00
22 Sugar, 3400/16	20.00
30 Sugar, 3400/68	20.00
17 Sugar, indiv., 3500/15	25.00
Sugar, indiv., 3900/40	25.00
Tray, creamer & sugar, 3900/37	15.00
Tumbler, #3121, 5 oz., juice	30.00
35 Tumbler, #3121, 10 oz., water	28.00
Tumbler, #3121, 12 oz., tea	35.00
34 Tumbler, #3900/115, 13 oz.	40.00
Vase, #3400/102, globe, 5"	60.00
Vase, #6004, flower, ftd., 6"	65.00
Vase, #6004, flower, ftd., 8"	75.00
Vase, #1237, keyhole ft., 9"	110.00
36 Vase, #1528, bud, 10"	110.00
Vase, #278, flower, ftd., 11"	125.00
Vase, #1299, ped. ft., 11"	150.00
Vase, #1238, keyhole ft., 12"	135.00
Vase, #279, ftd., flower, 13"	225.00

Note: See pages 252 – 253 for stem identification.

Color: crystal; crystal with gold named Goldwood

Woodland is an early Fostoria pattern that is gaining attention from collectors. There is a wide range of items found but stemware leads the way. The pattern is called Goldwood when found with gold trim. I'm sure gold trim added some to the production cost; thus, it was a way to provide a new pattern with a higher price and not have to make additional moulds.

4

Item	Price
Bottle, salad dressing w/ stopper #2083	75.00
Bowl, 4½" finger #766	12.00
Candy jar w/lid, ½ lb. #2250	60.00
Candy jar w/lid, ¼ lb. #2250	50.00
Comport, 5"	25.00
Comport, 6"	25.00
Creamer, flat #1851	17.50
Decanter, 32 oz. #300	75.00
Jelly w/cover #825	25.00
Marmalade w/cover #4089	37.50
Mayonnaise liner, 6"	7.00
Mayonnaise, ftd. #2138	35.00
Mustard w/cover #1831	35.00
Nappy, 5", ftd.	18.00
Nappy, 6", ftd.	20.00
Nappy, 7", ftd.	22.50
Night bottle, 23 oz. #1697	65.00
Night tumbler, 6 oz. #4023	15.00
Oil bottle, 5 oz., w/stopper #1465	40.00
Oil bottle, 7 oz., w/stopper #1465	50.00

#	Item	Price
3	Pitcher, 65 oz. #300	175.00
	Plate, 5", sherbet #840	5.00
	Plate, 6", fingerbowl liner #1736	6.00
	Plate, 7", salad #1897	6.00
	Plate, 8¼", luncheon #2238	8.00
	Plate, 11", torte #2238	12.50
	Shaker, pr. #2022	40.00
	Stem, ¾ oz., cordial	20.00
	Stem, 2¾ oz., wine	14.00
	Stem, 3 oz., cocktail	12.50
	Stem, 5 oz., low sherbet	10.00
2	Stem, 5 oz., saucer champagne	11.00
	Stem, 6 oz., parfait	14.00
1	Stem, 9 oz., water	15.00
4	Sugar, flat #1851	17.50
	Sweetmeat #766	25.00
	Syrup, 8 oz. w/cut-off top #2194	95.00
	Tumbler, 3½", 5 oz., juice #889	8.00
	Tumbler, 4½", 10½", water #4076	10.00
	Tumbler, 5½", 14 oz., tea #889	14.00

1   2   3

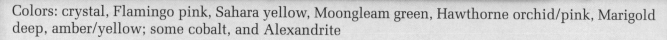

Colors: crystal, Flamingo pink, Sahara yellow, Moongleam green, Hawthorne orchid/pink, Marigold deep, amber/yellow; some cobalt, and Alexandrite

Yeoman in much treasured Hawthorne color is pictured on page 249. It is different from Alexandrite, which changes hues due to light sources. Hawthorne is consistently a pale amethyst, regardless of lighting.

Etched designs on Yeoman blank #1184 will bring 10% to 25% more than the prices listed below. Empress etch is the most frequently found pattern on Yeoman, as well as the most collectible for plain ware. You will find many pieces with sterling silver decoration; these were not done at the Heisey factory. Sterling decoration today does not add much to the price and in many cases will keep an item from selling at all. Yeoman has some very desirable pieces for item collectors such as cologne bottles, oil bottles, and sugar shakers.

	Crystal	Flamingo	Sahara	Moongleam	Hawthorne	Marigold
33 Ashtray, 4", hdld. (bow tie)	10.00	20.00	22.00	25.00	30.00	35.00
9 Bowl, 2 hdld., cream soup	12.00	20.00	25.00	30.00	35.00	40.00
Bowl, finger	5.00	11.00	17.00	20.00	27.50	30.00
20 Bowl, ftd., banana split	7.00	23.00	30.00	35.00	40.00	45.00
4 Bowl, ftd., 2 hdld., bouillon, w/liner	10.00	20.00	25.00	30.00	35.00	40.00
Bowl, 4½", nappy	4.00	7.50	10.00	12.50	15.00	17.00
Bowl, 5", low, ftd., jelly	12.00	20.00	25.00	27.00	30.00	40.00
Bowl, 5", oval, lemon and cover	30.00	60.00	65.00	75.00	90.00	90.00
Bowl, 5", rnd., lemon and cover	30.00	60.00	65.00	75.00	90.00	90.00
Bowl, 5", rnd., lemon, w/cover	15.00	20.00	25.00	30.00	40.00	50.00
Bowl, 6", oval, preserve	7.00	12.00	17.00	22.00	27.00	30.00
Bowl, 6", vegetable	5.00	10.00	14.00	16.00	20.00	24.00
28 Bowl, 6½", hdld., bonbon	5.00	10.00	14.00	16.00	20.00	24.00
Bowl, 8", rect., pickle/olive	12.00	15.00	20.00	25.00	30.00	35.00
Bowl, 8½", berry, 2 hdld.	14.00	22.00	25.00	30.00	35.00	50.00
Bowl, 9", 2 hdld., veg., w/cover	35.00	60.00	60.00	70.00	95.00	175.00
Bowl, 9", oval, fruit	20.00	25.00	35.00	45.00	55.00	55.00
Bowl, 9", baker	20.00	25.00	35.00	45.00	55.00	55.00
11 Bowl, 10", floral plateau #10	30.00	40.00		45.00	65.00	
Bowl, 12", low, floral	15.00	25.00	35.00	45.00	60.00	55.00
36 Box, puff w/insert	95.00	150.00		175.00		
Candle vase, single, w/short prisms & inserts	90.00			150.00		
21 Candy, hdl., 8½"	25.00	45.00		50.00		90.00
34 Cigarette holder (ashtray), bottom	25.00	60.00	65.00	70.00	80.00	100.00
Cologne bottle, w/stopper	100.00	160.00	160.00	160.00	170.00	180.00
22 Comport, 5", high ftd., shallow	15.00	25.00	37.00	45.00	55.00	70.00
15 Comport, 6", low ftd., deep	20.00	30.00	34.00	40.00	42.00	48.00
29 Comport and cover, #3350	55.00	85.00		85.00	110.00	175.00
25 Creamer, #1189	20.00	35.00	35.00	40.00		
7 Creamer	10.00	25.00	20.00	22.00	50.00	28.00
16 Creamer, #1001	40.00	60.00				
Cruet, 2 oz., oil	20.00	70.00	80.00	85.00	90.00	85.00
31 Cruet, 4 oz., oil	30.00	70.00	80.00	85.00		
3 Cup	5.00	20.00	20.00	25.00	50.00	
26 Cup, after dinner	20.00	40.00	40.00	45.00	50.00	60.00
30 Cup, coffee, Russian, 5 oz., #3312		45.00				
24 Egg cup	20.00	35.00	40.00	45.00	60.00	60.00
5 Goblet, #3325		40.00			65.00	
Gravy (or dressing) boat, w/underliner	13.00	25.00	30.00	45.00	50.00	45.00
Marmalade jar, w/cover	25.00	35.00	40.00	45.00	55.00	65.00
35 Mustard and cover	60.00	110.00	125.00	125.00		
Parfait, 5 oz.	10.00	15.00	20.00	25.00	30.00	35.00
1 Pitcher, quart	70.00	130.00	130.00	140.00	160.00	180.00

YEOMAN

	Crystal	Flamingo	Sahara	Moongleam	Hawthorne	Marigold
Plate, 2 hdld., cheese	5.00	10.00	13.00	15.00	17.00	25.00
10 Plate, cream soup underliner	5.00	7.00	9.00	12.00	14.00	16.00
Plate, finger bowl underliner	3.00	5.00	7.00	9.00	11.00	13.00
Plate, 4½", coaster	3.00	5.00	10.00	12.00		
Plate, 6"	3.00	6.00	8.00	10.00	13.00	15.00
27 Plate, 6", bouillon underliner	3.00	6.00	8.00	10.00	13.00	15.00
Plate, 6½", grapefruit bowl	7.00	12.00	15.00	19.00	27.00	32.00
6 Plate, 7"	5.00	8.00	10.00	14.00	17.00	22.00
Plate, 8", oyster cocktail	9.00					
Plate, 8", soup	9.00					
Plate, 9", oyster cocktail	10.00					
Plate, 10½"	20.00	50.00		50.00	60.00	
Plate, 10½", ctr. hdld., oval, div.	15.00	26.00		32.00		
Plate, 11", 4 pt., relish	20.00	27.00		32.00		
Plate, 14"	20.00					
2 Platter, 12", oval	10.00	17.00	19.00	26.00	33.00	
14 Salt and Pepper, #49	30.00	40.00				
Salt, ind. tub (cobalt: $30.00)	10.00	20.00		30.00		
Salver, 10", low ftd.	15.00	50.00		70.00		
Salver, 12", low ftd.	10.00	50.00		70.00		
3 Saucer	3.00	5.00	7.00	7.00	10.00	10.00
26 Saucer, after dinner	3.00	5.00	7.00	8.00	10.00	10.00
32 Stem, 2¾ oz., ftd., oyster cocktail	4.00	8.00	10.00	12.00	14.00	
Stem, 3 oz., cocktail	10.00	12.00	17.00	20.00		
Stem, 3½ oz., sherbet	5.00	8.00	11.00	12.00		
Stem, 4 oz., fruit cocktail	3.00	10.00	10.00	12.00		
Stem, 4½ oz., sherbet	3.00	10.00	10.00	12.00		
Stem, 5 oz., soda	9.00	8.00	30.00	20.00		
Stem, 5 oz., sherbet	5.00	5.00	7.00	9.00		
Stem, 6 oz., champagne	6.00	16.00	18.00	22.00		
Stem, 8 oz.	5.00	12.00	18.00	20.00		
23 Stem, 10 oz., goblet	10.00	15.00	45.00	25.00		
8 Sugar, w/cover	15.00	45.00	45.00	50.00	70.00	40.00
19 Sugar and cover, #1189	25.00	45.00	45.00	55.00		
17 Sugar shaker, ftd.	50.00	95.00		110.00		
Syrup, 7 oz., saucer ftd.	30.00	75.00				
Tray, 7" x 10", rect.	26.00	30.00	40.00	35.00		
Tray, 9", celery	10.00	14.00	16.00	15.00		
Tray, 11", ctr. hand., 3 pt.	15.00	35.00	40.00			
Tray, 12", oblong	16.00	60.00	65.00			
Tray, 13", 3 pt., relish	20.00	27.00	32.00			
Tray, 13", celery	20.00	27.00	32.00			
Tray, 13", hors d'oeuvre, w/cov. ctr.	32.00	42.00	52.00	75.00		
Tray insert, 3½" x 4½"	4.00	6.00	7.00	8.00		
Tumbler, 2½ oz., whiskey	3.00	20.00	25.00	40.00		
Tumbler, 4½ oz., soda	4.00	6.00	10.00	15.00		
Tumbler, 8 oz.	4.00	15.00	20.00	20.00		
Tumbler, 10 oz., cupped rim	4.00	15.00	20.00	22.50		
Tumbler, 10 oz., straight side	5.00	15.00	20.00	22.50		
Tumbler, 12 oz., tea	5.00	20.00	25.00	30.00		
Tumbler cover (unusual)	35.00					
18 Vase, 5½", #4157	40.00	65.00	75.00	70.00	85.00	
12 Vase, 6", #516-2		50.00		60.00	75.00	
13 Vase, 7", floral bowl, #3480		55.00		65.00	85.00	

Diane
1066
11 oz. Goblet

Tally Ho
1402
Brandy Inhaler (Tall)

Appleblossom
3025
10 oz. Goblet

Gloria
3035
3 oz. Cocktail

Cleo
3077
6 oz. Tall Sherbet

Elaine
3104
1 oz. Cordial

Diane
3106
9 oz. Goblet Tall Bowl

Cleo
3115
3½ oz. Cocktail

Gloria
3120
6 oz. Tall Sherbet

Wildflower
3121
10 oz. Goblet

Diane
3122
9 oz. Goblet

Portia
3124
3 oz. Wine

Portia
3126
11 oz. Tall Sherbet

Apple Blossom
3130
6 oz. Tall Sherbet

Gloria
3135
6 oz. Tall Sherbet

Apple Blossom
3400
11 oz. Lunch Goblet

Elaine
3500
10 oz. Goblet

Chantilly
3600
2½ oz. Wine

Chantilly
3775
4½ oz. Claret

Chantilly
3625
4½ oz. Claret

Chantilly
3779
1 oz. Cordial

253

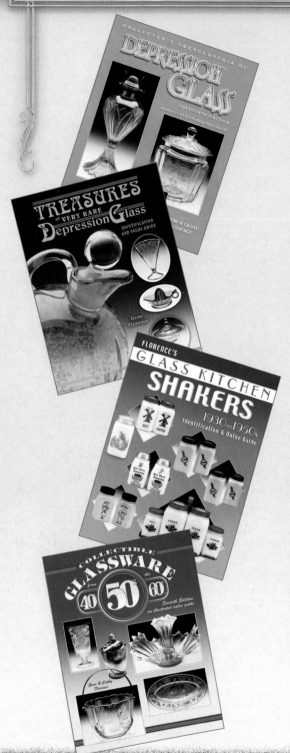
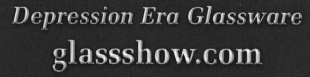

Anchor Hocking's FIRE-KING & More, Second Edition

Gene Florence

From the 1930s to the 1960s Anchor Hocking Glass Corp. of Lancaster, Ohio, produced an extensive line of glassware called Fire-King. Their lines included not only dinnerware but also a plethora of glass kitchen items — reamers, measuring cups, mixing bowls, mugs, and more. This is the essential collectors' reference to this massive line of glassware. Loaded with hundreds of new full-color photos, vintage catalog pages, company materials, facts, information, and values, this book has everything collectors expect from Gene Florence. 2002 values.

Item #5602 • ISBN: 1-57432-164-1 • 8½ x 11 • 224 Pgs. • HB • $24.95

Glass CANDLESTICKS of the Depression Era

Gene Florence

Florence has compiled this book to help identify the candlestick patterns made during the Depression era. More than 500 different candlesticks are shown in full-color photographs. The book is arranged according to color: amber, black, blue, crystal, green, iridescent, multicolor, pink, purple, red, smoke, white, and yellow. Many famous glassmakers are represented, such as Heisey, Cambridge, Fostoria, and Tiffin. The descriptive text for each candleholder includes pattern, maker, color, height, and current collector value. A helpful index and bibliography are also provided. 2000 values.

Item #5354 • ISBN: 1-57432-136-6 • 8½ x 11 • 176 Pgs. • HB • $24.95

KITCHEN GLASSWARE of the Depression Years, Sixth Edition

Gene Florence

This exciting new edition of our bestselling *Kitchen Glassware of the Depression Years* is undeniably the definitive reference on the subject. More than 5,000 items are showcased in beautiful professional color photographs with descriptions and values. Many new finds and exceptionally rare pieces have been added. The highly collectible glass from the Depression era through the 1960s fills its pages, in addition to the ever-popular Fire-King and Pyrex glassware. This comprehensive encyclopedia provides an easy-to-use format, showing items by color, shape, or pattern. The collector will enjoy the pages of glass, from colorful juice reamers, shakers, rare and unusual glass knives, to the mixing bowls and baking dishes we still find in our kitchen cupboards. 2003 values.

Item #5827 • ISBN: 1-57432-220-6 • 8½ x 11 • 272 Pgs. • HB • $24.95

Florences' Glassware PATTERN IDENTIFICATION Guides

Gene & Cathy Florence

Florences' Glassware Pattern Identification Guides are great companions for the Florences' other glassware books. Volume I includes every pattern featured in *Collector's Encyclopedia of Depression Glass, Collectible Glassware from the 40s, 50s, and 60s,* and *Elegant Glassware of the Depression Era,* as well as many more — nearly 400 patterns in all. Volume II holds nearly 500 patterns, with no repeats from Volume I. Volume III also showcases nearly 500 patterns with no repeats from the previous volumes. Carefully planned close-up photographs of representative pieces for every pattern show great detail to make identification easy. With every pattern, the Florences provide the names, the companies that made the glass, dates of production, and even colors available. These guides are ideal references for novice and seasoned glass collectors and dealers, and great resources for years to come. No values.

Vol. I • Item #5042 • ISBN: 1-57432-045-9 • 8½ x 11 • 176 Pgs. • PB • $18.95
Vol. II • Item #5615 • ISBN: 1-57432-177-3 • 8½ x 11 • 208 Pgs. • PB • $19.95
Vol. III • Item #6142 • ISBN: 1-57432-315-6 • 8½ x 11 • 272 Pgs. • PB • $19.95

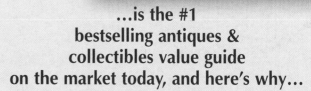
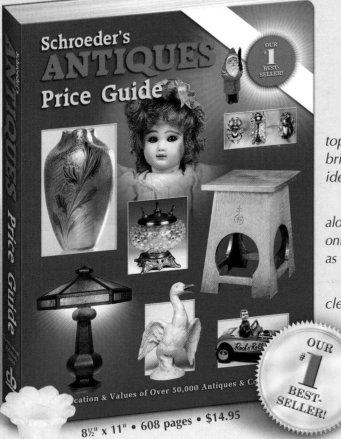